WELFARE RACISM

PLAYING
THE RACE CARD
AGAINST
AMERICA'S
POOR

Kenneth J. Neubeck
Noel A. Cazenave

ROUTLEDGE
NEW YORK LONDON

To my lovable and loving granddaughters, Yssis Amina Neubeck
and Lucy Sinclair Neubeck

KJN

To the memory of my mother, Mildred Depland Cazenave,
and my father, Herman J. Cazenave, and to my wonderful wife,
Anita Washington Cazenave, daughter, Anika Tene Cazenave,
and sister, Andree Cazenave Carter

NAC

Published in 2001 by
Routledge
29 West 35th Street
New York, New York 10001

Published in Great Britain by
Routledge
11 New Fetter Lane
London EC4P 4EE

Routledge is an imprint of the Taylor & Francis Group.

Library of Congress Cataloging-in-Publication Data

Neubeck, Kenneth J.
    Welfare racism: playing the race card against America's poor / Kenneth J. Neubeck and Noel A.
Cazenave.
        p. cm.
    Includes bibliographical references and index.
    ISBN 0–415–92340–9— ISBN 0–415–92341–7 (pbk.)
        1. Public welfare—United States. 2. Welfare recipients—Government policy—United States. 3.
Minorities—Government policy—United States. 4. Social service and race relations—United States. 5.
Racism—United States. I. Cazenave, Noel A., 1948– II. Title.

HV95 .N4368 2001
362.84'00973—dc21
                                                                                            00–068417

Contents

univ. high

22n-129

Preface and Acknowledgments

PREFACE

For decades now, we—along with millions of other people in the United States—have been exposed to racist comments and images about those who receive welfare. The racialization of welfare has reached the point where politicians can now exploit racial animus to promote their political ambitions and goals simply by speaking the word *welfare*. When, in the last decade, even liberal politicians joined in playing the welfare "race card" as a strategy in rising calls for meanspirited welfare reform, we could stomach no more.

We have written this book out of concern for the plight of the millions of impoverished people—mostly women and children—who have been hurt by such "reform." They reside in small towns, rural areas, metropolitan suburbs, central cities, "ghettos," barrios, and reservations. Families receiving welfare come in many skin colors, but all tend to experience the oppression of economic destitution in similar ways. The energies of mothers whose families must rely on welfare are consumed by the monumental challenge of protecting and nurturing their children with chronically inadequate resources. Many of these women have spoken out and fought against highly racialized and punitive welfare policies. Their desperate struggles—sometimes visible and collective, more often quiet and personal—are motivated by the fact that it is their children who are most ravaged by these policies.

Racism in public policy is an unpopular topic to raise in this nation's conservative political climate. Most European Americans, including academics, seem to be in a state of denial as to the very existence of racism in the United States. Given that we would be raising critical questions about elite decision making and the racial status quo, we expected to have difficulty finding government or foundation funding to conduct our research. While some of our colleagues were supportive of our interests, others gave us blank looks or awkwardly changed the subject when we talked about our plans to write a book on "welfare racism." We wondered then how such a book would be received by mainstream social scientists and welfare policy analysts. After all, scholars of U.S. welfare policy had apparently concluded long ago, without bothering to actually research the topic, that racism does not play a significant role in the formation and implementation of welfare policy in the United States. We even considered the possibility that the social science mainstream would simply ignore this book in the same way that it had chosen over the past few decades to largely ignore systemic white racism.

Mindful that a narrowly conceived manuscript addressed only to scholars and policy analysts might more easily be ignored, we decided to write a book that would be accessible and of interest to a broader audience, including people who are active in or supportive of movements for economic and racial justice. We reasoned that if people outside the confines of academia begin to understand the prevalence and significance of welfare racism, and to see this as an important public issue, then even "racism-blind" scholars and policy analysts might suddenly find themselves healed and their sight restored.

Our worries briefly materialized when we looked into funding sources for our research. Foundation grant officers, for example, seemed impressed with our letters of inquiry, but advised us that our research topic did not fit the ways in which they were framing research priorities when it came to welfare. The priority of one foundation was typical. Echoing the rhetoric of the many politicians who were calling for punitive welfare-reform measures, it informed us of its preference for research that would help develop "self-sufficiency" among recipients. Clearly our research topic was not only "politically incorrect," but "foundationally incorrect" as well.

Despite this somewhat unsupportive climate, after we began our research we quickly came to a profound and humbling realization: "We are not alone!" Indeed from our very first step toward the writing of this manuscript we had never really been alone. As we labored away on the historical components of our research, we began to hear courageous, caring, committed, and creative voices that clearly understood the importance of our topic. Many were rooted in the grassroots social movements that contested racism and poverty in the 1960s. We heard the inspiring voices of rank and file members of the National Welfare Rights Organization, and the voice of Martin Luther King Jr. proclaiming his commitment to a guaranteed annual income. As we continued our work there were also contemporary voices that seemed to echo the energizing message that we were now part of something much larger than ourselves. The University of Connecticut Research Foundation spoke to our efforts with a small grant which enabled us to expand our archival research and hire a research assistant. There were the sounds of progressive university faculty and graduate students from numerous departments with whom we formed the University of Connecticut American Welfare Policy Study Group, where we agonized over the meaning and implications of Bill Clinton's 1992 campaign pledge to "end welfare as we know it." There were welcome voices of encouragement for our research from activists/scholars whose work we hold in high regard, such as Frances Fox Piven and Joe Feagin.

We ducked, however, upon hearing of Bill Clinton's signing of the draconian Personal Responsibility and Work Opportunity Reconciliation Act of 1996 (PRWORA). This federal welfare "reform" legislation callously abolished Aid to Families with Dependent Children (AFDC), a sixty-one-year-old program that entitled impoverished mothers and children to public assistance. As we absorbed the likely consequences of this incredible welfare policy development and moved to document the role that welfare racism played in bringing it about, Routledge discovered us through the good words of Joe Feagin. Urged on by Joe and another Routledge author, Tom Shapiro, to our gratification we in turn found a book publisher that considered our topic and ideas to be within its mainstream.

As our writing slowly drew to a close, we found ourselves joining conferences of scholar-activists, legal services attorneys, and grassroots organizers who clearly understand the need to address racism in efforts to bring about economic justice for all poor people. We became aware of how political elites' attacks on the poor were being vigorously contested by progressive organizations such as the Kensington Welfare Rights Union, the Applied Research Center, and the Center for Community Change. These organizations are trying to force the issue of what we call "welfare racism" onto the national political agenda. With the PRWORA up for congressional reauthorization in 2002, such a movement cannot occur too soon.

The ease with which political elites abolished the Aid to Families with Dependent Children program—the primary safety net protecting poverty-stricken mothers and children—would have been impossible had not many politicians, along with policy analysts and the mass media, spent decades framing and morphing welfare into a supposed "black problem." Political elites relied upon often subtle racist stereotypes about welfare and its recipients to escalate antipathy toward public assistance. They then "reformed" it by removing all poor families' entitlement to aid, regardless of their skin color. The federal welfare-reform legislation enacted in 1996 does little more than make finding a way out of poverty the "personal responsibility" of the mothers and children who suffer it. It is clearly an antiwelfare program, not an antipoverty program. The hateful message put in place by the architects of contemporary welfare reform is quite simple: "You're poor? So, deal with it!"

If there is any wisdom to be obtained from hindsight in this post-AFDC era, it is this: *Punitive welfare reform underscores the challenge that white racism poses for progressive movements that seek to put an end to poverty as a matter of economic justice.* Too often, a call to fight racism is heard by "whites"—progressive or otherwise— as little more than a plea to rescue people of color from discriminatory treatment. But in a racialized social system, racism harms everyone, regardless of their skin color. Indeed, in some instances racism may be color-blind in its harmful consequences, as suggested by this book's subtitle: *Playing the Race Card against America's Poor*. This process of collective harm is very clear in the case of punitive welfare reform. The racialized attitudes, policies, and practices that constitute what we call "welfare racism," and which are embedded in contemporary welfare-reform legislation, have a negative impact on *all* poverty-stricken families, including white families.

Why a new term, *welfare racism*? For all practical purposes, social problems do not exist until they are named. For example, the arbitrary harassment and even the arrest and jailing of innocent people of color by police have been going on for a long time in the United States. However, it was not widely viewed as a systemic social problem that merited research and public policy attention until the 1990s, when the term *racial profiling* was coined. In the 1980s we witnessed a similar development related to the social policy–relevant concept of "environmental racism," which draws attention to policies under which communities of color have been systematically and disproportionately targeted for the location of hazardous waste facilities and other polluting facilities.

A major obstacle to understanding the effects of racism on welfare policy is the absence of straightforward, well-defined, and specific language about the phenomenon. Before an adequate theory regarding the role of racism in the realm of welfare policy can be developed, it is necessary to build a strong conceptual foundation. While we do not claim to have reached the theory formulation stage, the cornerstone of the conceptual framework we employ in our analysis is the concept of welfare racism. We hope that by naming the phenomenon it will be more easily placed into public policy discourse and into academic teaching and research.

However, unlike many professional discourse analysts we would not dare to suggest that naming the problem is enough. We are well aware that symbols are effective only when they are backed by power. Whether the topic of welfare racism, or whatever it might be called, assumes a central place in discussions of U.S. welfare policy will ultimately be determined by the ability of well-organized welfare rights advocates, antiracists, and other progressives to force it from the margins of political discourse and into the center. We hope that this book will be a resource and an inspiration for that movement to challenge welfare racism. If it is, *Welfare Racism* would not only help nurture the growth of more humane and rational welfare policy discourse but ultimately, by addressing forthrightly the problem of racism blindness, would help make possible an effective multi-ethnic movement for economic justice.

ACKNOWLEDGMENTS

We wish to thank the following scholars for their supportive and at times critical reactions to ideas in progress, unpublished papers, or pieces of what would become early manuscript drafts: Alex Dupuy, Joe Feagin, Myra Marx Ferree, Davita Silfen Glasberg, Susan T. Gooden, Frances Fox Piven, Jill Quadagno, Ellen Reese, Sanford Schram, Tom Shapiro, Susan L. Thomas, Steve Valocchi, Lucy Williams, and Ann Withorn. We are grateful for similar reasons to participants in the University of Connecticut American Welfare Policy Study Group, which often served as a sounding board for our thoughts: Marcia Bok, Nancy Chance, Nancy Churchill, Sandra Enos, Daryl Harris, Len Krimerman, Kalpana Kutty, Darryl McMiller, Mary Alice Neubeck, Jerry Phillips, Suzanne Reading, Louise Simmons, Archibald Stuart, and Steve Wisensale. For other helpful contributions to and encouragement of our efforts, we thank Laura Able, Richard Camble, Millie Charles, Ditmar Coffield, Jocelyn Freye, Patricia Green, D. Clive Hardy, Margaret Hallock, Chester Hartman, Morris Jeff, James Jennings, David Klaassen, Donetta Klein, Chrishana Lloyd, Wilbur Meneray Jr., Sandra Morgen, Doris Ng, Cay Petty, Andrew Simons, Judith D. Smith, Makani Themba-Nixon, and Wayne Villemez.

Timely completion of this research would have been impossible without a grant from the University of Connecticut Research Foundation and graduate research assistantships supported by the university's Institute for African American Studies and the Department of Sociology. Our work is heavily reliant on the contributions made by sociology graduate students Laurie Gordy, Beth Merenstein, Barbara Nangle, David Nielsen, Karen Powell, Jim Pritchard, Rachel Sullivan, Dena Wallerson, and Laura West. Many thanks as well to Arlene Goodwin and Jeanne Monty, sociology department staff, for all their help with administrative and secretarial tasks.

The historical component of our research was greatly aided by the cooperation we received from the following libraries or archives: the Amistad Research Center, the Center on Social Welfare Policy and Law Library, the Earl K. Long Library of the University of New Orleans, the Hill Memorial Library of Louisiana State University, the Howard-Tilton Memorial Library of Tulane University, the Lyndon Baines Johnson Library, the National Archives, the Newburgh, N.Y. public library, the New Orleans Public Library, the Roper Center Archives of the University of Connecticut, the Social Welfare History Archives, the State Historical Society of Wisconsin, the State Library of Louisiana, the Thomas J. Dodd Research Center of the University of Connecticut, the Tulane University Law

School Library, the University of Connecticut Library, and the U.S. Social Security Administration archives. In addition, we thank Joseph P. Ritz, who kindly gave us a personal file of documents that he gathered while a journalist with the *Newburgh News*. Valuable guidance to some of the most recent developments in welfare racism was provided by Su Sie Ju of the National Partnership for Women and Families and Shane Goldsmith of the Center for Community Change.

A number of persons graciously participated in either taped phone or personal interviews regarding their memories or other knowledge of important events. Those interviewed regarding their knowledge of punitive 1960–61 Louisiana welfare-reform legislation were William T. Carpenter, Raphael Cassimere, Adrian Duplantier, Joseph Logsdon, Rosa Keller, Revius O. Ortique Jr., Mary Evelyn Parker, Risley C. Triche, and Ursula Victorianne. Interviews on the controversial 1961 welfare policies initiated in Newburgh, N.Y., were conducted with Raymond Boyer, Elaine Disnuke, Eunice Shatz, and Joseph P. Ritz.

We thank the editors at Routledge, Jayne Fargnoli and Heidi Freund, who provided us with early encouragement, and Ilene Kalish, who enthusiastically helped us see this book to completion. Thanks also to Nicole Ellis, production editor, and to Norma McLemore, copy editor, for their thorough attention to details. We express special appreciation to Routledge reviewer Carter A. Wilson, whose contributions to the study of racism provided us with both inspiration and knowledge, and who gave our entire manuscript a careful and critical reading.

Both of us treasure the usual great patience, good humor, and strong support of our spouses, Mary Alice Neubeck and Anita Washington Cazenave. We are very grateful to them for believing in this project and for being willing to hear both our ideas and our gripes.

Finally, we want to express our gratitude to those individuals like Susan T. Gooden, and organizations such as the Kensington Welfare Rights Union, the Applied Research Center, and the Center for Community Change, for their commitment to challenging welfare racism.

1

SEEING
WELFARE RACISM

It's like we're all in the same room, and there's
this huge pink elephant in the middle of the
room. That pink elephant is racism. But
nobody wants to look at it; people walk around
it; they don't want to see it. But we can't begin
to move forward until we name it and get other
folks to actually see it. Until we can do that, we
can't really change anything, we can't get the
pink elephant out of the room.

Janet Robideau, coordinator,
Indian People's Action,
Montana, summer 2000

and in everyday conversation, mothers and their children who rely on welfare in the United States have overwhelmingly and erroneously been depicted as "black."[1] African-American women of all socioeconomic statuses have found themselves stereotyped with the negative qualities associated with so-called welfare queens. Today, the words *welfare mothers* evoke one of the most powerful racialized cultural icons in contemporary U.S. society.[2]

The following "joke," from an early 1990s calendar sold by Waldenbooks, is indicative of how prevalent the racist stereotype of African Americans as welfare recipients has become:

> How come you never see an African-American family portrait? Because when the photographer says, "Say cheese," they all run to the welfare center and form a straight line.[3]

The racialization of welfare did not happen overnight. For decades, well-known U.S. politicians like Barry Goldwater, George Wallace, Robert Byrd, Richard Nixon, Ronald Reagan, David Duke, Newt Gingrich, and Bill Clinton forged and exploited the link between "race" and "welfare" to such a degree that the two terms are now politically and culturally inextricable. Today, whenever politicians want to exploit white racist animus for political gain they need not say the words *Niggers* or *Nigras*, as did white southern segregationists. They now need only mention the word *welfare*.

Politicians have blamed black mothers who must rely on welfare for nearly every social problem in the United States, including violent crime; the illegal drug epidemic; the decline of families, communities, and schools; the growth of rampant immorality; and even poverty itself. Black mothers receiving welfare have been cast not simply as prototypical villains, but as a collective internal enemy that threatens the very foundation of U.S. society. They are portrayed as dishonest and irresponsible individuals who purchase bottles of vodka with food stamps intended to help feed their children, or as immoral and promiscuous individuals who are said to breed children to rip off the welfare system for more benefits.

As a result of the racialization of welfare and its recipients, all mothers who must rely on welfare, regardless of their color or ethnicity, are now being dealt with in a way consistent with the hostility evoked by the racist image of the so-called welfare-dependent black mother. To understand how U.S. society has reached such a point it is essential to take a close look at what we call welfare racism.

PLAYING THE WELFARE "RACE CARD"

The belief that African Americans are welfare-prone is not found only in such crude efforts at humor as the calendar joke mentioned above. Throughout

U.S. society those on the nation's welfare rolls are stereotypically depicted as consisting primarily of an African-American urban underclass. Indeed, as we will see, national surveys reveal that many whites believe that African Americans prefer remaining on welfare to being self-supporting. Public opinion surveys also show that the perceived race of welfare recipients matters mightily in determining how recipients are viewed. When welfare recipients are seen as being mostly white they are likely to be thought of with compassion; when they are seen as being mostly black they are viewed with contempt.

Politicians and policy analysts often exploit and reinforce these stereotypes. For example, in 1996, President Clinton kept his 1992 campaign promise to "end welfare as we know it" by signing legislation that abolished Aid to Families with Dependent Children and instituted the Personal Responsibility and Work Opportunity Reconciliation Act. As if his racial message was not clear enough, President Clinton had African-American mothers at his side in press photographs of the White House ceremony in which he signed the welfare reform bill.

Why might Bill Clinton make such a promise? Survey data reveal that many European Americans believe that most people on welfare are black, when in reality African Americans and whites have been about equally represented on the welfare rolls for many years.[4] Those European Americans who view welfare as a "black program" have been found to have the most hostile attitudes toward welfare recipients. They tend to stereotype African Americans as lazy, unwilling to make the effort to take advantage of opportunities open to them, and thus undeserving of public assistance.[5] As we have noted, politicians have fueled and exploited such racial sentiments for their own political gain.

Prior to the passage of the PRWORA, politicians and other policy elites routinely linked race and welfare. This was done by employing code terms that thinly camouflaged overt racism. Terms like *welfare queens, welfare chiselers, generations of welfare dependency*, and *children having children* were commonplace in 1990s discussions of the need for welfare reform. Political discourse using such terms routinely conjured up images of an inner-city, largely African-American welfare population, notable for its allegedly deficient group values and pathological behaviors.[6]

In this highly racialized political environment neither voluminous government statistical data nor scholarly research findings on the widely diverse characteristics and the unmet needs of the nation's poor have had much influence on the direction and outcome of recent welfare reform debates. The unusually harsh and punitive character of the "welfare reform" policies that have been proposed or implemented in the wake of such debates has often reflected a preoccupation with controlling the alleged sexual immorality and supposed preference for welfare over work of one group: African-American females.

Congressional discourse preceding the passage of the Personal Responsibility and Work Opportunity Reconciliation Act largely reflected concern with young, single, inner-city mothers. The act's proponents argued that such mothers need the incentive of restricted benefits and strict time limits on welfare eligibility to motivate them to avoid out-of-wedlock pregnancies and establish economic self-sufficiency. A stereotype that women on welfare were typically inner-city "children having children" to get on the dole has long endured despite the fact that African-American teenage girls made up a tiny percentage of all mothers receiving welfare.[7] Given the racially charged discourse that culminated in the abolition of AFDC, it should not be surprising that mothers and children of color are disproportionately affected by welfare reform. Such families are much more likely than European-American families to be extremely poor (living below 50 percent of the poverty line)[8] and to have little alternative but to turn to the state for cash welfare assistance.

In the 1990s there was a great deal of welfare racist sentiment among members of the public for politicians to exploit. While the percentage of families receiving welfare in 1996 who were African American was almost identical to that for whites (37 versus 36 percent),[9] survey research in the first half of the 1990s revealed that many European Americans had come to view AFDC as a "black program." Moreover, many believed that African Americans as a group preferred to live off welfare instead of working. One survey, commissioned by the Anti-Defamation League, found that 35 percent of those who identified themselves as white believed African Americans preferred welfare to work.[10] Data from the National Opinion Research Center showed that, when asked to directly compare themselves with African Americans, fully three-fourths of white respondents rated African Americans as less likely than whites to prefer to be self-supporting.[11]

Yet another survey found that almost half of the respondents, the vast majority of whom were white, held erroneous beliefs that most people who are poor are black, and that most people who are on welfare are black.[12] Most of those polled believed that lack of effort was to blame for people being on welfare and that most welfare recipients really did not want to work. These beliefs were most likely to be found among poll respondents who believed that most people on welfare are black. Political scientist Martin Gilens, analyzing still other survey data, has argued that the most important source of European Americans' hostility toward public assistance is their stereotypical beliefs about African Americans, especially the belief that they are lazy.[13]

It might be expected that public attitudes reflecting racist stereotypes about and hostility toward welfare recipients, the racialized tenor of the political discourse surrounding welfare reform legislation, and the fact that the PRWORA strips the safety net away from so many poor families of color would at least raise the question among policy analysts and social scientists: Is U.S. welfare policy racist? Unfortunately, the political and intellectual climate that has come to prevail in the United States discourages even asking this question. Broad-based insensitivity to the existence and significance of systemic racism, and even the denial of the salience of racism as a modern-day social force, are common.[14]

While perhaps more immediately visible in political elites' discourse than in academic writings, insensitivity to racism as a systemic social problem, and blindness to the race-based privileges possessed by all whites, extends to the work of all but a small number of social scientists and policy analysts.[15] Most European Americans today view the "race problem" as having been somehow solved by legislation passed during the 1960s, and simply do not believe that African Americans and other people of color continue to be deprived of "the dignity, opportunities, freedoms, and rewards that this nation offers white Americans."[16]

In stark contrast to this general insensitivity to the existence and significance of racism among European Americans, undeniably racist events and episodes do occur in U.S. society, sometimes taking horrific and violent forms. These are typically framed by European-American political elites as unfortunate aberrations and ignorant acts by a racially bigoted few.[17] This is the case even though it is difficult to open a daily newspaper or watch television news programs without coming across yet another example of white racism directed at people of color.

The larger social context of racist acts is ignored even though they are prevalent in every institutional and organizational setting in U.S. society. Those reported upon in the news include racially bigoted acts by European-American police officers, corporate executives, high school and college students, public officials, members of the military, athletes, and media figures. The fact that this behavior is ubiquitous and acted out by people from a wide cross section of the U.S. population tends not to be taken by European-American political elites as evidence that racial bigotry and systemic racism are serious matters in the United States with which we must contend. On this issue, the European-American public is generally in accord.

The majority of European Americans have difficulty seeing even blatant expressions of racial bigotry as indicative of a larger social problem. Not surprisingly, they are virtually blind to the often more subtle, systemic forms of racism that affect virtually every arena of social life. It is these systemic forms of racism that provide European Americans with their greatest present-day and cumulative advantages over African Americans and other people of color.[18]

In social arenas ranging from employment to housing, from education to politics and from law enforcement to health care, African Americans and others suffer collective disadvantages associated with highly systemic, albeit often subtle, institutionalized discrimination.[19] The absence of racism in welfare policy— given its presence in these other arenas—would be an exceptional situation indeed.

SEEING WELFARE RACISM

"Seeing is believing" is a popular expression in the United States. Clearly, welfare racism exists. It pervades this nation's politics and culture. And it is devastating in its consequences for all poor people. That something is obvious, however, does not mean that it will be seen or believed, much less acknowledged; people possess a remarkable ability to remain blind to what they choose not to see. At the opening of this chapter, we presented what we think is a powerful quote by a Native American community activist who compares racism to a big pink elephant in the middle of the room that no one sees. Metaphorically, welfare racism is that big, but apparently invisible, pink elephant.

Welfare racism is so pervasive in U.S. society that it is manifested in countless racist jokes and stories. While in U.S. public policy and social science welfare racism is a well-kept national secret, in U.S. society as a whole it is one of its worst-kept secrets. Most people have heard jokes like the one at the beginning of this chapter. When white politicians talk about welfare they know what part of their constituency they are appealing to and how. Unfortunately, as a society the United States, publicly at least, has closed its eyes and pretended not to see the gigantic pachyderm in its midst.

It is as if some time ago the nation's "welfare racism files" were classified "Top Secret." As we will show, this pretense is central to both U.S. public policy and its social science research on that policy. Unless those files are found, opened, read, and thoroughly understood—unless welfare racism is seen— it will be impossible to confront. In this book those files are presented for your inspection.

European-American insensitivity to and denial of racism as a social force— especially the systemic racism to which we have alluded—has been helped along and legitimized by a "scholarship of backlash" that emerged in the post–civil rights era.[20] This scholarship reflects and reinforces many European Americans' unwillingness to entertain the notion that racism is alive and well today. The "politics of denial"[21] regarding the present-day salience of racism make our current political and intellectual climate inhospitable to expressions of concern over the plight of poor African-American mothers and other impoverished people of color. Denial politics function to force the topic of welfare racism off the radar screen and thus eliminate it from discourse and study.

BEYOND RACISM? THE POLITICS OF DENIAL

While there is ample evidence that racist stereotypes and their exploitation by politicians have played an important role in discourse about welfare policy and subsequent policy initiatives, social scientists have paid relatively little attention to the significance of racism in their theorizing about how welfare policies originate and in their assessments of policy effects. To understand this omission we must examine the racial politics of contemporary U.S. social science. When it comes to white racism, the dominant politics enveloping U.S. social science is the politics of denial.

In 1978, sociologist William Julius Wilson published *The Declining Significance of Race*, a book that was widely read and commented upon both within and outside the social sciences. Wilson argued that the 1960s civil rights movement and responses to it by the federal government had largely solved the problem of racism. While he believed that racial discrimination had left some "historic effects,"[22] in Wilson's view it was no longer skin color but class membership that determined African Americans' life chances. Poor blacks were no longer mired in poverty due to racism. Rather, they lacked the human capital (education and skills) to take advantage of opportunities that had begun to open up for African Americans.

Wilson's analysis had an important impact, not only because he himself was African American and a prominent sociologist, but because his ideas were disseminated during a growing white aversion to government programs that were targeted at, or thought to be targeted at, assisting people of color.[23] Wilson did not intend to support such sentiments, but his ideas were consistent with European Americans' increasing rejection of the notion that, in the post–civil rights era, racism remained a major social problem in the United States. With bitter humor, one of his critics has commented that Wilson "seems to have convinced the entire Western world (with the exception of the ghetto population whom he had not previously consulted) that racism was 'of declining significance.'"[24]

Wilson's thesis helped to provide an umbrella of legitimacy for a whole procession of scholars committed to the politics of denial regarding racism. We use this phrase to refer to the view that racism is no longer a serious social problem and a major obstacle for people of color that requires government intervention. While most scholars who advance this ideology are European American, some are, like Wilson, people of color.

The positions taken by these scholars range from outright dismissal of the notion that racism is of any real importance in U.S. society to the argument that dwelling upon the topic of racism at this time is not useful or pragmatic, or may even be racially divisive. Besides their denial of the present-day salience of racism, such scholars generally share the notion that government social and economic policies should (and can) be race neutral. Let us take a brief look at some of this scholarship.

Dinesh D'Souza is a first-generation immigrant from India whose writings include *The End of Racism*, a book that has garnered a great deal of media attention. In D'Souza's view, "Racism undoubtedly exists, but it no longer has the power to thwart blacks or any other group in achieving their economic, political, and social aspirations."[25] If African Americans are, for example, disproportionately represented in the poverty population, this is explainable by their "dysfunctional and pathological" culture.[26] D'Sousa's views are typical of those who blame poverty among African Americans on their allegedly deficient group values.[27]

Not all scholars who are in denial regarding the present-day significance of racism blame racial inequalities on negative cultural traits that people of color alone allegedly possess. Even today, some still posit the existence of negative biological traits among people of color. In 1994, psychologist Richard Herrnstein and political scientist Charles Murray published their highly controversial book *The Bell Curve*.[28] These scholars argued that the United States now contains a "cognitive underclass," made up of low-income people with lower-than-average intelligence. Such low intelligence levels pose a serious obstacle to economic success. The subaverage intelligence of members of the cognitive underclass is, in Herrnstein and Murray's view, largely genetically based. Thus, the disproportionate representation of people of color in poverty is implicitly interpreted as an outcome of nature, not nurture.

Some scholars who deny the present-day salience of racism do so without basing their arguments on theories of cultural or biological inferiority of people of color. In rejecting the notion that racism is an important social problem today, so-called racial realists[29] are more likely to emphasize the positive advances made by many people of color over the last several decades. For example, in *America in Black and White*, historians Stephan and Abigail Thernstrom focus on the many ways in which things have changed for African Americans since 1940. In their words, "the serious inequality that remains is less a function of white racism than of the racial gap in levels of educational attainment, the structure of the black family, and the rise in black crime."[30] Once again, the burden of responsibility for the excessive representation of African Americans among the poor is placed squarely on the shoulders of the impoverished themselves.

The Thernstroms view government policies aimed at assisting people of color to overcome their economic disadvantage as unnecessary, and as having unwanted negative consequences. Their denial of the present-day significance of racism is coupled with the notion that programs targeted at helping people of color, such as affirmative action, are socially inflammatory. In rejecting race-targeted social and economic policies, they state: "We remain committed to race-neutral policies. Not simply because they are morally right; in a society already deeply divided along lines of race, we see divisive race-conscious programs as dangerous."[31]

Racial realists also argue that treating racism as if it actually was a serious social problem reinforces the notion among people of color that they are somehow "victims" and as such are owed special treatment. In *A Dream Deferred*,

African-American writer Shelby Steele blames the disproportionate presence of African Americans among the poor—a so-called black underclass—not on racism, but on overly generous welfare programs. In his view, it is welfare, not racism, that is the problem:

> Of course, the welfare system does not provide a luxurious life, but it has been a powerful system of incentives and reinforcements in which people—particularly women—were literally paid for having children out of wedlock, for failing to finish school, for not developing job skills, for not marrying, and so on. It is not at all an exaggeration to say that the welfare policies of the last thirty years . . . *created* the black underclass in America.[32] [emphasis his]

NOT SEEING THE FOREST FOR THE TREES: A CASE OF RACISM-BLIND SOCIAL SCIENCE

Even scholars who are apparently cognizant of the existence of widespread racial bias on the part of individuals in U.S. society seem blind to the systemic nature of racism, including welfare racism. And so they too contribute to the politics of denial. An excellent example is Martin Gilens's important and provocative book, *Why Americans Hate Welfare*.[33] Gilens presents compelling data on the negative attitudes that whites have toward welfare and the racial stereotyping that he found underlying these attitudes. Conceptually, however, he seems unmoved by the implications of his own powerful data. While acknowledging the role of "race" in affecting whites' attitudes toward welfare, he discounts the impact of *racism*.[34]

Gilens argues that "racial stereotypes play a central role in generating opposition to welfare in America." He notes, for example, "that the centuries-old stereotype of blacks as lazy remains credible for large numbers of white Americans."[35] He traces that stereotype, appropriately, to its historic origins in slavery. However, in explaining contemporary white racial attitudes toward African Americans, Gilens focuses on the low socioeconomic status of African Americans as the culprit that evokes the racial stereotypes. He makes no attempt to explain the origins of the current economic plight of African Americans. Consequently, he ignores the role played by systemic racism in accounting for African Americans' disproportionate presence in the poverty population today.

Unfortunately, Gilens stands too close to his data "trees" to see the "forest" of systemic white racism. Instead, he focuses almost exclusively on individual-level racial prejudice and whether whites bear blacks "ill will." With this conceptual blinder in place, Gilens confidently concludes,

> For most white Americans, race-based opposition to welfare is not fed by ill will toward blacks, nor is it based on whites' desire to

maintain their economic advantages over African Americans. Instead, race-based opposition to welfare stems from the specific perception that, as a group, African Americans are not committed to the work ethic.[36]

Gilens's failure to contextualize contemporary white racial attitudes, by placing them in the system of white supremacy and privilege within which they are generated, results in his underestimating the formidable impact of racial stereotypes on U.S. welfare policy.[37]

Further, Gilens's reduction of systemic racism to racial attitudes allows for a shifting of focus away from white racial hegemony to white perceptions of "the deservingness" of those harmed by such attitudes.[38] More specifically, he shifts the analytical focus to whether the work ethic of African Americans makes them deserving of public assistance in whites' eyes. When, as is the case in Gilens's work, the focus of analysis is on *racial* attitudes as opposed to *racist* attitudes, it is assumed that there should be an examination of the targets of those stereotypes rather than of the people who hold them or, more important, of the racially dominant groups and their institutions that generate and disseminate these attitudes. In brief, since most European Americans are not overtly racist, there must be something about African Americans themselves which evokes and sustains such negative stereotypes.

While Gilens's attitudinal data are important, his narrow focus on and interpretation of these data obscure the existence and workings of systemic racism—as is so often the case in social science. But even worse, he ends up analyzing the objects of racial stereotyping rather than the system of racial oppression from which those stereotypes emanate and to which they lend substantial support. In this manner, rather than challenging racist stereotypes, Gilens's analysis subtly serves to reinforce them.

THE SCOPE AND ORGANIZATION OF THIS BOOK

As a legacy of a white political backlash against African-American struggles for racial and economic justice that emerged in the 1960s, the intellectual and political climate in the United States has shifted away from addressing racism as a major social problem. A politics of denial has come to hold sway. Insofar as these kinds of ideas are allowed to prevail, our political and intellectual climate is going to be inhospitable to expressions of concern over the plight of impoverished African-American mothers and other people of color, whether they rely on welfare or not. Such a climate also discourages examination of the effects of racism on U.S. welfare policy formation and implementation.

In racialized societies, fundamental social change is impossible without successful challenges to their racial structures, including those of the state. As

Martin Luther King Jr. aptly put it shortly before his assassination, in a letter in which he sought support for the "Washington project" which became known as the Poor People's Campaign, "We have learned from bitter experience that our government does not correct a race problem until it is confronted directly and dramatically."[39] Unless welfare racism is challenged directly and relentlessly, there is no hope for humane poverty policies or for effective movements for economic justice in the United States and other racialized societies. Unfortunately, most advocates of movements for economic justice today seem not only to have ignored the important lessons of the inseparability of poverty and racism, but to have taken an approach which is in opposition to it. Economic justice–focused progressives now often operate under the erroneous and, indeed, dangerous assumption that such movements must be guided by a militant ideological ignorance of the racism which is at the root of both much of U.S. poverty and government's treatment of the poor.

We hope that this book will contribute to the struggle to overcome the politics of denial regarding racial oppression and that it will help to place the problem of welfare racism front and center in welfare policy discourse. Accordingly, in this volume we argue three major points. First, welfare racism exists. Second, welfare racism persists. Third, welfare racism changes. Welfare racism exists as a major force shaping contemporary public assistance attitudes, policies, and practices. Its continued existence has been ensured by its ability to adapt its form, functions, and processes over time. Welfare racism exists and persists because it serves three major social stratification and social control functions for racialized societies and their "racial states." Welfare racism provides: (1) *social* prestige for the general white population, (2) *political* and career power for its politicians and other elites, and (3) *economic* acquisition for the nation's economic elite in the form of a large and easily exploitable low-wage labor pool. Welfare racism persists because it is a *shape shifter*. It behaves like the shape-shifting organisms and machines common in contemporary science fiction. Welfare racism changes or "shifts" its shape both to adapt to the overall racial changes in the larger society and to better serve its changing racial functions.

This book provides ample evidence that racism shapes public assistance policies and practices. For example, it shows that welfare racist attitudes were a major force in the formation, evolution, and recent abolition of the Aid to Families with Dependent Children program. We also discuss research which shows that now, as in the past, when the federal government has given individual states great discretion in the administration of welfare policies and programs, the race of the clients is an important determinant in deciding who gets what, if anything. This constellation of welfare racist attitudes, policies, and practices—what we call welfare racism—is the focus of this book.

Here we wish to briefly mention a limitation of our study. Our analysis of welfare racism in the chapters that follow focuses primarily upon the role of racism in the formation and implementation of U.S. welfare policy with respect to African Americans. We deal most extensively with African Americans for two reasons. The most immediate reason is that, unfortunately, we found very little welfare-related research literature and data, historical or contemporary, that would allow us to adequately address U.S. welfare policy in connection with other populations of color.[40] In those instances where such literature and data were found to exist, we have included Latino/a Americans, Asian Americans, and Native Americans in our discussions. In many respects, their experiences with welfare racism appear to have been very similar to those of African Americans. The existence of such similarities, along with differences in experiences, needs more investigation. The second reason we focus primarily on African Americans is that white-on-black oppression has historically been the basis for racial classification and for white racial hegemony in the United States, and it has endured in this nation for more than four hundred years.[41] Not surprisingly, our research found that expressions of welfare racism have overwhelmingly revolved around concerns on the part of European Americans with the welfare participation of African Americans.

In chapter 2 we briefly review mainstream perspectives on the U.S. welfare state, perspectives that emphasize the importance of class, gender, or state-centered forces in shaping welfare policy. We, in contrast, offer a racism-centered perspective for understanding U.S. welfare policy. Our framework draws attention to the racialized nature of U.S. society as a whole and the existence of a racial state that has long served as the political instrument of societywide white racial hegemony. This racism-centered framework will guide the direction of the remaining chapters in this book.

Chapter 3 discusses expressions of welfare racism in public assistance from the mothers pension programs established by individual states early in the twentieth century to the federal/state Aid to Dependent Children program (later renamed Aid to Families with Dependent Children) that emerged from the New Deal. Through the first decades of twentieth-century welfare policy and on into the 1960s, racial discrimination, racial exclusion, and racist stereotyping of welfare recipients were key means by which welfare racism was expressed.

In chapter 4, we present three case examples from the early 1960s that illustrate some of the ways in which welfare racism has served functions of racial control for European Americans. In these instances, welfare racism was mobilized in response to threats against white racial hegemony posed by African Americans. These case examples show welfare racism being mobilized by racial state actors against the southern civil rights movement, being used in the North as a strategy aimed at discouraging African-American migration from the South, and as a vehicle of white "internal colonization" through which racial state actors sought to maintain control over disenfranchised African Americans in Washington, D.C.

Chapter 5 discusses the white political backlash that began in the mid-1960s and contributed to the racialization of national politics. In the late 1960s, there was a "welfare explosion," and the rolls of the Aid to Families with Dependent Children program grew dramatically, along with the proportion of African Americans admitted to the rolls. Enveloped by the growing white backlash and the racialization of national politics, welfare became the target of a decades-long campaign of subtly race-based attacks by political elites, policy analysts, and the mass media. As we will show, welfare racism proved central to AFDC's abolition in 1996.

Chapter 6 probes usually ignored aspects of the relationship between the Personal Responsibility and Work Opportunity Reconciliation Act of 1996 and some of the racial control functions of welfare racism. This chapter addresses the act's treatment of immigrants, its not-so-subtle attack on the reproductive rights of poor African-American women, and the support that the act's race-based premises regarding mandatory work requirements received from many white, middle-class feminists.

Fallout from the Personal Responsibility and Work Opportunity Reconciliation Act and earlier welfare reforms of the 1990s is examined in chapter 7. The federal government has handed enormous discretion to the individual states in forming and implementing their welfare policies. This "states' rights" approach to welfare policy allows policies and practices to flourish that harm impoverished African Americans and other poor people of color. In this chapter we provide an overview of recent indirect and direct expressions of welfare racism, stressing their apparent continuity with welfare racist policies and practices in past decades. The chapter also provides a critique of recent mainstream welfare reform–monitoring efforts, which largely ignore racism and the negative impact of welfare reform on people of color in assessing its outcomes.

Finally, in chapter 8, we argue that progressives must attack welfare racism for there to be a successful antipoverty struggle. We call upon antiracist, feminist, economic justice, human rights, and welfare rights groups to collectively and cooperatively struggle against welfare racism in their efforts to win policy changes that secure the well-being of all who are impoverished. The strategies for confronting welfare racism that we outline in chapter 8 invite European Americans to join their brothers and sisters of color in proactive anti–welfare racism and antipoverty battles from which all will benefit.

2

CONCEPTUALIZING "WELFARE RACISM"

The racialized gender politics of welfare have yielded reforms that subordinate women of color disproportionately, both ideologically and in their practical effects. Poor women of color suffer stigmas applied only to them (lazy, matriarchal, baby machines).

Gwendolyn Mink,
Welfare's End

we take to conceptualizing welfare racism. We begin this process with a brief overview of dominant, mainstream perspectives on U.S. welfare policy, indicating what proponents of each typically tend to stress in their analyses. These perspectives are, to varying degrees, "racism blind." Our overview of mainstream perspectives provides the background for why we believe it is important to offer a "racism-centered" perspective in order to more fully understand U.S. welfare policy and its consequences.

The racism-centered perspective we use draws upon radical political economy and radical black feminist or "womanist" perspectives, and employs concepts such as the "racial state," "racist culture," "controlling images," "gendered racism," and "policy as ideology." In this chapter we introduce and explain these concepts, together with our key analytical concept of "welfare racism." Such concepts will be used to draw attention to and analyze important phenomena that mainstream perspectives tend to ignore.

MAINSTREAM PERSPECTIVES ON U.S. WELFARE POLICY

The scholarly literature that seeks to explain the formation, implementation, and outcomes of U.S. welfare policy usually adopts one of three general perspectives. Welfare policy is seen as shaped primarily by class interests, or by patriarchal forces, or by organizational dynamics involving the polity and state actors. Scholars embracing any of these three perspectives do at times acknowledge that racism plays a role. However, as we will see, the significance and role they accord to racism vary.

Class-Centered Perspectives on U.S. Welfare Policy

Policy making by the contemporary welfare state is seen by class-centered theorists[1] as being shaped by dominant class interests,[2] by the state's need to respond to the operating requirements of the capitalist economic system,[3] or, by the outcome of interclass conflicts to which this system periodically gives rise.[4] Racism, when it is considered at all, is typically seen as being situated within and subordinate to class dynamics in importance. It is usually treated as but one element of working-class exploitation, or as a source of division and intraclass conflict that undercuts capacity for working-class consciousness and unity. In short, the systemic requirements of capitalism and class dynamics, not racism, are seen as the key factors shaping U.S. welfare policy.

An example of this perspective is Francis Fox Piven and Richard A. Cloward's classic study, *Regulating the Poor*.[5] Piven and Cloward maintain that U.S. welfare policy has been used by the state to stifle protest and to enforce submissive work norms. This is accomplished largely by the state's expanding or contracting welfare benefits in ways that serve dominant class interests. During periods of economic and political crisis, the state expands its welfare rolls to reduce the possibility of serious uprisings, in effect by pacifying, co-opting, or buying off the poor. In times of economic and political stability, the state turns around and expunges recipients from the rolls, forcing poor people to seek ways to survive in the market economy, and providing only the most meager assistance to those who would not otherwise survive. Those who must rely on welfare are condemned and negatively stigmatized for their "dependence on the dole." They serve as examples for others of how people will be treated who fail to accept whatever work is available, for whatever pay, and under whatever conditions are provided. In brief, Piven and Cloward see the principal function of welfare as that of allowing the capitalist class to maintain control over labor.

The role of welfare policies in buttressing dominant class interests and helping to meet capitalist labor needs is an important topic we will examine in this book. But in emphasizing dominant class interests and the economic functions of welfare, Piven and Cloward's class-centered perspective does not fully explore the role played by racism in U.S. welfare policy. To be fair, this was not their intention. While their analysis does include some rich data and valuable insights on the connection between racism, welfare policy, and dominant-class exploitation of the labor of impoverished African Americans, Piven and Cloward tell only part of the story regarding the functions played by racism in welfare policy.

Gender-Centered Perspectives

Gender-centered analyses address ways in which welfare state policies help to sustain and reproduce patriarchy.[6] The drive to maintain male dominance and the patriarchal family is assumed to be the principal force shaping the formation, implementation, and outcomes of U.S. welfare policy. Feminist scholars who address welfare policy from a gender-centered perspective often acknowledge the presence and impact of racism but, as with the class-centered perspective, typically accord racism a position of secondary importance in their analyses. Once again, to be fair, a full exploration of the role played by racism in welfare policy is not their aim, just as a full exploration of the impact of class and gender on U.S. welfare policy is not our objective in this book. The goal of feminist scholars is, of course, to expose the centrality and power of patriarchy in welfare policy and other social realms.

For example, in *Regulating the Lives of Women*,[7] Mimi Abramovitz seeks to understand welfare through a "gender lens." In analyzing U.S. welfare policy, Abramovitz observes that welfare has historically served the function of distinguishing the "deserving poor" (e.g., widows with children) from the "undeserving poor" (e.g., never-married and divorced mothers). Historically, the latter have often suffered exclusion from receipt of welfare benefits or condemnation for reliance on welfare. The state has sought to craft and implement welfare policy in ways that make public assistance unattractive for mothers to rely upon or difficult to get. This is done in order to enforce a patriarchal "family ethic" that calls for women to be wives and economic dependents of men, and which frowns upon the option of their being economically self-reliant and functioning independently from male partners.

Abramovitz does take note of ways in which white women and women of color have often received different treatment under U.S. welfare policy, and in doing so describes a variety of racist practices. She also draws attention to the special difficulties that African-American women have faced in living in accordance with the norms of a family ethic constructed around male dominance, given that so many black males have been unable to overcome discriminatory barriers that have prevented them from earning wages that will support a family. But even with the helpful contributions of Abramovitz and some other feminist scholars who are particularly sensitive to racism and its role in the lives of women of color, much more ground regarding the role played by racism in U.S. welfare policy remains to be explored.

State-Centered Perspectives

State-centered scholars tend to eschew the centrality of both class and gender, and instead view U.S. welfare policy as an historically contingent product of state-polity interactions, state institutional structure and capacity, previous policy legacies, and the like.[8] State actors are seen as having organizational interests and concerns that do not necessarily reflect group relations that prevail within the larger society (for example, those deriving from class, gender, or racial hierarchies). Nor is policy making by state actors seen as driven or restrained largely by the systemic requirements of capitalism. Instead, welfare policy is said to be principally a product of state-related factors.[9]

In comparison to class- and gender-centered perspectives on U.S. welfare policy, state-centered perspectives have been the least sensitive to the role of racism. As an example, racism is absent from the picture in sociologist Theda Skocpol's widely acclaimed, state-centered analysis of the origins of maternalist welfare programs of the early twentieth century, *Protecting Soldiers and Mothers*.[10] Other than a passing allusion to "cultural discrimination" against "subordinate racial and ethnic groups" that kept members of these groups from receiving welfare aid,[11] she ignores the topic. In later work, Skocpol's self-labeled "polity-oriented approach," when applied to African Americans' relationships to U.S. social policies, pointedly avoids exploring the existence and significance of racism.[12] At best, she allows racism to hover in the historical background, never acknowledging the possibility of its centrality as a social force.

Despite this general tendency to ignore or to look past racism, some state-centered scholars have recently begun to break ranks and to bring racism more forthrightly into their analyses. While her earlier scholarly work tends to be more class-centered in its perspective, in *The Color of Welfare* sociologist Jill Quadagno acknowledges the importance of racism in understanding decisions by state actors in the area of U.S. welfare policy.[13] Her concern is primarily with exploring why the United States has failed to develop a more broad-based and generous welfare state, in comparison to many European democracies. In Quadagno's view, racism has functioned as a key source of resistance to progressive state welfare programs largely because members of the white working class have tended to perceive such programs as primarily benefiting African Americans and have fought against them. In her view, race-based attitudes and actions on the part of the white working class, an important political and electoral constituency, have impeded those state actors who might otherwise have had the will to enlarge the role and largesse of the welfare state. Quadagno's focus on the racial attitudes of the polity is valuable. However, she has comparatively little to say about the role racism has played in the U.S. welfare policy that has been successfully adopted and implemented by the state, or about the racist welfare attitudes of state actors themselves.

Robert C. Lieberman, in *Shifting the Color Line*,[14] is likewise interested in the U.S. welfare state. His focus, however, is on the ways in which the U.S. welfare state has been institutionally structured. Racism, he notes, played a significant role in the politics surrounding the origins of the welfare state during the New Deal, influencing both the policies that were deemed politically possible by state actors and the kinds of institutions that they created to carry these policies out. Aid to Families with Dependent Children, a program that would eventually come to serve many impoverished African-American women and children, was from the very start institutionally structured in ways that made it politically vulnerable. It was, for example, administered at the individual state and local levels of government, where parochial and race-based political interests could most readily hold sway. In contrast, Old Age Insurance, another program created during the New Deal, from the start served an overwhelmingly white clientele. The program was structured so as to be centrally administered at the federal level, and it was set up in a way that insulated it from outside political meddling. In line with the state-centered perspective, Lieberman's emphasis is on state institutions and the importance of the nature of their originating structures. Yet his work provides useful insights into ways in which the administration of welfare policy may both reflect and help to perpetuate racial inequalities over time.

Another variant of the state-centered perspective is provided by Michael Brown in *Race, Money, and the American Welfare State*.[15] Brown argues that "questions of fiscal capacity—the ability of policy makers to raise revenues necessary to finance new policies—lie at the center of the development of the American welfare state."[16] In his view, the state actors who strove to initiate the New Deal had to first contend with minimizing the resistance of the people who would have to pay for its programs, namely investors and taxpayers. One way to minimize this resistance was to adopt a position of fiscal conservatism to hold down both taxing and spending, and to decentralize control over those welfare state programs likely to be most politically contested. Taxing and spending for Old Age Insurance were minimally controversial, so state actors made the decision to centrally administer it at the federal level. With regard to AFDC, a decision was made by federal state actors to give individual state and local governments broad discretion in the setting of benefit levels and administration, and thus control its costs. As this occurred in the mid-1930s, at a time when white racism was normative and segregation widespread at the individual state and local levels of government, Brown argues that such decisions set the stage for the racial stratification of the U.S. welfare state that continues to this day.

THE NEED FOR A RACISM-CENTERED PERSPECTIVE ON U.S. WELFARE POLICY

Proponents of each of the three mainstream perspectives on U.S. welfare policy—class-, gender-, and state-centered—at times suggest that racism plays a role in policy formation, implementation, and outcomes. However, as we have noted, none of these perspectives is aimed at fully exploring the significance and functions played by racism in this regard. We believe that this is largely due to the particular conceptual "lenses" that they employ and how these lenses shape scholars' perceptions of the nature of the state. In class-centered perspectives, scholars tend to view the state as serving the interests of the dominant class within capitalism. Those adhering to gender-centered perspectives envision a patriarchal state, one that serves the interests of male dominance. State-centered perspectives are less easy to characterize. With a few notable exceptions, such as those we have mentioned, its proponents too often seem to assume that state actors and the organizational networks in which they are involved are autonomous—or relatively so—from the class, gender, and racial hierarchies that have long organized social life in U.S. society. The question of whose or what interests are served by the state and its actors is sometimes treated as so historically contingent as to be left essentially undefined.[17]

In our view, gaining a fuller understanding of the role played by racism in the formation, implementation, and outcomes of U.S. welfare policy requires putting on a racial lens and taking a racism-centered perspective. A racism-centered perspective on U.S. welfare policy, while attempting to correct for the ways in which racism has often been accorded secondary importance by mainstream class-, gender-, and state-centered perspectives, should not in turn seek to "trump" them. Our approach here is not aimed at claiming racism is more important than other factors in understanding U.S. welfare policy. Rather, we wish to explore just what the importance of racism has been and is. We intend to be sufficiently flexible in our racism-centered perspective such that we can utilize and pay due credit to knowledge that has been generated by scholars using quite different conceptual "lenses."

In the next sections of this chapter we discuss the racism-centered perspective that will inform the chapters that follow. We begin by addressing the relationship between white dominance and the racial character of the state.

WHITE RACIAL HEGEMONY AND THE NATURE OF THE STATE

In his critique of the treatment of the state in the vast body of literature on U.S. racial and ethnic relations, Jack Niemonen draws attention to the fact that few scholars have paused to consider its "intrinsically racial character." In his view, scholars largely ignore the fact that "The state plays a significant role in forming, establishing, structuring, mediating, and reproducing racial and ethnic relations in specific historical contexts."[18] Niemonen's observations point to the need to reconceptualize the nature of the state in order to take its intrinsically racial character into account.

Social scientists really do not have a systematic theory that addresses the state's racial character, racist practices by the state, or the role of the state in maintaining racial inequalities. However, as U.S. scholars have begun to explore such topics, new ways of referring to the state are emerging. We are seeing more frequent use of terms like *racial state*,[19] the *racialized state*,[20] *white state power*,[21] and the *white supremacist state*.[22] The use of such terms signals a departure from conventional class-, gender-, and state-centered perspectives, as scholars grapple with the challenge of how best to bring racism into discussions of the state when the topic is government policies and practices adversely affecting people of color.

In a similar vein, a number of British scholars have drawn attention to "state racism."[23] Much of their work is in response to the shortcomings of a class-centered perspective for comprehensively handling racism.[24] Controversies surrounding state actors' efforts to control immigration from former colonies in Africa and Asia, and to fight violent crime committed by or aimed at people of color, have helped to energize British scholars' interest in theorizing about the origins and functions of racism in state policy.[25]

While developing or presenting a systematic theory of racism and the state is not our purpose in writing this book, in taking a racism-centered approach to U.S. welfare policy we do see the need to make our views about the link between the two explicit. We agree with the premise, advanced by Eduardo

Bonilla-Silva, that the United States is a "racialized social system"[26] in which white racism has long been endemic. As many scholars have pointed out, people of European descent historically created the concept of "race" and have used it as the basis for an ideology that denotes a hierarchy of human biological categories in which they, as "whites," assumed superiority.[27] For more than four centuries now, European Americans have relied on this socially constructed hierarchy, and the alleged inherited attributes of different "races," to explain and therefore justify seemingly intractable disparities in power and privilege along color lines. Once having set into motion an ideological justification for these race-based disparities, "whites" have worked relentlessly to keep the disparities intact.[28]

In the United States, race-based disparities in power and privilege both reflect and reinforce an ongoing system of societywide *white racial hegemony*. White racial hegemony refers to European Americans' systemic exercise of domination over racially subordinate groups. Today this domination is maintained not so much through coercion or force, but by exercising control over cultural beliefs and ideologies, as well as the key legitimizing institutions of society through which they are expressed (e.g., the state and mass media). Consequently, European Americans have been able to maintain a position of advantage politically, economically, and socially when it comes to enriching their own life chances over those of people of color.

This system of white racial hegemony has continued even though its critics have pointed out that both the concept of race itself and its notion of a hierarchy of human racial categories are inherently racist ideas, and that such modes of thinking exist and take on meaning only in a society in which racism is practiced.[29] White racial hegemony has also continued in the face of various forms of resistance and rebellion in the United States by the racially oppressed, namely people of African, Latin American and Caribbean, Asian, and Native American descent.

In our view, insofar as it is a fundamental component of the social organization of U.S. society, the state must be seen as more than a political apparatus driven primarily by class-, gender-, or state-centered forces. Such perspectives deny what Niemonen has called the state's "intrinsically racial character." The *racial state*—operating within the context of a racialized social system—has more often than not historically functioned as the *political arm of white racial hegemony*. Its policies have helped to protect and reinforce systemic inequalities along the lines of skin color, both during the United States' long-term history of outright white supremacy and on into the contemporary period, when there is much denial on the part of European Americans that racism is any longer a serious social problem. Few scholars capture the historical and ongoing relationship between racism and the state as well as political scientist Carter A. Wilson in

Racism: From Slavery to Advanced Capitalism.[30] His ideas help to inform our racism-centered perspective on U.S. welfare policy.

THE POLITICAL ECONOMY OF THE RACIAL STATE

Carter A. Wilson, along with proponents of the class-centered perspective that we discussed earlier, views capitalism as having always been a fundamentally exploitative economic structure. Drawing from Marxist theory, Wilson argues that in the United States, a dominant class of white property owners has historically derived disproportionate benefits from this economic structure in terms of income and wealth. The latter is, of course, often used as the foundation for claiming high prestige or social status and gaining political power. One way in which members of the dominant class pursue financial gain is by private ownership of profit-making operations that exploit the labor of subordinate, nonpropertied classes. In order to survive, members of the latter are ordinarily forced to sell their labor power to enterprises (such as plantations, farms, business firms) run by members of the dominant class or its agents. However, as employees, workers are paid less than the actual value that their labor is worth to their employer. The difference accrues to the dominant class in the form of profit, and profit is the fundamental basis of the capital accumulation on which this class's affluence and political power rest.

In Wilson's view, this capital accumulation process has been especially well served by racially oppressive social arrangements which have rendered the labor of people of color particularly subject to exploitation. Such social arrangements have ranged from slavery to employment discrimination and race-based labor market segregation. He sees the dominant class as having played an active role in creating, promoting, and disseminating ideas that legitimate and reinforce such racially oppressive social arrangements. African Americans have, for example, historically been defined as being capable of filling only certain kinds of jobs, in certain types of settings, where the work is dirty and hard and the pay is low. To Wilson, such ideas are part of a socially omnipresent *racist culture* built around notions of white supremacy.[31] Members of subordinate classes at times may uncritically accept or internalize its ideas.

While originating from the dominant class, over time, in Wilson's view, racist culture has become "a social force of its own, quite apart from its creators."[32] This culture does not, however, hover about, independent of social organization, but is deeply embedded in and helps to guide the functioning of virtually all major societal institutions, including the state. Wilson's neo-Marxist perspective thus departs from conventional class-centered approaches by acknowledging that racist ideas and practices are not simply and at all times explainable with reference to economic interests or determinants, a point with which we most emphatically agree. While racist culture informs policies that help to maintain economic inequalities between whites and people of color, it also helps to maintain social and political inequalities as well.

Wilson notes that ideas about "race" have been disseminated and kept alive "in just about every medium and institution in society: newspapers, magazines, books, theaters, cinema, and later in television and radio, as well as in Congress, courts, public schools, and universities."[33] Why is this the case? In a society predicated on white racial hegemony, racist ideas and practices serve not only important economic functions, but also social, political, and even psychological functions for people who define themselves as "white."[34] We thus believe it important to emphasize, even more than does Wilson, that no matter how racist culture originated it has been energized and sustained in a variety of institutional settings, by whites at varying class levels, and for reasons that go well beyond the strictly economic.[35]

Unfortunately, Wilson tends to unduly emphasize the role played by the dominant class in energizing and helping to sustain racist culture, and in our view underestimates the important contributions of other segments of U.S. society. In particular, we feel that he fails to give sufficient weight to the agency and self-activity of state actors, who not only operate within the environment of racist culture, but who help to shape this culture. State actors may, as Wilson maintains, be responsive to and supportive of racially oppressive social arrangements in order to serve the needs of the dominant class, and to be protective of the economic benefits this class derives from these arrangements. However, state actors may also be active agents in their own right when it comes to fashioning, using, or promoting elements of racist culture. For example, political elites have frequently introduced rhetoric or taken actions that have stimulated or exploited racist sentiments among members of the public, either while pursuing their own personal political fortunes or seeking to advance their political party agendas.[36]

We do agree with Wilson that racist culture, while omnipresent, has been dynamic and changing rather than static and fixed. The ideas and practices that constitute racist culture are subject to both construction and reconstruction. While in Wilson's view, the leading role in this process has been played by the dominant class, again we would stress the contributions made by other sectors of the racially dominant white population, especially state actors, but also those in policy-proposal and idea-generating positions in universities, think tanks, and the mass media. Moreover, although the ideas and practices of racist culture tend to become a part of the natural order of things for the majority of society's members, from time to time some important changes in this culture are wrought through countercultural challenges by antiracist or racial justice social movements.

Wilson sees the dominant class as facing an ongoing need to capture or put pressure upon the state so that state power is used to help maintain the labor-exploitative capital accumulation process. The dominant class depends upon state actors' general acceptance of the basic canons of the racist culture and the racially oppressive social arrangements sustained by this culture that help the accumulation process along. Yet, because the state is open to political challenges from those outside the dominant class, for example from racially subordinated groups, in Wilson's view the state's racial role is somewhat indeterminate rather than inflexible and constant. Social movements have periodically arisen that have challenged state actors' adherence to the canons of racist culture. Such movements have struggled to interfere with or even reverse the use of state power to prop up social arrangements that are racially oppressive. At times, as in the case of the 1960s civil rights movement, they have achieved some success.

In response to antiracist social movements, the state has occasionally resembled a contested terrain and been forced into shifting or even contradictory racial roles. Buffeted by pressures from racially subordinated groups and their allies, the state may maintain, or it may ameliorate, racially oppressive social arrangements. Or it may do both simultaneously, choosing to address some arrangements and to ignore others. Thus, in Wilson's view, the racial role of the state is not only indeterminate; at times it is paradoxical. He sees the state as a somewhat fragmented social structure, "sensitive to interest group pressures while at the same time biased in favor of upper-stratum interests."[37] And because racist culture is dynamic, and is constantly being built and rebuilt, the ways in which racism is expressed and employed by state actors take different forms over time.

In taking a racism-centered approach to U.S. welfare policy, we acknowledge Carter A. Wilson's argument that the United States' dominant class set a racist culture into motion in order to advance its quest for financial gain. However, we depart from Wilson in that we wish to underscore the stake that all whites, as members of the racially dominant group, have had in helping to keep racist culture energized and sustained, since it legitimates whites' advantaged access to race-based economic, political, and social privileges. Unlike Wilson, we want to place particular emphasis on racism's social and political functions, and not simply its economic functions, especially since racist ideas and practices are frequently present even when discernibly economic interests and determinants are not. We depart from Wilson in that we wish to heavily stress the important role played by state actors and others whose ideas and practices have frequently expressed and reinforced elements of racist culture, in its various and changing forms.

In U.S. society, state actors have historically been extremely important pilots of the racial state. Our use of the term *racial state* in this book will not only refer to state structure at the federal level. In the United States, the formation and implementation of racial state policy has involved not only the federal government but relatively autonomous individual state and local governments as well.[38] As we will see, by its actions, the federal racial state has affected welfare policy across U.S. society. Yet, by its regulatory omissions and permissions, the federal racial state has also given lower-level governmental bodies political space to tailor policies and practices in ways that meshed with regional or localized race-based mores and patterns of racial inequality. We consider levels of governance below the federal level to be part of the overall racial state structure. The racial state thus operates at multiple levels and, as we will see in subsequent chapters, not always with interlevel consensus and unity.

Wilson does not use the term racial state in setting forth his heavily racism-centered perspective. But we will use the term in this book to emphasize the intimate and interactive relationship between the state and white racial hegemony. It is clear, however, that Wilson is sensitive to the fact that those who have been routinely most successful in capturing key state positions, or in pressuring the state from without, have been racially dominant as well as class dominant. It is the intersection of racial oppression and class exploitation contained in Wilson's political economy model with which we feel an affinity, for the dominant class in the conventional class-centered perspective is often treated as if it had no color, or else its whiteness is not treated as if it is significant. Wilson has introduced a racism-centered perspective on the state that neither ignores class nor subordinates its influence by fiat to racism. At the same time, by employing the concept of racist culture to characterize the operating environment within which state actors function, Wilson opens the door to the fact that policy decisions by racial state actors may serve functions for white racial hegemony that go well beyond the economic.

What Wilson does largely ignore, which we will not, is gender. Members of the dominant class to which he alludes, along with racial state actors, have not only historically been white; they have also been male. Those persons rendered most subordinate to, and whose labor has been most intensively exploited by, the dominant class within U.S. capitalism have historically been women of color.[39] Moreover, the racist culture set in motion by the dominant class is uniquely negative and oppressive in its treatment of African-American women. The significance of this feature of racist culture for our racism-centered perspective on U.S. welfare policy is perhaps best understood with the help of Philomena Essed's concept of "gendered racism,"[40] which we will discuss shortly.

In our view, ultimately U.S. welfare policy generated by the racial state must be understood within the context of racial, class, and gender forces, since "exploitation, sexism, and racism are intimately intertwined and constantly affect one another."[41] Being sensitive to all elements of this multidimensional context is particularly important to a consideration of U.S. welfare policy, given the disproportionate numbers of poor women of color that this policy has harmed and continues to harm today.[42]

U.S. welfare policy has always been very much about how poor women of color, particularly African-American women, are going to be dealt with within a system of white racial hegemony. Unfortunately, the "gender lens" adopted by many white feminist scholars has not provided us with the tools to look at U.S. welfare policy from the vantage point of those at whom it has largely been targeted. Consequently, we will turn our attention here to the work of African-American scholars who have put forth a radical black feminist or "womanist" perspective as an alternative to "white feminism."

WOMANISM, GENDERED RACISM, AND CONTROLLING IMAGES

Sojourner Truth, a nineteenth-century black abolitionist and feminist, has long been emblematic of the courage and determination that fuels the African-American freedom struggle. Unfortunately, the narrative of Sojourner's truth is also a sad testimony of the racial and class divisions within this nation's women's movements. Indeed, the truth of Sojourner's womanhood could not be taken for granted. At an antislavery rally in Indiana, Sojourner Truth responded to a white male heckler's challenge that "I don't believe you are a woman" by bearing her breasts for all to see.[43] Before giving her eloquent "Ain't I a Woman?" speech at an important convention of the women's rights movement, Sojourner Truth endured still more indignities. This time they came from white women who warned, "Don't let her speak!"[44]

Unfortunately, the womanhood (or womanliness) of African-American women was far from settled by Sojourner Truth's bold actions in the mid-nineteenth century. Now, well over a century later, African-American women intellectuals question the relevance of the modern feminist movement to their lives. This time it is they who, through their writings, "heckle" the color and class persona of what they sometimes deride as the "white women's movement." In the view of many black feminists, the white- and middle-class–dominated feminist movement that has been active and visible since the late 1960s is out of touch with the experiences and needs of women of color, and of poor women in general.

It is within this context of their continuing struggle for recognition of their womanhood, and against racial and class exclusion or marginalization from the largely white, middle-class women's movements that many African-American feminists have rejected "white feminism" for a "womanist" perspective.[45] More than any other single perspective, the *womanist perspective* has influenced our thinking about U.S. welfare policy. A radical black feminist or womanist perspective challenges the foundations of not only patriarchal but also racist and class-exploitative forms of social organization and oppression. The womanist perspective and the present study have a common distinguishing feature: each sees racism as central to its analysis. With the possible exception of their social class backgrounds, the sounds of the voices of womanist intellectuals ring more experientially true to those most likely to be stereotyped as "welfare mothers." It should not be surprising, therefore, that a womanist perspective offers rich intellectual insights for analyses of racism in the realm of welfare.

Consistent with the long struggle of African-American females to gain recognition of their womanhood, the approach crafted by radical black feminists calls for the linking of the struggles of African-American women to "a wider struggle for human dignity, empowerment, and social justice."[46] This approach was termed a "womanist" perspective by black feminist Alice Walker. From the womanist perspective, gender oppression of African-American women can not be separated from the racial and economic oppression they and others of color (including males) endure.

Dorothy Roberts, an African-American legal scholar, puts the point this way: "Black women experience various forms of oppression simultaneously, as a complex interaction of their race, gender, and class that is more than the sum of its parts."[47] From the womanist perspective, women's political action is valued not merely as a source of power but as a means to achieving the ultimate end to race-, class-, and gender-based oppression.[48] Among womanists there is, however, general agreement as to the primacy of dealing with the racism faced by African Americans.[49]

The existence and raison d'être of the womanist perspective helps to underscore the limitations of mainstream perspectives in helping us to fully understand the formation, implementation, and outcomes of U.S. welfare policy. The womanist perspective reminds us that analyses of U.S. welfare policy must be sensitive to the vantage point of those at whom this policy has largely been targeted, African-American women. A racism-based perspective must pay attention to this vantage point, and to how U.S. welfare policy portrays and deals with women of color. Adopting such a perspective can be aided by two black feminist concepts: "gendered racism" and "controlling images."

Gendered Racism and Controlling Images

Philomena Essed's concept of *gendered racism* draws attention to the fact that racism often manifests itself in ways that are not gender neutral. That is, while both racially oppressed males and females are affected by racism, the treatment each receives and how racism is experienced are often gender specific. The violent black man and the sexually promiscuous black woman are examples of gender-specific negative stereotypes, beliefs that have long been embedded in racist culture. The concept of gendered racism can be used in analyzing the gender-specific racist portrayal, treatment, and experiences of both men and women of color. It assumes that for racially oppressed people of a specific gender, the lines of racism and sexism are not only overlapping, but often indistinguishable.[50]

Gendered racism is a concept that can also help us to understand the intensity of white hostility toward the supposedly ubiquitous and stereotypical "welfare queen." She is typically portrayed in the mass media and in everyday discourse as an African-American woman who is living fraudulently, lazily, and "royally" off generous welfare benefits provided by taxes paid by overworked European Americans. Even the less racially charged term "welfare mother" is heavily burdened with welfare queen stereotypes. The intense white hostility toward the welfare queen and the welfare mother stems from the fact that the stereotypes do not originate from a single ideological source. The explosive bonding of patriarchal thinking with racist stereotypes results in a new formulation that magnifies their effects exponentially, rather than in a simple additive fashion.

Gendered racism, like racism more generally, is best viewed not as a thing or as a structure, but as a process. Thinking about racism as a process leads us to ask how and why racism occurs in policy arenas such as welfare. By focusing on gendered racism as a process, one can analyze ways in which negative class-, race-, and gender-based images of impoverished, public assistance–reliant mothers are effectively mobilized by racial state actors and others who contribute to welfare-related discourse. It is important to ask why racial state actors choose to single out women of color in this discourse (or use race-coded terms for such women), given that there are plenty of white women who rely on welfare. It is also revealing to explore the functions that effective mobilization of such images serves for whites and for white racial hegemony more generally.

While a structural approach to racism focuses on racism as a highly organized system of racially oppressive social arrangements, a process approach to racism highlights racism as a continuous and dynamic process of social control. Susan Thomas, for example, defines racism as "a process of systemic oppression directed against people who are defined as inferior, usually in pseudobiological terms such as skin color."[51] Cheryl Townsend Gilkes takes the process-driven definition of racism to yet another level. In Gilkes's view, to understand racism as "a system of social control, it is important to understand that the process of creating and maintaining group subordination is an act of social control."[52] That is, racism is not just maintained through a system of social control. Racism is both a system and a social control process.

In applying a process approach to racism, Gilkes finds sociologist Howard Becker's sociological concept of "outsiders" relevant to an understanding of *racial control*.[53] Outsiders are people who are considered and treated as a deviant Other by dominant groups, sometimes because their behavior is considered non-normative, and sometimes in response to their very being. Gilkes argues that as "perpetual outsiders," African Americans have historically served the profit-making interests of capitalists either directly as superexploitable labor, or as a buffer against interclass tensions between capitalists and white workers that would likely have been heightened if African Americans did not serve that buffer role. To keep African Americans as outsiders, they have been "isolated and contained" through moral stigmatization by numerous agents of social control.[54]

As we will show in this book, the moral stigmatization of African-American women in welfare discourse and the process of racial control of which it is a component have not come only from those occupying positions in the racial state—from Congressmen on down to welfare office officials. They have also come from the mass media, policy research and think tank analysts, university-based social scientists, independent intellectuals, and members of the general public.

Why have African-American women been a particular target of attack? Gilkes argues that because of their historic and contemporary roles as opponents of white racism, as "biological and social producers" of African Americans (the unwanted Other), and as persons who have often penetrated the racial boundaries of the dominant culture, African-American women are considered to constitute a threat to white racial hegemony. Threats to this hegemony are typically countered with bombardments of system-sustaining ideas that emanate from the omnipresent racist culture. Gendered racist stereotypes that morally malign African-American women represent efforts to control their real and potential threats not only to white racial hegemony but to capitalism and patriarchy.[55]

The perceived threats to white racial hegemony posed by the reproductive activities of African-American women have long been the subject of moral malignment by whites, according to Dorothy Roberts. She maintains that by framing procreation by African-American women as a problem, and by falsely claiming that African-American women are "breeding" indiscriminately and without concern for their ability to provide for the children they bear, whites attempt to make them carry the blame for black poverty and racial inequality. This moral malignment thus deflects attention away from white racial hegemony and the highly organized social structures and processes that bring about and sustain it, whose unraveling requires nothing short of radical change.[56]

In Roberts's words, "Blaming Black mothers then, is a way of subjugating the Black race as a whole."[57] Moral malignment of African-American women serves multiple functions in the interest of racial control. First, it can excite, harness, and express white racist sentiment. Second, it can buttress the omnipresent racist culture in promulgating everyday, taken-for-granted understandings about black moral inferiority and irresponsibility. Third, it can provide a rationale and impetus for racial state policy that reflects these understandings, such as recent provisions of welfare reform that seek to control childbearing by African-American women.[58] Such policy is not simply shaped by racist ideology. In Roberts's view, *policy as ideology* is a useful way to view the ideological function of welfare policy. Barbara Cruikshank adds to the policy-as-ideology idea her observation that, in welfare policy set in motion by racial state actors, "The stereotype does not justify practices; rather, practices justify stereotypes."[59]

In *Black Feminist Thought*, Patricia Hill Collins employs the concept of *controlling images* to explore the powerful functions that racist stereotypes of African-American women play in the maintenance of racial, class, and gender oppression.[60] Controlling images are another way of talking about the process involved in effective racial control. As you will see in the chapters that follow, one way in which racial state actors and other European Americans have managed welfare policy discourse is through the use of controlling images that denigrate African-American women, particularly their moral character and quality as mothers.[61] Portrayed as moral "outsiders" who are incapable of operating in accordance with the racially dominant group's white middle-class norms, impoverished African-American women are marginalized as Other. Their negative stigmatization and treatment through controlling images serves to reinforce and to reify the boundaries of both who and what is morally normative within white racial hegemony.[62]

Collins examines the functions of "the mammy," "the matriarch," the "welfare mother," and "the Jezebel" as "interrelated, ideologically constructed controlling images of Black womanhood."[63] The mammy is an image derived from slavery, and from generations of poorly remunerated domestic service by African-American women in white people's homes. The mammy is the "the faithful, obedient domestic servant" who spends more time caring for white people's children than her own.[64] Ironically, Collins notes, this is the only image of African-American women that has been viewed favorably by European Americans.

Although she may be forced by economic circumstances to spend far more time caring for white children than she can ever allot to members of her own family, the mammy is deemed to be socially responsible. The controlling image of "the mammy" suggests that how socially responsible African-American women are judged to be is less a product of how well they care for their own children than how they serve the interests of the racially dominant group. Moreover, as a "good" colored, Negro, or black, the mammy is not threatening to the racial status quo or any other system of social inequality. Indeed, she is prominently displayed for commercial purposes as "Aunt Jemima" on boxes of pancake mix even today. In this controlling image, racial accommodation and social responsibility are synonymous. Being socially responsible means accepting white racial domination.

As we will discuss in a later chapter, the controlling image of the matriarch was promulgated as part of the white political backlash against African-American struggles for civil rights and economic justice that reached an explosive head in the mid-1960s. Racial state actors played a major role in the dissemination of this controlling image. It is seen, for example, in the so-called Moynihan Report, whose chief author was Daniel Patrick Moynihan, a U.S. Department of Labor official who would later become a U.S. senator and an "expert" on U.S. welfare policy.[65] The widely discussed Moynihan Report had the effect of helping to align the Lyndon B. Johnson administration with the emerging white backlash against challenges to white racial hegemony posed by the civil rights movement and black urban unrest. Continuing in character, Moynihan would later advise President Richard Nixon, in a confidential government memorandum, that "the time may have come when the issue of race could benefit from a period of 'benign neglect.'"[66]

The controlling image of the black matriarch invoked the notion that the two-parent nuclear family structure, said to have been already weakened among African Americans by slavery, was being further undermined by the behavior of African-American women. Portrayed as domineering, emasculating, and overly independent, African-American women were seen as contributing to marital dissolution and being responsible for increasing rates of single motherhood and female-headed families. The inference was that they cared more for their own selfish interests than for the well-being and needs of their children. Subtly using this controlling image of the matriarch, the Moynihan Report shifted blame for African Americans' deep-rooted poverty away from white racial oppression and onto the backs of black women.[67]

The gender role independence implied by African-American single motherhood apparently threatened not only the racial order but the white-dominated patriarchal order as well. Use of the controlling image of the matriarch constituted yet another blow in the centuries of attacks on African-American womanhood, but it also had special implications for white women.

According to Collins,

> the image of the Black matriarch serves as a powerful symbol for both Black and White women of what can go wrong if White patriarchal power is challenged. Aggressive, assertive women are penalized—they are abandoned by their men, end up impoverished, and are stigmatized as being unfeminine.[68]

The controlling image of the matriarch was a potent way to morally malign and stigmatize black women, while sending a message as to what could happen to white women who opted for independence from males and control over their reproductive decisions.[69]

Collins argues that the controlling image of the "welfare mother" functions to provide an ideological justification for restraining the fertility of poor women of color. The modern stereotype of the morally irresponsible, sexually promiscuous welfare mother is rooted in a much older image of black "breeder" women that originated under slavery. Then and now, these various portrayals of black women as breeders have been used to justify "efforts to harness Black women's fertility to the needs of a changing political economy."[70] Under slavery, impoverished women of African descent were forced to reproduce to provide laborers who would generate profits for their "owners." Under modern-day capitalism, where their offspring are more often seen as a tax burden than a source of profit, state actors have used U.S. welfare policy as a way of discouraging impoverished African-American women from bearing children. The controlling image of the overprocreating welfare recipient promotes the racial control process and gains potency by drawing not only upon racist culture, but on more general ideologies in support of patriarchy and capitalism.[71]

Labeling African-American mothers who must rely on welfare as immoral is a signal that the process of employing negative controlling images to assert racial control is in play. Like the controlling image of the matriarch, that of the stereotypical "welfare mother" is built on the assumption that women of color are bad mothers. Moreover, it is assumed that not only are they bad mothers, but they are the root cause of many contemporary social problems. African-American women, under the welfare mother image, behave badly themselves and transmit the wrong values to their offspring. Their alleged social pathology is portrayed as contagious in other ways as well. For example, impoverished African-American women serve as negative role models whose non-normative behavior could conceivably spread to traditional, decent middle-class white women.[72] From this logic it is not difficult to conclude that society can best be protected from poor African-American women's social pathology by curtailing reproduction by these women.

The last controlling image that Collins identifies is the Jezebel or "whore." She is the sly, conniving, manipulative, materialistic, sexually aggressive African-American woman whose appetites are subject to very little self-control. The stereotype of the Jezebel bears an ironic resemblance to many of the female European-American characters on popular television soap operas and comedies, whose behavior results in little public hand-wringing no matter how outrageous it seems. But racialized and aimed at African-American women, the image of the Jezebel carries with it the weight of centuries of European-American male obsession with black women's supposed craftiness and hypersexuality.

It is important to note that the various controlling images of African-American women sometimes overlap. For example, the power of the assault on mothers receiving welfare is intensified by its linkage to the controlling images of the matriarch and the Jezebel. The overlapping of the images results in a vision of domineering, amoral, welfare-dependent single mothers who are impoverished because of their failure to control their sexual urges. Collins argues that the Jezebel "is central in this nexus of controlling images of Black womanhood. Because efforts to control Black women's sexuality lie at the heart of Black women's oppression, historical Jezebels and contemporary 'hoochies' represent a deviant Black female sexuality."[73]

Let us now examine this book's central concept, welfare racism.

WELFARE RACISM

To reiterate points made earlier in this chapter, at the core of U.S. society is a racist culture that originated in connection with dominant-class economic interests, that has taken on a life of its own, serving important social and political, as well as economic functions, and that has been kept alive in "just about every medium and institution within society,"[74] including the racial state. The racial state, along with other institutions, has historically supported white racial hegemony through welfare policy as part of the process of racial control. This control process has largely focused on African-American women, often through the medium of various expressions of gendered racism. The latter has rested upon a variety of racist stereotypes and negative controlling images that morally malign and otherwise degrade African-American women, images which are often utilized by racial state actors and others involved in U.S. welfare policy discourse and debate.

The formation, implementation, and outcomes of U.S. welfare policy are thus rife with what we term *welfare racism*. We will use this umbrella concept to refer to the various forms and manifestations of racism associated with means-tested programs of public assistance for poor families that will be described in this book.

We define welfare racism as the organization of racialized public assistance attitudes, policy making, and administrative practices.[75]

Here the term *racialized* refers to the social processes of welfare racism. Our use of this term does not imply that racialization is a discrete historical event, but instead it refers to a continuous process through which racism drives the various forms that welfare takes. In U.S. society, welfare has been driven by racism from its beginnings. Consequently, our use of the term *racialized* does not imply that at one time welfare attitudes, policies, and practices were not racism driven, but later became so. Instead, the racialization process refers to the persistence of racism at varying levels of intensity as a force shaping public assistance.

In our conceptualization of welfare racism, attitudes refer to a set of negative beliefs and judgments about welfare recipients that often manifest themselves in racist stereotypes. For example, racist stereotypes held by European Americans about African Americans suggest that African Americans are overrepresented on the welfare rolls, are lazy, and are undeserving of aid. In this chapter we have made the point that such stereotypes are embedded in racist culture.

Policy making includes government structures and processes, and the policy products they formulate, affecting public assistance. In the chapters to come, for example, we will see that racist attitudes and stereotypes on the part of state actors—federal, state, and local—often result in punitive welfare policy initiatives intended to minimize the presence of people of color on the welfare rolls. Administrative practices refers to the ways in which these public assistance agencies implement policies. Subsequent chapters will make reference to systematic racial discrimination in day-to-day policy implementation, as well as evidence of more informal practices of discouragement or harassment directed toward people of color applying for or receiving aid.

In addition to their damage to public assistance programs, racialized attitudes, policy making, and administrative practices negatively affect recipients in two principal ways. First, they affect benefit eligibility, the criteria used to determine who may or who may not receive public assistance, for how long, and under what conditions. Benefit eligibility may involve the stipulation of behavioral standards recipients must meet as a condition of their receiving aid. As we will show, often these behavioral standards are built around controlling images associated with gendered racism. Second, these components of welfare racism affect how much aid applicants may receive.

As we will show in subsequent chapters, welfare racism first manifested itself with the definition of people of color as undeserving and denial of their access to the welfare rolls. When outright racially exclusionary policies could not readily be maintained, policy makers often stiffened the criteria for initial eligibility and the behavioral conditions for continuing to receive aid. Similarly, welfare officials at times provided higher benefit levels to European-American recipients than to recipients of color. As more of the latter made up the welfare rolls, the ways in which welfare racism was expressed shifted to meet the changing conditions. Racial state actors allowed the dollar value or purchasing power of benefits to progressively decline, and instituted new behavioral standards to discourage applications for aid and to pressure existing recipients off the rolls. Thus, not only racially oppressed groups felt the negative effects of welfare racism, but so did members of the European-American poor who had to deal with inadequate benefits and restrictive welfare policies. As this book will show, welfare racism serves multiple functions and is adept at shifting its shape in keeping with the changing needs of systems of white racial domination. The ultimate expression of welfare racism—thus far—has been, in our view, the abolition of AFDC and the substitution of punitive welfare reform policies for the safety net needed by impoverished families.

Racialization of welfare discourse has kept debate far away from what might otherwise be a more rational discourse over what can be done about poverty. Instead, racial animus has been stirred by the resilient racial myths that envelop contemporary politics. Not surprisingly, the U.S. welfare policy that has been proposed and implemented in the wake of these debates can best be described as racially punitive, both in motivation and effect.

In this book, we hope to make clear the social, economic, and political functions served by welfare racism. The existence and persistence of welfare racism can best be understood when placed in the context of ideologies, policies, and practices which serve multiple functions in the sustenance of a highly racialized society.

In the post–World War II period, for example, welfare racism has played a major role in European Americans' efforts to shore up and reproduce their eroding system of white racial hegemony. Negative controlling images of African-American women, often informed by gendered racism, have led to highly punitive, racially subjugating welfare policies. These policies have been employed as part of a process of racial control in response to a variety of real or perceived threats posed to white racial hegemony by racially oppressed groups. Both the discourse calling for punitive welfare policy and the actual policy adopted by the racial state have signaled and reinforced the notion that African Americans as a group possess characteristics that make them inferior to whites, whether they are poor or not.[76] Chief among these characteristics is moral inferiority, a tag that is routinely placed on African-American women whenever welfare is discussed. Advocates of "welfare reform" have often couched their arguments in the language of a moral crusade in order to justify the need to intensify control over those who have traditionally been subject to racial domination. One important side effect of the welfare-related moral demonization of African-American women, and African Americans more generally, is that many whites today will not lend any support to government programs that they even suspect might be targeted at helping "those undeserving" black people. This adversely affects *all* poor people who need help from such programs, regardless of skin color.

In the contemporary United States, the racialization of welfare policy is an important vehicle through which members of the dominant European-American population (and recently some highly visible African-American male allies) have successfully realized partisan political or professional gains. In the cynical and shameless manipulation of the electorate that passes for democratic politics in the United States today, few political candidates are even willing to mention the "R-word" (i.e., racism), no less point out the ways in which U.S. welfare policy reflects and reinforces it. Through this book we hope to challenge welfare racism by exposing its structure, functions, and processes to critical examination.

In the chapter that follows, we begin our analysis of welfare racism with an examination of its early years.

3
WELFARE RACISM
IN THE EARLY YEARS
OF PUBLIC
ASSISTANCE

The number of Negro cases is few due to the unanimous feeling on the part of the staff and board that there were more work opportunities for Negro women and to their intense desire not to interfere with local labor conditions. The attitude that "they always have gotten along," and that "all they'll do is have more children" is definite.

Southern welfare program
field supervisor, 1939

welfare racism back to mothers pension programs, through which local governments provided limited financial aid to impoverished mother-headed families between 1911 and 1935. Welfare racism often led to the outright exclusion of African Americans and other persons of color from these programs. Mothers pensions were replaced by Aid to Dependent Children (ADC), a program of federal/state public assistance for poor families that was much more far-reaching and comprehensive than mothers pensions. As we will see, in its operation, ADC tended to be similarly biased toward serving impoverished white families. Even those families of color who managed to gain access to the ADC rolls were subject to racially discriminatory treatment up through the post–World War II era.

We will also see how, as welfare policy evolved, outright expressions of racism were masked or camouflaged. In the words of black Marxist feminist Angela Davis, racism that is camouflaged involves "hidden racist arguments [that] can be mobilized readily across racial boundaries and political alignments."[1] Arguments on behalf of restrictive public assistance policies that focus on welfare costs, fraud, moral standards, the work ethic, and the like have often been favored by political elites and policy analysts who cannot or will not openly acknowledge the existence of racism. Such camouflaged expressions of welfare racism often coexist alongside discourse by other elites and policy analysts that openly uses gendered racism, the mobilization of negative controlling images of African-American women, and morally maligning stereotypes to justify excluding such women and their children from public assistance.

The racially exclusionary practices and attacks on black welfare recipients by white racial state actors that we discuss in this chapter clearly functioned as actions and as ideology in support of white racial hegemony. That is, their chief function was racial control.

WELFARE RACISM IN THE PROGRESSIVE ERA

The Mothers Pension Movement and Its Impact

At the beginning of the twentieth century, no federal or state programs existed to provide public assistance to the nation's poor families, no matter what their skin color. The local government aid that did exist was very limited. Moreover, economic hardship was largely considered to be a personal matter, as opposed to a public issue. Even though an estimated 40 percent of the U.S. population lived in poverty in 1900,[2] the plight of the poor was not widely viewed as a systemic problem requiring government intervention. Women rearing families alone faced particular hardships.[3] It was not unusual for poor mothers, finding themselves in desperate straits and having no way to adequately provide for their children, to give them up to adoption, foster homes, or orphanages in the hope that they would be better off.[4]

Concerns over the well-being of the nation's impoverished children were voiced by many prominent social reformers during the Progressive Era (1890–1920). Reformers argued that providing limited financial assistance to deserving, needy mother-headed families was an appropriate responsibility for governments to undertake. Following an unprecedented national White House Conference on Dependent Children held in 1909, a surge of political activism emerged on the part of women's groups to bring such government involvement about.[5] They and their allies, engaging in what has been called the Mothers Pension Movement, pressured state legislators to pass bills establishing "mothers pensions."[6]

Mothers pensions, advocates held, would reduce the need for impoverished mothers to be in the labor force, scrabbling for wages in exhausting, low-paid factory, agricultural, or domestic service jobs or, worse still, performing long hours of even more poorly paid drudgery in the home as laundresses or seamstresses.[7] Moreover, advocates argued, keeping children in their homes with their mothers would save money, given the greater costs of institutional care in orphanages and other settings to which children were frequently sent.[8] In making their arguments, advocates portrayed children as an asset to the nation, and their proper nurturing by mothers was deemed to be in the national interest.

Shortly after the 1909 White House Conference, state legislatures began to pass bills endorsed by the Mothers Pension Movement, beginning with Illinois's "Funds to Parents Act" in 1911. Ten years later, forty more states had some kind of mothers pension law. By 1934, forty-six of the then forty-eight states had such laws, as did Washington, D.C., Alaska, Hawaii, and Puerto Rico.[9] In most states, the legislation that was adopted approved the establishment of mothers pension programs at the local community level, but did not require that localities do so. Moreover, few state governments with mothers pension laws actually provided any funding to local communities for the programs. Consequently, in most of the states that enacted mothers pension programs very few poor mother-headed households actually received assistance.

Not only were relatively few mother-headed families provided with aid, but those families that did receive mothers pensions were often aided begrudgingly. The aid that was provided to mothers was nowhere near sufficient to allow families to move out of poverty.[10] Indeed, the amounts of assistance provided were typically so low that most mothers had little choice but to supplement it with low-paid jobs in or outside of the home.

Racial Exclusion from Mothers Pensions

The Mothers Pension Movement that emerged during the latter part of the Progressive Era was one of many social reform movements. These movements addressed such issues as the need for regulation of the activities of industry, politicians, and landlords, as well as protections for immigrants, workers, consumers, women, and children. But while they may have been "progressive" in many other ways, none of the reform movements of the Progressive Era addressed the United States's rigid apartheid-like conditions of racial segregation or the racially discriminatory practices maintained by whites to uphold their supremacy over people of color. Indeed, Bruce S. Jansson, author of *The Reluctant Welfare State*, argues that "many progressive reformers saw no contradiction between social reform and racism."[11]

Scholars of the Mothers Pension Movement like Theda Skocpol[12] tend to ignore the fact that it arose within a system of white racial hegemony that was heavily governed by Jim Crow racial segregation laws intended to protect white racial supremacy. Given this fact, it should not be surprising that the racial state officials who organized the 1909 White House Conference on Dependent Children did little to encourage consideration of the plight of impoverished families of color. Of the hundreds of invited participants, only two were African Americans. They were described by one black historian as being southern men who "verbalized acceptance of segregation. Their selection as the sole Black participants among the hundreds at this historic conference was not accidental; it was fully representative of the view of Black people held by the callers of the conference."[13]

The plight of African-American children was not the topic of any of the policy papers presented by white participants in the conference, despite the fact that such children were much more likely to be deeply impoverished than were white children. Statements by the two African-American participants, one of whom was the renowned racial conservative Booker T. Washington, president of Tuskegee Institute, focused only on children in the strictly segregated South. Consistent with his racial accommodationist approach, Washington indicated that African-American children were being adequately cared for within their own racially segregated communities and were "not the responsibility of the white child-caring system."[14]

In the individual states, racial state officials were often hostile to the notion that government aid should be provided to impoverished African-American mothers. Hostile sentiments were strongest in the southern states, where they reflected the strength of racist culture and the negative controlling images of lazy, immoral African-American women that whites had constructed to help justify slavery. However, such sentiments existed across the nation. Consequently, welfare racism was widely manifested through the exclusion of African-American women from eligibility for mothers pension assistance.

Decisions to exclude African Americans and other women of color from mothers pensions were made at the local level of the racial state. Those families receiving mothers pensions were in most cases headed by white widows.[15] By today's standards, statistical information from that period is skimpy. However, a federal study, conducted twenty years after the first mothers pension program was launched in Illinois in 1911, suggests the degree to which local programs practiced racial exclusion. Racial group membership data, available on half of the families known to be receiving mothers pensions in 1931, indicate that 96 percent of the mothers being aided were white, 3 percent were black, and 1 percent were other women of color. While the vast majority of the nation's African Americans resided in the southern states at that time, most of the African-American mothers receiving mothers pensions lived in Ohio and Pennsylvania. North Carolina and Florida, with relatively large African-American populations, each had only one such family receiving mothers pension aid.[16] Even when aid was made available to African-American widows, it was not equally doled out. One study found that in Washington, D.C., white recipients received higher levels of assistance than did black recipients.[17]

It is worth taking note of the fact that the ideological construct of "race" has at times been applied by whites in ways that construed certain European-American immigrant groups as inferior.[18] Nationality and culture have often played an important role in immigrants' "racial" classification. In the early part of the twentieth century, persons who today are commonly thought of as being "white," such as southern and eastern Europeans, were often viewed by persons of Anglo-Saxon European ancestry as belonging to lesser "races."[19] Indeed, the desire of white Anglo-Saxons to maintain racial supremacy in the United States was a key factor in the nativist sentiment that arose in opposition to the heavy waves of immigrants that came into the United States between 1880 and 1920.[20]

It is within this more broadly racialized context of nationality and culture that some historians of the Mothers Pension Movement have pointed to practices favoring mothers pension aid only for native-born white mothers and immigrant mothers of the Anglo-Saxon "race."[21] A 1922 federal report, for example, found that Mexican, Italian, and Czechoslovakian families in some locales were either excluded from aid or received less aid than did other families.[22]

In large northern cities, however, where poor European immigrant families lower in the "racial" hierarchy were most likely to be heavily concentrated, mothers pension advocates often favored providing them with aid. The intention was to use the award of aid as an opportunity to intervene in immigrants' lives and assist in bringing about their "Americanization." In practice, this meant encouraging their conformity to white, middle-class, Anglo-Saxon cultural habits and values.[23] Unlike impoverished African-American mothers, poor immigrant women of southern and eastern European ancestry were thought to be capable of rising above their station in life with proper guidance and a little help.

One study of mothers pensions in Chicago found that African-American mothers were underrepresented, while most recipients of aid in that city were foreign born, and a high percentage of these mothers came from southern and eastern European immigrant groups.[24] But the outreach of Americanization was not equally extended to all immigrants outside the white Anglo-Saxon "race." In Los Angeles, Mexican-born widows were excluded from mothers pension aid because it was assumed that their "feudal background" would predispose them to abuse the program.[25]

Local officials' rules for mothers pension eligibility usually required that a mother be maintaining a "suitable home" for her children. The term "suitable" meant the invocation of strict moral standards of behavior on the part of mothers as a condition of aid, and was part of the reason nonwidowed mothers were often excluded from eligibility. African-American women were routinely denied mothers pension aid, but not simply because they were more likely than European Americans to be divorced, deserted, or unwed mothers. Gendered racism, and the controlling images it fostered, invoked stereotypes of African- American women that harkened back to slavery, including their supposed laziness, immorality, and sexual promiscuity. Such stereotypes rendered black mothers' homes "unsuitable" by definition, even if they were widows.[26] African-American mothers were viewed as incapable of being adequate caregivers and thus unworthy of assistance. They were frequently morally maligned and negatively stereotyped as "breeders, sluts, and the caretakers of other women's homes and children."[27]

In short, in the nation's first significant step toward providing public assistance to poor families, welfare racism limited aid to a highly select group of "gilt-edged widows."[28] This group consisted of white women who were judged by local welfare workers to be living up to the very highest standards of adult female behavior, and to be providing "suitable homes" for their children. Because African-American women were deemed incapable of meeting these criteria by virtue of their racial inferiority, they were customarily excluded from assistance at the local level of the racial state, no matter what their marital status, level of impoverishment, or family needs. In a polite reference to racist culture, Winifred Bell described mothers pension aid as an "'elite' program, intimately based in parochial and regional values."[29] For both eligibility rules and benefit levels, these values accommodated the widespread expression and everyday acceptance of welfare racism.

THE RACIALIZED WELFARE STATE

The New Deal Accommodation to White Racial Hegemony

The Great Depression of the 1930s spurred passage of the Social Security Act of 1935. That act was the centerpiece of President Franklin D. Roosevelt's New Deal package of social legislation and the foundation of this society's welfare state. Of interest to us is the section of that act that established the Aid to Dependent Children program, or ADC.

President Roosevelt's New Deal social legislation has long been criticized by political conservatives as an example of liberal excess. However, as we saw in the case of the Mothers Pension Movement, welfare racism can readily be a by-product of "progressive" politics. This observation is confirmed by both federal-level racial state actors' legislative handling of the Aid to Dependent Children program and by the way it was implemented by the racial state at lower levels of governance.

As was true of mothers pensions programs, the ADC program did not challenge the existing system of white racial hegemony. Such New Deal programs were enacted and implemented within a society in which racial discrimination in all institutional spheres, including welfare, was taken for granted. Steve Vallochi characterizes that historical period as follows: "The creation of the New Deal welfare state was a racially-based affair. Many of the programs and policies of the New Deal, while improving the conditions of the poor and working class, discriminated against African Americans or were implemented in a discriminatory manner."[30]

Surprisingly little discussion occurred in Congress regarding ADC when President Roosevelt's Social Security bill was under consideration. Members of Congress did not appear to be particularly interested in proposals for aid to impoverished children.[31] Instead, they devoted most of their attention to the bill's proposals to establish old-age and unemployment insurance in which the attitudes of racial state actors pertaining to "the handling of the Negro question"[32] were most clearly revealed in congressional debate and actions. The same race-based attitudes on the part of members of Congress, however, also shaped the legislation establishing ADC. The power over the program granted to the individual states made it possible for them to allow welfare racism to dictate policy regarding ADC eligibility and benefit levels.[33]

Interestingly, President Roosevelt's principal legislative architect for this legislation, Edwin E. Witte, claimed that it never occurred to him or any of his bill-drafting colleagues that the "Negro question" would come up in connection with the Social Security bill. Only when congressional hearings began, so he claimed, did it become clear that providing aid to African Americans at all, no less aid equal to that provided to whites, would be an issue to members of Congress from southern states. To get a bill passed, according to Witte, "it would be necessary to tone down all clauses relating to supervisory control by the federal government" over individual states.[34] In this way, in contradiction of his claim that the Roosevelt White House itself was little concerned with race in political decision making, Witte blithely explained away the willingness of the White House to accommodate this legislation to the wishes of powerful congressional racial state politicians who were concerned with its impact on white racial hegemony.[35]

As the Social Security bill went through hearings and drafts, three specific political compromises were won by powerful members of Congress from the South.[36] First, all language that directly outlawed racial discrimination was removed from the bill. In this way the U.S. Congress signaled to the individual states that they had license to discriminate. Racial state actors in the White House and Congress were in broad consensus when it came to respecting individual states' rights, meaning in this case that the bill would not require the federal government to act aggressively to interfere with racially oppressive public assistance policies and practices.

In a second compromise, initial wording was stricken from the bill that required states to offer "assistance at least great enough to provide, when added to the income of the family, a reasonable subsistence compatible with decency and health."[37] This was done to assuage the concerns of white southern members of Congress that uniform and unacceptably high national aid standards would be imposed on southern states. By striking this wording, members of Congress allowed the individual states to provide as little financial assistance to impoverished families as they wished.[38]

The issue of public assistance benefit levels was closely tied to the threat they could pose to white racial hegemony. Nationally set aid standards would disrupt local wage rates in the South by reducing the economic desperation that forced most African Americans in southern states to take extremely low-paid agricultural jobs.[39] Jill Quadagno has documented the resistance of southern members of Congress to requiring states to provide African-American workers with unemployment insurance and old age assistance "compatible with decency and health" and on a par with whites. As Quadagno put it, "High rates for old age assistance grants would, they feared, subsidize the children of aged blacks, who would then be more independent and less willing to perform farm labor for low wages."[40] Likewise, had Congress mandated a national minimum standard of ADC assistance, relations between employers and impoverished African-American women workers whose families received ADC could have been similarly disrupted. Thus, the "compatible with decency and health" phrase was struck from wording in the bill pertaining to assistance under ADC as well.[41]

Other members of Congress had their own concerns about the relation between ADC and white racial hegemony. As one chronicler of the legislative history of the 1935 Social Security bill tells it, "In fairness to the south, it should be added that there were Congressmen from other sections of the county where there were unpopular racial or cultural minorities who wanted to have their states left more or less free to treat them as they wished."[42] People of Mexican and Native American ancestry were no doubt among those whom some in Congress had in mind as "unpopular racial or cultural minorities." Welfare racism in individual states, as we will see, often functioned to exclude members of these groups from ADC along with African Americans.

In the third area of legislative compromise, states were allowed to "design and administer their own welfare programs." This meant that ADC programs were rendered so open to the influence of customary practices regarding discrimination against people of color that "the possibility that local prejudices might become a matter of official practice was guaranteed."[43] As with the mothers pension program, the individual states turned most of the day-to-day administration of ADC over to the local racial state, where race-based attitudes of welfare agency officials and caseworkers often determined who would be aided and how.

In a related action, white southern segregationists in Congress also insisted that the Social Security bill be revised to keep the federal government out of the "selection, tenure of office, and compensation of personnel" who administered welfare in the individual states. This, of course, left the door open to racial discrimination in the hiring and assignment of state and local welfare program staff. In the South, for example, it meant that it was unlikely that African Americans would be hired as welfare caseworkers, and almost unimaginable that black caseworkers would be assigned to investigate and determine the eligibility of white mothers for ADC.[44]

Silencing the Racially Oppressed

The potential for the exclusion or mistreatment of people of color under the racial state's ADC policy was contested early on by organizations that sought to represent the interests of the racially oppressed at congressional hearings. Such organizations objected to the direction in which the Social Security bill was going, and expressed concern that African Americans would not gain a fair share of benefits under New Deal assistance programs. Many of their dire predictions came true.

The National Association for the Advancement of Colored People (NAACP), founded in 1909 with a dual agenda of "civil rights and progressive social welfare,"[45] was worried about what would happen if the individual states were left free to determine standards of economic need, eligibility policies, and assistance levels. According to civil rights historian Dona Cooper Hamilton, "Programs administered at the federal, rather than the state and local, level were considered by the NAACP less likely to discriminate against African Americans."[46] Unfortunately, this concern was not to be given much of a hearing by racial state actors.

At congressional hearings on the Social Security bill, only two persons out of the scores who turned out to testify drew attention to the need to deter racial discrimination in ADC. Attorney Charles H. Houston, a representative of the NAACP, pointed out that the proposed bill would exclude many African Americans from old age assistance and from unemployment compensation. Then, addressing ADC, Houston wasted no words:

> There are states in which, according to the law, separate institutions are maintained for Negro and white citizens. I think there should be a provision written into the bill in such states at least that where the money is allocated to the states, and by law in public institutions you have a separation of races, there must be an equitable distribution between the white and colored citizens.[47]

Houston's words made explicit the racially oppressive arrangements made lawful by the U.S. Supreme Court's "separate but equal" doctrine established by the Court's *Plessy v. Ferguson* decision in 1896. That racial state doctrine legalized segregation and legitimized the discriminatory practices required to maintain it.[48]

Members of Congress also heard from George E. Haines, who represented the Department of Race Relations of the Federal Council of Churches. His testimony was even more pointed than that of the NAACP representative. Haines specifically requested there be "a clause in this bill against discrimination to protect those who are discriminated against under existing legislation of similar type."[49] Haines went on to detail numerous examples of "repeated, widespread, and continued discrimination on account of race or color as a result of which Negro men, women, and children did not share equitably and fairly in the distribution of the benefits accruing from the expenditure of such federal funds."[50]

Haines pointed out provisions within the proposed bill under which racial discrimination could readily take place at the individual state and local levels. He remonstrated against the exclusion of African Americans from benefits or the payment of unequal benefits based on race and complained that the bill failed to protect African Americans from being excluded from employment in agencies administering benefits. Haines called for language to be inserted in the bill that would outlaw any such discrimination and would deny funds to states unless they showed they "will so distribute the funds so that the benefits shall be offered to eligible persons irrespective of race or color."[51]

Needless to say, organizations such as the NAACP and the Federal Council of Churches had insufficient political influence to prevent the federal racial state from ceding a great deal of power over ADC to the individual states. Many African Americans were politically disenfranchised and unable to vote or hold elective office in the southern states where their population strength was concentrated. They were also unable to gain cooperation from white-run northern urban political machines that could have had an impact on legislative decision making by federal racial state actors.[52] The "progressive" Roosevelt administration remained silent in the face of civil rights organizations' demands for guarantees of racial justice. Thus, what finally passed Congress and was signed by President Franklin D. Roosevelt was a Social Security bill with provisions that said nothing directly about racial discrimination and that provided for only limited federal supervision over states' ADC activities.

Provisions of the Racial State's Aid to Dependent Children Program

Under Title IV of the Social Security Act of 1935, the federal government was to pay a part of the costs to the individual states of providing financial assistance to needy and dependent children. Children aided through ADC had to be less than sixteen years of age and "deprived of parental support by reason of the death, continued absence from the home, or physical or mental incapacity of a parent."[53] While the wording left some flexibility regarding the types of family situations to which ADC could be extended, the imagery that racial state actors had of the typical household that would be helped was much like that of mothers pension programs: dependent children in homes headed by white widows. As the first executive director of the appointed federal board that oversaw ADC put it, "The ADC example we always thought about was the poor lady in West Virginia whose husband was killed in a mining accident, and the problem of how she could feed those kids."[54]

Individual states were not required to participate in ADC. However, if they chose to do so and to accept the federal share of their ADC costs, states had to meet certain general conditions and requirements.[55] In this they would be supervised by a federal Social Security Board, established by the 1935 law.

Among the law's requirements were these:[56]

(1) Individual states had to have their plans for administering ADC approved by the Social Security Board. Moreover, it was mandatory that the approved plan be carried out uniformly across all of a state's counties or other local political subunits.

(2) All children who met the criteria of age and need were to be considered eligible to apply for ADC. Children could not be denied assistance without the right to a fair hearing before the individual state's welfare department. (Thus, in theory, eligible children of color could not be excluded from aid.)

(3) Children needed only to reside in a state for a year as a condition for assistance. Children less than one year of age would be considered eligible if their mother lived in the state for a year or more.

Unfortunately, the Social Security Board was given little in the way of negative sanctions to enforce individual states' conformity to these requirements and conditions. However, the Social Security Act provided that in cases where a state deviated from its board-approved plan, "after reasonable notice and opportunity for hearing to the State agency,"[57] the board could choose to cease federal ADC payments to the offending state.

Welfare Racism in ADC: The Pre–World War II Years

Welfare racism manifested itself immediately in ADC programs. This occurred primarily but not exclusively in the southern states. African-American children and other children of color were often left without assistance. In his classic work *An American Dilemma*, Swedish economist Gunnar Myrdal describes the situation in the late 1930s: "Aid to dependent children is intended primarily for broken families with children. In view of the great number of widows and widowers in the Negro population, and its high divorce, separation, and illegitimacy rates, it is quite apparent that Negroes need this assistance much more than do whites."[58] Thus, if part of the purpose of ADC was to provide for the disproportionate numbers of needy African-American children, the racial composition of the ADC rolls should have immediately reflected this.

Nationwide statistics on the numbers of children applying and the proportion in turn receiving ADC, by race, do not exist. Data from ADC's early years show only how many African-American children were accepted as recipients. A Social Security Board report indicated that from 1937 to 1940 between 14 percent and 17 percent of children accepted to receive ADC were African American. These figures were compared in the board's report with the fact that 11 percent of all children under age sixteen in 1930 were African American.[59] These overall statistics on acceptance into the ADC program surely obscure the existence of many never-tendered or rejected ADC applications. A much higher percentage of African-American than white children were impoverished and living in single-parent (usually mother-headed) or parentless family circumstances. This was especially true in the southern states.

Indeed, states in the North and Midwest with board-approved state plans and African-American populations of one hundred thousand and more were typically far more racially inclusive than comparable southern states. They thus held up the overall average percentages reported above. When one focuses only on southern states, the extent of underrepresentation and the indications of racial exclusion become much clearer. Myrdal, for example, noted that in seven southern states the percentage of African-American children accepted for ADC was smaller even than the proportion of children under age sixteen living in these states who were African-American. Offering Georgia as an example, he pointed out that from 1937 to 1940 only 11 percent to 12 percent of children accepted were African American, while they constituted 38 percent of all Georgia children in 1930.[60] Given that data were not available in the late 1930s for some southern states with board-approved plans, such as Kentucky, Mississippi, and Texas,[61] the degree of racial exclusion in the South was no doubt undercalculated.

Studies conducted in North Carolina and Georgia reveal the size of the gap between eligibility and the extension of ADC coverage in those two states.[62] While African-American children made up less than 25 percent of North Carolina children accepted for aid in the mid-1930s, it was estimated that they made up 50 percent of those eligible. In Georgia, the disparities were far worse. A study using data from the late 1930s found that while many more African-American than white children were eligible for aid in Georgia, not many of those eligible of either race received ADC. In comparison to the numbers of white recipients, the numbers of African-American children receiving aid were negligible.

Regional and racial differences also appear when one examines the limited data that exist on the size of ADC benefits provided to children. Social Security Board data reported for children accepted in ADC during 1939–40 show, for example, that Arkansas paid an average of $3.52 per month to African-American children, but $4.24 to whites. In South Carolina the ratio was $4.03 to $6.46. This race-based aid differential prevailed in most southern states for which the board had data.[63]

In contrast, many northern states provided higher benefits on average to African-American children than to white children, perhaps reflecting greater willingness to recognize the magnitude of need those children experienced. New York, for example paid $24.15 per month to African-American children and $22.08 to whites. In Pennsylvania the ratio was $18.13 to $14.42.[64] Given African-American children's overrepresentation in extreme poverty, one should not assume that their needs were adequately met by the aid granted, even in those instances when their benefits were on average higher.

In summing up these data, Richard Sterner, whose analysis of the economic plight of African Americans helped to inform Myrdal's *An American Dilemma*, observed that "it cannot be said . . . that the various state programs, especially in the South, have given full recognition to the extent of need among Negro children or to their particular problems. . . . Negro children in a number of states have not shared equally with white children in the [ADC] program."[65] How is this to be explained? In 1943, Sterner wrote,

> This is not the fault of the Social Security Act, which contains only the framework for the state plans. Neither are the provisions of the state plans openly discriminatory. Experience has shown, however, that community attitudes and traditions which favor differential treatment are strong enough to hold their own where rules and regulations are not sufficiently explicit or leave too much to the initiative of individuals, and this unfortunately is widely evidenced in the case of needy children.[66]

Day-to-day decisions regarding administration of ADC were made at the local level, often in ways that openly served white racial hegemony. Frequently, there were clear economic motivations linked to racial discrimination. This was particularly but not exclusively true for the South. By denying ADC benefits, or keeping them so low that they made very little material difference in the lives of impoverished people of color, black women who performed the most menial work for the lowest wages were forced to keep doing that kind of work.[67]

The justifications for keeping African-American mothers off ADC, when a steady supply of black low-wage labor was needed by white employers, flowed seamlessly out of gendered racism and its controlling imagery of the stereotypical lazy, immoral, African-American "breeder" mother. As is clear from the quote which appears at the opening of this chapter, the racist attitude that African-American women and their children could and should get by on less than whites was another key assumption underlying racial discrimination in the administration of welfare benefits.[68]

Sterner's position that racial differentials and disparities were simply due to local community attitudes and traditions strikingly failed to acknowledge the significant role played by racial state actors at the federal and individual state levels. Many racial state actors outside of local communities knowingly supported legislation and contributed to an overall political environment in which racial discrimination against people of color was not only possible but tolerated in ADC programs. Welfare racism has never been simply a matter of local attitudes and traditions, but has been nurtured along by the race-based actions and inactions of those racial state actors who occupy elite political positions.

For years, under "states' rights" and "welfare localism," customary racist practices informed ADC policies without significant federal intervention.[69] In what for her was a rare scholarly acknowledgment of the importance of racism for the implementation of New Deal welfare legislation, sociologist Theda Skocpol commented: "The great leeway left to the states in the legislation of the 1930s ensured that conservative or racist interests would be able to control welfare coverage, benefit levels, and methods of administration in large stretches of the nation, and especially in the South, where the vast majority of blacks lived in poverty and political disenfranchisement."[70]

Putting Limits on Welfare Racism: The Federal Racial State Reins in Racist Exclusion

While the Social Security Act of 1935 granted the individual states enormous discretion in the implementation of ADC, and the states similarly gave their localities free rein in handling everyday matters, federal-level racial state actors were not able to completely look the other way in the face of racial discrimination. The act stated that all children who met the criteria of age and need were eligible to apply for ADC, not just white children, and that eligible children who applied could not be turned down without the right to a fair hearing. It is true that the racial state acted as the political arm of white racial hegemony in upholding the legality and legitimacy of racial segregation in most areas of social life. But while the U.S. Supreme Court permitted segregation under the "separate but equal" doctrine, the Court was bound by constitutional restraints that prohibited the outright denial of access to ADC on the basis of race.

The racial state actors overseeing ADC at the federal level had little in the way of sanctions to work with when there were violations involving racial discrimination. However, under the law the Social Security Board was authorized to hold hearings on serious violations of provisions of the act. Such hearings could lead to the cutting off of federal ADC contributions to an individual state. Steps in this direction were taken in a few instances when there were documented practices of welfare racism involving the blatant exclusion of children of color from ADC.

Jane Margueretta Hoey served as director of the Social Security Board's Bureau of Public Assistance from 1936 to 1953. The bureau, which reported to the Social Security Board, was responsible for dealing with all the individual states on ADC matters. In an oral history interview, Hoey, while at first reluctant to discuss the topic, revealed that when blatant racial exclusion of children occurred, she did try to end it. Here are her comments on handling statewide discrimination against African Americans in Mississippi.

> Q: Were there any problems in administering the programs in the
>   southern states, when it came to the question of providing benefits
>   for Negroes?
> Hoey: Really, that shouldn't be in.
> Q: I think it's worth talking about.

> Hoey: I can tell you. Down in Mississippi, I found, from the staff (because I know the workers from all over the country), I got word that in that state a quota had been put in every county—but nothing in writing—that there was to be 10 percent quota for Negroes.
>
> Q: Even though the Negro population would be higher?
>
> Hoey: Some would be 50 percent, or 60 percent Negroes in a county, and 10 percent quotas. I had a staff at that time, that did these special things. I sent them in to study a cross-section of cases in that county, and found exactly that. So I telephoned the chairman.
>
> Q: The state chairman?
>
> Hoey: State welfare. And I asked him what date, that I would like to recommend a time that would be convenient for him to have a hearing before the board. "What do you mean?" he said. "You know, and I know exactly what we're talking about." He said, "What do you want?" I said, "I want a letter to every county in the state, and I want to receive a copy of that letter and have it for the record and to present to the board, that there are to be no quotas in your state." We had no hearing.[71]

As in the case of mothers pension aid, African Americans were not the only people of color singled out for exclusion from ADC. Children of Native American ancestry were subject to racial exclusion in southwestern states. Hoey describes the situation she confronted:

> As long as we're talking restrictions, the states of New Mexico and Arizona sent out word to Indians. Somehow we learned that word had gone out to the Indians not to apply, because they would not get anything. I could get no records. I would go to the lawyers and say, "What will we do?" and they'd say, "Get your records." But how could I? There wasn't anybody refused because they didn't come in. . . . Finally, fortunately, a new board member on the New Mexico Board had a resolution that no assistance would be given to the Indians. Well, that was one thing. That came to me fast, and I presented it to the [Social Security] Board and asked for the calling of a hearing.[72]

From their examination of county records in Arizona, Hoey's staff "found applications that had been accepted but never acted on. They'd been there six months or a year."[73] Hoey called for Social Security Board hearings to be held for Arizona as well as New Mexico. Whereas New Mexico state welfare officials quickly gave in and agreed to take the resolution banning aid to Native Americans off the records, Arizona officials went to court for relief from this federal interference with their ADC program. According to Hoey, Arizona's court case was thrown out.

While other states discouraged applications from or denied aid to families of color, Nevada refused to even start up an ADC program for twenty years in order to avoid providing benefits to Native American children. It became the last state to implement an ADC program, in 1955. Hoey describes the situation, about which she could do little:

> There are other forms of discrimination that I wanted to mention. Nevada. Nevada refused to take the initiative to ask for Aid to Dependent Children for twenty years. Only when the women's organizations in the state, somebody taking the initiative in that state, got them together and forced through a program. They did not want to take Indian children; that was the reason. Isn't that incredible? And nothing I could do.[74]

Finally, Hoey informed her interviewer of individual state ADC policies requiring recipients to be U.S. citizens. Those policies were subtly crafted to exclude Mexican children from ADC:

> Q: Was there a similar problem with the Mexican population in Texas? Or in New Mexico?
>
> Hoey: Yes, without any question. That was why they had the citizenship requirement in the laws, that I mentioned to you, for children. Think of having a citizenship requirement for a child![75]

The federal Social Security Board, responding to revelations of scandals involving political patronage and fiscal irregularities in states' administration of the new Social Security Act programs, successfully persuaded Congress to approve a merit system requirement in 1939 as one of the revisions to the act that it made that year.[76] While this was not intended as a civil rights measure, a merit-based system of hiring by definition opened up employment possibilities for people of color who were racially excluded from working in the welfare system. Apparently, some of Hoey's efforts were drawn to addressing the conflict between merit-based hiring and complaints of racial discrimination in the staffing of welfare agencies.

A Virginia study cites comments by the first African-American social worker hired by a local public welfare agency in that state.

> My offer of employment [in 1947] was the result of Virginia's fear of losing funds from the federal government. After their battle to get the state's plan approved [in 1938], the state began to receive warnings about not having any blacks working for the bureau. They

didn't want to do it [hire blacks], but they finally accepted the fact that they would have to or face the very real possibility of losing federal funds.[77]

She described how officials there instituted a merit system with competitive examinations for the hiring and promotion of welfare workers. However, she also characterized Virginia's merit system as "corrupt," and administered in ways that minimized the hiring and career mobility of African Americans.

According to this social worker, Virginia's local welfare agencies abided by racial state legal doctrines allowing segregation in their offices, including racially segregated restrooms for clients and personnel. African-American social workers, if they succeeded in getting hired, received unequal on-the-job treatment even when they were, by all objective measures, better educated and qualified for the job than many whites who held positions. African Americans were only assigned African-American cases, were banned from doing home assessments of white families, and were denied access to benefit scales used to determine aid for white recipients.[78]

Under the Social Security Act of 1935, individual states could be brought to a hearing if their state plans departed from the act's requirements, or if the administration of the state's plan departed significantly from what the Social Security Board had approved. Under the law, "a substantial number of cases" had to be affected by these deviations. And even then, hearings would not be called unless federal negotiations with the states failed to bring about compliance. It is not surprising, therefore, that very few such hearings or court reviews took place. From 1936 to 1951 there were only thirteen, and in the next decade there were but three.[79] It is not clear just how many of these hearings involved racially discriminatory practices. It is clear, however, that plenty of race-based exclusion occurred that could not be acted on by threatening or calling hearings under the auspices of the Social Security Act.

While some hearings did indeed take place, it was apparently rare for them to result in the cutoff of federal funds. Such a cutoff of funds occurred in 1938, after Georgia was discovered to have instituted a racial quota system much like the one Hoey described for Mississippi. This financial sanction against Georgia was temporary, and it was rescinded when the state's welfare director agreed to end the quotas. Even so, data indicate that with the quotas rescinded, African-American children in Georgia continued to be underrepresented on the state's ADC rolls.[80]

Emerging Institutionalized Patterns of Welfare Racism in ADC

The children of poor southern African-American women were often barred or removed from the ADC rolls under the rationale of "suitable work" or "employable mother" rules which prohibited their mothers from refusing employment whenever local ADC administrators said it was available. Application of these rules typically corresponded to seasonal agricultural and other low-wage labor needs of white employers. Because the rules were most likely to be implemented in areas where seasonal workers were nearly all people of color, they supported the economic interests of those who prospered from white racial hegemony.[81]

Such labor-exploitative welfare policies stand in sharp contrast to the maternalist philosophy associated with the white-dominated mothers pension programs that preceded ADC, which at least paid lip service to the importance of mothers being at home with their children instead of in the labor force. Employable mother policies at times forced everyone out of the home. In 1943 Louisiana adopted a policy requiring that children be cut off from ADC whenever they or their mothers were needed to pick cotton.[82] Mothers and children were together, but in the cotton fields.

Likewise, some individual states adopted the mothers pension program practice of providing aid only to those in "suitable homes" and used it to restrict African Americans' eligibility for ADC.[83] The notion of a suitable home was vague and subjective. It took on almost whatever meaning that local welfare officials and caseworkers decided. Typically, the concept was associated with judgments about the character and moral quality of the mothers forced to seek ADC for their children.

In the case of African-American women, the judgments were negative more often than not. They reflected gendered racism and the use of negative controlling images of "welfare mothers" that justified denial of ADC. Commenting on suitable-home policies, Gunnar Myrdal observed: "According to popular belief in the South, few Negro low income families have homes which could be called 'suitable' for any purpose . . . and since often practically all Negroes are believed to be 'immoral,' almost any discrimination against Negroes can be motivated on such grounds."[84]

When the Social Security Act of 1935 was passed, the vast majority of ADC recipients were European American. In 1939, Congress agreed to allow the widows of retired workers and their children to receive financial assistance under the old-age insurance provisions of the act. Since the widows of only certain types of workers were covered under the act, namely workers in occupations from which whites almost entirely excluded African Americans, one effect of this racial state action was to allow many white widows an alternative to ADC. It was a preferable alternative, since families receiving old-age insurance benefits did not have to demonstrate economic need.[85]

Widows with children on old-age insurance were not subject to any morality tests, suitable-home policies, or compulsory work requirements. Because most were white widows, they were considered to be among the "deserving poor," and thus were not required to live under what feminist Gwendolyn Mink refers to as a "welfare police state" of regulations and intrusive surveillance.[86] Eligible white widows rapidly began leaving ADC and "ADC became the last resort for divorced, single, and deserted women. Many of these women were African-American."[87] As African Americans and other people of color slowly but perceptibly began to develop a noticeable presence on the ADC rolls, the individual states moved to adopt or tighten up enforcement of restrictive eligibility rules.

A 1942 federal Social Security Board report concluded its analysis of the ADC program in sixteen individual states by stating:

> Practices in the administration of aid to dependent children in some States apparently result in assistance to fewer Negro and Indian children than white children in relation to the number of needy children in the respective populations.[88]

Children of color were less likely to be approved for ADC by local welfare offices even when their families were as large and as poor as families who were European American.[89] While acknowledging these racial disparities, the board's report made no recommendations as to how they might be alleviated. As we will discuss shortly, such racial differentials in benefits were observed to exist into the 1960s.[90]

In the period before and during World War II, the presence of African Americans on the ADC rolls was minimized by actions of various levels of the racial state. But welfare racism would be widely manifested in ADC programs in the postwar period as well. Its principal manifestations did not necessarily involve outright exclusionary practices. Rather, welfare racism, a shape shifter, increasingly took the form of policy restrictions on eligibility that ostensibly were not racial in nature, but that still had a disproportionately adverse effect on African Americans.

CAMOUFLAGED WELFARE RACISM IN THE POST–WORLD WAR II PERIOD

In the period following World War II, welfare racism took a number of camouflaged forms. As we will discuss, seemingly "race-blind" welfare policies, usually by intent, had a disproportionately adverse effect on impoverished families of color.

Suitable-Home Policies

After World War II, individual states and localities vigorously fought to control growth in the size and costs of their ADC rolls, often by enacting new or more restrictive policies that would make it more difficult for impoverished families to be eligible for ADC. In the period from the end of the war to 1960, more and more states enacted "suitable-home" policies. By late 1960 some twenty-three states had some version of such policies in place. They were but one way in which the "welfare police state" attempted to keep down the growing and ever darker complexioned ADC rolls.

Individual states' use of suitable-home policies to racially discriminate sometimes took rather subtle forms. For example, some states encouraged local welfare offices to deny aid to the children of unwed mothers, no matter what their race, on the grounds that it was self-evident such mothers could not provide morally "suitable homes." This is a good example of camouflaged welfare racism. Suitable-home policies per se ostensibly had nothing to do with racism.

In the African-American community, placing a child up for adoption by strangers was traditionally seen as undesirable. With the support and encouragement of their families the vast majority of unwed African-American mothers kept their children. Indeed, there were few options, since most maternity homes and adoption agencies reserved their services for whites. In contrast, members of the European-American community operated with a different set of "family values"and options. In European-American communities, pregnancy outside marriage was more heavily stigmatized, and great efforts were expended to deny or hide such pregnancies and their outcome. For the most part, abortion was illegal and dangerous. Unmarried white women who became pregnant were often expelled from their families and communities, or sent away to maternity homes and encouraged to give their newborns up for adoption by infertile European-American married couples.[91] Consequently, the impact of suitable-home policies denying ADC to unwed mothers rearing their children fell disproportionately on African-American women.

Man-in-the-House Policies

In addition to suitable-home policies, many individual states implemented "man-in-the-house" or "substitute father" policies that denied ADC to families whose female heads were suspected of consorting with and thus allegedly receiving financial assistance from adult males.[92] Suspect households were often subject to surprise midnight or middle-of-the-night raids by local welfare caseworkers. These raids entailed searches not only for overnight male guests, but for any sign that males had been around. A man's suit or hat in a closet was often enough to cause a family to be cut off from ADC. Such policies and practices were common not only in the southern states, but elsewhere as well. They were most frequently aimed at African-American households. In such cases they were driven by the controlling images of immorality and promiscuity to which black women were subject. According to feminist writer Rickie Solinger, an investigative raid in Phoenix, Arizona, was referred to in the local media as a "'pre-dawn safari' to emphasize the African connection."[93]

Residency Requirements

Other individual state policies besides suitable-home and man-in-the-house rules were used to disqualify African-American households from ADC eligibility.[94] Many states adopted residency requirements, which we noted earlier were provided for under the Social Security Act. Such policies usually required that a family reside in a state for no less than a year before becoming eligible for ADC. When welfare racism was behind individual states' use of residency requirements, the latter often functioned as a form of geography-focused "race population control" which restricted migratory movement by African-American families in the interest of maintaining white racial hegemony. While our examples in this section are of geographic control, the topic of race population control, both in terms of immigration-focused control and procreation-focused control, are dealt with in more detail in the chapters that follow.

In the South, residency requirements impeded the ability of impoverished mothers to freely move with their children across state lines in search of better-paying work or to join other family members, lest the children lose eligibility for the meager aid ADC provided. Whether they migrated or not, such mothers had little choice but to accept the exploitative labor conditions to which they were subjected by white employers in their state of residence. Residency requirements were thus a form of geographic race population control that ensured a steady supply of compliant, low-wage, African-American women workers, whose job opportunities were largely limited to working for whites in agriculture and domestic service.

Strict residency requirements were also used as a form of geographic race population control in individual states in the North. Some northern racial state actors considered these requirements to be a way of discouraging poor southern African-American families from migrating northward. Their presence in predominantly or all-white communities was not commonly desired or welcomed. Racial state actors also feared that poor African-American families would migrate to get the higher ADC benefits that most northern states offered and thus drive welfare costs further upward. There is, of course, no evidence that families made decisions to move out of southern states based on the attraction of higher ADC benefits, as opposed to a desire to join other family members, to find better work opportunities, or to escape the racially oppressive social arrangements of the South.

Both North and South, residency requirements had an especially negative impact on the families of migrant farm workers, whose constant seasonal movement from job to job across state lines often rendered them ineligible for ADC at all. Many migrants who found themselves ineligible for or regularly removed from the ADC rolls were impoverished families of color. The geographic race population control provided by residency requirements in this instance increased poor migrant families' already high vulnerability to race-based labor exploitation by white employers.[95]

Compulsory Work Rules

Another form that camouflaged racism often took was the use of racially discriminatory compulsory work rules. In Georgia, for example, such work rules were openly tied to gendered racism and the racist stereotype of the African-American "breeder" woman. In 1952, that state adopted an "employable mother" rule explicitly with the intention of discouraging out-of-wedlock births by African-American women. This rule illustrates how welfare racism could be used not only for geographic race population control, but for race population control in the area of procreation. The rule remained in force until it was outlawed by a federal court in 1968. The court found that Georgia was discontinuing ADC to African-American mothers "when suitable seasonable employment was presumptively, but not necessarily, available. All aid had been denied these women and their children even when their wages from stoop labor did not reach the pitifully low welfare budget levels."[96]

THE DARKENING COLOR OF THE ADC ROLLS IN THE POSTWAR PERIOD

In the post–World War II period, impoverished families of color were subject to various forms of welfare racism across the nation, and received scant protection from the federal government. The ADC rolls were still principally made up of European Americans, but increasing numbers of African-Americans and other persons of color received ADC. The reasons for this increase include:

- Dissolution of two-parent households associated with the stresses and demands of World War II on families, and family disruptions accompanying the postwar wave of African-American migration from the rural South to the North;

- High rates of black unemployment and underemployment as the military and defense industries reduced personnel and the nation settled back into a peacetime economy in which "white-skin privilege" gave whites the advantage in competition for civilian jobs;

- The inability of many employed black men to earn wages sufficient to support and house a family, which slowed or undercut their ability to enter permanent and formal marital relationships and contributed to out-of-wedlock births;

- The somewhat more liberal approach to approving mother-headed African-American families' applications for ADC that existed in the North, particularly in large northern cities where they were less likely than in the South to experience racial exclusion;[97]

- Inroads—although limited—made by the federal overseers of ADC in stopping the blatant and unlawful exclusion of families of color from individual states' welfare rolls, particularly in the South.

A federal study of sixteen states found that in 1942 some 21 percent of ADC families were African Americans or others of color. This figure rose to 30 percent in 1948. Nationwide data revealed that by the end of the 1950s a little more than 40 percent of ADC families were of color; the vast majority of which were African American.[98] The steady movement of the black population out of the rural South and into northern cities, combined with natural rates of city population growth, made this increase ever more visible and thus troubling to whites.

As has been well documented, whites in the North had reacted with hostility to the migration of African Americans from the South since the early part of the twentieth century. White communities enforced, often through threats and acts of violence, formal and informal practices that maintained racially segregated residential arrangements. By World War II, the groundwork for racially segregated ghettos in cities across the nation had been laid. This happened with the direct help of the federal government and that of individual states, and certainly with the general support of the white population.[99]

The fact that large numbers of often impoverished people of dark skin color were residing in crowded, racially segregated housing in spacially circumscribed city neighborhoods rendered the color line conspicuously visible.[100] But changes in ADC's racial composition and in the residential demographics of poor families of color were also accompanied by a change in the marital status of ADC family heads. As mentioned earlier, ADC at first served mostly families headed by white widows, but revisions made in the Social Security Act in 1939 shifted certain workers' widows and their children, who were predominantly white, to the old-age insurance program. As we pointed out, this policy changed the racial composition of the ADC rolls. It also changed the predominant marital status of recipients. By 1960, only 8 percent of those heading ADC households were widows. An additional 18 percent were mothers with disabilities. In more than two-thirds of ADC households, the father of the children was absent, usually because of desertion, separation, or divorce. In 21 percent of ADC households, mothers whose children were receiving aid had never married.[101] Both the changing color composition of the ADC population and the fact that so many of the mothers in ADC families possessed a "deviant" marital status made it increasingly difficult for the general public to accept the notion that those receiving ADC were among the "deserving poor."

As the proportion of the ADC rolls made up of African Americans grew, whites' attitudes toward recipients of color "became openly punitive and antagonistic."[102] Whites mobilized the racist controlling image of the lazy, immoral African-American "welfare mother" to condemn blacks for being on the rolls. They ignored the fact that nationally, as of 1960, most of those receiving ADC were European Americans. Moreover, whites ignored the fact that the aid being received by African-American ADC recipients and other recipients of color, such as Native Americans and Latino/a Americans, was in no respect proportionate to their economic needs or to their overrepresentation as impoverished populations.

While the increasingly subtle practices of welfare racism could not hold back African Americans' growing presence on the ADC rolls, individual states and localities could and did hold down costs by limiting recipients' ADC benefits. Studies of aid eligibility policies and public assistance benefits at the local level compellingly demonstrate the existence of race-based patterns. For example, a U.S. Civil Rights Commission investigation in Cleveland in the mid-1960s found that African-American families there received less in aid than similarly sized white families.[103] A study of Virginia counties in the late 1960s found that predominantly white counties were more generous in their aid to recipients than counties containing a high percentage of African Americans.[104] Research on thirty-four standard metropolitan statistical areas found that those with higher levels of racial inequality had less generous welfare benefits.[105]

Researchers found that states whose populations contained greater proportions of African Americans had more restrictive welfare eligibility requirements than did other states.[106] Studies also found that, in general, the higher the proportion of African Americans in a state's population, the less aid welfare recipients received.[107] Social scientist Gerald Wright concluded that "the racial basis for hostility to welfare is reflected in the policymaking processes of the states."[108]

The racial disparities in benefits depicted in these studies may seem to be a minor matter, given low levels of benefits paid to whites and African Americans alike under ADC programs, particularly in the southern states. But, like the outright denial of welfare eligibility, the maintenance of racial disparities in benefits contributed to the exacerbation of the poverty experienced by African-American women and their children, increased the vulnerability of such women to exploitation of their labor by white employers, and helped to institutionalize existing social and economic inequalities along skin color lines.

TOWARD AN UNDERSTANDING OF WELFARE RACISM AS RACIAL CONTROL

In this chapter we provided an overview of how and why welfare racism was expressed at various levels of the racial state over roughly a fifty-year period ending around 1960. Many of our examples speak to the importance of welfare racism as a strategy of racial control. As we have seen, at times this control was used to advance the exploitation of African-American mothers' labor and even to discourage their bearing children. Two questions are central to analyzing welfare racism and to understanding how systems of racial inequality are structured and maintained. When examining such systems, it is useful to ask: "Who is there?" and "What are they doing?"

Our next chapter contains three case examples from the early 1960s in which racial state actors at various levels of governance made use of welfare racism to control who was there and what they were doing. These case examples reveal some important ways in which racial state actors have employed welfare racism as a weapon against threats that racially subordinated African Americans have at times posed to white supremacy.

4

WELFARE RACISM AS A DEFENSE AGAINST CHALLENGES TO WHITE SUPREMACY

When three civil rights workers disappeared during the summer of 1964, the FBI launched an intensive search, fearing they had been murdered. While they dragged a river in Mississippi in search of the bodies, a local white farmer told them: "Hey, why don't you hold a welfare check over the water. That'll get that nigger to the surface."

Michael K. Brown,
Race, Money, and the
American Welfare State

movement approached the height of its intensity and threatened to overthrow domestic racial apartheid. Racial state actors who were virulently committed to protecting white supremacy and fearful of the civil rights movement had many weapons to draw upon. Welfare racism was an important part of their arsenal. This chapter examines three case examples of ways in which welfare racism was aggressively used in the defense of white racial supremacy in the early 1960s.

The racist stereotypes and negative controlling images of welfare recipients revealed in these three cases have roots that were evident in whites' objections to black participation in mothers pension and Aid to Dependent Children programs. With the help of the events we will describe in this chapter, such stereotypes and controlling images were further reinforced and became indelibly ensconced in white racial thinking across the nation. They helped welfare racism make its transition from largely a manifestation of states' rights to a shaper of national politics. Today welfare racist attitudes both shape welfare policy and are reinforced by welfare policy itself in its function as ideology.

BATTLING THE CIVIL RIGHTS MOVEMENT: WELFARE RACISM IN LOUISIANA

The Challenge to White Supremacy in Louisiana

The antagonistic and punitive nature of race-based attitudes toward ADC recipients in the postwar period is well illustrated by actions taken against recipients in Louisiana in 1960.[1] To be understood, these actions must be considered within the larger context of institutionalized white privilege that had been carefully cultivated and maintained throughout that state for many years.[2] In 1960, nearly one-third of the Louisiana population was black. Like other southern states, Louisiana maintained a system of Jim Crow laws that kept African Americans in racially segregated schools, restricted their employment opportunities and access to public accommodations, denied them legal rights and court protections, kept them out of elective office, and minimized their ability to register and to vote. And, like other southern states with large African-American populations, Louisiana had a long history of single-minded commitment to states' rights and objection to federal intervention or interference in individual states' affairs.

In the 1950s, a growing movement for African-American civil rights was forcing the federal racial state to cautiously reverse its putative hands-off approach to de jure racial discrimination and segregation. This movement was viewed as posing serious threats by Louisiana political elites as well as the state's white population in general. In 1954, the U.S. Supreme Court finally responded to a long series of suits filed by civil rights lawyers by outlawing racially segregated school systems in the case of *Brown v. Board of Education of Topeka, Kansas*. In Louisiana and in the rest of the South the Court's decision was denounced as a direct attack both on the assumption of white racial superiority and on states' rights. The Court's order that the desegregation of schools commence with "all deliberate speed" incited immense public opposition in Louisiana and elsewhere. This opposition included widespread calls for defiance of what was depicted as federal intrusion into individual states' internal affairs.

Many of Louisiana's political elites had long been outspoken on both segregation and states' rights. They responded to the Court's decision by sharply escalating their pro-segregation rhetoric and actions. From Louisiana's congressional delegation to its state and local officials, there was widespread condemnation of the U.S. Supreme Court's actions. Louisiana's state legislature established a "Joint Committee on Segregation" to develop ways to get around desegregating the state's schools. At the local level, white supremacist organizations such as the White Citizens Councils and the Ku Klux Klan worked energetically to encourage local school systems and white parents to hold on to traditional racial separation. In Louisiana as in the rest of the South, pro-segregation rhetoric often equated school desegregation with community and family destruction. Opponents of school desegregation typically claimed that it would bring about increased crime and violence, interracial dating, sexually transmitted diseases, out-of-wedlock births, intermarriage, and the bastardization and mongrelization of the white race. In late 1959, a federal district court judge ordered the school board of New Orleans to produce a desegregation plan. Despite board members' resistance, Judge J. Skelly Wright acted aggressively to force the city to start the state's desegregation process. In response to Judge Wright's orders, in 1960 the Louisiana state legislature passed a "segregation package"of twenty-nine pieces of legislation. Most of that legislation was directly aimed at helping local school boards resist federal school desegregation mandates. Among the measures adopted were bills that removed final legal jurisdiction over public schools from local school boards and gave it to the state of Louisiana, allowed the governor to close schools threatened with court-ordered policies that were contrary to state law, and denied accreditation to racially integrated schools.[3]

The assumption of white superiority that held sway in the all-white Louisiana legislature in 1960 also prompted the inclusion of certain other bills in the legislators' "segregation package." These other bills were not aimed at engineering new administrative moves to keep schools segregated. Rather, they were designed to reinforce the prevailing system of white racial supremacy that was threatened by the school desegregation orders. These racial backlash bills were intended to keep people who were deemed racially inferior "in their place."

To help achieve their racial control objectives, members of the Louisiana legislature passed bills that made it a crime for a woman to have more than one child out of wedlock and criminalized men and women who had a common-law marriage. Such family situations were closely linked with abject poverty and thus were consequently more common in the African-American than in the white community.

Legislators also acted to remove the right to vote from certain categories of persons who were defined by law as "not of good character."[4] Louisiana already had a voter registration system that was creatively designed and made complicated in ways that kept African Americans from exercising the franchise. The new legislation was intended to make voter registration even more difficult for black applicants.[5] Persons registering to vote were required to fill out a form on which they had to indicate whether they had been convicted of felonies for which they were not legally pardoned, or misdemeanors for which they had been sentenced to jail. Given the institutionalized racism that guided Louisiana's criminal justice system, African Americans were far more likely than whites to be screened out of the voter registration process for having been convicted of a crime and jailed. Along with these items was a series of questions which asked if in the last five years the applicant had lived in a common-law marriage, given birth to an "illegitimate child," or fathered such a child.[6] Persons owning up to any of these other signs of "bad character" conformed to the images of those whose behavior should be controlled by the Louisiana racial state and were therefore prohibited from becoming voters. Again, African Americans were most likely to be denied the franchise for such reasons.

The Mobilization of Welfare Racism by the Louisiana Racial State

Of central interest to us is the component of that 1960 "segregation package" of legislation that pulled the subsistence rug out from under thousands of African-American families receiving ADC. That legislation removed over a quarter of Louisiana's ADC recipients from the state's welfare rolls by eliminating the eligibility of 6,000 families with 22,500 children—95 percent of whom were African American. At the time, two-thirds of the children in the state's ADC caseload were African American. This number was an indicator of their situation of extreme impoverishment and of Louisiana's inability to maintain outright racial exclusion in the face of federal racial state safeguards and a tide of incredibly impoverished applicants of color.

Modeling their new suitable-home law after Mississippi's, Louisiana racial state officials took the position that the children they removed from ADC were not residing in morally suitable homes. The children's homes were proclaimed unsuitable primarily because their mothers had given birth to a child out of wedlock, or had given birth to a child after receiving their first ADC payment, or were partners in common-law marriages, which the Louisiana legislature chose not to recognize as legal. The new suitable-home law was intended to be retroactive. Families affected were given little or no information or encouragement that would have made it possible to exercise their legal right to appeal or to participate in a fair hearing prior to their children's loss of aid. Moreover, Louisiana welfare officials removed children from the rolls without adequately investigating and establishing proof of their ineligibility. Instead, the burden of proof was placed upon the recipients' families, and children were assumed to be ineligible unless their mothers or other adult caretakers in their families could demonstrate otherwise.

Under the Louisiana suitable-home law, mothers in common-law marriages could reapply for eligibility for ADC if they could offer proof to local welfare officials that they had "entered into a valid marriage or ceased their relationship" with their male partner.[7] A mother of out-of-wedlock children could reapply for eligibility if there was proof "showing that the mother has ceased illicit relationships and is maintaining a suitable home for the child or children."[8]

Louisiana's Democratic Governor Jimmie H. Davis took office in early 1960 after campaigning across the state as a fervent segregationist. He was a sponsor and proponent of the segregation package of legislation that included the welfare bill, and was highly outspoken on what he saw as the need to crack down on the use of the public's tax dollars to support the allegedly immoral behavior of mothers who gave birth out of wedlock and whose children received ADC.[9] After Davis's election, one of his first official acts as governor was to address the Louisiana legislature, where he expressed concern over "the existing policy regarding public assistance to unwed mothers who have proved by their past conduct that they engage in the business of illegitimacy in the same way that a cattleman raises beef."[10] Davis successfully advocated passage of the suitable-home law as a form of procreation-focused race population control "to stop this practice." The law became effective July 6, 1960.

In a news conference held in September 1960 to explain the state's adoption of a policy that had by then denied almost twenty-three thousand children ADC, some five thousand of whom lived in New Orleans, because they did not live in "suitable homes," Governor Davis referred to their mothers as a "bunch of professional prostitutes."[11] This slur was consistent with racist controlling images of the immoral, promiscuous, African-American "welfare mother." In a "clarifying comment" released later, the governor explained the statements he made at his press conference by complaining that some of the state's welfare recipients were making a "business" of having illegitimate children while on welfare. Governor Davis also asserted, "I have no intention of seeing our tax money used as a subsidy for those whose actions attack the basic concepts of our civilization."[12] Of course racial segregation and white racial supremacy were core values of "civilization" as Governor Davis and other southern segregationists saw it.

Camouflaged beneath the expressions of gendered racism and the rhetoric of outrage over the allegedly immoral behavior of mothers in ADC families, Louisiana's segregationist political elites were in fact reacting to challenges to the southern racial caste system. The issue of the morality of African-American mothers was introduced and exploited as part of a political strategy that sought to maintain the legitimacy of white racial hegemony and the strict segregation along color lines that it demanded. As one historian put it, "The state's meanspirited welfare cutoff was not directly related to the schools issue, but it was most assuredly part of the legislature's overall strategy of resistance to integration."[13]

Risley C. Triche is an attorney who served as a Louisiana state representative and a coauthor of the Louisiana House bill containing the suitable-home policy. In an interview three and a half decades later, this is how Triche—after first indicating that he did not specifically remember that event—placed the welfare bill in its broader racial context:

> We must remember that at that time we were concerned about *Brown versus Topeka, the Board of Education,* which ordered the integration of public schools—with celerity—with haste. And we were concerned about the effect that would have here, and we were concerned—at the time—about what it would do to our public school system. That was, maybe, the principal concern. And most of these types of bills were very frankly racially motivated to prevent the black population from becoming enfranchised; to be able to go to the polls in numbers and effect their own agenda . . . those things at that time was a part of a package of bills designed to prevent and slow down the political movement in the black population.[14]

Louisiana racial state actors used the pretext of their suitable-home policy to harp on the alleged immorality, dishonesty, and irresponsible nature of African Americans; to raise fictitious allegations about African-American male and female sexuality and promiscuity; and, to denigrate African-American family values by pointing to rising rates of single parenthood and out-of-wedlock births. Indeed, the policy itself was a form of racist ideology.

The Racial State as Contested Terrain: Challenging Welfare Racism

Civil rights organizations in Louisiana and elsewhere publicly condemned the suitable home policy as a punitive response to African-American litigation and protest against racial segregation. In September 1960 the National Urban League took a leadership role in publicizing Louisiana's policy and its effects. The Urban League complained in a widely circulated statement that "there has been little public indignation over the Louisiana situation." [15] The organization noted that 593 national organizations had gathered at the White House for the Golden Anniversary White House Conference on Children and Youth to express concern for care of the young. The Urban League then chided such advocacy groups for their silence and urged that strong protests over the ADC cutoffs be directed at racial state actors, including President Eisenhower, federal welfare officials, and the Louisiana Board of Welfare.

The National Urban League statement pointed directly to the thinly camouflaged racism associated with the ADC cutoffs. It described the bill as "an act of reprisal or intimidation against a Negro population which has been insistently pressing for an end to racial segregation in education and other areas of living." [16] The Urban League report also criticized Governor Davis for the "segregationist package" that he sponsored.

New Orleans's *Louisiana Weekly*, an outspoken African-American publication, referred to the legislature's actions as "states' rights, southern style . . . the right to take whatever legal means available to thwart, discourage, and harass Negroes in their fight to be recognized as first-class citizens exercising the right to vote and other rights accorded American citizens." [17] The *Louisiana Weekly* reported regularly and in depth on the effects of the ADC cutoffs, and reprinted editorials condemning the cutoffs that had been published in other African-American papers. One such editorial addressed the question "'Why must such cruelty be heaped upon children already so unfortunate as to be objects of public charity?'":

> The answer to this question shows the motive to be even more horrifying than the deed itself. These children are the deliberate victims of politically applied economic pressure. The purpose is to force the adults into abandoning their efforts to desegregate public schools and to register and vote. Political economic pressure is worse than that applied by private organizations such as the White Citizens Councils. This is because the evil is perpetrated by public officials whose duty it is to represent fairly and justly all elements of the population. [18]

By September 1960, the federal racial state was confronted by outcries from civil rights and child advocacy groups, organized social work professionals, liberal whites, and the African-American community. There was also a National Urban League–sponsored "Feed the Babies Project" which, in response to a nationwide appeal, received donations of money, food, and clothing for the Louisiana children cut off from ADC. Donations poured into New Orleans from twenty-one states and a number of nations, including Canada, England, and Ireland. A group of women on the Newcastle-on-Tyne, England, city council not only sent donations for the children removed from ADC but announced their intention to bring as many of these children as possible to their country so they could be adequately cared for.[19]

Race-Blind Intervention by the Federal Racial State

In response to growing pressure to take stronger action, federal welfare officials finally wrote to Louisiana officials on October 1, 1960, advising them that a hearing was to be held to determine whether Louisiana's welfare law was out of conformity with the requirements of the Social Security Act of 1935.[20] If this proved to be true, federal officials had the statutory authority to cease all ADC contributions to the state.

Hearings were conducted through November and December of 1960. Louisiana welfare officials testified that the state was only following similar suitable-home policies that already existed in six other states (Arkansas, Georgia, Michigan, Mississippi, Texas, and Virginia). They camouflaged the racist intent of Louisiana's governor and legislative racial state actors by arguing that the policy that was crafted in Louisiana "was concerned only with the 'moral uplift' of some of its citizens."[21] Those officials pointed out that the federal government had never banned suitable-home laws, and that almost half the states had one or another version of such a law in 1960. Louisiana welfare officials vociferously denied that racism was involved in any way. They argued that the suitable-home law applied equally to blacks and whites. The reason so many African-American children were denied aid, officials said, was that they were more likely to live in unsuitable homes. They also claimed that children were being put back on ADC "as fast as a suitable home can be proved."[22]

A variety of national organizations, such as the Child Welfare League of America, the Family Service Association of America, the American Civil Liberties Union (ACLU), and the National Urban League rebutted Louisiana racial state actors. Those organizations provided briefs or memoranda that condemned Louisiana's actions and argued against the appropriateness and legality of its suitable-home law. In its memorandum, the ACLU urged U.S. Department of Health, Education, and Welfare officials to consider the importance of the racial context within which the Louisiana law had been passed: "We urge the Department . . . to look behind the statute. If it is satisfied that it was in fact adopted to threaten Louisiana's Negro citizens' pursuit of equal treatment, it would be unnecessary to examine further into the subtleties of Louisiana's ADC program."[23]

The ACLU went on to argue that racist motivation or intent need not be overt for the suitable-home policy to be considered racially discriminatory:

> (A) statute, not discriminatory on its face, may be designed to deprive a single class of citizens of rights to which they are otherwise entitled. Whether or not it is so designed, may be inferred from its impact. We believe the impact of the Louisiana statute can lead to the fair inference that it was designed to exclude a large number of Negro recipients of the benefits of ADC funds.[24]

The National Urban League also attacked white racism in its hearing memorandum, noting that the cutoff of ADC "has caused, by all reports, incalculable hardship and deprivation" to black children and mothers. The memorandum cited a letter from its New Orleans chapter, which stated that "a vast majority of the welfare cases which have come to our attention are women who are mentally and physically incompetent for employment which would assure them of wages adequate to care for their families."[25]

The federal commissioner of Social Security, William L. Mitchell, ultimately issued a decision on January 16, 1961. In it he concluded that Louisiana, having made appropriate procedural changes and having promised to abide by such procedures in the future, was no longer out of conformity with the Social Security Act. However, consistent with our argument about the bill's procreative-focused race population control function, Mitchell went on to suggest that there was reason to suspect that the Louisiana suitable-home law was more about controlling out-of-wedlock births and punishing mothers than it was about ensuring that children would be provided with wholesome family surroundings. He commented harshly on the privation and suffering inflicted upon thousands of children by the Louisiana suitable-home law. Mitchell ended by announcing plans to immediately issue a revised federal policy that would not allow states with suitable-home laws to leave children in "unsuitable homes" without ADC. In his report of findings on Louisiana's actions Mitchell did not mention racism or segregation at all.[26]

The following day, January 17, 1961—just before Democratic President John F. Kennedy's administration took over the White House—U.S. Secretary of Health, Education, and Welfare Arthur S. Flemming sent a message to all state agencies administering ADC plans under the oversight of the federal Bureau of Public Assistance. In that message he ruled that the individual states could not deny aid to dependent children on the basis that their homes were unsuitable so long as the child continued to reside in the home. Assistance had to be continued while ADC caseworkers made efforts to improve the home conditions or made arrangements for the child to live elsewhere.[27] With this ruling, Louisiana racial state officials pulled back and the legislature revised its 1960 suitable-home law to conform to the new federal requirement.[28]

Flemming's new ruling on suitable homes would not become effective until 1962 when the U.S. Congress made it a part of revisions to the Social Security Act. Meanwhile, only a little over half of the families whose children had been cut from Louisiana's ADC rolls and had reapplied were deemed to be eligible once again and were put back on. Thousands of impoverished children permanently lost ADC benefits either because their families did not reapply or because they were turned down by local officials upon reapplying. Those put back on the rolls went without ADC assistance for months. In the interim, they endured serious deprivation and hardships.[29]

The six other individual states that had adopted policies barring ADC to children living in unsuitable homes were forced to adapt to the new requirement. Flemming's ruling marked the first time since 1935 that the individual states were required to abide by federal restrictions on the conditions under which they could cut off ADC from homes found be "unsuitable."[30]

It is extremely important to emphasize that federal racial state actors did not come right out and ban suitable-home policies, even in the face of their awareness of the race-based exclusionary uses to which these policies were frequently put. The Social Security Act included absolutely no mandate to monitor the morality of mothers. It was instead worded in such a way as to place first priority on the needs of impoverished children. But federal racial state actors were unwilling to challenge suitable-home policies that were launched with the publicly stated pretext of discouraging promiscuity and "illegitimacy," and promoting acceptable family behavior. These were issues on which politicians at the state level had overwhelming public support.

The Louisiana case is notable for two major reasons. First, it demonstrated the efficacy of collective action by people of color and their supporters in forcing federal racial state actors to act against legislation embodying welfare racism at the individual state level. This case example supports Carter A. Wilson's view of the state as contested political terrain which, because it is open to challenges from racially subordinated groups, has a racial role that is more shifting and indeterminate than constant. Efficacious collective action by the racially oppressed had to be undertaken if Louisiana's welfare racism was not to run free and rampant under "states' rights" and federal inaction. It seems clear from the cautious and reluctant federal response to the Louisiana suitable-home policy and from federal officials' noticeable failure to acknowledge or challenge its racist intent and consequences that without political protest little would have happened to reverse this legislated act of white oppression.

The second lesson offered by this case is the strict limits on the federal racial state's willingness to challenge individual states on ADC policies and practices that were clearly racist and were targeted to harm people of color. While conservative and racist interests shaped the Social Security Act of 1935 in ways that may have tied federal welfare officials' hands, one might have thought that by 1960 the act could have been changed or new legislation passed by Congress to discourage racially discriminatory ADC policies. The failure of the federal racial state to do so, or to even openly identify racism as an issue and to challenge it in the Louisiana case, was a telling sign of its continued willingness to capitulate to the politics of white racial hegemony when it came to welfare.

Louisiana Lost the Battle and Won the War

As political scientist Gilbert Steiner noted: "Louisiana was not to be penalized for outfoxing the federal people. . . . Governor Davis did not do badly. In the end, even his law survived. . . . On the basis of the outcome of the suitable home issue, neither Louisiana nor any other state had reason to feel that the federal leash was shortening." [31] Likewise, as sociologist Joe Feagin observed, "The state of Louisiana had in effect won, because no federal money had been withheld for noncompliance. Although Louisiana authorities had to support these needy children, they soon adopted other strategies to reduce the number of [ADC] families." [32] Indeed, in 1964 Louisiana began using a revised suitable-home law to cut off payments to mothers who were living with men other than their husbands. By 1968 almost sixteen thousand Louisiana children, 63 percent of whom were black, had again been cut from the welfare rolls. Many couples were forced to separate so that children could continue to receive aid. In 1968, a federal district court ordered Louisiana welfare officials to reinstate the children who had been denied aid. Months later, Louisiana officials cut state welfare benefits by 10 percent. [33]

Louisiana's actions in 1960 and the federal racial state response helped to provoke nationwide discourse among European Americans over whether poverty-stricken African-American families were deserving of public assistance at all. This debate sharply escalated the following year in connection with harsh welfare policy initiatives in upstate New York.

COMBATING THE BLACK DIASPORA: THE NEWBURGH, N.Y. CONTROVERSY
Challenges to White Supremacy in an "All-American" City

Displays of welfare racism were no doubt less frequent and less blatant in the North than they were in the South in the postwar era. However, while there is a paucity of systematic data, we do know that racist welfare practices were certainly not limited to the South. In 1961, for example, welfare racism clearly was expressed through a series of policies announced by the city manager in Newburgh, New York. Those policies moved the ADC program further into the national spotlight.[34] In the words of journalist Edgar May, it "was here for the first time on a major scale that public welfare really became public." May went on to say that Newburgh's policies provoked "an outpouring of words that dwarfed any previous public welfare issue." They became a matter of nation-wide debate and dispute. "The dispute inked across the front page of America, blared from radios, and flickered on the television screen."[35]

Newburgh is a small city in upstate New York on the Hudson River. Long a thriving river port and manufacturing city, its economy began to undergo marked changes in the post–World War II period.[36] While it received a national award as an "All American City" in 1952, its stable base of industrial employment, on which local and nearby residents depended, was eroding. In the 1950s a number of important local manufacturers closed down operations entirely or moved their plants to the South, with its lower taxes and non-union labor.

The loss of a good deal of factory employment and thus a steady flow of income from manufacturing jobs provoked a marked decline in Newburgh's downtown retail and business service sectors. The downtown area began to suffer visible signs of economic decline and physical deterioration. Empty windows and boarded-up storefronts replaced vibrant offices and shops. The bustle of downtown business activity sharply dwindled as Newburgh residents with money and transportation traveled to suburban shopping plazas and retail centers outside the city.

In addition, many of those residents who could afford to do so moved away from the crumbling downtown area. Some left Newburgh altogether. In their wake, housing in that area underwent marked deterioration. Rental housing replaced owner-occupied housing, and rental units were often provided with little maintenance or upkeep. Homes that had once been occupied by single families were divided into multiple family living units. People crowded into this housing despite the dilapidation, substandard conditions, and housing code violations that prevailed and often menaced the health and safety of occupants. This was especially true for people of color.

Due to racial discrimination in the sale and rental of housing in Newburgh and other northern communities, African-American single adults and families in search of affordable living quarters often had little choice but to take shelter in these deteriorating neighborhoods. The jobs available to African Americans living in Newburgh paid substantially less than those of white workers. Consequently, the few city neighborhoods in which African Americans were concentrated had a higher rate of poverty, and thus a greater need for welfare assistance, than did white neighborhoods.

As the demographics of Newburgh underwent change, the presence of the black population and its poor was made a public issue within the city. And it was an issue to which welfare was inextricably linked. This kind of demographic change occurred in numerous cities outside the South in the postwar period as southern African Americans left in search of better economic opportunities and to escape white racial oppression.[37] Most of Newburgh's African Americans were visibly concentrated in the several racially segregated neighborhoods that had undergone the greatest white abandonment and physical blight.

The demographic change—to quote Newburgh journalist Joseph Ritz—"created apprehension and resentment among white residents."[38] White residents' reactions to the changes in color that Newburgh's population underwent during the 1950s included fear. Interviewed more than three decades later, Ritz recalled, "It was threatening, it was frightening, because people remembered it as it used to be—predominantly white."[39] In Newburgh, the racial fears of whites mixed and mingled with their economic anxiety. Elected officials were unaccustomed to and disturbed by the downward economic spiral of the city, and seemingly powerless to reverse it. Moreover, members of Newburgh's white community, including most key elected leaders of its local racial state, tended to blame the city's plight on African-American residents.[40]

Local Racial State Actors' Struggle to Uphold White Dominance

In 1959 one of the five members of the Newburgh's all-white City Council publicly criticized the city's African Americans. In a reaction to a local school official's report of street conflicts involving a small number of white and African-American children, Republican Councilman George F. McKneally issued a call for racial control:

> The colored people of this city are our biggest police problem, our biggest sanitation problem, and our biggest health problem. . . . We cannot put up with their behavior any longer. We have been too lenient with them. They must be made to adhere to the standards of the rest of the community. If necessary, we will enforce our own ideas on them.[41]

McKneally went on to castigate the local chapter of the National Association for the Advancement of Colored People. "Their real function should be to advise Negro parents on bringing up their children properly,"[42] he said.

The president of Newburgh's NAACP chapter quickly responded to McKneally's statements with comments which were critical of the local racial state:

> The real trouble is a basic disregard by this city's government for the Negro and his needs. If there is any trouble we will, of course, do our best to work it out. But it remains that the Negro in Newburgh has been neglected.[43]

McKneally stated that his comments reflected those of "a majority of city residents," among whom there was a "rising tide of resentment" against Newburgh's African-American leaders.[44] He thus shifted the causes of problems in the black community away from white racism and onto blacks themselves. He specifically targeted the leaders of local civil rights organizations.

Insight into the tenor of relations between Newburgh's white power structure and the African-American community in 1959 is revealed in letters to the editor that quickly appeared in the city's daily newspaper, the *Newburgh News*. Most of these letters condemned McKneally's statements. Those letters were most likely to come from members of Newburgh's African-American community. A few came from sympathetic whites. Here are two examples.

- A letter from an African-American clergyman commented on how McKneally's disparaging comments about troublemakers cast a shadow over all African Americans in the city:

  It is incredible that an eminent City Official who proposes to foster high Democratic ideals and ethical standards is punishing both the innocent and the guilty by his loosely chosen words. . . . The fact that there is a tendency on the part of some people to place all Negroes on the same low level is depriving the deserved ones of their stature in the community.[45]

- A letter from a sympathetic white Newburgh resident focused on the racial control implications of McKneally's comments:

  Mr. McKneally sounds as if we should combat this problem with the same method that was used for the Indian population. Fencing the Negroes in on a reservation. Has it ever occurred to him that Negro leaders have helped in building the government we have today? I am surprised that Mr. McKneally should voice a public segregationist opinion when he is seeking an elective office depending on the Negro votes.[46]

McKneally held silent in the face of such letters to the editor for a couple of weeks. He then publicly defended his position in the *Newburgh News*. Once again he made reference to the need for racial control:

Newburgh is a tightly organized society, and it cannot be run at all, let alone be made to advance, if the people living within its limits refuse to have a due and proper regard for the law and the spirit of community living.[47]

He called for the leaders of the African-American community to come forward and assist in controlling the behavior of its members, because, in McKneally's words:

> 1. We shall never have enough police to accompany all the children to and from school.

> 2. We shall never have enough police to investigate, as we're attempting to do, every case of illegitimacy among relief children, every case of mothers living in sin, on relief, while their children go needy.

> 3. We shall never have enough police to watch every house holder who dumps his garbage or trash into the gutter.[48]

In a clumsy and racist stereotype–laden attempt to camouflage the racism embedded in his public message, McKneally went on to say, "I am not anti-Negro; I am anti-knifings. I am not anti-Negro; I am anti-delinquents. I am not anti–relief chiselers."[49]

The fact that a key elected official in the local racial state felt free to speak openly and publicly in this way indicates that there was strong support for such views within Newburgh's white community. McKneally certainly had no hesitation in speaking out publicly in ways that morally maligned African Americans receiving welfare. On one occasion he asserted, "Many Negroes are taking money from the Welfare Department here under false pretenses. If a real check were made you would find many cases just on the legal borderline. They are at least violating the spirit of the law. It is shocking."[50] And, "When you come right down to it, [welfare is] a Negro problem."[51]

According to journalist Joseph Ritz, McKneally's principal solution to the city's urban blight was to curtail welfare funds, which he believed were attracting "jobless southern Negroes" to Newburgh. McKneally thus was a staunch advocate of geographic race population control. Ritz described his ideas as making sense to and fitting in with the prejudices of many of the white Newburgh natives to whom he spoke. Here is Ritz's version of a typical McKneally message, presented to a group of local white businessmen: "The people who live in the slums create them; the slum dwellers are Negroes; therefore, keep the Negroes from moving into the city."[52]

McKneally portrayed welfare benefits, such as ADC, as a magnet attracting African Americans to Newburgh. Consistent with his advocacy of geographic race population control, he supported the notion of a strict residency requirement that would discourage African Americans who (he claimed) were coming to Newburgh with no means of support and with the goal and intention of going on welfare.[53]

McKneally's 1959 statements and some of the reactions to them provide a backdrop that helps make sense of the tumultuous events that followed two years later. The full significance of McKneally's views regarding welfare and African Americans, which went largely uncontested if not accepted by the community's white majority, would not become fully apparent until 1961. At that time, officials of Newburgh's local racial state would approve harsh welfare policy initiatives that caused this All-American City to become a household word in the national discourse on welfare.

Welfare Reforms and the Mobilization of Controlling Images in Newburgh

In October 1960, Newburgh hired a new city manager, Joseph McDowell Mitchell. Mitchell came to Newburgh as the first choice of Councilman McKneally. The latter was a driving force on the five-member city council and was able to swing the other four members of the council to agree to this hiring decision. Despite the numerous problems facing a city suffering from economic stagnation and decline, at the city council's request, City Manager Mitchell quickly homed in on welfare. Consistent with McKneally's concerns, Mitchell wasted no time in taking steps to identify "welfare cheats," reduce the welfare rolls and welfare budget, and develop punitive policies to discourage people from even applying for aid. The city manager's policies, as we shall see, included steps aimed at "migrants" and "newcomers." These words were used and understood to be meant as euphemisms or code terms for African Americans.[54]

In early 1961 the city faced unexpectedly high snow removal costs. Mitchell sought to balance the budget by ordering cutbacks in payments to ADC families and in unemployment relief payments to adults.[55] He also requested that all "borderline" cases be closed and removed from the rolls. Upon learning of his actions, New York state welfare officials quickly declared the budget cuts illegal and asked that they be rescinded. Most of the thirty cases removed from the rolls were reopened at their prompting. This was be the first, but by no means would be the last, of Mitchell's attacks on welfare recipients to draw a rebuke from higher-level racial state actors.

Later, in the spring of 1961, Mitchell secretly issued orders to his staff mandating that welfare recipients pick up their assistance checks in a May 1 "muster" at the city's police headquarters. While there, they would be evaluated for their eligibility. Those found ineligible would lose their benefits. The appointed day was abruptly announced in letters put in the mail to recipients on April 29. The surprise muster drew mothers of ADC families with children and infants in tow, as well as others receiving income assistance or relief, such as the unemployed, the elderly, and people with disabilities. Some two hundred fifty persons stood in lines waiting to be processed by police. Eighty-six persons were too ill or disabled to come to police headquarters and were visited at home by police officers. When all was said and done, no welfare chiselers were found.[56]

This time Mitchell's action sparked angry words of protest from some city residents as revealed by letters to the editor of the city's daily newspaper. It elicited public condemnations from a group of Newburgh clergy as well as representatives of local private charitable and community service agencies. The muster was defended by the four Republican members of the city council. The only non-Republican council member, the Democratic mayor, clearly opposed the muster. He took sharp issue with Mitchell's views of and approach to welfare in Newburgh. As it turned out, this was a role he alone would continue to play among key officials of the local racial state. The mayor and other local critics uniformly decried the muster as harassment and public humiliation of the needy.[57]

The muster was endorsed in an editorial in Newburgh's daily newspaper, whose executive editor was very supportive of Mitchell's views on welfare matters. The editorial stated: "There is no doubt that the needy should be helped. At the same time, there is no doubt that the pretender or fraud should be exposed."[58] In general, Mitchell's push to crack down on welfare recipients seemed to have widespread support in the city, even though the muster had exposed no fraud. Mitchell was undaunted by the muster's failure to uncover welfare cheats among the recipients: "If nothing else, it scared the daylights out of them. This was a routine governmental exercise. I intend to hold one whenever necessary."[59]

However, news of the muster—which hit the front page of the *New York Times*—generated a visit to Mitchell and Newburgh's mayor from state welfare officials. They released a statement calling the muster a borderline violation of the law and a "highly irregular method" of which the state of New York could not and would not approve. The officials later wrote to Mitchell and threatened to cut off state and federal funds for Newburgh's welfare programs. Mitchell denied violating any laws, and the four Republican members of the city council denounced higher-level racial state actors' reaction to the muster as "arrogant" and "an interference in justified local efforts to reduce welfare expenses."[60]

Almost immediately after the May 1 muster, Mitchell released the results of a study of welfare operations in Newburgh, which was widely reported upon and even serialized in the daily newspaper. Not surprisingly, the report reflected McKneally and Mitchell's mantra of unsubstantiated allegations of abuses of welfare by recipients, welfare's magnetic power to attract "migrants" to Newburgh from southern states, the contribution of welfare recipients to urban blight, and social instability associated with welfare recipients' nonconformity to mainstream moral values. Little care was taken to veil the inference that African Americans were the principal focus of the report's concern.[61]

In reality, hardly any of Newburgh's funds were paid to "migrants." In 1960, home relief, which provided aid to jobless families, totaled only $205 in payments to those who were residents for less than a year. The state government reimbursed the city that cost. In that same year no ADC funds had gone to new arrivals. In the previous two years, in all forms of public assistance, Newburgh had paid a total of $1,395 to newcomers.[62] Moreover, most newcomers receiving public assistance of any type in Newburgh were white.

In 1960, only 39 percent of persons receiving some form of income assistance in Newburgh were persons of color. Most African Americans who received assistance received it in the form of ADC. Nor were black welfare recipients characteristic of Newburgh's African-American community. The 359 African Americans on the welfare rolls in 1960 constituted only 7 percent of Newburgh's black population.[63] These facts went largely unacknowledged by Mitchell's report on welfare operations and were certainly lost in his antiwelfare rhetoric.

The study report also called for more local control to improve welfare operations. Shortly thereafter, at Mitchell's request, the four Republican city council members voted to turn over all of Newburgh's welfare operations to him to run as he saw fit, even if it meant the loss of federal and state aid. The city manager and his supporters thus threw down the gauntlet to federal and New York racial state actors who oversaw ADC. The latter announced that if Newburgh went ahead with its plans to run its own welfare programs, not only Newburgh but the state of New York as well could lose federal ADC contributions. If state officials were to permit Newburgh to go its own way regarding welfare operations, New York would be in violation of the Social Security Act provision requiring the individual states to have uniform welfare programs across all their local political subunits.

The Racially Punitive "Thirteen-Point Program"

Armed with the city council majority's endorsement of his authority over the city's welfare programs, Mitchell proceeded to act. The findings of the welfare study report, most of which were authored by Mitchell himself, laid the groundwork for what would become his "thirteen-point program" of welfare policy initiatives.[64] This program was announced by Mitchell and approved by the city council in mid-June 1961. Mitchell's thirteen-point program contained new and restrictive measures aimed not only at ADC families but at anyone applying for or receiving assistance through the city's welfare department. They were to go into effect on July 15.[65]

Prior to publicly announcing the thirteen points, Mitchell had sent a confidential memo to the four Republican members of the city council. In this way he bypassed the Democratic mayor, who was an open critic of the study report and its findings. In his confidential memo, Mitchell frankly acknowledged that his welfare policy initiatives were unlikely to be accepted at the New York state and federal levels. Nor was the local racial state in any position to pay for welfare programs on its own if the city's outside funds were cut off. Publicly, however, Mitchell expressed willingness to go to court, if necessary, to uphold his new welfare measures.[66]

Thus, Mitchell proposed the thirteen-point program which, although never publicly acknowledged, served as ideology for his own political gain. With the welfare racism of his policy proposals subtly camouflaged, Mitchell played to the state- and national-level mass media. He decried the inability of local governments to run their welfare programs any way they wished, and condemned federal and state "interference" in local welfare matters. Mitchell demanded sympathy by portraying himself as a righteous but frustrated local official forced by state and federal bureaucrats to waste taxpayers' money on the lazy, undeserving, immoral, and fraudulent.

There is no need to enumerate all thirteen of Mitchell's proposed welfare measures[67] (the reader will find striking parallels between the draconian character of those mentioned here and that of contemporary "welfare reform"). One provision stated that monthly budgetary limits would be set on all categories of welfare expenditures. Except for the blind, aged, and disabled, no one would receive aid for more than three months out of a year. Vouchers for food, rent, and clothing were to be issued in lieu of cash welfare payments. Mothers of children born out of wedlock would be stricken from the welfare rolls upon birth of another such child. Children on ADC found living in homes whose environment was not satisfactory would be removed and placed in foster care. Applicants for relief who were new to the city would have to show they came to Newburgh because of an offer of employment, "similar to that required of foreign immigrants."[68] They would then be limited to two weeks of aid. While, in keeping with camouflaged racism, nowhere were African Americans named or singled out in the thirteen-point program, their presence on Newburgh's welfare rolls was a significant policy subtext.

The harshness of Mitchell's thirteen-point plan would have fallen most heavily on African Americans. The three-month limit on aid applied only to ADC recipients and those jobless families who needed home relief. The limit did not apply to those who were aged, disabled, or blind. Indeed, as was true in Louisiana, those most punished by the three-month limit would have been African-American children. Three-quarters of the African Americans receiving aid fell into the two most vulnerable categories of ADC and home relief. This was the case for a far smaller percentage of whites receiving some form of public assistance. While Mitchell's plan was "race-blind" on its face, whether by intention or by impact, African Americans would disproportionately feel the adverse effects.[69]

In its geographic race population control provisions, Mitchell's thirteen-point program was not simply aimed at discouraging African-American "newcomers" and "migrants" from coming to Newburgh (ostensibly in search of generous welfare benefits). The policies, according to Newburgh journalist Joseph Ritz, were also intended to "drive blacks out." They played upon many white residents' fears that the city population might turn black if demographic trends were not reversed.[70] Mitchell and those who supported him apparently thought that many African Americans already in Newburgh could be pressured to leave. Councilman McKneally was quoted as saying, "I don't think we need any more [of these people]. They should return to their point of origin."[71] Indeed, McKneally introduced a resolution before the city council calling for the city to pay one-way transportation home for migrants who were on the welfare rolls for over three months.

In Mitchell's view, Newburgh's African Americans ideally should not have been permitted to reside in the city in the first place, and would not have if adequate geographic race population control measures existed:

> It's not simply a race question. It's a problem of low-class people, for lack of a better term. I mean it might be Puerto Ricans or the Mexicans someplace else. What we should do is have laws, similar to the immigration law, to prevent them from moving from one section of the country to the other unless they have a definite job where they're going. But, of course, you can't do that.[72]

Mitchell's statement, "It's not simply a race question," clearly implies that "race" was indeed an issue. Moreover, it is telling that his examples of "low-class people," used to illustrate his race-blind approach, are people of color.

Newburgh Welfare Policies Become a National Issue

Cloaking himself in the rhetoric of "local control" and "fairness to taxpayers," the city manager played to the mass media. As the major New York City newspapers and the national wire services picked up on the thirteen-point program, what became known as "The Battle of Newburgh" set off racialized discourse about welfare that went well beyond local or state boundaries. Indeed, Mitchell quickly became a national celebrity. Some called him a hero. Thousands of letters and telegrams poured into city hall from people across the country.[73] Many requested further details on the thirteen-point program and advice on how to implement such policies. Most of the communications were, according to Mitchell, supportive of his ideas.

Mitchell was invited to speak all across the nation on his proposals to combat immorality and dependency among the welfare poor. One of his talks was deemed significant enough to be published in *Vital Speeches*. In this talk, delivered in 1961 in Detroit, Mitchell characterized his actions in Newburgh in a way that revealed both their procreative and geographic race population control intent:

racial welfare stereotypes political framing

We challenged the right of social parasites to breed illegitimate children at the taxpayer's expense. We challenged the right of moral chiselers and loafers to squat on the relief rolls forever. We challenged . . . the right of people to quit jobs at will and go on relief like spoiled children. We challenged the right of citizens to migrate for the purpose of becoming or continuing as public charges.[74]

In the meantime, the contents of Newburgh's daily newspaper reflected the controversy kicked off by the study report on welfare operations, Mitchell's assumption of authority over all welfare programs administered by the city, and his thirteen-point program. While there was division apparent in the community, Mitchell clearly retained a great deal of community support. But it did not come from Newburgh's African-American population.

The local NAACP condemned the proposed thirteen-point program at an emergency meeting, at which time a visiting official from the national NAACP office drew a direct parallel between Mitchell's welfare measures and welfare racism in Louisiana, "where 23,000 children were cut off and some of them starved."[75] Meanwhile, consistent with more recent racially camouflaged ideas justifying mandatory work requirements for welfare recipients, Councilman McKneally was quoted as making the following racist statement while denying *stereotype* the racial intent of the Newburgh actions: "This is not a racial issue. But there's hardly an incentive to a naturally lazy people to work if they can exist without working."[76] Clearly, one racial control function of Newburgh's welfare policies was to modify the assumed laziness of African Americans. As we will see in chapter 6, the various racial control functions of Newburgh's policies anticipated provisions of the welfare reform legislation adopted in the 1990s.

The response of the New York racial state actors responsible for overseeing local ADC programs was not long in coming. Just before the announced July 15 implementation date of the thirteen-point program, Mitchell and other Newburgh officials were called to a hearing by the New York State Board of Welfare. That hearing focused upon the legality of almost all of the measures Mitchell proposed to implement under state or federal law.[77] Shortly thereafter, state welfare officials ordered Mitchell not to implement these measures. They concluded that the measures consisted of "an illegal program to push around unfortunate men, women and children; and even if they are not carried out, they constitute psychological warfare against the needy and helpless."[78] But Mitchell refused to give in.

Meanwhile, the thirteen-point plan had entered welfare discourse among racial state actors at the federal level. U.S. Senator Barry Goldwater, a conservative Republican looking to garner support in his bid for the party's 1964 presidential nomination, wrote a letter to Mitchell in which he stated that Mitchell's welfare stand was "as refreshing as breathing the clean air of my native Arizona."[79] And, he went on say, "This took courage on your part, but it is the kind of courage that must be displayed across this nation if we are to survive. . . . My thanks to you as an American."[80] Goldwater later stated that he "would like to see every city in the country adopt the plan."[81] *political figure supports racist idea*

Governor Nelson Rockefeller, a moderate Republican with similar presidential aspirations, cautiously announced his opposition to the plan by expressing disbelief that Newburgh officials would actually follow through on it. Rockefeller indicated that he would "carry out his constitutional responsibilities" if the plan went into effect and Mitchell thus flouted state and federal laws.[82] One of Rockefeller's champions for the 1964 Republican presidential nomination, New York Republican Senator Jacob Javits, openly condemned Goldwater's position. Javits stated that the thirteen-point program represented "a grave reverse to humane concepts of relief and welfare."[83]

Dissent between Levels of the Racial State

As the July 15 program implementation date arrived, Mitchell ignored all demands by New York welfare officials and ordered his thirteen-point program to be implemented. New York state officials almost immediately requested that the attorney general take legal action to stop this from occurring. After efforts behind closed doors to resolve the conflict over the thirteen-point program failed, state officials went to court to obtain an injunction. While awaiting the judicial decision, Mitchell attracted further attention by announcing that, as part of the effort to more strictly police the welfare rolls, he was instituting a policy of photographing those persons receiving checks for ADC and home relief. Those who were disabled or bedridden, and the children in ADC families, would be exempt from his new policy.[84] Mitchell was no doubt buoyed by the news of a national Gallup poll conducted to tap some of the issues raised by his stance. Results showed that 55 percent of those surveyed approved of local communities' having more say in setting up and implementing their own welfare programs.[85]

Throughout the turmoil, federal racial state ADC overseers kept careful track of what was happening in Newburgh, but took no formal action. In a memo from Bureau of Public Assistance Director Kathryn D. Goodwin to U.S. Commissioner of Social Security William L. Mitchell, Goodwin reviewed developments in

Newburgh, actions taken by New York state officials, and the public response to the issues that Joseph Mitchell's actions had provoked. She raised the possibility of federal action, but not in response to welfare racism in Newburgh. Instead, she concluded: "The Federal agency will become involved only if the final action by the State agency fails to assure that its plan conforming to the Social Security Act requirements is in effect throughout the State."[86]

Finally, in mid-August 1961, a temporary court injunction against Newburgh's thirteen-point program was issued.[87] Almost immediately after this occurred, Roy Wilkins, then a top official of the national NAACP, blasted the thirteen-point plan by stating: "Newburgh, while pretending to be trying to reduce its welfare costs, is really—and falsely—smearing Negro citizens. . . . There is much talk of illegitimacy, of laziness, of drinking and carousing, of slum districts—all of this to slander the race in the public mind without using the designation. . . .[Mitchell's] hidden message is anti-Negro all down the line."[88]

At the end of August, Governor Rockefeller appointed a special investigative commission to study welfare in New York state. He denied that the call for this study had anything to do with the attention swirling around Newburgh. Needless to say, his study plans did not reflect concerns with welfare racism. Rockefeller's rationale for the study was instead couched in concerns about fraud and waste that were being expressed by conservative politicians and that were obviously resonating with members of the public.[89]

Rockefeller's action was followed in mid-December by the first sign of movement on welfare issues at the federal level. U.S. Secretary of Health, Education, and Welfare Abraham A. Ribicoff announced a ten-point program, said to have been approved by newly elected Democratic President John F. Kennedy, "to eliminate abuses and help people get off relief rolls."[90] Among the program's provisions was a change in the name of the federal Bureau of Public Assistance to the "Bureau of Family Services." This change was said to be "an attempt to avoid the concept of handing out money instead of helping families become self-supporting."[91] Other steps included ordering the individual states to increase measures to locate deserting parents and to tighten procedures for detecting fraud. Ribicoff claimed that his office had been working on these issues for some time and vehemently denied these steps were in any way a reaction to Newburgh. He did say, however, that "Newburgh may have sensationalized this, and it may have had a salutary effect."[92]

The Thirteen-Point Program Unravels

In December 1961, the New York state Supreme Court granted a permanent injunction against the implementation of twelve of the thirteen points (it allowed only the provision that required aid recipients to report to the welfare office once a month to have their eligibility checked).[93] By this time some of City Manager Mitchell's support in Newburgh had begun to erode. This process was hastened by a highly critical NBC television exposé on "The Battle of Newburgh," broadcast in January 1962, which many residents thought brought embarrassing and unwanted attention to the city and generally made their community look bad. The hourlong NBC "white paper" focused on Newburgh's economic and social problems. It sympathetically portrayed Newburgh's poor while indicting the degradation to which Mitchell's welfare policies exposed them. Mitchell was portrayed as a political demagogue. The program pointed out the factual inaccuracy of Mitchell's rhetoric on the frequency of welfare fraud, the ability of recipients to work or to become self-sufficient, the color of the welfare population, and recipients' alleged "newcomer" status.[94]

Mitchell and his supporters took issue with the program. They charged NBC television journalists with bias and distortion. Meanwhile, New York state welfare officials began new investigations into Newburgh's welfare operations. In March they reported that the city had "denied relief arbitrarily to some applicants and had used various pressures to keep needy persons off the relief rolls."[95] Progressively, residents grew weary of all the controversy that Mitchell's initiatives had engendered and of the often nasty local tensions and conflicts his actions prompted. Newburgh's welfare rolls had not fallen, the city's welfare costs continued to rise, hardly any fraud had been detected among recipients, a great deal of social discord had been created in the city, and many residents wondered if the attack on welfare had been worth all the tumult.[96]

In December 1962 Mitchell was arrested and accused of accepting $20,000 in bribery money in connection with a property zoning matter in the city.[97] Even though he was found innocent and claimed to have held on to a good deal of his local support, a poll of Newburgh residents found that 74 percent felt he should not stay on as city manager.[98] Even Councilman McKneally withdrew his support. In July 1963 Mitchell announced his resignation, and from Newburgh he went on to take a position as field director in Virginia, Maryland, and Washington, D.C., for the segregationist Citizens Councils of America.[99] But the Battle of Newburgh would be remembered for years to come.[100]

Fallout from Welfare Racism in Newburgh

As journalist Edgar May observed, once the harsh welfare policies proposed in Newburgh hit the national media, "[Newburgh] became the catalyst for welfare discussion in scores of social work forums, from city councils to state legislatures, and, finally, in the taverns and living rooms of these United States."[101] Intense mass media coverage of events in Newburgh—through television, news articles, cartoons, editorials, and articles in popular magazines like Life and Look—helped both to make welfare a national partisan political issue and to frame it (and its recipients) as a problem that both conservative and liberal political elites would find ways to exploit for years to come.

Mitchell's arguments on behalf of highly restrictive public assistance policies were based upon the unspoken premise that the ADC population was composed largely of undeserving, welfare-prone African Americans. Events in Newburgh and the discourse around welfare to which Mitchell's actions contributed helped to further imprint welfare reliance as a racial phenomenon in the public mind. As was the case in Louisiana, racist stereotypes and controlling images regarding African Americans' work and reproductive behaviors were at the center of Mitchell's antiwelfare discourse and actions. And, similar to what happened in the case of Louisiana, federal welfare officials were silent on the subject of Mitchell's subtly racist portrayals of welfare-reliant mothers and on the harm that Mitchell's thirteen-point program would have done to impoverished families of color in Newburgh if implemented. This silence provided political space allowing for the further spread of meanspirited, race-based attacks on public assistance. Mitchell's efforts to introduce punitive welfare reforms, while frustrated at the time, turned out not to be for naught. Thirty years later, in an article examining the significance of the harsh welfare measures that Joseph Mitchell proposed in Newburgh, a *New York Times* journalist observed, "A symbol of welfare meanness and bigotry in 1962 is a trend today."[102]

MAINTAINING INTERNAL COLONIALISM IN WASHINGTON, D.C.

Internal Colonialism Perspectives and Their Relevance

Before we begin our third case example, an analysis of West Virginia Democratic Senator Robert C. Byrd's 1962 hearings on alleged welfare fraud, we will present a brief overview of the "internal colonialism" perspective that will guide this case example. The internal colonialism literature that we employ consists primarily of writings that focus largely on racial oppression. This literature is distinct from that which approaches internal colonialism from a radical, typically neo-Marxist, critique of capitalism, in which attention to racism often becomes secondary to class exploitation.[103] Both bodies of literature assume, however, that for African Americans and other people of color, public assistance, like other institutions run by white "colonial" state powers, is employed as an instrument of racial control.

One of the first explicit uses made of the colonial analogy to emphasize primarily racial oppression was by African-American intellectual Harold Cruse. In the early 1960s Cruse argued that the key to understanding the essence of African Americans' oppression is recognition that "the Negro has a relationship to the dominant culture of the United States similar to that of colonies and semi-dependents to their particular foreign overseers."[104] Cruse described the condition of African Americans in the United States, beginning with their enslavement, as "domestic colonialism."[105] After the abolition of slavery, white racial oppression persisted in other forms, and, in Cruse's view, African Americans have never fully achieved independence from their colonized status.[106]

In his use of the colonial analogy, Cruse was careful to stress that African Americans had obtained at least semi-independence after slavery. Moreover, he anticipated what would become a major criticism of the domestic or "internal" colonialism analogy. Cruse argued that in contrast to "a pure colonial status," African Americans' "semi-colonial status" does not require geographic distance between the colonizing country and those it colonizes. The semicolonial status of African Americans is "maintained in the 'home' country in close proximity to the dominant racial group."[107]

The internal colonialism analogy is valuable for our analysis of welfare racism because it can help us to better understand the nature of the relationship between welfare recipients of color and the whites who decide on and administer welfare policy. As we will show, the type of relationship which existed between Washington, D.C.'s African-American welfare recipient population and its white congressional overseers in the early 1960s can fruitfully be viewed as analogous to the relationship between colonial-like racial state actors and members of their racially distinct colony.

Racial Change and Tensions in Washington, D.C.

In the early 1960s, Washington, D.C., underwent transformations in its racial demographics, race relations, crime rates, and politics. "White flight" to the suburbs, a common occurrence in U.S. cities in the 1950s and 1960s, was especially pronounced in the nation's capital. The District of Columbia lost a third of its European-American population during the 1950s. The European-American proportion of the city population dropped dramatically, from 65 percent in 1950 to 45 percent in 1960. By 1960, African Americans constituted a majority of the District's residents.[108]

In her study of the politics of the city of Washington, Martha Derthick emphasizes the profoundness of this demographic transformation. To Derthick, racial composition was "the central fact of demography in the nation's capital, and the central fact of politics as well."[109] Racially, Washington, D.C., in the early 1960s was very much a southern city. It was a segregated city whose racial relations were greatly influenced by racist culture. This fact enhanced the impact of the dramatic shift in the city's racial demographics.[110]

There seemed to be two Washingtons—one white, the other black. This stark racial contrast was compounded by the virtual political disenfranchisement of the city's population. District of Columbia residents lacked "home rule" and the ability to exercise political control over their own internal affairs. As the African-American majority of the District was well aware, the U.S. Congress basically ran the city. The city's black residents endured intense racial oppression under the District's semicolonial status.[111]

In the early 1960s, European Americans were fearful of the social volatility of the District's large and politically disenfranchised African-American population. Many were also concerned with increases in juvenile delinquency and other crimes occurring in the city. Rising crime rates increased the strain on racial relations.[112] At that time liberal observers believed that the District's social problems were linked in a self-perpetuating cycle. For example, it was argued that the conservative racial politics of the members of the U.S. Congress who oversaw the District prevented the city from taking effective measures to address its rising crime rates and other social ills.[113]

The Nature of Internal Colonialism in the District of Columbia

The District of Columbia has always lacked the high degree of local political autonomy characteristic of other U.S. municipalities. Even today, the ability to make key political decisions affecting the District rests in the hands of the executive and legislative branches of the federal racial state. In the District, for all practical purposes, local politics are dominated by the U.S. Congress, and to a much lesser degree, by the executive branch of the federal government. Not surprisingly, in the early 1960s Congress was known to District residents as Washington's "city council" and the Capitol as "city hall."[114]

Because the District of Columbia is the location of the nation's capital, the U.S. Constitution grants Congress a great deal of political authority over the city. Congress exercises this authority both directly and indirectly. While through various legislative acts Congress has delegated some authority to other political entities,[115] it exercises the political authority it retains over the District through congressional committees.[116] Up to 1960, Congress had not allowed African Americans much share in the District's governance.[117]

While appreciating the District of Columbia's unique constitutional status is essential to understanding the relative political powerlessness of Washington, D.C., residents, that fact alone does not explain their colonial-like predicament.[118] Throughout much of its history the city has been the subject of rule by a federal racial state that was also a colonial state. Early on, Congress made a decision to take the vote away from Washington, D.C., residents, who at the time included both European Americans and African Americans. This is how U.S. Senator John Tyler Morgan, an Alabama plantation owner and former officer in the Confederate army, justified the disenfranchisement of District residents: "It was necessary . . . [to] burn down the barn to get rid of the rats . . . the rats being the Negro population and the barn being the government of the District of Columbia."[119]

Although the District's colonial-like governance structure was not initially established for racial reasons, racial state forces became the main fuel source for its maintenance. Given this background, we can better understand the following statement regarding the political status of the District made in 1960 by Representative Adam Clayton Powell Jr., an African American from Harlem who was very much concerned with the plight of black District residents. Powell stated, "We are colonials here in the District. The District of Columbia is the Canal Zone of the United States."[120]

In the early 1960s, the House District Committee, the federal racial state entity in which most congressional political authority over the city was lodged, was dominated by southern segregationists. Critics charged that the actions of the committee seemed to be motivated primarily by the desire of its members to retain the city's racial status quo. Such actions included opposition to home rule and to expanding financial appropriations for the District.[121] A May 19, 1961, *Washington Post* editorial, for example, criticized the House District Committee's conservative and racialized approach to the city's crime problem. That editorial also scolded the committee's opposition to efforts to promote racial integration in the city, and thus reduce the alienation felt by many African-American residents.[122]

Other congressional committees and subcommittees in addition to the House District Committee had various spheres of colonial-like authority over District affairs. There was a Senate District Committee, and both a House and Senate District Appropriations Subcommittee, which exercised considerable control over the city's affairs through their hold on federal purse strings.[123] These committees and subcommittees did not have as much national visibility and prestige as some others in Congress. However, they were attractive to white, southern, usually rural, segregationists who saw their colonial-like control over the city's African-American population as consistent with the racial politics upon which their political careers were based.[124] Chairing such a congressional committee or subcommittee could be especially attractive to a young, ambitious politician eager to make a name for himself.[125] This was the case in the early 1960s with regard to Senator Robert C. Byrd, a Democrat from West Virginia.

In the early 1960s the nation's civil rights movement was expanding and becoming more intense. The sit-in protests of 1960 were followed by the southern freedom rides the following year. The pinnacle of the civil rights movement's escalating protest activity would occur not long after, in Birmingham,

Alabama.[126] These types of widely reported events represented a threat to white racial hegemony and in many instances stimulated white racial backlash. Indeed, our two earlier case examples of welfare racism revealed how punitive welfare policy initiated by racial state actors in Louisiana and in Newburgh, New York, were a part of white backlashes.

Beyond the civil rights movement, an additional challenge confronted the colonial racial state actors ruling the nation's capital at that time. In Washington, D.C., the District's semicolonial status was threatened. With the ratification of the Twenty-Third Amendment to the U.S. Constitution in the spring of 1961, D.C. residents would be allowed to vote in presidential elections beginning in 1964.[127]

At the time, not all branches of the federal racial state were in full accord regarding how to handle the District politically. In racial matters, the White House at times served as a countervailing force against the more extreme conservative bias built into the District's other governance structures. For example, Washington, D.C.'s public schools were desegregated through presidential mandate.[128] President John F. Kennedy was sympathetic to critics who saw a need for some changes in the District's governance system. As a segregationist and staunch conservative, however, Senator Byrd was not likely to support Kennedy, a fellow Democrat, on such issues. Indeed, Byrd had been a leader in the unsuccessful Stop Kennedy movement in the West Virginia Democratic presidential primary.[129]

The Byrd Hearings

The Byrd hearings on welfare fraud in the District of Columbia were not simply a local event. They must be understood as part of a growing nationwide attack on expanding welfare rolls and expenditures. Historically, growth in public assistance has often evoked "public hostility toward relief agencies." [130] In the District of Columbia, the ADC caseload increased almost threefold over an eight-year period. It grew from 2,114 cases involving 8,951 persons in 1954 to 5,444 cases involving 25,175 people in 1962.[131] This increase occurred at the same time that racial composition of the District was changing. As Senator Byrd would note at one hearing session, "Negro families now make up more than half the population of the District." [132]

The growing welfare rolls, and the increase in African Americans as a proportion of the nation's urban residents who were on those rolls, fueled growing hostility toward welfare across the United States. Not surprisingly, this hostility would soon be openly and loudly expressed by southern conservatives in the U.S. Congress.[133]

By focusing on the growing welfare rolls in the District, members of Congress took advantage of a unique opportunity to express their dissatisfaction with public assistance. They were able to focus on the issue of welfare fraud in a way usually possible only for state and local governments.[134] By conducting hearings on welfare abuses in the District, Senator Byrd was able to establish himself as an expert on welfare and a national leader on the need for welfare reform. He did this at a time when the national political spotlight was focused on welfare as a serious problem.[135]

The Senate Committee on Appropriations, in its report on the 1962 House appropriations bill for the District, expressed concern about the growing welfare rolls in the city. The Senate committee requested the District's Department of Public Welfare to assign investigators "to ferret out any so-called freeloaders who may be benefiting under the public assistance program."[136] The committee thus set into motion an investigatory process that led to the Byrd hearings themselves.

Robert C. Byrd: From the Klan to the U.S. Senate *political framing*

Early in his political career, Robert C. Byrd was a Ku Klux Klan member, organizer, and leader.[137] Although Senator Byrd later said that his membership in the Ku Klux Klan in the early 1940s was a "mistake," his political behavior two decades later suggests that his racial attitudes had not fundamentally changed.[138] The form and tone of his public utterances on racial matters remained consistent with the racial mores and politics of the segregationist South that would be conducive to his re-election.

Byrd's actions to expose welfare fraud in the nation's capital, while pursued with a pile of government agency–commissioned reports and a bevy of statistics, were consistent with what had been "the Klan's main function" since the abolition of slavery: making sure "that black people were honest and not sexually promiscuous."[139] Byrd's hearings were built on negative, gender-racist controlling images of African Americans. Consistent with his Klansman background, the hearings entailed a search for lazy, shiftless, dishonest, and irresponsible African-American men who were involved in predatory relationships with immoral, sexually promiscuous African-American women. Byrd's actions resembled a crusade, and were driven by underlying white racist stereotypes and the perceived need to enforce "white" moral rectitude on the District's largeley "black" residents. To Senator Byrd the differences seemed to be as simple as black and white. His vision was color struck.

Color Struck: Poverty in Black and White

Like many racial state actors, Senator Byrd was often subtle in his expressions of racism. In a widely publicized *U.S. News and World Report* article published after the 1962 hearings, Byrd was careful to only imply that the race of welfare recipients was related to the scandal his hearings had exposed. In a section of that interview titled "Problem of Race," Byrd was asked, "Is the Aid to Dependent Children largely a race problem?" Byrd responded with a dry and careful reporting of the relevant facts:

> I can only answer that by saying this: that, of the Aid to Dependent Children case load in the District of Columbia, 93 percent of the cases are nonwhite; 79.6 percent of the social workers are nonwhite; about 85 percent of the over-all public-welfare case load in the District involves non-whites.[140]

Senator Byrd was also very careful not to openly reveal his racial sentiments in the hearings. Instead, he made his case meticulously by piling seemingly objective fact upon fact. However, buried deep in the nearly twenty-five hundred pages of hearings transcripts are clear examples of the stark black-and-white contrast between the attitude Senator Byrd held toward the District's overwhelmingly African-American welfare recipients and the attitude he had toward his own experiences with poverty as a child and young man. Both were extreme portrayals with little of the complexity, ambiguity, and nuance that make for ordinary human being. While he depicted his own white poverty as wholesome, virtuous, and pure as the driven snow, black poverty was portrayed as vile and completely devoid of virtue.

In a display of his credentials as someone who knows "something about living in a family situation where there is need," Senator Byrd noted that his mother died when he was ten months old and that as a result he was separated from his brother and sister.[142] In referring to his foster parents, Byrd pointed out that although they had little in the way of formal education, "they worked hard and they were honest, and when the only dad who I ever knew died, at the age of 82, he did not owe anyone on earth a single penny." Byrd went on to state that it was not only he who had experienced poverty, but also others "who sit here" (before the congressional hearing) and many other people who are now successful.[142] According to Byrd, what distinguished himself and these other people from the District's poor was that

> their parents had the desire to work and their parents did work, and there was never a time when 5 cents worth of surplus commodities, clothing, public welfare money or anything of that kind, ever came to my home.[143]

These good parents raised good, hardworking children.

Finally, Senator Byrd reasserted his contention that this experience of having "lived right down in the mud with these people" (presumably African Americans) prepared him to understand their problems. He argued that his understanding was different from what one might see from an "ivory tower."[144]

Byrd's Racist Controlling Images of Welfare Recipients

If Senator Byrd's experiences provided him with greater appreciation of the trials and tribulations of "these people" of the mud, it was not apparent in his characterizations of District of Columbia welfare recipients. What is most evident is not his sense of a common humanity but of differences, and the nontranscendable social distance of race.[145]

In Senator Byrd's words,

> I cannot recall one instance in which a child has grown up to amount to anything where liquor in the home, and the mother's illicit relations with paramours are the order of the day. And seldom, if ever, do the lazy and slothful ever get anywhere. It is about time, therefore, that we stop encouraging indolence and shiftlessness, and that we quit furnishing money, food, and rent for indecent mothers and paramours who contribute nothing but illegitimate children to the society of this Federal City, most of whom end up roaming the streets and getting arrested for various crimes.[146]

In those three sentences, Senator Byrd unleashed a barrage of emotion-packed racist images of those who made up the District's African-American population. Like the lynching of African Americans in the Jim Crow South, or Ku Klux Klan cross burnings, congressional hearings are highly dramatic and very public rituals which can be used to reassert a dominant group's behavioral norms.[147] Senator Byrd was committed to restoring what he considered to be appropriate moral boundaries for the behavior of Washington, D.C.'s African-American mothers receiving welfare. To Byrd, these women were—consistent with gendered racist stereotypes rooted in American slavery—sexually promiscuous breeders:

> Not just one man hangs around—but two or three men frequent the home. The children don't know who their fathers are. These mothers and their paramours are breeding future citizens who are going to have no conception of law and order.[148]

Senator's Byrd's language is quite revealing. Animals are typically thought of as breeding, not humans; Byrd's use of words seems to deny even the humanity of welfare recipients. It is the language not of democratic philosophy, but of racial colonialism.

Increasing Waywardness by Narrowing the Path

The welfare "freeloader" cases the Byrd hearings were ostensibly supposed to "ferret out" were those cases that were deemed to be in violation of the District's ADC eligibility rules. In the absence of eligibility rules there would, by definition, be no freeloaders. The underlying premise of the Byrd hearings was that a significant number of the ADC cases on the District's rapidly expanding rolls were fraudulent. Given the District's eligibility requirements, Byrd could be confident that his inquiries could produce only one result: evidence of widespread welfare abuse. Such a conclusion was assured more by the unusual strictness of the District's ADC eligibility rules than by any morally irresponsible behavior on the part of its poor families.

Contrary to much of the contemporary rhetoric about "welfare dependency," impoverished mother-headed families have never been, and indeed could probably never be, dependent solely on public assistance to meet their needs. Since public assistance has always provided only a portion of the aid that such families have needed to survive, mothers receiving welfare have been forced to improvise. Mothers have, by necessity, devised complex survival strategies based on multiple and often unreliable sources of aid (e.g., public assistance, private charities, their children's fathers, boyfriends, kin, unreported earnings, etc.).[149] Strict public assistance eligibility rules outlaw much of this necessary financial improvisation. Consequently, both welfare recipients and their caseworkers have often been trapped in a moral dilemma. If they followed public assistance eligibility rules to the letter, basic family needs would likely go unmet. If they violated the eligibility rules, they would be labeled welfare chiselers or the abetters of welfare fraud.

In brief, where welfare recipients reside may, indeed, be the best predictor of epidemics in welfare fraud. In places with liberal eligibility rules there may be less inclination to initiate investigations to ferret out welfare chiselers. Moreover, were there to be such an inquiry, the behavior of mothers reliant on welfare in places with liberal rules would likely produce comparatively few cases of welfare fraud. On the other hand, in jurisdictions with strict eligibility rules any serious investigation is likely to expose rampant cases of welfare fraud. Consistent with its colony-like status, the District of Columbia had one of the nation's strictest sets of ADC eligibility requirements.[150]

Need was not the ultimate determinant of public assistance eligibility for District residents at the time of the Byrd hearings. Gerard M. Shea, the director of the District's Department of Public Welfare, began his testimony at the July 30, 1962, hearing by emphasizing that ADC eligibility rules were "restrictive." "The ability of the family to support itself is not a factor in the ineligibility determination in these situations," he said. The first rule he cited, directed at "employable parents," makes this clear: "Persons who are eligible to work are not eligible for aid regardless of the non-availability of jobs."[151] In other words, families in great economic need could be found ineligible for public assistance.

The District's ADC eligibility rules were oblivious to poverty in another important way. The rules assumed that the poor were able to maintain stable families as easily as the affluent colonial racial state actors who made these rules. The irony of this assumption is that eligibility rules (e.g., such as the District's employable parents and "man-in-the-house" rules) actually worked against family stability. The stabilizing role that many mothers receiving welfare served for children was, for example, severely challenged by the eligibility rule that denied public assistance to employable mothers (again, even when jobs were unavailable).[152]

Two other ADC eligibility rules threatened the mother's relationship with men who could have carried out important partnering and parenting roles. One of these rules denied aid to children in situations where the "mother associates with a man in a relationship similar to that of husband and wife, and the mother, her children and the man live in a family setting regardless of whether the man is the father of the children." The second rule forbade aid to children when the "mother maintains a 'husband-wife relationship' and the man continues a relationship with the children similar to that of father and child, even though the man claims to be living at an address different from the mother's address."[153] In short, these two ADC rules outlawed any type of "husband-wife relationship," be it with a man inside or outside of the home.

Welfare Fraud Uncovered: Man in the House Discovered

The second day of the Byrd hearings began on July 31 with a report by the comptroller general of the United States on an investigation into ADC recipients' program eligibility. The major finding of that investigation, involving 236 randomly selected ADC cases was that 133, or 57 percent, were ineligible.[154] Of those, 69 (52 percent) were in violation of the District's man-in-the-house rules.[155] The second most common ineligibility factor (29 cases) was a determination that the ADC parent was employable.[156]

In the overwhelming majority of ineligibility cases, children were penalized by the termination of ADC not because the aid was not needed, but because they were found to reside in quasi-intact family structures or their mother was found to be employable. The reassertion of moral boundaries by colonial racial state actors through the Byrd hearings would not only have a disproportionately adverse effect on many of the District's most impoverished African-American mother-headed families, but would especially affect these families' youngest and thus most vulnerable members.

When it came to the District's man-in-the-house rules, ADC mothers were presumed guilty until proved innocent. For example, the rule barring a mother from living with her husband or with the children's father states: "Only in situations where strong, convincing evidence is submitted that a parent is no longer in the home and has discontinued his relationship, shall the factor of continued absence be established."[157]

Senator Byrd seemed to be obsessed with enforcing the District's strict "man-in-the-house" rules and removing ADC eligibility from mothers who violated them. But the welfare "freeloaders" whom Byrd's moral crusade appeared most concerned with were these mother's "paramours." For example, later in the hearings Byrd complained that there were ADC families receiving money, "some of which would go to the whisky purchases of the paramour and the mother, and some of which would go for food and shelter for the paramours."[158] The senator went much further in a *New York Times* article when he asserted that "in most cases, the children aren't receiving much of this money anyhow. In most cases, most of it's going to this woman and her paramour."[159]

Senator Byrd's animus toward "paramours" blinded him to evidence that these men were not parasites. For example, in explaining why 94 percent of the children removed from ADC as a result of his hearings did not end up being institutionalized, Senator Byrd remarked, "There was other income involved here somewhere."[160] Consequently, the "paramours" were portrayed as being, on the one hand, men who exploited welfare-reliant mothers and their children, and on the other hand, as men who provided for them. Both actions violated ADC policy, and, taken separately, each depiction presented a very negative view of these men, their motives, and their actions.

Byrd's views ignored the fact that when a couple are involved in an intimate relationship, be they poor or not, there is usually much giving and taking on the part of both the male and female partners. Such relationships are much more likely to involve exchange than one-way exploitation. For mothers who had to rely on the limited financial assistance offered to their families by ADC, exchange relationships were no doubt crucial to family survival. However, once their male partners were labeled and disparaged as "paramours," there was nothing that these men could have done that would have been regarded positively by Senator Byrd and his like-minded colleagues. *Any* relationships such men had with mothers receiving welfare were by definition illicit.

One way to end the District's crisis of welfare ineligibility and "illicit" relationships uncovered during the hearings was simply to change the rules. Senator Byrd, however, would have none of that. He would not let "welfare mothers," "paramours" and the "illegitimates" they were "breeding" escape his moral crusade. In reference to a proposal by the District's Department of Public Welfare to alter eligibility rules, Senator Byrd warned that

> there is another side to this picture. It isn't all a dollars-and-cents side. I simply cannot understand the reasoning of those who would suggest that we permit a situation to continue in which public moneys are used to subsidize and reward illegitimacy.[161]

Senator Byrd's actions were analogous to those of a white colonial administrator concerned about the moral behavior of the dark-skinned natives.

The Byrd Hearings as Racial Colonialism

Can the Byrd hearings be considered an expression of racial colonialism? Even Senator Byrd was sensitive to such criticisms of his actions. "A lot of people may say, 'Well, who does he think he is? Does he think he is running the District of Columbia?' I don't have any such conception of my responsibility."[162] But having denied the charge of imposing his rule on the District, Byrd went on to sound very much like a colonial administrator as he commented to District welfare officials,

> I do think that a man must stand up for his convictions, and I insist that you rid the welfare caseload of cheaters and freeloaders. Let's help the needy but let's not make welfare a haven for people who are shiftless and undeserving of help. So, I suggest that you work this and put your best thinking into it.[163]

Coming from the chair of the Senate Subcommittee on Appropriations for the District of Columbia, Byrd's suggestion was nothing short of a mandate. And, as we will see when we discuss the consequences of the hearings, they would be treated as such by District officials.

To any informed observer of the Byrd hearings there was little doubt that, reflecting the city's colonial-like situation, District officials were not really in charge of the public assistance programs. While the White House exercised its authority to appoint three District commissioners to nominally "run" the city's affairs, including its public assistance programs, the commissioners did not actually have the power to do so.[164] Conflict between the District's appointed commissioners and Senator Byrd over the District's ADC eligibility rules is a case in point. On the one hand Senator Byrd claimed that it was the District commissioners, not himself, who had the power to change the ADC rules. On the other hand, making the rules less restrictive would have raised welfare costs and required an increase in federal appropriations. That increase had to be approved by Senator Byrd and his colleagues, who expressed opposition to such rule changes. As one reporter concluded, "In short, the Commissioners can act but they cannot do anything."[165]

Senator Byrd had reason to be sensitive to the charge that he was trying to run the District. He was depicted as a racial colonialist not only by African-American organizations, but in an establishment media institution, the *New York Times*. In one *Times* article, Sterling Tucker, the executive director of the Washington, D.C., chapter of the National Urban League, expressed his frustration with congressional rule of the city by saying, "Congress has no determination to make this a showcase of the nation. We are making a good community here in spite of Congress and this is not just an indictment of the House District Committee."[166]

A *Times* writer went much further than did Tucker in framing the Byrd hearings on alleged welfare fraud as an expression of racial colonialism:

> Congressional rule, with its deep Southern accent, is particularly resented in the Negro community, which is convinced that Congress's continued refusal to make the city self-governing grows out of racist fears in its committees and indifference to the masses.[167]

The *New York Times* reporter suggested not only that the District experienced colonial rule, but that this rule appeared to take the particular form of racial colonialism:

> The white minority inside the city appears contented with its colonial status. The influential *Washington Evening Star* and the Board of Trade, composed of the city business leaders, are actively opposed to self-government. The problems that disturb the northwest [a predominantly white part of the District] are more like those that disturb the white suburbs, to which Congress is sympathetic. . . . The Negro, however, has become resentful, not only of the absentee rulers on Capitol Hill, but of what he regards as an absentee ruling white majority decamped in segregated suburbs from which it governs the city.[168]

Exerting Racial Control over City Social Workers

Because of the huge social distance between those who colonize and those who are colonized, colonial rule typically requires the cooperation of members of the colonized group who hold key positions in controlling institutions. These include teachers, police officers, intermediate and lower-level government officials, and, of course, social workers. Apparently Senator Byrd and his colleagues who provided congressional oversight over the District did not feel that they had the compliance they needed from ADC caseworkers to control the city's black welfare masses.

We noted earlier, for example, that in an interview published in *U.S. News and World Report,* Byrd was not content, when asked, "Is the Aid to Dependent Children largely a race problem?" to give the high percentage of welfare recipients who were black. He also cited the exact percentage to the decimal point (79.6 percent) of Washington, D.C., social workers who were "non-white."[169] Clearly Senator Byrd saw the fact that the overwhelmingly majority of social workers were African-American to be a problem. Indeed, both his statements and actions suggest that he intended to bring those social workers under tighter control through his hearings so that he and his fellow colonial state actors could, in turn, gain greater control over the mostly African-American welfare recipients whose cases the social workers managed.

We also noted earlier that public hearings can be viewed as the mobilization of rituals to reassert moral and racial boundaries. When it comes to Byrd's welfare "abuse" hearings, the purpose was to point not to the need for reform of existing welfare policy, but rather to a need for better enforcement. Piven and Cloward, for example, have asserted that the goal of the Byrd hearings was to correct the "administrative laxity" that had allowed the District's welfare rolls to rise.[170] As Gilbert Steiner noted, "Byrd focused less on the inadequacy of policy and more on the inadequacies of petty administrators."[171]

It is understandable, in the context of racialized internal colonialism, that the African-American social workers would have been the subcommittee's prime target for weeding out laxity in the enforcement of public assistance eligibility by petty administrators. This is what Senator Allott, a Senate District of Columbia Appropriations Subcommittee member, had to say about what he deduced to be the lax attitudes of the District's social workers: "I must say, frankly, that I have not seen any real awareness, deep awareness, on the part of the people who administer this program of the fact that they are dealing with moneys that are not theirs."[172] Or, as Senator Byrd put it, "When it is patently evident that there is cheating going on and that the regulations are not being enforced, it is our responsibility to ask why and to demand that the Department of Welfare clean its own house."[173]

In responding to Senator Byrd's question as to why the District's strict ADC eligibility rules were not being better enforced, social work professionals indicated that the problem was a shortage of social workers. For instance, in hearing testimony it was noted that on average District caseworkers handled 180 cases and, with their other clerical and administrative responsibilities (it was noted that the average social worker had "21 different forms" of required paperwork

to fill out), spent only five hours each year per case in home visits. Consequently, they were unable to keep eligibility and other information about ADC
families current.[174]

Moreover, consistent with the internal colonialism perspective, Congress was
seen by social services experts as being at the root of ADC caseload administration problems. Anthony J. Celebrezze, the U.S. secretary of Health, Education,
and Welfare appointed by the Kennedy administration in 1962, shared this
view: "The whole problem here in the District is one of inadequate staff and you
are going to alleviate the situation if you get adequate staff here."[175] Celebrezze
suggested that having expended a great deal of effort in uncovering ineligibles,
Senator Byrd "ought to spend now as much time on seeing that the programs
are properly staffed."[176] Again, on the issue of public assistance, different
branches of the federal racial state were in evident conflict.

Because Byrd and his colleagues had concluded that social workers were a
major source of the problem, they were not open to appeals for more social
work personnel, which would of course have meant increased federal appropriations. Senator Byrd's solution to the problem of the need for more social
workers was simple. His "Catch-22" response was not to hire more social workers, but to decrease the ADC caseloads by removal of ineligibles.[177] And despite
his questioning of their competence, Senator Byrd was also the chief congressional critic of funding for a training program for District social workers.[178]

Unheard Voices

Colonizers are typically uninterested in hearing views from the colonized that differ from their own. In the District's case this was certainly true. The voices of the
mostly African-American rank-and-file social workers of whom Senator Byrd
and his colleagues were critical went largely unheard in the hearings. Robert G.
McGuire, president of the Washington, D.C., chapter of the National Urban
League, an organization which included many middle-class African-American
professionals with strong social work roots, urged the subcommittee to

> avail itself of the extremely knowledgeable corps of experts on pub-
> lic welfare programs which is present in the city, by extending to
> those persons an open invitation to appear before it and to present
> testimony on our welfare needs and possible solutions.[179]

Caseworkers were not being called to testify by the committee, and given their
position near the bottom of the hierarchy in the city welfare department, they
were unlikely to volunteer to testify.

Byrd's response was that, like anyone else, rank-and-file social workers could
testify if they wanted to, but that the District's top Department of Public Welfare

officials who were testifying were certainly social work experts.[180] Consequently, there was no significant dialogue between Byrd and his colleagues and the largely African-American staff of caseworkers whom the senators held to be as culpable for the city's welfare abuses as the overwhelmingly African-American welfare recipients themselves. Both the voices of the District's welfare caseworkers and recipients went largely unheard. Consistent with racial colonialism, the colonized of color were to listen, not to speak.

The refusal to hear the voices of the colonized was integral to the "success" of the Byrd hearings, which could more accurately be described as a congressional inquisition than a democratic forum open to the views of the District's African-American residents. With the autocratic rule of Congress firmly in place, the senators prevailed in their framing of the hearing as the ferreting out of welfare fraud. Had the voices of the District's African-American leaders, social work professionals, welfare recipients, and residents entered into how the issues surrounding conduct of the District's ADC program were to be framed, a news headline might have read "Senators and District Residents Clash over Welfare Policy." For, while the District's congressional overseers wanted to enforce and maintain the strict "man-in-the-house" and "employable parent" eligibility restrictions, the city's African-American residents favored not simply leniency in the administration of those two provisions, but their abolition.[181]

This racially charged policy dispute between the colonial state officials who ran the District of Columbia and its politically disenfranchised and majority African-American population would continue after the 1962 Byrd hearings. Senator Byrd persisted in his opposition to the liberalization of the District's ADC eligibility rules. He remained opposed to federal legislation supported by the Kennedy administration and passed by Congress which allowed all local welfare departments the option of liberalizing existing policies.[182] For example, in 1963 Senator Byrd opposed extension of and funding for the AFDC-Unemployed Fathers program for the District (ADC was by then renamed Aid to Families with Dependent Children, or AFDC). AFDC-UF gave states the option of allowing benefits to be received by welfare families with unemployed fathers present.[183] Resistance to the colonial-like congressional rule over the District was evident in a 1964 Democratic primary straw poll. District residents voted overwhelmingly (72,000 yes to only 1,600 no) for the AFDC-UF program.[184]

The Byrd Hearings As Seen through an Economic Lens

We noted earlier that there are both "race" and "class" varieties of internal colonialism theory. Though our focus in the Byrd hearings has been political forces, there were, of course, also powerful economic forces at work helping to maintain colonial racial state rule and seeking to exploit the labor of poor mothers that restrictive ADC policies had made available.

At that time the Washington, D.C., Board of Trade was the city's oldest and most powerful group of business leaders. In 1959, on the occasion of its seventieth anniversary, it was described by the *Washington Post* as having "played a central role in framing citizens' opinions on Congress, the District Building and the myriad other local and Federal agencies which help to govern the Nation's Capital."[185] As the board's vice president put it "We have stuck our nose into everything. We have been in some measure responsible for most of the important conclusions concerning the city of Washington."[186]

One of those important "conclusions" was that home rule for the majority African-American District should be vigorously opposed. In 1961–1962 the president of the Board of Trade was the associate editor of the *Washington Evening Star* and president of the Evening Star Broadcasting Company. The *Washington Evening Star*, the more conservative of the city's two principal newspapers, was a major source of influence, both inside the board and within the greater Washington, D.C., area more generally.[187] The Board of Trade, "the major conservative pressure group in the city," was known for "taking care of its friends on the House Committee."[188] At that time all of the board's approximately seven thousand members were white, and its major concerns were economic— with keeping taxes down a prime concern.[189] Senator Byrd's crackdown on welfare fraud in the midst of a dramatic increase in the ADC rolls was consistent with that tax goal, as was stricter enforcement of the District's public assistance eligibility rule regarding employable parents.

Piven and Cloward argue that to comprehend welfare fraud "rituals" like that of the Byrd hearings, it is important to remember that their main target "is not the recipient who ordinarily is not of much use as a worker, but the able-bodied poor who remain in the labor market. It is for these people that the spectacle of the degraded pauper is intended." That is, welfare fraud spectacles discourage many of the poor who might apply for welfare from doing so.[190] As welfare policy scholars Joel Handler and Yeheskel Hasenfeld put it, "*moral degradation* of the poor is used as a negative symbol to reinforce the work ethic."[191] Highly publicized welfare fraud scandals are especially useful during times of tight labor markets. Many who are eligible for aid are discouraged from applying. In addition, many of those who are receiving public assistance can be forced into the labor market by making eligibility rules more restrictive.

The transcript of the Byrd hearings quoted an August 4, 1962, *Washington Post* article which stated, "Washington area employment neared 800,000 and set an all-time high during June at a time when the Nation was struggling with a hard-core unemployment problem." It was also noted that this figure was thirty-one thousand higher than the previous year and that the increase was "largely the result of increased Government employment."[192] Federal employment was a major source of jobs for African Americans in the District, who were more likely to face racial discrimination in the private employment sector.[193] As relatively decent-paying and stable federal government employment became more available to the District's African-American residents, the ready supply of unskilled and low-skilled labor available to businesses in the area was threatened. This meant a reduced pool of African Americans who were competing for private-sector jobs and who were easily controllable and willing to work for low wages. District businesses were faced with having to raise their wages and compete with one another to attract a sufficient supply of such workers, thus cutting into their profit margins.

This is what Piven and Cloward had to say in arguing that the Byrd welfare fraud investigation was an instrument of labor regulation:

> In the several years immediately before the Byrd attack in 1962, about 6,500 District of Columbia families had applied for aid annually; during the attack, the figure dropped to 4,400 and it did not rise for more than five years—long after the scandal had subsided.[194]

The hearings and the subsequent attention that the city's Department of Public Welfare gave to enforcing the District's ADC eligibility rules clearly prevented some impoverished mothers from receiving ADC. This forced many to remain in the low-wage pool of labor from which white-owned District businesses benefited. Moreover, more active enforcement of the employable-parent rule forced many mothers receiving ADC into taking jobs who otherwise would have engaged in full-time family caregiving.

After the Hearings and Beyond

The Byrd hearings were a continuation of and a high point in highly racialized antiwelfare initiatives that were launched in the early 1960s. Like the Louisiana and Newburgh case examples, the Byrd hearings were expressions of welfare racism. This Washington, D.C., case differed, however, because it involved racialized attitudes, policy making, and administrative practices that were imposed onto politically subservient city officials by elected representatives of the federal racial state. Its colonial-like actions revealed Congress to be involved in welfare racism in its own backyard.

Moreover, the highly publicized Byrd hearings involved Congress in the further racialization of welfare as a national issue. Press and television coverage enabled race-based thinking on the part of these colonial racial state actors to affect welfare policy discourse across the United States. Expressions of gender racism ran rampant in the Byrd hearings, and the general public's racist stereotypes of African-American welfare recipients could not help but be reinforced by the references that came out of Congress to "breeders" with their "illegitimates" and "paramours."

The success of the Byrd hearings in launching the previously little-known senator from West Virginia into the national limelight demonstrated conclusively that welfare policy had emerged as a racially charged national issue and as an integral component of the policy agenda of the federal racial state. The hearings allowed Byrd to proclaim from the Senate floor that his challenge to administrative laxity in the District's Department of Public Welfare had resulted in reducing the city's welfare rolls by half.[195] In casting a shadow of inferiority over the majority African-American population of the District (and over African Americans generally), the Byrd hearings also reinforced the notion that Congress had no business giving "those people" the right to home rule. Thus, welfare racism promoted racial control over an African-American population that was—like African-American communities elsewhere around the nation—contesting its political powerlessness in the face of white racial hegemony.

Byrd used the highly publicized findings of his hearings to successfully demand a national investigation of public assistance eligibility. That study did not produce findings as sensationalistic as those in the eligibility-strict District of Columbia. Indeed, it found that the major cause of ineligibility was not fraud but problems in public assistance administration. But by this time Byrd's welfare expertise and senatorial clout had been established.[196] The praise and enthusiasm that his welfare-related actions received from both Democrats and Republicans in the Senate were emblematic not only of his rising political fortunes, but of the extent to which his racialized views on welfare either influenced or reflected the views of Congress generally.

THE SIGNIFICANCE OF LOUISIANA, NEWBURGH, AND WASHINGTON, D.C.

The harsh and punitive welfare policies initiated by different levels of the racial state, as represented by the Louisiana, Newburgh, and District of Columbia cases, must be understood as attempts at racial control in the interests of white hegemony. These attempts were in large part a response to social and geographic movement and political challenges to white supremacy by African Americans.

Consistent with punitive attacks on ADC elsewhere, racial state officials mobilized racist stereotypes and negative controlling images of welfare-reliant mothers to justify their defense of racial supremacy. In feminist scholar Mimi Abramovitz's view, such racial control efforts extended across the nation: "The ADC backlash . . . represented an initial reaction to the emergence of the post-War civil rights struggle which radically challenged institutionalized racism."[197]

Postwar attacks on ADC often singled out poor African-American mothers for moral malignment. Indeed, feminist writer Rickie Solinger suggests that childbearing African Americans served as "proxies for a race resisting white supremacy."[198] Political elites frequently mobilized controlling images of sexually immoral African-American women embedded in the racist culture on which white supremacist practices, such as de jure segregation, were premised. As Solinger describes it, attacks on childbearing African Americans were rationalized by the view that "black women used their bodies in ways that were morally and fiscally destructive to the nation."[199]

In the case of Newburgh, local officials were not reacting primarily to the challenges to white racial hegemony posed by the nation's civil rights movement, but to threats they perceived from African Americans' geographic movement. The growing appearance of people of color in locations where few if any had previously been present helped to precipitate punitive welfare policies aimed at racial control. Nor was this response to the black diaspora peculiar to Newburgh.

In a rare acknowledgment of the existence and impact of white racism, historian James Patterson notes that "the explosive growth of nonwhite populations in the poorest areas of large cities guaranteed that people would think of poor blacks and welfare together."[200] Support for the punitive welfare policies in Newburgh was, in Patterson's view, consistent with a broader current of thought in which "people readily assumed a connection among black migration, illegitimacy, and welfare."[201] In Patterson's words, "the unfavorable attitudes toward welfare in the 1960s in part reflected white hostility toward blacks."[202]

The Byrd hearings on alleged welfare fraud in Washington, D.C., occurred in a setting where the civil rights movement was sharpening the sense of colonial-like racial domination experienced by District residents. Their political restiveness was met in part with attacks by key federal officials like Senator Byrd, who—like those in Louisiana and Newburgh—used racist stereotypes of African-American welfare recipients to project images of all that was wrong with black people generally, thus explaining and justifying the need for racial control.

The events in Louisiana, Newburgh, and the District of Columbia are significant because in each case welfare racism was central and because of their immediate and long-term consequences. The controversies surrounding Louisiana and Newburgh, and the revelations of the Byrd hearings, received enormous publicity, helped to focus national attention on welfare as an issue, helped to influence or reinforce race-based public perceptions of welfare, and provoked a wider sharing of existing antiwelfare sentiments among members of the public. They also helped to make welfare a national and partisan political issue.

In their comments on "welfare recipient degradation rituals" in which aspersions are cast on the character and behavior of those poor people who receive public assistance, Piven and Cloward cite Newburgh as a case in point. As they put it, "Periodically the rituals of degradation are set forth for public display through legislative investigations and newspaper exposes in which recipients are branded as sexually immoral, as chiselers, and as malingerers. It is partly by such public spectacles that popular definitions of relief are formed."[203] What Piven and Cloward fail to acknowledge is the significance of the color of those being singled out for branding.

Piven and Cloward's comments suggest that the actions of state actors in these cases—in which policy clearly was ideology—encouraged and reinforced widespread negative public perceptions of welfare and welfare recipients. But the kind of discourse that surrounded and followed these actions also helped contribute to the racialization of welfare as a national issue, and to cast welfare as a problem for which blacks were to blame. Patterson notes that "by the early 1960s the stereotype [of those on welfare] was likely to evoke visions of 'hard core' black welfare mothers with hordes of illegitimate children."[204]

It is clear that these punitive policies had many supporters. In the absence of a national forum, however, strong race-based antiwelfare sentiments had previously remained largely submerged or restricted to localized issues. Louisiana, Newburgh, and the Byrd hearings stirred and activated these sentiments, and the mass media provided them with a forum through its reporting, editorializing, and publishing of letters to the editor. Whites who sympathized with punitive welfare policies certainly could not help but become aware that they had allies in many quarters nationwide, not only in their own locales.

Newburgh journalist Joseph Ritz, for example, found that "nationwide, initial reaction to the Newburgh welfare experiment was overwhelmingly favorable. . . . The city was lauded . . . not only by the press and a few thousand letter writers, but also by the masses of working people and businessmen."[205] And Ritz went on: "[S]upport for it was voiced on both sides of Congress," and "For a time, it looked as though local and state legislatures and welfare officials throughout the country might adopt some part of the Newburgh plan."[206] Like others who have written about Newburgh, Ritz drew attention to the broad antiwelfare sentiments that were exposed: "Mitchell tapped a deep reservoir of popular emotion which extends much further than Newburgh or New York State."[207]

Louisiana, Newburgh, and the Byrd hearings evoked manifest and latent themes that would be employed in subsequent national welfare debates. Punitive welfare policies in all three cases were said to be aimed at saving taxpayers' money, limiting assistance to the "deserving" poor, discouraging immorality and out-of-wedlock births, and encouraging work effort; to use a phrase central to contemporary welfare reform discourse, these policies were aimed at ending "welfare dependency." In latent terms, events in Louisiana and Newburgh, and the Byrd hearings, mobilized and coded the theme of welfare dependency as a racial phenomenon. The negative race-based attributes said to produce welfare dependency—often based on gendered racism—were stereotypes that historically had been used to rationalize and justify white hegemony over African Americans.

Well before the events in Louisiana, Newburgh, and the District of Columbia occurred, the conception of African-American *biological* inferiority had been the subject of attack by social scientists and other intellectuals, liberal politicians, and the civil rights movement. Biological inferiority was a central canon of racist culture. By 1960 public acceptance of the notion of biological inferiority was eroding, albeit more slowly in the South, where miscegenation laws remained and allegations of African-American biological inferiority often infused rationales for resisting school desegregation. The conception of African American *cultural* inferiority, which did not require reference to faulty genes, was supplanting the biological conception. Louisiana, Newburgh, and the Byrd hearings both expressed and reinforced the theme that value systems and associated behaviors differ along racial lines. This was a theme that would continue in subsequent welfare discourse.

Welfare racism, as a means of racial control, initially involved blatant denial of African Americans' civil rights by excluding or otherwise discriminating against a racially designated group deemed culturally, if not biologically, inferior. In their own ways, events in Louisiana, Newburgh, and the District of Columbia signified a nascent turn away from open racial discrimination in the realm of welfare. Such discrimination would no longer be possible under federal civil rights laws enacted in the 1960s in a climate of increased civil rights militancy. Instead, welfare policies championed in Louisiana, Newburgh, and the Byrd hearings embodied what today might be called race-blind, but highly restrictive, moral and behavioral standards for eligibility. African Americans and others whose alleged cultural inferiority got in the way of meeting these standards could be denied public assistance.

While participants in welfare policy debates years later would claim, "It is not about race," their discourse would often subtly reflect conceptions of race-based cultural inferiority. As we will see in the next chapter, the racialization of welfare as a national issue proceeded apace from the 1960s on, as did European-American hostility toward welfare and its recipients. A "white backlash" to the civil rights movement and other events in the 1960s will provide a starting point for understanding how and why the federal government came to pass the Personal Responsibility and Work Opportunity Reconciliation Act of 1996.

5
THE DEMISE
OF AFDC AS A LEGACY
OF WHITE
RACIAL BACKLASH

The culture of black America is the most significant for an understanding of today's nonwork and poverty. . . . Evidently, the worldview of blacks makes them uniquely prone to the attitudes contrary to work, and thus vulnerable to poverty and dependency.

Lawrence M. Mead,
The New Politics of Poverty,
1992

had achieved some notable successes. The federal racial state had been made to accede to many of the movement's key demands. As we will discuss in this chapter, influential white political elites responded to the movement and events that followed by lighting and fanning the flames of white backlash against African-American struggles for racial equality and economic justice. This political backlash helped to racialize national politics from the mid-1960s into the 1990s, and affected the discourse on welfare by racial state actors, political candidates, policy analysts, and the general public.

In the previous chapter we noted the role of the mass media in publicizing events in Louisiana, Newburgh, and Washington, D.C. Extensive media coverage of these conflicts helped to foster and reinforce the notion that race and welfare were inextricably linked. As we will see in this chapter, the mass media have played a key role in promulgating racist stereotypes and negative controlling images of impoverished African Americans who must rely on welfare. The media have thus contributed to a national political environment in which hostility toward welfare and its recipients could be easily exploited by racial state actors and others riding the legacy of the 1960s white political backlash.

By the 1990s, the national political environment had changed such that those federal racial state actors and other political elites who were the most concerned with shoring up white racial hegemony, or who were willing to use the "race card" to advance their own or their party's political fortunes, felt free to launch the most audacious project in welfare racism to date. Their efforts were aimed at no less than the dismantlement of Aid to Families with Dependent Children (AFDC; Aid to Dependent Children was renamed Aid to Families with Dependent Children in 1962 when mothers of the children receiving aid were made eligible to receive assistance) and abolition of the entitlement to public assistance that it guaranteed many millions of impoverished mothers and children. As we will discuss, political elites were aided in their attacks on welfare by conservative social scientists and other policy analysts who put the responsibility for African-American poverty squarely on the backs of poor blacks themselves. Overall, racial state actors have been shockingly successful in riding and milking the institutionalization of the white political backlash as "welfare reform" in the 1990s.

L) Code word

WHITE BACKLASH AND RACIALIZED WELFARE POLITICS

We realize that there are conceptual difficulties inherent in employing the notion of white backlash to analyze events over a period extending from the 1960s to the 1990s. To some, the term *backlash* implies the existence of a sudden spikelike reaction in a given historical period. We are not arguing here that there has been a three-and-a-half-decade long white *backlash* spike in the United States. Neither are we implying that there have been a number of discrete and identifiable racial backlash spikes during that historical period. Rather, we are arguing that the white backlash that emerged in the 1960s left a *legacy* of racialized politics that, consistent with a process approach to racism, was kept in motion by an organizational base of racial state actors and other political elites.

In the popular media and in U.S. social science and history, "the white backlash" is typically depicted as being a single historical event which began and ended in the mid- to late 1960s. The white backlash is erroneously portrayed as little more than a brief reaction to the excesses of the increasingly militant and violent "black power" phase of the civil rights movement. When analysts portray it in this way, their primary focus is whites' reactions to the black urban rebellions and other socially disruptive behavior by African Americans in that decade.[1]

Invisible to such an analysis is the ongoing and overarching system of white racial domination and its equilibrium-maintaining mechanisms and processes. Those mechanisms and processes become visible through historical trend analysis. Only through the latter is it possible to see white backlash for what it is: a process rather than an event. More specifically, white backlash is a process of racial control by which white racial hegemony, when threatened and disturbed, is brought back into equilibrium. As a racial control process it existed well before and has extended well beyond the 1960s. In the United States white backlashes are not unusual. Rather, they are an integral adjustment mechanism of U.S. race relations.

In the twentieth century alone there were at least three other major white backlashes. Prior to the onset of the 1960s there was a largely southern white backlash to the U.S. Supreme Court's 1954 *Brown v. Board of Education* decision outlawing racially segregated public schools.[2] Years earlier, in 1918–1919, and then again in the late 1940s, there were two white backlashes aimed at thwarting the rising social and economic expectations of returning African-American veterans of World War I and World War II. Both postwar backlashes included vicious acts of violence against African Americans.[3] What these white backlashes had in common with backlash activity occurring later is the function they served for whites in restoring the status quo of white supremacy, seen to be threatened by African Americans. The racially fueled attacks on welfare and its recipients discussed in the previous chapter can be viewed as a part of the same racial status quo–maintaining process involving white backlash.

In its racial content, the attack on welfare which ultimately proved fatal to AFDC in the 1990s can be understood as a legacy of the white political backlash

that emerged in the 1960s. The white backlash of the 1960s focused first on condemnation of the perceived excesses of the civil rights movement, which many
European Americans linked to the urban rebellions. These excesses were most
frequently expressed in political discourse by one word: "riots." By the early
1970s, the civil rights movement had run its course, and the urban rebellions
had been stilled. But by then the nation's AFDC rolls had exploded, and the
numbers of African Americans on the roles had increased dramatically. Not surprisingly, white backlash politics shifted focus from "riots" to another issue that
was symbolic of white discontent: "welfare." The African-American target population and whites' sentiments toward it remained largely the same. Only the
issue had changed.

From the very beginning, the racist sentiments harnessed by the white backlash that emerged in the 1960s were central to the agendas of political elites.
They not only exploited such sentiments but played a key role in both their
design and maintenance. Once an easily evoked and exploitable sentiment has
proved to be politically useful to politicians, parties, and their backers, it is likely
to become institutionalized. This was the case with racial sentiments embedded
in the white political backlash that emerged in the 1960s. In the absence of a
fundamental change in the racial structure of U.S. society, including the nature
and functioning of the racial state, it is not surprising that contemporary racial
attitudes and practices not only reflect but in many ways duplicate the racialized
sentiments that this 1960s backlash contained.

We maintain that because of the important political functions that the racial
sentiments accompanying white backlash serve, such sentiments have become
institutionalized into U.S. politics through the mobilization of racially loaded
terms like *welfare* and the use of racist controlling images of welfare recipients.
Chief among these functions is the furtherance of the ambitions of politicians
who are skilled at playing the welfare race card to advance their careers. Since
the 1960s, white backlash–era sentiments much like those involving welfare
have been structured into the highly racialized platforms of mainstream political
parties (e.g., the Republican Party's "Southern Strategy") and the racist coalitions that they helped to cement.

Consequently the racist sentiments mobilized by the 1960s white political
backlash never went away. Racialized politics are a permanent feature of U.S.
national, individual state, and local politics. What varies is their intensity. That
intensity changes with changes in the larger society, such as the overall state of
race relations and the state of the economy. The intensity of racialized politics
also varies in response to the needs of the racial state and the ambitions of its key
actors. The intensity has been generally high since the 1960s and has shown no
signs of abating.

Shifting Targets of Backlash Politics: From Civil Rights to Economic Justice

Important social and historical processes are lost in snapshot-type analyses that reduce white political backlash to a logical response of hapless whites, whose supposedly expansive racial tolerance was pushed beyond reasonable limits by militant black power "extremists" in the 1960s. Such analyses ignore the changes in the nature of the demands that African Americans have made on the racial state over time. New, and increasingly militant, demands for racial equality and for economic justice on the part of the racially oppressed were what provoked a white backlash in the 1960s and set the stage for today's highly racialized politics of welfare reform. Without understanding this historic shift in demands, it is impossible to comprehend the unfolding of events which culminated in the abolition of the Aid to Families with Dependent Children program in 1996.

Explanations of a white political backlash in the 1960s that focus on the shift in civil rights strategy from nonviolent direct action to threats or acts of violence overlook an equally if not more important development: a change in the civil rights movement's goals. For all members of U.S. society, regardless of their skin color, the black urban rebellions were emblematic of a substantive shift in African-American aspirations. For many African Americans, the rebellions were an expression of frustration and anger stemming from the realization that significant change in their collective socioeconomic plight was unattainable. For many European Americans, on the other hand, the rebellions symbolized nothing less than a fundamental challenge to white racial supremacy.

By the mid-1960s, it was increasingly clear to most African Americans that gaining fundamental legal civil rights in the South was not enough. The primary goal of the civil rights movement began changing to economic equality with whites for African Americans everywhere, North and South. This goal threatened the race-based economic privileges enjoyed by all whites. At the same time as the civil rights movement shifted from a regional movement concerned with civil rights to a national movement for economic justice, the post–World War II migration of African Americans to the northern states and into urban centers continued apace.[4] Thus, the white political backlash that emerged in the 1960s was precipitated not only by the civil rights movement and its shifting goals, but by the highly visible African-American geographic movement into whites' "space" as well. It is not surprising, therefore, that the changing size and color of the AFDC rolls became a ready target for growing white racial antipathies.[5]

In the late 1960s, both eligibility rules and benefits for AFDC recipients were liberalized.[6] Racial exclusion from the rolls began to be replaced with racial inclusion.[7] Many of the barriers to eligibility that had been put in the way of

African Americans broke down. Consequently, AFDC became much more of a true entitlement for impoverished families. Indeed, the second half of the 1960s is usually characterized as a period of "welfare explosion." Between 1965 and 1970 the number of AFDC recipients more than doubled, from 3.3 million to 7 million. Many of those added to the roles were black. By 1970, African Americans constituted some 45 percent of AFDC families.[8] By then, the numbers of African Americans on AFDC, when combined with those Latina/o Americans receiving aid, produced an AFDC population in which people of color were in the majority for the first time.[9]

Among the factors that have been cited to account for the growth in the AFDC rolls is the impact on welfare policy of the increasingly militant civil rights movement and ghetto-based rebellions.[10] The welfare regulation process was further loosened by pressures placed on welfare officials by a contentious welfare rights movement dominated by African-American participants and leaders. As we will see, however, as AFDC rolls visibly darkened, the response of racial state actors progressively shifted from these liberalized policies to policies of racial containment and racial control. This policy shift culminated in the elimination of AFDC. In a whirlwind three decades, the racial state would go from public assistance policies of racial exclusion, to inclusion, to racially motivated abolition of the AFDC program.

WHITE BACKLASH AND THE TRANSFIGURATION OF THE RACIAL STATE

The conventional wisdom on white backlash leads to erroneous conclusions not only about its causes, but about its nature and workings. We have said that white backlashes cannot be meaningfully reduced to finite moments in history. When they are viewed instead as a process, we can better understand how the racial sentiments they contain become institutionalized as features of the racial state, transfiguring the state along the way.

The spread of the civil rights movement to northern cities in the 1960s resulted not only in the transformation of that movement, but in the transfiguration of the federal racial state as well. It changed from a relatively racially benign state during the Eisenhower administration (1953–1961), to one which under the Kennedy and Johnson administrations (1961–1969) became actively involved in the amelioration of poverty, to the white backlash-driven racial state of President Nixon (1968–1974). The racialized politics that commenced in the Nixon administration still reverberate. Contemporary federal racial state actors and policy analysts often justify their calls for more conservative social policies by making reference to the alleged excesses of the civil rights movement, and a decline in moral values that was supposedly encouraged by "liberal" domestic social policies such as the War on Poverty.[11]

President Lyndon B. Johnson initiated the federal War on Poverty in 1964, shortly after Kennedy's assassination. The War on Poverty undertaken by the federal racial state mirrored and articulated the civil rights movement's shift to a national economic justice agenda. In *The Neoconservatives*, Peter Steinfels argues that what upset prominent policy analyst Daniel Patrick Moynihan and others about the turbulent 1960s was that it constituted a threat to social order and stability. A major threat Steinfels identifies was the challenge to white authority.[12] The civil rights movement greatly influenced the federal racial state's decision to launch the War on Poverty, and in response to the growing militancy of the civil rights movement, many War on Poverty community action programs would become highly activist and militant.[13] Ironically, the Johnson administration's focus on poverty reflected a retreat from civil rights to an agenda which, while attractive to African Americans, was less race specific and race targeted than they deemed necessary.

The Johnson administration's seemingly "race-blind" attack on poverty was not enough, however, to appease the many whites who felt threatened by the protests and changes demanded by civil rights militants as the movement spread its efforts beyond the South. Most whites had been appalled at media images of African-American children being chased and bitten by police dogs as they participated in peaceful civil rights marches during the height of the civil rights movement in the South. Many showed little patience with those white supremacists who were outspoken in their support for southern segregation, and who condoned the use of violence to protect "the southern way." But as the civil rights movement extended its activities into the North, it faced complex problems that were not easy to target. White racism in the North was rooted in highly institutionalized but largely invisible structures of white racial privilege. Unlike de jure segregation, it typically had little formal basis in racial state laws and statutes that could be contested in the courts. Civil rights movement excursions into northern terrain evoked little sympathy from most whites, and drew great reproach from many as movement actors sought to contest the workings of institutions—from de facto segregated school systems to white-dominated trade unions—on whose racial status quo whites depended. In this climate of increased racial antipathies, Johnson's ostensibly race-blind War on Poverty, along with other "Great Society" programs that his administration initiated, were seen by many whites as "a veiled attempt to further help blacks."[14]

One aspect of the federal War on Poverty that piqued many whites was its contribution to what conservative policy analyst Daniel Bell has lamentingly called the "participation revolution" of the 1960s.[15] Using federally funded community action programs as a base, people of color challenged local white power structures. They protested disruptive urban renewal projects as "Negro removal," and they challenged racist school systems, police brutality, and slum landlords. Participation and leadership in such programs helped to launch the careers of many African-American politicians, some of whom would win election to city councils and mayoral offices. Finally, community action programs were also used in the struggle for welfare rights, and helped support the militant and flamboyant battles of the African American–dominated National Welfare Rights Organization.[16]

It should be noted, however, that President Johnson held a very negative attitude toward welfare in comparison to the support he gave his own War on Poverty, which was primarily intended by its racial state architects to provide services to the poor with which they were expected to engage in "self-help." Johnson's contemptuous and racialized attitudes toward AFDC were akin to those of many European Americans. He expressed this contempt in a manner that was consistent with slavery-rooted racist stereotypes of African-American women as breeding animals. In discussing public assistance for families with "illegitimate" children with his chief budget officer, Johnson complained:

> The unemployed parents, the ones that just stay up there and breed and won't work and we're feeding them. You've got two-and-a-half million [dollars] in your budget and I told you that we didn't want, we don't want to take care of all these illegitimate kids. And we want to make them [parents] get out there and go to work.[17]

By 1968, the civil rights movement faced growing antagonism from whites in the North. Not only did many whites see the movement as being responsible for the destructive and frightening black urban rebellions that had been taking place in the nation's cities, but they objected to its advocacy of school desegregation policies like busing and open-housing policies intended to desegregate whites-only neighborhoods.[18] The black urban rebellions and insurrections of the mid- to late 1960s were emblematic of the frustration many African Americans felt in not having their aspirations for economic justice taken seriously by the racial state. But for many European Americans, the rebellions—coming on top of the civil rights movement's activities and the War on Poverty—signaled the need for an end to this period of racial state liberalism and a return to the racial status quo.

Public opinion polls indicated whites' desire for a retrenchment in race relations. The civil rights movement reached its peak of activity in 1963 with the highly publicized and successful Birmingham, Alabama, demonstrations and the historic March on Washington, D.C. Not surprisingly, public opinion polls showed that civil rights peaked as a national issue in the years 1963 through 1965.[19] Beginning in 1965, however, there was a dramatic decline in public support for federal racial state efforts on behalf of African-American civil rights.

Poll results showing public agreement that the Johnson administration was "pushing racial integration" either "not fast enough" or "about right" dropped from 71 percent in April 1965 to 64 percent in August 1965—the month that Los Angeles's huge Watts rebellion occurred—and fell to 48 percent in September 1966 "after riots and related disorders in Chicago, Cleveland, and forty-one other communities." In that poll, the majority (52 percent of those polled) indicated that the Johnson administration was pushing too hard for civil rights.[20] Republican Party leaders urged their party's candidates for elected office to exploit these racial sentiments. In doing so they cited their own poll data showing that racial unrest had become the top domestic issue.[21] This trend in public opinion was underscored by the "long hot summer" riots of 1967, after which social control was ranked in national public opinion surveys as the nation's most important problem.[22] The U.S. white citizenry was thus ripe for exploitation of its racial sentiments by political candidates and racial state actors.

Political Elites as Agents in the Racialization of National Politics

Both popular and social science literature often assume that somehow, when white racial sentiment reaches a certain critical mass, it is articulated through the political process. Typically, racial state actors are portrayed as mere puppets of public opinion. This portrayal ignores the active role of racial state actors and other political elites in helping to generate and inflame these white racial sentiments and the periodic white racial backlashes they in turn fuel. Moreover, political elites and political parties provide an organizational base for keeping white racial backlash sentiments alive well after the backlash itself peaks. In looking for clues as to the origins of how contemporary national politics became racialized, it would not take long for a good detective to find the fingerprints of political elites such as Barry Goldwater, George Wallace, Richard Nixon, and Ronald Reagan.

Edward Carmines and James Stimson argue that the 1958 congressional elections were a racial "turning point" in the reshaping of American politics "for the remainder of the twentieth century."[23] Through the election of many liberal congressional Democrats and the decimation of the ranks of moderate and liberal Republicans, that election set the stage for the white political backlash against what many European Americans in the mid- to late 1960s saw as federal policies targeted to benefit undeserving African Americans. As a result of that white backlash and its electoral effects, conservatives came to dominate the Republican Party, and by the 1980s and 1990s would make significant inroads into dominating national politics in the United States.[24] Speaking of the national political picture today, Edsall and Edsall state that "considerations of race are now deeply imbedded in the strategy and tactics of politics."[25]

While racial state actions in Louisiana, Newburgh, and Washington, D.C., were watershed events that helped to turn welfare into a highly racialized, national political issue in the early 1960s, the 1964 presidential campaign of Arizona Republican Senator Barry Goldwater was a pivotal event in the racialization of post–World War II national politics more generally. Senator Goldwater won only his home state and five southern states, but he showed the nation that Republicans could win states in the Deep South, a longtime bastion of Democratic Party politics.[26]

In his campaign against Democratic incumbent Johnson, Goldwater framed support for white supremacy around conservative political principles without using overtly racist language. He was thus able to demonstrate how racial sentiments could be tapped for political advantage by candidates for national office, without their taking the risk of appearing to be racial bigots. In this way Goldwater made an early and significant contribution to what historian Michael Goldfield has referred to as "the building of the white racist coalition," a development which continues to be a powerful force in the shaping of mainstream American politics.[27] In his presidential campaign, Goldwater also demonstrated the viability of using welfare as a racialized political issue in general elections.

It is important to note that in 1964 Senator Goldwater received the political support of a man who would later become the nation's top elected racial state actor and a nemesis of welfare, Ronald Reagan. Like Goldwater, Reagan was also supportive of maintaining white privilege, and was likewise skilled in communicating this to whites without demonstrating overt racism. Reagan, for example, made a political name for himself by opposing a California fair housing referendum that would have combated residential racial segregation. Moreover, he was elected governor of California after taking a tough "law and order" stance against outspoken African Americans. In doing so, he played on whites' fears and negative racial sentiments evoked by the urban rebellion in the Watts section of Los Angeles.[28]

Of course, Republicans were not the only ones who helped mold the racialization of national politics in the late 1960s. Many Democrats were supportive and helpful in this regard as we have shown, such as Senator Byrd with his Washington, D.C., welfare fraud hearings and continued racialized condemnations of AFDC. But none made an impact like Alabama's Democratic governor, George M. Wallace. In 1968, Wallace—a diehard segregationist—ran for president as a third-party candidate against Democrat Hubert Humphrey and Republican Richard Nixon. Like Goldwater, Wallace was also skillful in engaging in racist politics without being overly explicit. Lacing his campaign with racialized code words, Wallace "enlarged both the southern and national base for white racist politics." Wallace's ability to attract large numbers of European-American voters in the North was especially impressive to Republicans.[29]

In his successful bid for the presidency in 1968, Nixon also exploited the white political backlash that was under way. Nixon used a "Southern Strategy," designed to appeal to supporters of white supremacy in the South without using racially explicit language that could have cost him the support of politically moderate European Americans. Nixon was not simply impressed with Wallace's success,[30] but viewed Wallace as a political threat to his own Southern Strategy, to the possibility of his re-election in 1972, and to the national political ambitions of the Republican Party.

After concluding that Nixon could not win re-election in 1972 if Wallace captured much of the South, the Republican Party leadership planned an aggressive campaign of race-based politics for that year's presidential campaign.[31] However, this pragmatic political move on the part of the Republicans should not lead one to conclude that Nixon himself did not believe in white racial supremacy. Here is an April 28, 1969, diary entry by one of Nixon's chief White House aides. It was recorded after a discussion about the need for changes in federal welfare policy ("P" refers to President Nixon):

> P emphasized that you have to face the fact that the *whole* problem is really the blacks. The key is to devise a system that recognizes this while not appearing to. Problem with overall welfare plan is that it forces poor whites into same position as blacks. Feels we have to get rid of the veil of hypocrisy and guilt and face reality.[32]

The white backlash–driven assault on welfare increased the need for the voices of welfare recipients to be heard. Unfortunately, that same racial backlash contributed to the demise of the civil rights movement and the War on Poverty, which were key fuel sources for the most effective collective voice that mothers reliant on welfare ever had: the National Welfare Rights Organization (NWRO). At its peak in 1969, the NWRO had twenty-two thousand members—mostly women of color—who voiced their concerns through hundreds of protests[33] organized through some eight hundred local groups which operated in all fifty states.[34] The brief existence of the NWRO came to an end in 1973 when the white backlash was still strong.[35] Its voice was sorely missed some two decades later, when the legacy of the same backlash that precipitated the end of the NWRO contributed mightily to the abolition of AFDC. Not surprisingly, the congressional hearings on the legislation abolishing AFDC were conspicuous for the absence of the voices of welfare recipients.

Michael Goldfield notes that although a national-level white racist political coalition had been set in place by the early 1970s, in Nixon's second term, "The full-fledged emergence of a dominating racist coalition . . . only took place during the presidencies of Ronald Reagan and George Bush."[36] Like Goldwater, Wallace, and Nixon before him, Reagan was adept at using camouflaged racism to exploit white racist sentiments.[37] As a former movie actor, Reagan was especially skilled in using the mass media in appealing to these sentiments. For example, although Reagan did not specifically refer to race, in his unsuccessful 1976 campaign for the Republican Party presidential nomination he evoked a powerful racialized controlling image with his reference to a Chicago "welfare queen" who allegedly lived lavishly on money she cheated from AFDC. Reagan used this image repeatedly in campaign speeches that were widely covered by the media to personify what he argued was wrong with the U.S. welfare system.

In a speech in New Hampshire during the Republican presidential primary Reagan made the following comments in reference to a "woman in Chicago" whom he depicted as a welfare queen:

> She has 80 names, 30 addresses, 12 Social Security cards and is collecting veterans' benefits on four nonexisting deceased husbands. . . .
>
> She's collecting Social Security on her cards. She's got Medicaid, getting food stamps and she is collecting welfare under each of her names. Her tax-free cash alone is over $150,000.[38]

Although Reagan selected an extreme case of welfare abuse to characterize the behavior of AFDC mothers, and though a *New York Times* article noted that many of Reagan's facts were erroneous,[39] the gendered racist stereotype of the welfare queen proved to be an effective political campaign tactic in appealing to the sentiments of white voters. Prior to the abolition of AFDC, it remained one of the chief negative controlling images of African-American mothers on welfare that was used by political elites and others who were outspokenly critical of welfare.

As we will show, the Reagan administration (1981–1989) achieved some legislative changes from its attacks on AFDC, which were then implemented by the Bush administration (1989–1993). The Reagan administration attacks, together with the growing clout of the white racist political coalition in national politics, set the stage for Bill Clinton's 1992 campaign promise to "end welfare as we know it." The conservative Republican-dominated Congress that the Clinton administration had to deal with in the mid-1990s, and the importance of the issue of welfare reform to his prospects for re-election, pushed him to go much further in meeting this campaign promise than he had originally intended.

The white political backlash that emerged in the 1960s, and the legacy of racialized national politics to which it contributed, were given a good deal of support by the mass media from the 1960s onward. The media played a major role in hardening the link that was forged between "race" and welfare by political elites, thus contributing to the overall power and resiliency of welfare racism. Before examining events leading up to the abolition of AFDC, let us look at the media's role in the racialization of welfare.

RACIALIZED IMAGES OF THE POOR: THE ROLE OF THE MASS MEDIA

Gilens's Provocative Data on the Media's Racial Bias

As Carter A. Wilson has noted, one of the chief commodities of the U.S. media is racist culture. Members of this nation's dominant economic class and its racial state actors have long exploited racist culture in pursuing their goals. Thus, the media are an important analytical site for the study of racism generally, and welfare racism in particular.[40] Members of U.S. society depend upon mass circulation magazines, newspapers, and television for information on welfare issues. To the degree to which the media, in concert with political elites, link "race" to welfare, elements of racist culture are disseminated and reinforced in the minds of whites.

Dominant economic and political interests, such as preserving class inequalities and white racial hegemony, are served by the mass media's highly racialized representations of poor people and, more specifically, welfare recipients. In *Why Americans Hate Welfare*, political scientist Martin Gilens argues that the media's highly racialized portrayal of the poor played a major role in changing popular attitudes toward poor people. In making this case, Gilens examined the photographs of poor people in *Time, Newsweek,* and *U.S. News and World Report* over a forty-three-year period.[41] He found that during the period studied (1950–1992) most of the poor people pictured (53 percent) were African Americans, when, in fact, on average only 29 percent of the poor during that entire period were African American. Moreover, he found that the proportion of African Americans presented in the photographs varied both over time and according to the type of poverty story presented in the accompanying magazine text.[42]

Gilens's findings that the overrepresentation of African Americans pictured in these magazines varied over time is very revealing of the dynamic nature of race relations in the United States. They challenge the popular notion that racism has progressively diminished and thus will eventually disappear. Consistent with the 1960s white political backlash and its legacy, Gilens found a major difference in the racialization of poverty prior to the mid-1960s and afterward. "From the beginning of this study through 1964, poor people were portrayed as predominantly white. But starting in 1965 the complexion of the poor turned decisively darker."[43] During the entire decade of the 1950s, African Americans were underrepresented in poverty photos (18 percent), as they were in 1964, the year

more neg. stigma attached 2 black poor

the War on Poverty was initiated (27 percent). In 1967, as the white political backlash to the civil rights movement and its aftermath grew, so did the proportion of African Americans portrayed in pictures of the poor (72 percent).[44] As the complexion of the poor darkened, the media depiction of African Americans and their poverty became decisively more negative and unsympathetic in comparison to the depiction of whites in poverty.

Let us take a closer look at the link between the color of the poor people found in the photographs in these three magazines over time, and how they were depicted. According to Gilens, there were few stories on poverty and few African Americans pictured in the stories that were published from 1950 through 1964. In the early 1960s, when the Kennedy and Johnson administrations launched poverty-related initiatives, both the number of poverty-focused stories and the proportion of African Americans in those stories increased somewhat. Still, the "policy-focused stories were illustrated almost exclusively with pictures of poor whites." In stark contrast, photographs of African Americans accompanied stories on the Newburgh controversy, and pictures related to Senator Byrd's 1962 investigation of alleged welfare fraud in Washington, D.C., contained both African Americans and European Americans. Thus the trend began of using darker images to illustrate poverty-related stories involving controversy and scandal.[45]

As we noted earlier, the War on Poverty was initiated by the Johnson administration in 1964. In 1965 the media began to focus on various antipoverty program controversies.[46] In that one-year period, the proportion of African Americans pictured in poverty stories in *Time*, *Newsweek*, and *U.S. News and World Report* increased dramatically, from 27 percent to 49 percent. Gilens suggests that a factor associated with that increase was the increased focus of civil rights leaders on the War on Poverty. Consistent with a racial control thesis, Gilens notes that while the black rebellion in Los Angeles' Watts section, which occurred in August 1965, intensified awareness of African-American poverty, concern with African-American inner-city poverty was not a major focus of those magazine stories (although a fourth of them mentioned the "riots").[47]

The three news magazines' coverage of poverty changed in response to the black urban rebellions of 1966 and 1967. In 1966 there was a major increase in stories on urban poverty. By 1967 there were nearly as many stories on urban poverty as on the federal War on Poverty.[48] "Urban" increasingly became a synonym for the word "black," as would become true for the terms "inner-city" and, later, "underclass." The increasing focus on inner-city people of color was accompanied by decreasing coverage of the War on Poverty, as the media shifted their focus away from economic justice issues to the issue of the control of the behavior of low-income inner-city African Americans. This shift fueled the racial

Shift in media portrayal of poor

stereotype that most mothers receiving AFDC benefits were African-American inner-city women.

The black face that the magazines put on poverty did not change after the black urban rebellions of the 1960s. There were significant fluctuations in African Americans' photographs in *Time*, *Newsweek*, and *U.S. News and World Report*, but never a return to the time when African Americans' photographs were underrepresented in poverty stories. The peak periods for poverty's black face was 1972 and 1973, while the face of poverty whitened dramatically "during the economic recessions of 1974 and 1982–83." [49] White poverty was benignly portrayed as an outcome of economic forces over which whites had no control.

According to Gilens, during the 1972–73 recession some poverty stories in the three magazines focused on the "welfare mess." They exposed welfare waste, mismanagement, and fraud. Many highlighted various racial state initiatives in punitive welfare reform. When these negative stories on the poor appeared, the color of poverty was pictured as being black. For 1974–1975, more than three-quarters (76 percent) of the people in welfare-focused stories were African American. This was more than twice the proportion of AFDC families in the United States who were black. [50]

Gilens notes that this increase in African Americans pictured in welfare-related stories cannot be explained by the changing racial composition of the welfare rolls. The color images of the poor in the magazines changed dramatically between the late 1960s and the early 1970s while the racial composition of the welfare rolls "hardly changed" during that time. [51] Moreover, during the same time period there were significant color variations by the *type* of poverty story covered. For example, while photographs of European Americans dominated articles that focused on unemployment policy during the 1974–1975 economic recession, African Americans were more likely to be pictured in general poverty stories. [52]

During the 1982–1983 recession, when there was increased national concern about unemployment-related poverty and some strong opposition to government cutbacks in poverty-related programs, the proportion of African-American poverty stories in the three magazines surveyed was 30 percent. That was the lowest it had been since 1964, the year the War on Poverty was declared. [53] Again, it appears that problems that media decision makers were prone to portray sympathetically, such as recession-linked rises in the nation's unemployment rate, were pictured as "white" problems. Those poverty-related problems of which they were critical were colored "black." The color of poverty's face was and continues to be a key factor in its treatment by the mass media and by the nation as a whole.

Racism Blindness in Gilens's Explanation for Evidence of Media Bias

Gilens's data are extremely valuable in showing racial bias in media depictions of the poor and welfare recipients. Unfortunately, his analysis in *Why Americans Hate Welfare* fails to link these data to systemic white racial hegemony.[54] In his book, and in a website posting on "Media Misrepresentations" of welfare recipients, Gilens limits the search for reasons for the highly racialized magazine images of the poor that his study found to isolated decisions of individual photo editors.[55] His analysis is restricted to the possible impact of editors' own racial prejudices on magazine photograph selection. Individual racial bigotry therefore receives a quick glance from Gilens. Systemic white racial hegemony, the mass media's role in it, and the economic and political interests that help to drive that role go ignored.

In "Media Misrepresentations," Gilens concludes that "in my conversation with photo editors at the three weekly news magazines, I found none had any clear sense of how their magazines had portrayed the poor. Photographs are chosen story by story." So what could explain his findings? As we noted earlier, there were disproportionately more African-American faces in magazine photographs than there were poor African Americans. In addition, racial differences existed in the photos, depending upon whether the magazine was reporting on so-called good poverty (e.g., whites pictured in stories of poverty based on recession-driven unemployment) or bad poverty (e.g., blacks pictured in the case of poverty-related controversies, or scandals involving politically unpopular programs such as welfare).

Gilens was content to trust an explanation by one of the photo editors that those patterns of racial differences could only be explained by a type of "subtle racism"[56] at the individual attitudinal level. Yet Gilens's trend data suggest that both the manifestation and the magnitude of this "subtle racism" were strikingly consistent with the changing structure and tenor of race relations in U.S. society. More attention to the history of U.S. race relations, racist culture, and racialized national politics could have gone a long way in providing Gilens with the structural context required to understand this "subtle racism" on the part of editors. He acknowledges this to some extent when he allows that journalists are not only professionals who observe and chronicle world events, but are "also residents of that world and are exposed to the same biases and misperceptions that characterize society at large."[57]

In focusing on individual prejudice, not systemic racism, Gilens fails to treat *Time, Newsweek,* and *U.S. News and World Report*—three very popular commercial magazines—as reflecting the thinking of organizational components of a powerful institution in U.S. society: a multibillion-dollar mass media industry. This industry has important transactions with and effects on other key institutions that collectively constitute the racialized social system. Again, putting a context to racial bias in editors' selection of photographs would require moving beyond consideration of racially prejudiced individual attitudes to a structural or systemic approach to racism. Fortunately, some approaches to the study of racism and the mass media aim to do just that.[58]

THE WHITE BACKLASH LEGACY HOMES IN ON AFDC

The centrality of the federal racial state as an organizational base for white political backlash sentiments shows that those rank-and-file white members of U.S. society who want to maintain racial dominance need not protest, riot, or even organize. U.S. society is already structured to represent their racial interests. They don't need a "participation revolution" for this to happen. Old-fashioned electoral politics works just fine. In brief, for European Americans the system works quite well in the maintenance of white racial hegemony. Any challenges—real or imagined—are efficiently met through a hyperresponsive political system and the racialized public policy it produces.

We have said that white backlash is best viewed as a process. In the post–civil right era, the legacy of the white racial backlash that emerged in the 1960s has sometimes resembled an avalanche, affecting almost everything in its path. Welfare, as a national political issue, was wholly encompassed in the legacy of white backlash politics by the 1980s. Welfare racism, as a component of this backlash legacy, would come to be manifested in a variety of ways. By the end of the 1980s, for example, the federal racial state had legislated broad "workfare" requirements for AFDC mothers under the Reagan administration's Family Support Act of 1988. Racial state actors also began handing out "waivers" to the Social Security Act to individual states. These waivers allowed the states to impose new and more restrictive rules requiring mothers receiving AFDC to adhere to a variety of behavioral conditions in order to maintain their families' eligibility for aid.

Moreover, racial state actors at the federal and individual state levels largely refused to act to stem the dramatic drop in the cash value of AFDC benefits that had begun in the 1970s. That drop progressively fell short in the face of the rising costs of living. Between 1970 and 1994, with inflation taken into account, the median maximum monthly state benefit for a mother with two children on the AFDC rolls dropped by 47 percent.[59] Widespread and ongoing resistance to funding benefit increases for AFDC families coincided with a color change in the AFDC population wherein whites became a numerical minority. In 1967, 53 percent of AFDC families were white.[60] By 1996—the year the program was abolished—the percentage had dropped to only 36 percent.[61]

In their treatment of AFDC and its recipients over the thirty-year period after the mid-1960s, political elites at the federal and individual state levels rarely revealed overt racist intent. Manifestations of welfare racism were much more indirect and subtle in their intent than those that prevailed up to that time. Yet while the racist intent of racial state actors' welfare policy actions was frequently camouflaged and opaque, and thus readily deniable, the adverse effects that their actions disproportionately inflicted on impoverished African Americans and other persons of color remained profound. Political elites were supported in these actions by the negative and highly racialized body of public opinion about welfare that they themselves, along with the mass media, helped to generate and sustain.

The Legacy of White Backlash and Public Opinion about Welfare

The legacy of the 1960s political backlash and the racial sentiments accompanying it were directly reflected in public opinion polls on poverty and welfare. A poll taken in 1989 showed that 48 percent of the U.S. public was inclined to blame the high rate of poverty among African Americans on lack "of motivation or willpower," and 49 percent rejected the notion that "white society hasn't given blacks a fair chance" as a way of explaining why African Americans on average have a much lower socioeconomic standing than do whites.[62]

By the 1990s, the public's race-based hostility toward AFDC had reached a level where it could be almost effortlessly fanned and inflamed by political elites. The mix of racist ideology and beliefs about welfare had crystallized to the point where it was no longer necessary for there to be direct threats to white racial hegemony for welfare racism to become salient in the political process. At every level of politics the very word "welfare" had been racialized in the public's mind and in the minds of racial state actors. Like "the drug problem" and "the crime problem," welfare had become an effective resource in the lexicon that politicians could mobilize to exploit whites' racial fears and animosities.[63]

The effect of the constant dissemination of these images was clearly revealed in public opinion polls. For example, a 1993 survey commissioned by the Anti-Defamation League found that 35 percent of respondents who identified themselves as white believed that African Americans prefer to live off welfare.[64] Data from the National Opinion Research Center showed that, when asked to directly compare themselves with African Americans, fully three-fourths of the white respondents rated African Americans as less likely than themselves to prefer to be self-supporting.[65]

In a poll conducted a little more than a month after Republicans captured control of Congress in 1994—using the need for welfare reform as a key issue—

almost half of the respondents thought that most people who are poor are black and that most people who are on welfare are black.[66] Significantly, more than half of those polled believed that: (1) lack of effort is to blame when people are on welfare (as opposed to circumstances beyond their control); (2) most people who receive money from welfare could get along without it if they tried; and, (3) most welfare recipients really don't want to work. These three beliefs were most likely to be found among poll respondents who thought that most people on welfare were black.

Another poll conducted around the same time revealed just how racialized the images of welfare recipients had become. Forty-four percent of its respondents chose "black" in answering the question "Of all the people who are on welfare in this country, are more of them black or more of them white?" (Only 18 percent responded "white," with the remaining respondents indicating "equal" [17 percent] or "Don't know/ No answer" [21 percent]).[67]

Perceptions of the color of those on AFDC affected whether members of the public believed recipients were deserving of assistance. Negative racist stereotypes about African-American irresponsibility and laziness were quite widespread. For example, the 1994 poll mentioned above revealed that there had been a shift from 1990 poll results, with fewer respondents blaming economic circumstances for poverty and more blaming the poor themselves. Those respondents polled in 1994 who thought that most welfare recipients were "black" were more likely than those who thought most recipients were white to believe that persons were on welfare "because of lack of effort" (61 percent), that "they don't want to work" (65 percent), and that "they could get along without welfare benefits" (60 percent).

In stark contrast, of the far fewer respondents who thought that most welfare recipients were "white," only 38 percent indicated that lack of effort was the reason for people being on welfare, and only 43 percent believed that most persons on welfare did not want to work. About an equal number expressed the belief that those who were on welfare needed it (48 percent) compared to those who indicated that they did not (49 percent).[68]

Commenting on yet another poll conducted in 1994, a reporter for the *New York Times* observed that despite a healthy economy, "American voters have become less compassionate about the problems of the poor and minorities." The public expressed "growing resentment toward immigrants" and was said to be "less inclined to express concerns for the plight of black Americans than they were only two years ago." The poll found that the majority of white respondents (51 percent) agreed "that equal rights had been pushed too far." Only 42 percent had agreed with that view in 1992. This decline in support for efforts to advance the civil rights of African Americans was accompanied by "a striking decline in support for social welfare programs."[69] It appears that, indeed, the legacy of the 1960s white racial backlash persisted into public opinion of the 1990s.

From the 1970s to the early 1990s, political elites skillfully exploited the economic anxieties, sense of stagnation, and fears of downward mobility suffered by many working- and middle-class whites.[70] Across the country, consummate attacks on AFDC were orchestrated by conservatives and right-wing ideologues who saw putting an end to AFDC as a key step in dismantling all federal welfare state programs.[71] They took great pains to portray AFDC as perhaps the most wasteful example of welfare state spending and AFDC's recipients as the principal source of U.S. social problems. Indeed, welfare itself was portrayed as a social problem.

Conservatives were well aware that the suffering of the welfare poor had long failed to generate much sympathy from the white public, and thus was likely to receive little from their own political opponents, including liberal Democrats. Widespread race-based hostility toward AFDC, politicians' success in using poor people of color as scapegoats for many European Americans' sense of economic distress, and the lack of an effective counterresponse from the poor and their traditional political allies would all combine to allow the federal racial state to end public assistance entitlement for this nation's poorest families.

The attacks on AFDC took a turn in the 1980s in which the alleged cultural deficiencies of the African-American poor were made central. This attack strategy would continue until, and be enshrined in, the Personal Responsibility and Work Opportunity Reconciliation Act of 1996. As the AFDC rolls became darker, and as the public perception of the typical welfare recipient was racialized well beyond the actual numbers of African Americans and other people of color receiving AFDC, the real dollar value of welfare benefits dropped precipitously. Moreover, mothers reliant on welfare were required to relinquish more of their remaining dignity and freedom to receive that lower level of support. This was accomplished largely through "New Paternalism" racial state welfare reform policies.

CONTROLLING WELFARE QUEENS: THE "NEW PATERNALISM"
Old and New Paternalisms

"Paternalism" refers to a dominant group's treatment of others whose life chances are closely tied to its actions and dependent upon its largesse. Paternalistic practices bolster the prestige and power of members of the dominant group. They also help maintain systems of social, cultural, and economic oppression by stigmatizing and controlling the behavior of those who are subordinated. Dominant groups seek to govern others by creating rules to regulate their behavior and by threatening or employing negative sanctions to punish those who deviate. The rules and sanctions are presented and rationalized as being in the best interests of those who must abide by them. That is, subordinates are bonded into systems of social hegemony through the adhesive of dominant group ideologies. They are dealt with as if they are incapable of understanding their own best interests or functioning autonomously without guidance by their social superiors. Paternalism can be found in many settings in which unequal power relations prevail. For example, the dynamics of paternalism are often apparent in fathers' relations with their children, traditional relations between men and women, and slavemasters' relations with their slaves.[72]

From a womanist perspective, U.S. welfare policy is an ideology-based process of racial control. The racial control process is targeted at controlling the behavior of mothers, or *what* mothers receiving welfare can do. This process stands in contrast to procreation-focused and geographic-focused race population control, which together seek to manage a population's racial composition and distribution. These latter two types of population control—which we will discuss in the next chapter—focus primarily on *who* is present in a highly racialized society. Paternalistic welfare policy as a racial control process is fueled by the image of the "welfare queen" and other negative controlling images of mothers on welfare that are based on racist stereotypes. These images and stereotypes provide the justification for paternalistic racial control. In the 1980s, paternalism became an integral theme in welfare reform policy debates, proposals, and initiatives associated with what was then the nation's largest welfare program, AFDC.[73]

The "New Paternalism," as it was called by policy advocates such as political scientist Lawrence M. Mead, advocated making welfare assistance contingent on mothers' willingness to shape their own and their families' personal behaviors to conform with values and norms dictated by the racial state.[74] In reality, New Paternalism reflected what Gwendolyn Mink has called "racialized morality."[75] We believe that the term "New Paternalism" obscures the degree to which there has been continuity in the paternalistic policy treatment of welfare recipients over the years. New Paternalism welfare policies were really no more than a resurgence of the kind of blatant, hard-nosed old paternalism toward welfare recipients that had become well established by the 1950s and that was expressed through the punitive welfare policies that were overturned in response to welfare rights protests and court actions in the 1960s. Despite some apparent differences between the old and new paternalisms, we believe that there was far more continuity than discontinuity between the two.

New Paternalism as Racial Control

Let us take a closer look at the so-called New Paternalism. For the reasons we noted earlier, by the 1980s, assaults on AFDC and its recipients gained substantial legitimacy during and in concert with welfare cutbacks by the Reagan administration.[76] President Reagan, voicing the view long advanced by other conservatives, framed the problem needing solution as "welfare dependency."[77] He joined with highly visible conservative figures, including former Ku Klux Klan Grand Dragon David Duke of Louisiana, in playing upon racist stereotypes held by many European Americans. Such stereotypes included the notion that not only did such dependency exist, but that it was primarily a problem involving African Americans. Referring to the role of welfare issues in Duke's successful campaign for the Louisiana House of Representatives, as well as to President Reagan's favorite anecdote about fraud by a so-called welfare queen, Jill Quadagno observed, "Welfare reform is the policy issue that most readily translates into a racial code."[78]

Conservative critics of AFDC were energized and inspired by congressional passage of the Reagan administration's Family Support Act of 1988, through which federal racial state actors hoped to capture greater control over the work behavior of mothers receiving AFDC benefits. The act effectively changed AFDC from a program of public assistance for poor mothers caring for children into one that called for mandatory work in return for aid.[79] In this way, welfare policy served as an ideology supporting the notion that African-American mothers receiving welfare, due to their alleged slothfulness and indolence, must be coerced to seek employment outside of the home. Any failure on their part to do so would be confirmation of their laziness and would simply reaffirm that they were undeserving of aid.

Critics of welfare began to press for even more policies to control the allegedly offensive behaviors of "welfare queens" and their children.[80] They argued that new demands on welfare recipients were necessary to instill "responsible" behavior in them. In essence, they issued a call for stronger measures of racial control. Greater control was said to be essential in order to reverse the supposed permissiveness of existing AFDC policies and to end the coddling of recipients that encouraged them to languish on the dole over generations.

The conservatives' arguments were, again, consistent with the widely held racist stereotype of African Americans' laziness. Such subtly race-based messages had an appeal to many European American voters, a fact not lost on moderate and liberal politicians. Because welfare and its recipients had been racialized and encompassed by the legacy of 1960s white backlash, such racist stereotypes could easily be mobilized as negative controlling images of all mothers who rely on welfare. In the 1980s, liberal and moderate politicians quickly came to join conservatives in making the need for new control-focused welfare policies a key national political issue.[81]

By the late 1980s, conservative critics of welfare had begun calling for the implementation of paternalistic welfare policies at the individual state level.

They proposed strict AFDC eligibility requirements reminiscent of those out-lawed by the courts two decades earlier.[82] Federal racial state actors in the Bush and Clinton administrations indicated their willingness to approve "waivers" to the Social Security Act so that individual states could "experiment" with new AFDC policies. Consequently, state-level New Paternalism took a variety of dif-ferent forms.[83] Policies mandated that mothers reliant on welfare participate in job programs or undergo job training,[84] and commence or continue with educa-tional programs.[85] Other New Paternalism policies financially penalized AFDC mothers who gave birth to additional children while receiving welfare,[86] pro-vided financial incentives to mothers on the welfare rolls who got married,[87] and denied AFDC benefits to mothers who did not cooperate in establishing paternity for their children.[88]

Some New Paternalism policies called for financial penalties for mothers on welfare whose children were truant from or dropped out of school,[89] as well as for mothers who could not present evidence their children were receiving rou-tine preventative health care, such as immunizations.[90] Other policies reduced AFDC payments to recipients who did not pay their rent, or who "doubled up" with other families to reduce housing expenditures.[91] There were New Paternal-ism policies that placed a limit on how long mothers could continue to receive AFDC benefits before losing their eligibility.[92] Other policies called for all AFDC applicants to be fingerprinted and checked against a central registry to help detect fraud.[93]

New Paternalism advocates called for welfare to be paid to teenage mothers only if they remained living with their parents, other family members, or guardians.[94] More extreme proposals would have made young unwed mothers ineligible for welfare unless they and their children lived in group homes or other institutional settings.[95] There were even proposals that AFDC mothers give up any additional children born to them to adoption or to orphanages.[96] Indeed, conservative policy analyst Charles Murray suggested that "government should spend lavishly on orphanages" to properly rear the children removed from single mothers who cannot afford to support them.[97] Some AFDC critics called for mothers receiving welfare to use the long-term contraceptive known as Norplant to prevent additional childbearing.[98] Perhaps the most radical New Paternalism proposal called for AFDC to be eliminated entirely, under the ratio-nale that welfare is an enabler of out-of-wedlock births. It was argued that elimination of AFDC would force a sharp drop in such births and encourage partners to marry if pregnancy occurred.[99]

In brief, according to New Paternalism advocates, drastic changes in existing AFDC requirements were said to be necessary to encourage mothers who were reliant on welfare to become "self-sufficient," and to force them to abandon the so-called culture of welfare dependency that burdened the taxpaying public. This welfare "dependency" notion was built around the racist stereotype that lazy African Americans used welfare to avoid work. But it was not the only negative controlling image that fueled the sentiment for punitive welfare measures. Gendered racism informed this and other arguments of New Paternalism advocates, who implied that African-American women were sexually promiscuous people whose rate of out-of-wedlock births was out of control.

This stereotype was often linked with yet another racist stereotype, which held that poor African-American women bore children to gain or increase their welfare benefits. Such a view was expressed by Lawrence Townsend, welfare director for Riverside, California, a city which instituted one of the nation's most stringent work requirements for AFDC mothers. Reminiscent of an infamous statement attributed to U.S. Senator Russell Long of Louisiana, who is said to have characterized mothers receiving AFDC as "brood mares" in 1967,[100] welfare director Townsend stated in 1993: "Every time I see a bag lady on the street, I wonder, 'Was that an AFDC mother who hit the menopause wall, who can no longer reproduce and get money to support herself?'"[101]

An important characteristic of racist stereotypes is their amazing ability to persist no matter how strongly or how often they are challenged by contradictory evidence.[102] This durability supports the view that such stereotypes do, indeed, serve important racial control functions. For example, data show that the fertility rate of women who received AFDC was not significantly higher than that of women not on welfare. The typical welfare recipient had two children. And researchers found no evidence that AFDC mothers had children to receive welfare benefits or had additional children to increase their benefits.[103] Yet the stereotype of low-income African-American women giving birth to large numbers of children to gain financially from AFDC persisted, and helped to fuel discourse calling for more controlling and punitive welfare policies.

As we have seen, the discourse surrounding the New Paternalism linked—sometimes directly, sometimes implicitly—welfare dependency to people of color. Racist stereotypes were endemic. Indeed, welfare policy analysts, including some social scientists, made significant contributions to the racialization of New Paternalism welfare discourse. Welfare recipients were made victims of a dominant ideology that used pseudo–social science jargon and code words to mask the racism implicit in its underlying premises and implications. Policy analysts' application of racist ideas to welfare policy was not usually outwardly apparent. This was unlike welfare discourse by right-wing, white-supremacist political elites such as David Duke, whose racist attitudes toward African-

American mothers receiving welfare were there for all to see in his 1992 campaign for the Republican presidential nomination.

The racist ideas of present-day white supremacists such as David Duke remind us of the recent period in America's history when racial inequalities were both legal and widely accepted. In that period, "race" derived its validity from assumed *biological* differences that rendered some races inferior to others. But biological differences are still occasionally posited, even by social scientists. Richard J. Herrnstein and Charles Murray drew national attention in 1994 with their claims that differences in the genetic makeup of white and black "races" are responsible for supposed differences in their respective cognitive abilities.[104] The widespread controversy that their biologically driven claims generated indicates that today, in comparison to the era of legally enforced segregation, many more people are willing to criticize assertions that some groups are biologically inferior or superior to others.

There is, however, a great deal of societal tolerance for assertions that significant *cultural* differences exist between "races," even among those who would deny that such differences are necessarily biologically based. People in the United States readily embrace the notion that race matters because of differences in race-based culture.[105] Indeed, as we shall see shortly, the assumption that there are cultural characteristics that differentiate the "white race" from the "black race" is central to the construction of arguments by contemporary advocates of punitive welfare policies. It was this cultural view of race and justification of racism that made the logic of the New Paternalism so popular and politically enduring.

Policy Analysts' Attack on the "Culture" of the Impoverished

European Americans have held certain fundamental stereotypes about African Americans from slavery to the present which are central to the canons of racist culture. Moreover, as radical black feminist or womanist scholars recognize, race relations have been managed largely through the mobilization of negative controlling images, which provide ideological justifications for oppressive actions taken by the racially dominant. Racist stereotypes depicting African Americans as lazy, irresponsible, and sexually promiscuous are central to restrictive welfare policies related to the important and overlapping spheres of work, family, and reproduction.

The stereotype of African-American women as baby-making machines, who have children to obtain additional welfare dollars, is inextricably linked to the stereotype which emerged during slavery of African-American women as indolent but supersexed breeding animals.[106] To many European-American citizens, who tend to view themselves as hardworking, responsible, and moral, such behavior is reprehensible. The affluent, largely European-American male decision makers who represent these citizens in the name of the racial state are therefore expected to discipline the unacceptable behaviors of impoverished female welfare recipients of color. We contend that such racialized thinking underlay the broad support surrounding the punitive AFDC policy initiatives referred to as the "New Paternalism."

Negative controlling images were frequently mobilized in 1994 congressional and gubernatorial election campaigns. Following up on President Bill Clinton's then-unfulfilled 1992 electoral promise to "end welfare as we know it," campaign rhetoric from candidates of both major parties called for making "welfare reform" a top priority. Both this rhetoric and the policies it justified frequently played on and fanned European Americans' negative controlling images of African Americans, while functioning to divert attention away from systemic sources of poverty, un- and underemployment, falling real wages for most workers, and other economic problems being experienced by members of the public irrespective of their "race."[107] *Political elites play on racist images*

Policy analysts, as well as political candidates and other racial state actors, subtly exploited or contributed to the production, legitimation, and dissemination of racialized controlling images concerning the composition and characteristics of the poverty population.[108] Many used the term *poor* interchangeably with the highly racialized term *urban underclass*. By doing so, they conjured up images of a U.S. poverty population that is primarily composed not only of inner-city ghetto residents of color, but of an alien people whose values and behavior are markedly different from (and, by implication, inferior to) that of most middle-class European Americans.[109]

New Paternalism social science ideologues skillfully exploited such popular racist sentiments. This certainly was true in the case of Lawrence Mead, the chief theoretician of the New Paternalism movement. He views the causes of American poverty-related problems largely in racial terms,[110] and traces the origins of the contemporary politics of poverty to challenges that African Americans posed to the social order and to the white backlash those challenges provoked.

In *The New Politics of Poverty*, Mead presents a very negative and stereotypical view of "black culture" as the chief force behind "nonwork" and the poverty that (he contends) results from it. Consistent with racist stereotypes that originated during slavery, Mead asserts, "the worldview of blacks makes them uniquely prone to the attitudes contrary to work, and thus vulnerable to poverty and dependency."[111] He mentions no such poverty-inducing culture for the millions of poor people who might be described as white.

Mead refers to the current stage of welfare politics as "dependency politics." The key focus of dependency politics today is, in his view, quite frankly racial.

Such politics involve deciding, according to Mead, "how to respond to the disorder of the inner city." As he puts it, "This new agenda goes back to the late 1960s, when the welfare rolls doubled, crime soared, and riots erupted in the ghettos of major cities."[112] He asserts that today the issue at hand is not economic inequality or economic justice, but poor people's conduct.[113] As Mead puts it: "In the current dependency politics, competence is at issue rather than justice. The dispute is over whether the poor can be responsible for failing to function, but fundamental questions about society cannot be raised."[114]

In 1992, Mead both openly acknowledged and exploited the racial politics of welfare when he warned Democrats that they dare not oppose the New Paternalism policies that were by then appearing in many individual states under federally granted waivers. In prepared remarks before a U.S. Senate hearing on state-level welfare reform, Mead stated:

> I need hardly add that a controversy over welfare could be fatal to Democratic hopes in the upcoming presidential election. Democrats have lately pressed economic issues such as the recession and health care to their advantage. A battle over welfare would shift attention back to the disorders of American cities, questions where the majority are clearly conservative. Dependency already bids fair to become the "Willie Horton" issue of 1992.[115]

Since the 1988 presidential election, the name "Willie Horton" had become synonymous with the effective racialization of politics. In Mead's view, welfare dependency was becoming "Hortonized," a situation to which his own and other conservative policy analysts' writings had directly contributed. Apparently, Mead, an important intellectual architect of punitive welfare reform, was keenly aware of the power and politics of racialized controlling images.

Mead and other conservative policy analysts routinely raised and, by repetition, reinforced racist stereotypes regarding African Americans' supposed laziness, immorality, dishonesty, and irresponsibility. By doing so they not only contributed to the overall racist culture of U.S. society; they mobilized negative controlling images of African Americans specific to the task of bringing about the type of racialized welfare reform they advocated.

Critics of the New Paternalism decried its requirements as meanspirited; a threat to personal liberty and privacy; evasive of the real problems poor people who must rely on welfare face; ineffectual in the achievement of its stated goals; and based on erroneous and harmful negative stereotypes of the poor, women, and people of color.[116] Despite such criticisms, New Paternalism initiatives came to enjoy a remarkable degree of political acceptability. By the early 1990s, racial state actors and political candidates of both major political parties were embracing the idea that states should be encouraged to experiment with or be free to adopt New Paternalism–style policies. New Paternalism themes had permeated welfare reform policy debates, proposals, and initiatives at all levels of the racial state by the early 1990s.

When the November 8, 1994, elections gave the Republican Party control of both houses of the U.S. Congress for the first time in forty years, Republican leaders immediately issued a package of proposed legislation that they titled "Contract With America." This "contract" was said to represent commitments made to Republican candidates' supporters during their campaigns. One part of the package contained a set of proposals consistent with the New Paternalism and the racialized politics underlying it. Republicans proposed an end to the federal government's treatment of AFDC as an entitlement program, major cutbacks in federal spending on AFDC benefits (as well as on other programs serving the poor), severe restrictions on the number of years recipients would be allowed to receive AFDC, denial of monetary aid to unwed mothers under eighteen, mandatory drug testing for aid eligibility, and policies that would allow states to devote funds to orphanages to house children of unmarried mothers who could not afford to care for them.[117]

Consistent with New Paternalism thinking, the Republicans' proposed welfare reform legislation, introduced in the U.S. House of Representatives in 1995, was called the Personal Responsibility Act. The name of the act implied that the responsibility for and the solutions to poverty rested with impoverished individuals themselves, not the state.[118] While not all of the Republicans' punitive proposals for welfare reform survived congressional deliberations, their "Contract With America" initiative dominated congressional welfare reform discourse and in large part framed the stated rationale and key provisions of the Personal Responsibility and Work Opportunity Reconciliation Act that President Clinton signed into law in August 1996. This act replaced AFDC with the "Temporary Assistance for Needy Families" program.

THE USES OF RACIALIZED WELFARE POLICY AS IDEOLOGY

We have emphasized that as one key legacy of the white political backlash of the 1960s, national political elites routinely crafted welfare policies that are informed by racism. As we have shown, racialized welfare policy has functioned as ideology in the interests of maintaining white racial supremacy. In discussing the significance of welfare policy aimed at restricting procreation by African-American women, Dorothy Roberts argues that restricting the reproductive choices of these women is not the primary function of such policy. Political elites have used racialized welfare policy as an ideology to "persuade people that racial inequality is perpetuated by Black people themselves." This use of welfare policy not only deflects attention away from the need for "radical change in America," but provides "a principal means of justifying the perpetuation of a racist structure."[119]

In the context of the legacy of white political backlash, welfare policy as ideology has proved especially dangerous to African Americans in recent years when political elites have called for more punitive welfare measures based on the argument that "liberal" antipoverty policies had failed. They have blamed this failure on the supposed race-based characteristics of those whom they portrayed as the intended policy beneficiaries.[120] Political elites framed the failure of people of color to obtain upward mobility, and to compete successfully with others for social and economic resources, as results of biological or cultural inferiority, not of highly structured systems of social and economic injustice.[121]

Once blamed on the supposed deficiencies of people of color, the perceived failure of welfare and antipoverty policies can also be used by political elites to justify opposition to other racial state policies that advocates argue will ameliorate racial inequalities. These include, but are not limited to, antiracist employment policies like affirmative action and policies intended to reduce discrimination and segregation in education and housing. In brief, as Robert C. Lieberman argues, U.S. welfare policy is not shaped only by race relations. Welfare policy also plays a major role in shaping race relations,[122] as well as the contours of the racial state.

6

WELFARE REFORM
AS RACE
POPULATION
CONTROL

They come in rags and Chebby trucks,
I buy big house with welfare bucks . . .
We have a hobby; it's called breeding.
Welfare pays for baby feeding.

1993 poem by
California state assemblyman
William Knight

changes not only its face but its entire socially structured body to meet the changing needs of its white beneficiaries. It is a shape shifter. When the building of individual and national fortunes was predicated on cheap or unpaid labor from abroad, racial state policies encouraged both the importation of such labor and, once it arrived, high fertility rates, so that first slave labor, and then immigrant labor, would reproduce itself. However, racial state policies shifted once the national infrastructure had been built, and technological and economic changes diminished the need for cheap labor from abroad. And as white needs have changed, so too has welfare racism.

The ability of racism to adapt to meet the changing labor and other needs of racialized societies helps to explain why, as the United States moves deeper into a new millennium, the color line persists. As this line is redrawn it increasingly takes the form of a boundary line which enforces the sentiment that certain types of people should not be here. That is, "those people"—the racialized Other—should not be allowed to come into the United States. Moreover, so goes the sentiment, poor people of color who are here, whether immigrants or native born, should be discouraged from reproducing.

Even a quick glance at the rationale and provisions of the Personal Responsibility and Work Opportunity Reconciliation Act of 1996 (PRWORA) suggests that one of its authors' major goals—in addition to other racial control functions like forcing indolent African-American mothers receiving welfare to take jobs— was *race population control*. As we will show, the act focused on two types: procreation-focused race population control and immigration-focused race population control. In this chapter, we examine how the act's provisions addressed the sentiment of many white political elites and other European Americans that the federal racial state must respond decisively to reproductive and immigration threats to the United States' white racial demographic status quo.

As a shape shifter, welfare racism has also created conundrums for groups who might be expected to unite in the struggle against it, such as white feminists. We will close this chapter by examining some reasons why many affluent white feminists failed to fight against the PRWORA, particularly the mandatory work provisions of the Temporary Assistance for Needy Families (TANF) program, despite the fact that these provisions threatened great harm to their impoverished sisters of color. As we will see, many feminists conflated their experiences and needs as members of the white middle class with those of impoverished mothers who receive welfare. Caught up in their ideological support for women's workplace participation, they capitulated to mandatory work requirements that took the freedom to choose caregiving at home over outside employment out of the hands of poor women. In effect, they either actively supported or capitulated to racial control policies aimed at the stereotypical "lazy welfare mother."

WELFARE REFORM AS IMMIGRATION-FOCUSED RACE POPULATION CONTROL

The PRWORA and the Color Line at U.S. Borders

As we noted earlier, in the 1990s many European Americans believed that AFDC was essentially a "black program." It is important to stress, however, that welfare racism is not simply a matter of black and white. Latino/a Americans and other people of color are subject to welfare racist stereotypes similar to those imposed on African Americans, albeit to different degrees.[1] The impact of welfare racism on Latino/a Americans, Asian Americans, and other people of color becomes evident when we examine the link between racism, immigration, and welfare reform built into certain eligibility provisions of the Personal Responsibility and Work Opportunity Reconciliation Act. Indeed, consistent with demographic changes in the United States, it has been suggested that the stereotypical face of the undeserving welfare recipient is changing from the African-American "welfare queen" to the "Hispanic immigrant."[2]

A major goal of the framers of the PRWORA was to eliminate what was considered to be the welfare inducement for immigration to the United States. In chapter 4 we discussed the threat to white supremacy posed not only by social movements for equality by African Americans, but by their physical or geographical movement within U.S. society as well. The PRWORA and other immigration-focused race population control efforts were initiated in the 1990s by political elites who were concerned with the threat to white supremacy posed by those coming into U.S. society.

To reduce the numbers of poor people of color migrating to the United States, the PRWORA made both legal and illegal "aliens" ineligible for most federal programs. Illegal aliens were declared ineligible for Temporary Assistance for Needy Families; legal aliens were deemed not eligible until five years after they entered the United States. It was also stipulated that the individual states and public housing agencies were to report names, addresses, and other pertinent information regarding noncitizen recipients to the U.S. Immigration and Naturalization Service. Clearly the act was intended to serve a major immigration control function.[3]

When it comes to race population control policies the avoidance of overtly racist language by racial state actors is necessary. The passage of legislation to implement such policies typically requires that the racial sentiment upon which they are based remain camouflaged or out of sight. Consequently, what are essentially racial arguments tend to be couched in cultural rather than biological terms.

Racializing "Foreign" Culture, Demonizing Dark-Skinned Immigrants

The racial state actors who framed the immigration provisions of the PRWORA treated certain immigrant groups as foreign "aliens" who threatened to undermine the core U.S. value of "self-sufficiency." The tone of the act, and the rhetoric surrounding it, implied that large numbers of racially different aliens were coming to the United States ill prepared or unwilling to work, expecting public assistance and other government benefits, and with the goal of being dependent on government and hardworking taxpayers.[4] As is the case in science fiction movies, "aliens" from abroad were clearly depicted as Other—creatures unlike the socially dominant "us."

Immigrants, however, tended not to be treated explicitly by racial state actors as a racial Other. This covert tactic is effective both as an offensive and defensive maneuver. That is, the "race card" can be simultaneously played and denied. The racial contours of welfare policies aimed at keeping "aliens" out of the country are clearly visible, however, in the writings of some conservative policy analysts. Nowhere was this racial sentiment communicated more clearly than in the writings of Peter Brimelow, author of *Alien Nation*,[5] a book extremely critical of U.S. immigration policy. In that book, Brimelow expresses concern that immigration is bringing about an unprecedented racial and ethnic transformation of U.S. society. His ultimate nightmare is, as he put it, "the fateful day when American whites actually cease to be a majority."[6] Brimelow expresses concern as well with what he sees as the tendency of recent immigrants of color to join the welfare rolls.

Four years prior to the 1996 enactment of the PRWORA, Brimelow, a senior editor for *Forbes* magazine, published a lengthy article in the *National Review* on the need for tighter immigration control in the United States. Indeed, Brimelow was part of "a panel of opinion makers" featured in a November 27, 1995, *Time* magazine article on immigration. That distinguished panel included a U.S. senator, a former New York City mayor, a former congressman and secretary of the U.S. Department of Housing and Urban Development, and a former congresswoman and then current chair of the U.S. Commission on Immigration Reform. Another senator thought the article important enough to enter into the *Congressional Record* two days later.[7] Brimelow's policy goals in this article and in *Alien Nation* were congruent with the immigration-focused race population control provisions that would be included in the PRWORA.

Understanding racism as a process requires examining the emotions that fuel it. While recent immigration-focused race population control policies have typically been justified by carefully selected facts and arguments regarding the benefits to society of restricting "our" borders, they are ultimately based largely on white racist sentiment toward people of color. As applied to certain groups of "aliens," that sentiment can be summed up as follows: "We don't want them here!" Such sentiment is vividly clear in the poem about Latino/a immigrants cited at the opening of this chapter.

This kind of overt racial sentiment is usually difficult to find in most public policy analysis, which tends to be couched in the methods of social science. With its claim to value neutrality, social science is even more skillful at camouflaging racial sentiment than are political elites.[8] This is obvious in painstakingly dispassionate "scientific" studies with patently racial agendas, such as Herrnstein and Murray's *The Bell Curve*.

Immigration Control through Welfare Denial

After the PRWORA was passed in 1996, welfare benefits were denied to impoverished immigrant families who needed help in their struggle to gain an economic foothold in U.S. society. We do not believe it was any accident that this attack on immigrants occurred in an era when, as was documented in great detail in *Alien Nation*, a high proportion of those who were coming to the United States were people of color from Latin America, the Caribbean, and Asia. After all, the very same racial state actors who incorporated highly racialized, New Paternalism–style, mandatory work and reproductive control provisions into the PRWORA also voted in its immigration control provisions.[9]

As an expression of welfare racism, the immigration-focused race population control provisions of the PRWORA parallel the racially exclusionary policies by which many impoverished African-American families were kept off the welfare rolls for many years. African Americans were not driven out of the United States in response to such expressions of welfare racism. Likewise, it is extremely doubtful that immigrants of color—legal or illegal—will avoid coming to the United States, or that many of those already here will leave because of being denied access to public assistance. After all, as with African Americans, there is no evidence that welfare motivates immigrants' decisions to come, remain, or go, despite the claims of Brimelow and other political conservatives.[10] Instead, immigrants of color will continue to come across U.S. borders, legally or illegally, and many will choose to stay. But without access to Temporary Assistance for Needy Families, those who arrive impoverished will be much more vulnerable to the kinds of labor exploitation by employers to which native-born people of color denied welfare have always been vulnerable. Moreover, as immigrants' desperation for work swells the pool of labor seeking low-wage jobs, this puts downward pressure on wages for all low-wage workers—including whites. It seems unlikely that racial state actors who framed the immigration provisions of the PRWORA did not know this. While Brimelow and others anguish and wring their hands over fear that the United States will cease being a "white nation," the federal racial state's denial of welfare to immigrants does serve the interests of European-American economic elites and other members of the dominant class who are looking for cheap domestic labor.

In the next section we will make clear just how potent racist sentiments and stereotypes were in shaping the PRWORA's welfare reform policies when they were combined with patriarchal and class-elitist images of mothers receiving welfare. We will explore how the act advanced procreation-focused race population control policy which, like immigration-focused race population control, helps to determine the racial structure and composition of U.S. society.

CONTROLLING AFRICAN-AMERICAN REPRODUCTION THROUGH WELFARE RACISM
Welfare Reform as Procreation-Focused Race Population Control

Congressional discourse preceding the passage of the Personal Responsibility and Work Opportunity Reconciliation Act of 1996 largely reflected concern with young, single, inner-city mothers. The act's proponents argued that such mothers need the incentive of restricted welfare benefits and strict time limits on welfare eligibility in order to motivate them to avoid out-of-wedlock pregnancies and to encourage them to marry. People from varying political viewpoints have drawn attention to the goal of procreation control in connection with the PRWORA and other recent welfare reforms.

From the political left:

 Ensuring that poor women do not reproduce has become one of the most popular welfare reform proposals of the 1990s.[11]

Susan L. Thomas, political scientist, Hollins University

From the political right:

Today everyone recognizes that dealing with births out of wedlock is the central issue of welfare reform.[12]

Douglas Besharov, American Enterprise Institute

And from those stuck in the middle:

I think they trying to say, trying to tell us to stop having kids.[13]

African-American mother receiving welfare, Boston

A "natalist perspective," which examines the social locations of different views concerning who should and who should not reproduce, provides a powerful lens through which to view the intersection of "race," class, gender, and the state. We agree with Susan Thomas that there is ample evidence that recent welfare reform legislation has been used to promote racially and class driven fertility control. First, low-income African-American women are disproportionately affected by such racial state legislation. Second, childbearing by low-income African American women in the United States has long been both devalued and discouraged by European Americans, having lost its economic value to dominant-class whites with the abolition of slavery. This observation is supported by an abundance of historical evidence on involuntary sterilization. Third, contemporary welfare discourse seems to be driven by racist stereotypes and negative controlling images of African-American women that stress their supposed hypersexuality, promiscuity, and enormous fecundity (e.g., the welfare queen).[14]

White Political Backlash and Black Motherhood as a Social Problem

Expressions of welfare racism have changed shape as the racial state moved away from public assistance policies of racial exclusion. When, in the 1960s, impoverished African-American mothers and their children could no longer be legally denied access to the welfare rolls and eligibility rules loosened, the rolls progressively expanded and their racial composition became visibly darker. It was seemingly inevitable, as part of the white political backlash fueling welfare racism, that mainstream political elites and policy analysts would become concerned with how welfare policy could be used to contribute to procreation-focused race population control. The latter had been openly called for by white supremacists for many years.

Because of their relative intensity and overtness, periods of white backlash are especially instructive of how procreation-focused race population control works, even under ordinary circumstances. Examining the white backlash process offers important insights into the dynamics of shifts in the racial state and its welfare policy discourse. An important public policy discourse accompaniment to the white political backlash that emerged in the 1960s was a gender shift in who was blamed for the intergenerational reproduction of poverty among African Americans.[15]

Emblematic of the white backlash that commenced in the 1960s was the so-called Moynihan Report on the changing composition of African-American families.[16] In this 1965 report, social scientist Daniel Patrick Moynihan, then a top official of the U.S. Department of Labor, presented Census Bureau statistics that documented African Americans' high rates of: 1) marital dissolution, 2) out-of-wedlock births, and 3) female-headed families.[17] The data Moynihan resented were not, however, the major source of the widespread controversy t his report generated when it became public. Indeed, in the decades since that report was published, the statistical portrait of African-American family structures has if anything become grimmer. The major locus of controversy was not the data in the report but their interpretation.

As the civil rights movement became more militant, the white political backlash began to manifest itself. By the mid-1960s, at a time when the Johnson administration was searching for a way to back away from its verbalized commitments to civil rights and economic justice,[18] the 1965 Moynihan report conveniently concluded that "at the heart of the deterioration of the fabric of Negro society is the deterioration of the Negro family."[19] With this conclusion Moynihan provided members of the Johnson administration and other racial state actors with the social science–legitimated ideology that they needed to redirect the blame for the poverty status of many African Americans from white racism to the supposed pathology of their families.[20]

As we discussed in chapter 2 in connection with negative controlling images of African-American women, the specific target of blame in the Moynihan Report was the assumed dysfunctionality of "black matriarchy."[21] As both a family structure and process, the black matriarchy was assumed to be dysfunctional because it was different from the two-parent nuclear family considered normative by most European Americans and was seen as incapable of providing proper socialization of and control over rebellious young African-American males.[22] By its targeting of supposedly overly assertive and independent African-American female family heads at a time when the feminist movement in the United States had begun an important resurgence, the Moynihan Report also served an important early gender backlash function.[23]

With the publication of the Moynihan Report, the social science notion of a "culture of poverty," which blamed poverty on the values of the poor, was racially re-gendered. The report shifted attention away from the supposedly deficient values of African-American men as the chief cause of black intergenerational poverty and social pathology[24] to the deficient values of the "culture of single motherhood."[25] This revised culture of poverty focus would come to dominate the thinking of New Paternalism advocates and helped to frame provisions of the PRWORA.

A key ingredient in the re-gendering of the culture of poverty was the slavery-rooted, gendered racist controlling image of sexually promiscuous and irresponsible African-American women. In this image, free of and unburdened by either sexual or marital controls, low-income African-American women were seen as constituting a threat to the entire society's normative order and moral character. Not surprisingly, the principal solutions that political elites developed for the problem of the culture of single motherhood were public policy–pressured birth control and marriage.[26]

By the 1990s, a major goal of welfare reform was the reassertion of racial, gender, and class control over impoverished African-American mothers and, through them, control over their children. Concern with the effect of the culture of single motherhood on black children was most crudely put to one of this book's coauthors in the late 1980s at an informal social gathering held at the Philadelphia home of an African-American social worker. The host calmly informed his guests that, if he had his way, his solution to the problem of unsupervised, low-income, inner-city African-American children would be to smash their heads against the pavement.[27]

Examining the Discourse over Unwanted "Breeding"

Our brief discussion of the Moynihan Report and its significance reveals the importance of viewing welfare racism in the broader context of race relations during a given historical period. In any historical period, welfare racism, like other forms of racism, is a process of racial control.[28] Analyses of social structures and processes can be framed around two key questions posed by distant observers: 1) *Who is there?* and 2) *What are they doing?*

Our discussion in chapter 5 of New Paternalism welfare policies directed at mothers of color, and the racist stereotype-driven mandatory work provisions of the PRWORA to be discussed later in this chapter, primarily focus on the second question of "What are they doing?" The other question, "Who is there?," is relevant to analyzing policies aimed at procreation-focused race population control, as well as policies aimed at immigration-focused race population control. Underlying these forms of race population control and the welfare policies to which they give rise is the racist sentiment that certain people of color should not be in a certain place in society, should not reside within its borders, or should not exist at all. Immigration-focused race population control and procreation-focused race population control are opposite sides of the "Who is there?" control coin.

While often presented by their advocates as if they were ostensibly concerned with the issue of overpopulation, U.S. reproductive control policies have tended to be fashioned by white male elites who impose their ideas about who should not reproduce on women from groups judged to be inherently inferior and undesirable.[29] Unfortunately, like many other expressions of white racism, procreation-focused race population control initiatives are often barely visible as such. Racial state actors are skilled at camouflaging them. Consequently, the racial sentiment underlying policies that might prove controversial and be contested by racially subordinated groups can be difficult to detect, much less to analyze or to oppose.[30] How explicit procreation-focused race population control advocates are in their proposals varies with both the nature of race relations at a particular point in time and with how deeply the proposals penetrate the political policy formation process.[31]

In the early 1960s the white segregationist Louisiana legislature pushed pro-creation-focused race population control legislation as a part of a white political backlash against court orders to desegregate public schools. But as the civil rights movement grew in strength and spread nationally, overt mention of procreation-focused race population control faced quick and powerful responses. Such measures could not be proposed without considerable risk of a counterattack. With the emergence of white political backlash against the movement later in the 1960s, the climate for race population control discourse and initiatives changed again. By the early 1970s, as the backlash was blossoming nationally and after the Moynihan Report had recast the problem of widespread African-American poverty as a problem of single motherhood, physicians engaged in widespread involuntary sterilization of low-income African-American women.[32]

A revealing example of the raw racist sentiment and stereotypes around which procreation-focused race population control proposals are sometimes organized is J. Philippe Rushton's *Race, Evolution, and Behavior*. Published in 1995, only a year after Herrnstein and Murray's controversial *The Bell Curve*, Rushton's book likewise employed the methods of scientific racism to provide ideological justification for racially targeted human eugenics. Both of these books exploited one of the U.S. society's oldest and most powerful racist stereotypes, the low intelligence of African Americans.

What made Rushton's book so effective in stirring up white racist animus and as a justification of racist human eugenics was its pseudoscientific linking of the stereotype of low African-American intelligence to the stereotype of African-American hypersexuality and fecundity. From his statistical analysis of race data, Rushton concluded that Mongoloids (or Asians) and Caucasoids (or "whites") had "the largest brains," while "Negroids" (or "blacks") had the greatest reproductive capability.[33] Consistent with popular welfare racist stereotypes of African-American mothers having at state expense large numbers of children that they do not properly care for, Rushton argued that because of genetics, different races employ divergent reproductive and caregiving strategies to ensure their survival. Those high in intelligence (Asians and whites) have fewer children and make a higher "parental investment" in the children that they do have. In contrast, less intelligent "blacks" have more children and make less parental investment in them.[34]

Rushton's ideas and research did not emerge in isolation. Like much racial human eugenics research in the United States, his work was funded by The Pioneer Fund, a nonprofit foundation more than six decades old that makes grants of about a million dollars each year to academicians. Most of the researchers receiving foundation funds have dedicated themselves to establishing that racial differences in intelligence and personality are genetically based. Academicians whom the foundation has funded include not only Rushton, but William Shockley, Arthur Jensen, and Michael Levin.[35] The racist beliefs of these "scholars" is often evident from their public pronouncements. For example, in an interview with a reporter for *Rolling Stone* magazine, Rushton made the following summation of his research findings in response to the charge that he is in fact arguing that whites are racially superior to black people: "It's a trade off: more brain or more penis. You can't have everything."[36]

The Pioneer Fund's grant recipients lobbied for changes in immigration-focused race population control as a form of racial human eugenics.[37] They have also been vocal in advocating procreation-focused race population control policies targeted against welfare recipients. Stanford University's William Shockley, a longtime advocate of the view that African Americans are genetically inferior in intelligence to whites, "proposed sterilizing welfare recipients." Shockley's "Bonus Sterilization Plan" of cash incentives for low-I.Q. welfare recipients provoked controversy in the 1970s and 1980s.[38] City College of New York's Michael Levin, who complained that "the country is being overrun by people who don't work and have illegitimate children," blamed African Americans for many of society's social problems. His solution to these problems was simply stated: "End welfare . . . End welfare." According to Levin, ending welfare, by "ceasing to subsidize them . . . would automatically have a very excellent demographic effect."[39]

We believe that, while seldom expressed so overtly and publicly, such racial sentiments lie not far beneath the surface of much of the mainstream political discourse that has surrounded welfare reform. Periodically, however, such sentiments rise to the surface among political elites. The year before the PRWORA was passed in 1996, New Jersey Governor Christine Todd Whitman told a London publication about the "jewels in the crown" game she said was played by young African-American males, in which they compete to see who can impregnate the most women.[40]

In 1996, as welfare reform legislation moved through Congress, the Reform Party founder and presidential candidate, Ross Perot, provided television celebrity David Frost with his imitation of how black men approach reproduction. Note the multiple racist stereotypes that Perot mobilized:

> I'm just kind of a dumb dude who never finished the fourth grade. I'm wandering around the streets with my baseball hat on backward and $150 tennis shoes I knocked another kid out to get. I'm looking for real trouble to prove that I am a man. Well, how do I define what

a man is? I define what a man is from the rap music I hear. . . . A man is defined in that culture as a breeder who gets the woman pregnant and then she gets welfare.[41]

This kind of overt racist stereotyping of black sexuality has occasionally leaked out of the mouths of political elites in one or another context. For example, a few years later, commenting on the likelihood that George W. Bush would become the Republican presidential nominee for the 2000 election, Utah's Republican Senator Bob Bennett stated that "unless George W. steps in front of a bus or some black woman comes forward with an illegitimate child that he fathered within the last 18 months," he would be the Republican nominee.[42]

The implications of such sentiments for procreation-focused race population control policy on the part of racial state actors and other political elites were apparent in pressures for mothers on the welfare rolls to use the Norplant contraceptive device.

Norplant: The New Technology of Procreation-Targeted Race Population Control

> If you don't want government in your business, then you don't have to [ask the government for] any money.
>
> Marion Barry, mayor-elect, Washington, D.C., 1994

In the 1990s, some political elites expressed interest in how new technology could be used to control the reproductive activities of poor women, especially welfare recipients. Forced sterilization was for many decades the most common form of reproductive control targeted at welfare recipients unfortunate enough to find their bodies under the control of racial state institutions or the courts. In the early 1990s, political elites would perceive the new Norplant contraceptive device as a functional equivalent.[43]

The Norplant contraceptive device consists of six capsules containing contraceptive chemicals that are placed under a woman's skin, usually in the upper arm, and are left in place for five years. Approved by the federal Food and Drug Administration in December 1990, the device is so effective that it has been described as being "a form of temporary sterilization."[44] Four years later Norplant had become so widely accepted that even Marion Barry, an African-American who was then mayor-elect of Washington, D.C., advocated its mandatory use by some mothers receiving welfare.[45]

It quickly became clear how the availability of Norplant would figure into contemporary welfare policy discourse. Two days after its approval, Norplant was the subject of a *Philadelphia Inquirer* editorial titled, "Poverty and Norplant: Can Contraception Reduce the Underclass?" Its focus was specifically on the "black underclass." This editorial's title and focus were emblematic of the extent to which the impoverishment of the racially oppressed had been reframed from a problem requiring a War on Poverty to provide "equal economic opportunity" in the 1960s to one requiring racial human eugenics in the 1990s.[46]

Consistent with changing race relations and the legacy of the white political backlash of the 1960s, in three decades the focus of many political elites had shifted from helping poor African Americans to keeping "them" from procreating. The type of proposal that would only be expected by someone with the racist reputation of Professor Shockley a decade earlier now bore the editorial imprimatur of one of the nation's most respected and widely read newspapers. Although the *Philadelphia Inquirer* later issued a printed apology for its editorial in response to protests, support for the ideas it contained came from magazines such as *Newsweek* and *The New Republic*, as well as newspapers such as the *Richmond Times-Dispatch*. The head of population sciences of the Rockefeller Foundation wrote a supportive letter that was published by the *Washington Post.*[47]

In *Killing the Black Body*, Dorothy Roberts had the following to say about the significance of the *Philadelphia Inquirer* editorial:

> The *Inquirer* episode inaugurated a new wave of birth control politics, with Norplant at the center. . . . Lawmakers across the country have proposed and implemented schemes not only to make Norplant available to women on welfare but to pressure them to use the device as well.[48]

The Norplant wave did indeed spread quickly. Roberts reported that within the first two years of the device's availability, twenty measures were proposed in thirteen states "to implant poor women with Norplant." Among the proposals was one by David Duke, who as a Louisiana gubernatorial candidate proposed that mothers on the welfare rolls be paid a yearly grant of $100 to use the device.[49]

In Roberts's view, a driving force behind such procreation-focused race population control initiatives was white fear that the changing racial demography of the country threatened white racial supremacy. Roberts also expressed concern that in the future, with the development of more sophisticated and less detectable birth control methods (e.g., Depo-Provera injections and contraceptive vaccines), the potential for procreation-focused race population control policies will increase.[50]

Given the preoccupation of many political elites with "breeding" by the African-American poor, race population control measures such as the mandatory use of Norplant must have seemed logical. In 1994, at a hearing on some of President Clinton's ideas on welfare reform, Daniel Patrick Moynihan, by then a

U.S. senator and acknowledged welfare expert, expressed deep concern with the "ominous" trend toward uncontrolled out-of-wedlock births. Moynihan stated that "if you were a biologist you would be talking about speciation here"— meaning that the high rate of such births could somehow result in the creation of a whole new species. He was joined in this bizarre conclusion by West Virginia Democratic Senator Jay Rockefeller.[51]

Family Caps: Enforcing Birth Control through Increased Impoverishment

As proposals for the use of reproductive technology were becoming more racialized in the hands of political elites, so was welfare reform legislation more generally. Along with proposals for the use of Norplant, racial state actors called for "family caps" or "benefit caps" intended to discourage mothers reliant on welfare from having additional children by denying the very small monthly increases in cash benefits they usually received with the birth of an additional child.[52] Since a mother receiving welfare would have to support an additional child without additional aid, the effect of the family cap would be to reduce the amount of public assistance available to her and her children. Family cap advocates thought that this would provide the negative financial incentive that they assumed poor mothers needed to avoid additional pregnancies and births.

The most famous and influential family cap policy was the "child exclusion" provision enacted in 1992 as part of the New Jersey Family Development Act.[53] The New Jersey legislation illustrates the power of racialized images of the reproductive activities of mothers receiving welfare in the formation of contemporary welfare policy. The preoccupation with the reproductive activities of African-American women and, more specifically, the notion that "Black women increase their number of children to increase their government assistance checks," are pervasive. They appear everywhere from white supremacist literature[54] to European-American political elites' welfare discourse.

As we have shown, people of color are not immune to the internalization of the pervasive white racist stereotypes that abound and that are an integral part of racist culture (e.g., African-American U.S. Supreme Court Justice Clarence Thomas publicly portrayed his own sister as a "welfare queen").[55] Although the architect of the New Jersey bill, Assemblyman Wayne Bryant, was an African-American state legislator who claimed to be acting in the best interests of low-income African Americans, the NAACP Legal Defense and Education Fund filed an administrative complaint with the U.S. Department of Health and Human Services charging that the New Jersey Family Development Act's additional child provision was racist not only in its consequences but in its intent as well.[56]

The NAACP brief argued that the provision would have a racially discriminatory impact, in that the New Jersey AFDC population was overwhelmingly

African American and Latino/a-American. These two groups would therefore bear the brunt of its harmful effects.[57] The NAACP administrative complaint also quoted public hearings and news articles in which Bryant made statements suggesting that the policy was targeted at African Americans in an attempt to change their behavior. For example, as evidence of "the racial character of the additional child provision," the brief cited the following statement by one of the act's supporters in the New Jersey state Senate. "It would be very difficult for a white to raise (welfare issues). . . . A white raising the same question would be called a racist." The senator concluded that Bryant "is doing all of us a favor by focusing the debate."[58] Indeed, it would have been difficult for a European American to escape charges of racial bigotry if he or she had used the very explicit language Bryant did in spelling out the act's racially targeted intent. Bryant's champion in the state Senate apparently accepted the erroneous premise that African Americans can neither internalize white racist beliefs and sentiments nor express such beliefs about other African Americans.

The authors of the NAACP administrative complaint also argued that the New Jersey legislation was based on negative racial stereotypes that portray people of color as "sexually irresponsible, inclined to bear children outside of marriage, and encouraged by AFDC benefits to bear numerous children."[59]

These stereotypical traits are linked to the offensive idea of a moral deficiency among African-American and Latino welfare recipients which causes them to reject marriage, legitimate births and limited family size. It is this racial stereotype of a lack of "family values" that is rarely applied to poor whites and which is often blamed for the poverty of the Latino and African-American communities.[60]

Legislating Male Patriarchy through Gendered Welfare Racism

Our focus on the racist premises upon which the New Jersey Family Development Act was built should not obscure its sexist premises. The act was designed to enforce what feminist writer Mimi Abramovitz refers to as a "family ethic," built on a traditional, heterosexist patriarchal ideology, which holds that women are best suited for certain social roles vis-à-vis men and have a proper gendered "place."[61]

In Abramovitz's view, there has been a shift over time from familial patriarchy to a social patriarchy enforced by the welfare state. The shift that Abromovitz depicts is consistent with welfare rights activist Johnnie Tillman's description of the dilemma of impoverished women. She describes a mother's need to rely on welfare as trading "'a' man for 'the' man."[62] As *the* man, the racial state regulates the family, reproductive, and work lives of poor women to

reinforcing patriarchal domination [handwritten]

ensure that they serve the interests of both patriarchy and capitalism. By making welfare benefits hard to get and impossible to live on, the racial state puts economic pressure on poor women to marry and become "dependents" of husbands, and reinforces patriarchal domination of family life. Such economic pressure is also used by the racial state to get mothers reliant on welfare to limit their fertility, and to render them more useful in meeting capitalists' need for an easily exploitable and plentiful pool of low-wage labor.[63]

When viewed from Abramovitz's perspective on how the lives of women are regulated by state policies, the New Jersey Family Development Act clearly served gender control functions, as well as the racial control functions we have stressed. Gender control is inherent in the act's "child exclusion" provision that financially penalized AFDC families for an added child and in its "bridefare" provision that financially rewarded AFDC mothers who got married. Such provisions were initiated with the purpose of changing "the size and composition" of the state's AFDC families and to impose "family ethics" on recipients. Operating under the patriarchal assumption that all women must enter into enduring relations with men, the law pushed for marriage to promote "women's traditional role in the family as the key to economic success."[64] Reflecting not only this gender domination but social class dynamics as well, the chief legislative sponsor of the Family Development Act was an affluent African-American male legislator.[65]

promote marriage + less kids → gender subordination [handwritten]

The heterosexist subtext of New Jersey state actors' efforts to promote marriage through the New Jersey Family Development Act should not be lost on the reader. Discourse emphasizing the desirability of marriage for poor women has been common among political elites and was embedded in the rationale for the Personal Responsibility and Work Opportunity Reconciliation Act of 1996. It is noteworthy that conservatives' attacks on the "family values" of single welfare-reliant mothers have typically employed much of the same pro-family, pro-marriage rhetoric used in their attacks on the gay, lesbian, bisexual, and transgender community. Not surprisingly, many of that community's impoverished members have been subject to harassment and discriminatory treatment under patriarchy-oriented welfare reform.[66]

While the New Jersey Family Development Act was widely touted as a national model for family cap welfare reform legislation, such legislation had an unintended consequence that would severely challenge the conservative political consensus. The early evidence on the New Jersey legislation's impact suggested that it did not lower birthrates among mothers receiving AFDC but did prompt a significant increase in the number of abortions by women on welfare.[67] That increase set off an early alarm about family cap provisions for religious conservatives and other pro-life groups, who later broke with conservative political elites at the national level to oppose similar family cap provisions for the PRWORA. Let's take a closer look at those provisions and the problems they posed for welfare reform advocates in the U.S. Congress.

The PRWORA as Procreation-Focused Race Population Control

By the 1990s the sentiment for procreation-focused race population control policies seemed to be very broad, if not very deep. While the racial sentiment behind support for such policies remained just beneath the surface, the successful pursuit of such policies required that their distinct racial tinge remain hidden. As Dorothy Roberts put it, "After the commotion over the *Inquirer* article . . . few politicians are likely to link birth control specifically to Black poverty, even if that is their intention."[68] The consequences of political pressures to camouflage procreation-focused race population control measures can be seen by observing how, as the PRWORA moved through the congressional process toward enactment, racial state actors' legislative language became less explicit in targeting specific social groups reducing the political risks that overt racial intent involved.

This camouflaging process is evident if one compares the explicit race and reproduction language of an initial bill introduced by Republicans into the U.S. House of Representatives, "The Personal Responsibility Act of 1995,"[69] to the House- and Senate-enacted bill signed by President Clinton, the "Personal Responsibility and Work Opportunity Reconciliation Act of 1996."[70] An examination of these and related documents confirms that as the welfare reform policy formation process proceeded, its legislative products lost their explicit markings of racially targeted procreative population control. As we will show, what ended up as the PRWORA clearly began as a birth control measure fueled by racist stereotypes of "welfare mothers" as oversexed and superfertile black women. However, in stark contrast to its race population control origins, by the time the welfare reform bill was actually signed by President Clinton its content appeared to be "race blind" and not especially focused on the reproductive behaviors of welfare recipients.

Procreation-focused race population control policies are particularly difficult to detect when, as is the case with federal welfare reform, their provisions are not always explicitly targeted toward that goal. In such cases, the true intent of a specific piece of legislation may be apparent in other sections of the bill, especially its rationale statement. The stated rationale of the Republicans' proposed Personal Responsibility Act of 1995 was "To restore the American family, reduce illegitimacy, control welfare spending and reduce welfare dependence."

The 1995 bill's first title was "Reducing Illegitimacy." It began with a "Sense of Congress" section that listed more than three pages of statistics and other findings about the prevalence, correlates, and consequences of so-called "illegiti-macy."[71] Moreover, the first set of statistics cited in the bill referred to the "illegitimacy" rate of "black Americans." It noted that rates of "illegitimacy" increased from 26 percent in 1965 to 68 percent "today." Recall that 1965 was the year the Moynihan Report was published, and when what Susan Thomas refers to as the "culture of single motherhood" became the favored explanation for the high rate of poverty among African Americans. Further, consistent with the racial and gender control implications of the Moynihan Report and its con-cern with the dysfunctions of "black matriarchy," the House bill noted that "the likelihood that a young black man will engage in criminal activities doubles if he is raised without a father."[72] *bill based on statistics done in 65' → racist stereotypes based on*

The Personal Responsibility Act of 1995 also contained a number of repro-duction control–related provisions. These included federal mandates to deny benefits to unwed teenage mothers and to prohibit benefits for additional chil-dren born to a mother receiving welfare. In addition, the individual states were allowed to deny benefits to mothers ages eighteen through twenty. The states were also to receive funds to implement their own programs to reduce "illegiti-macy." The bill specified that funds could be used to remove children from financially destitute mothers and place them for adoption or in orphanages.[73] From its rationale and these provisions it could reasonably be concluded that the goal of the Republican bill was to reduce births among poor women, with par-ticular emphasis on impoverished African Americans. It seems unlikely that someone reading the bill's "Sense of Congress" section could conclude that the legislative intent was simply to reduce the availability of public assistance.

The welfare reform bill that was actually passed by both the House and Sen-ate and signed into law by President Clinton did not place nearly as much emphasis on nonmarital births. In contrast to the earlier House bill, the Personal Responsibility and Work Opportunity Reconciliation Act of 1996 did not contain a specific title on what was referred to as "illegitimacy," and "illegitimacy" statis-tics were not as prominently placed as part of its rationale. The PRWORA contained few reproduction-focused provisions; rather, the emphasis was placed on mandatory work requirements.

The individual states were granted two options by the PRWORA. They could deny benefits to teenage mothers if they wished, and they could impose family caps barring additional aid to children born to welfare recipients. Neither the Sen-ate welfare reform bill that had to be reconciled with the House bill, nor the final version of the bill signed by President Clinton contained race-specific statistics.[74] The "race-blind" Senate version may have reflected, at least in part, the fact that U.S. senators are generally accountable to a more racially diverse political con-stituency than is the case for many members of the U.S. House of Representatives.

↳ make it race blind b/c of constiuents

The reproductive choice implications of the House bill were obvious to African-American lawmakers. For example, Democrat William L. Clay of Missouri said of the bill's goal to reduce the number of out-of-wedlock births to teenage girls by denying them cash assistance: "If that doesn't work, what's next? Castration? Sterilization?"[75] Ignoring such criticisms, the House Republican leadership was successful in getting the proposed Personal Responsibility Act of 1995 through the House with major procreation control provisions. However, it also inadvertently mobilized an unlikely alliance of pro-life, pro-choice, and other normally divergent groups. Such groups followed the issue of welfare reform to the Senate, where they felt that they could assert more political leverage over bill provisions.[76]

In addition to opposition from both pro-life and pro-choice forces, the House bill faced significant opposition from political elites who represented larger and more racially diverse constituencies. Even before the House bill was passed and taken under consideration by the Senate, President Clinton promised to veto it if it were approved as is by that body.[77] In addition, there was strong opposition from the very influential Republican governors who, although they helped shape the proposed Personal Responsibility Act of 1995, complained that it placed too many federal restrictions on the individual states. To address this concern, the Republican governors submitted a new proposal to the Senate that would allow states to decide whether to use federal funds to provide welfare benefits to unmarried teenage mothers, children born to women already receiving welfare, and legal aliens.[78] The welfare reform bill approved by the Senate's Finance Committee reflected the governors' wishes.

Presidential campaign politics were yet another powerful force that helped shape what the Senate called its "Work Opportunity Act of 1995" welfare reform bill.[79] Senator Bob Dole, who at the time was seeking the Republican presidential nomination, had expressed his inclination to eliminate the most contentious procreation control provisions from the Senate Republican version of the welfare reform bill. However, Senator Phil Gramm, a major Dole rival for the nomination, claimed that Dole had agreed to the demand of conservative Republicans that single welfare-reliant mothers be denied, as Gramm put it, "more and more cash . . . for having more and more children on welfare."[80]

Phil Gramm was not the only Republican senator who advocated welfare reform as a way of reducing births to low-income single mothers. The importance of welfare reform as a mechanism of procreation control targeted at this group was evident in a statement made by Senator Spencer Abraham of Michigan. In defending against an attempt to remove from the Senate welfare reform bill the House provision to financially reward states for reducing the number of out-of-wedlock births, Abraham protested: "If we strip this provision from the bill, we will have to go back to our constituents and explain why we did not do one significant thing to address the No. 1 social problem in America today."[81] That provision was passed.

To the consternation of conservative Republicans, however, a coalition of Democrats and moderate Republicans defeated the provisions that would have forbidden states from using federal funds for benefits to teenagers who had babies out of wedlock and for mothers on the welfare rolls who had additional children. In response to the defeat of these two reproduction-related measures some conservative policy analysts concluded that welfare reform had failed. For example, Robert Rector of the Heritage Foundation not only lamented that the Senate bill was "a complete failure" but accused the Senate of voting "to keep in place a system that promotes illegitimacy and destroys marriage."[82] Again, for conservatives, the procreation control provisions of welfare seemed just as important as or indeed more important than the abolition of the AFDC program and the entitlement to public assistance it provided, benefit time limits, mandatory work requirements, and other stringent non–reproduction-related provisions of the bill.

Procreation-Focused Race Population Control Policy, Patriarchy, and Class Dominance

In keeping with our racism-centered perspective, we have primarily discussed the reproduction-related provisions considered in the congressional legislative process as forms of procreation-focused race population control. Of course, things are not quite that simple. As we have seen, those policies were formulated largely by affluent European-American men to control what they considered to be the wayward reproductive behavior of low-income African-American women. A more complete view of the procreation-focused race population control function of welfare reform can be had only by examining the intersections of class, "race," and gender.

Feminist scholars operate from the premise that even *within* racial and class segments of U.S. society, male decision makers impose their will on the reproductive choices of women, making use of the patriarchal structure of families, religion, and the state. In brief, when it comes to reproduction control policies, male patriarchy is viewed as being paramount. Mimi Abramovitz, for example, has explained how gender was associated with what she referred to as the "attack" on the Aid to Dependent Children program, later AFDC, during the post–World War II period. In the 1960s, the dramatic expansion of AFDC rolls, together with the outlawing of restrictive eligibility rules, resulted in a reduction in racial state actors' ability to "regulate" the lives of poor women by excluding those whose sexual and reproductive behavior was said to render them "undeserving." Consequently, if welfare was to continue to serve its patriarchal functions, adjustments would have to be made.[83]

The patriarchal functions of the PRWORA are evident in its pro-marriage provisions and the political discourse that surrounded the act. In the logic of conservative political elites and policy analysts, poverty is not a major cause of single motherhood. Instead, the politically correct, conservative policy logic is that single motherhood causes poverty. Under this ideologic, poverty is not seen as an outcome of class dynamics resulting in economic inequality, and thus a structural problem requiring the intervention of the state. Instead, poverty is held to be an individual morality problem whose solution requires that women who have children marry or, in the case of divorce, remarry.[84]

Earlier we referred to a comment by welfare rights activist Johnnie Tillman, who in the mid-1970s explained why welfare is a women's issue: "AFDC is like a supersexist marriage. You trade in *a* man for *the* man." Tillman also had a keen response to the widely accepted belief that mothers receiving welfare have additional children to get extra welfare benefits. "Having babies for profit is a lie that only men could make up, and only men could believe."[85] In Tillman's view, welfare policy was an expression of patriarchal state power intended to make single mothers suffer for their independence from in-house male dominance by a husband.

Of course, procreation-focused race population control policy is also a class issue. Human eugenics movements have often been predicated on the assumption that certain social classes of people, presumed to be genetically deficient, should not be encouraged or, indeed, allowed to reproduce. A mid-1920s American Eugenics Society slogan, "Some people are born to be a burden on the rest," seemed to anticipate contemporary European-American attitudes toward welfare recipients.[86] Consistent with this class-centered view is sociologist Thomas Shapiro's assertion that "a major achievement of the capitalist class has been to incorporate population policy within the welfare state."[87]

Dwight Ingle's *Who Should Have Children?*, published in the early 1970s, is an example of the sentiment and ideology behind class-based eugenic appeals linked to welfare. Although Ingle advocated a program of "positive" (i.e., noncoercive) human eugenics, his thinking revealed ideas and emotions consistent with dominant class-based attacks on welfare recipients. In *Who Should Have Children?* the size of the welfare state and reproduction by women on welfare were identified as social problems that could be addressed by "selective population control."[88] Ingle argued that "a substantial percentage of steady welfare clients should not have children." Not only would the size of the welfare state be reduced by encouraging such women not to procreate, but in Ingle's view there would be improvement of the genetic makeup of the average child.[89] Building

*prevent more
welfare babies*

on the racist and class-elitist stereotype that mothers on the welfare rolls "have additional children in order to increase the size of their welfare check," Ingle proposed that they be provided incentives "to remain childless."[90]

In *The Legacy of Malthus*, human eugenics critic Alan Chase offered an insightful analysis of both the centrality of class to eugenics movements and of similarities in the dynamics of racial and class oppression. Chase argued that inferred biological differences (e.g., genetic dispositions for feeblemindedness or criminality) are exploited by such movements to promote reproductive control targeted at the lower classes. This is done by dividing people generally thought to belong to the same "race" into distinct class-specific racial groups. Chase argued that the foundation upon which such races are constructed is really class. Following this logic, Chase maintained that human eugenics movements, from early-nineteenth-century Europe to contemporary U.S. society, have been aimed primarily at the ethnic and racial majorities of nations, not their minorities.[91]

Unfortunately, in his focus on class, Chase's analysis of what drives human eugenics movements failed to attach significance to the fact that their leadership has typically come overwhelmingly from white males. More generally, Chase minimized the importance of patriarchy and white racial hegemony in shaping the thinking of people leading those movements. Consequently, he did not really address the significance of the triple oppression (i.e., racism, sexism, *and* classism) that is imposed upon and experienced by poor women of color by racial human genetics. However, Chase's analysis did make a key point about class relations as *an* important (Chase would say *the* important) driving force behind coercive human eugenics movements.

Both race- and class-based procreation control sentiments are strongly embedded in the work of one of contemporary welfare reform's most influential intellectuals, Charles Murray. Perhaps no single individual was more influential in framing the contemporary welfare reform discourse that led up to the PRWORA. Murray's success came from his ability to simultaneously appeal to racist, class-elitist, and patriarchal sentiments. He accomplished this by evoking the specter of out-of-control black "illegitimacy" and an emerging "white underclass."[92]

Both of these images infused a 1993 newspaper essay which seemed to serve as an ideological and policy blueprint for the House Republicans' proposed Personal Responsibility Act of 1995. As was true for the Personal Responsibility Act, Murray's essay focused on race-specific statistics on "illegitimacy." In his essay, however, Murray added a new twist when citing the statistics for white mothers. Having called attention to the high rate of out-of-wedlock births for black mothers, Murray seemed to dismiss this as "old news." The new news he wanted to stress in his essay was the dramatic increase in "illegitimacy" among white mothers which "threatens the U.S." with the emergence of a "white underclass."[93]

As he did as a coauthor of *The Bell Curve*,[94] Murray offered a Social Darwinian solution to this "illegitimacy" crisis. From his perspective, solving the problem of out-of-wedlock births required that "the state stop interfering with the natural forces that have done the job quite effectively for millennia." The needed economic penalties to discourage single motherhood could best be restored by ending all economic support for poor mothers.[95] Murray went on to make proposals identical to those offered later in the Personal Responsibility Act of 1995. These included an end to AFDC payments and withdrawal of subsidized housing and any other benefits for which poor single mothers were eligible. As was articulated in a provision of the House welfare reform bill, it was anticipated that such economic support cuts would result in many single mothers placing their babies for adoption. Consequently, as we noted earlier, Murray proposed that "the government should spend lavishly on orphanages."[96] In brief, the Republicans' proposed Personal Responsibility Act of 1995 seemed to have felt Murray's influence not only in its rationale and statistics, but in specific policy proposals as well.

While some might argue that Murray's arguments do not evoke racist sentiments, his position fits quite comfortably into white supremacist thought. For example, in an analysis of white supremacist literature, Jessie Daniels made reference to a National Association for the Advancement of White People article that cited Murray's 1984 highly publicized book attacking AFDC, *Losing Ground*, in justification of that organization's position that the "welfare quagmire" could be solved by not allowing mothers receiving welfare to reproduce. Those who had additional children would face forced sterilization or the lost of welfare benefits.[97]

There was, however, a significant difference between the House Republicans' bill and Murray's proposals. While both were committed to the patriarchal concern of providing incentives for poor women to marry, Murray argued that toward encouraging this end, unmarried mothers should not be entitled to make any claims against their children's biological fathers for child support. In contrast, the House welfare reform bill contained a provision to pressure single mothers to cooperate in establishing the paternity of their children's fathers. Such information was to be used in the enforcement of policies aimed at increasing the numbers of fathers who paid child support. But despite some differences, both Murray's proposals and the proposed Personal Responsibility Act of 1995 seemed to be driven not only by racial undercurrents, but by class and patriarchal considerations as well.

"What Are They Doing?"

In this chapter we have thus far explored how recent welfare reform policy was informed by concerns with immigration-focused race population control and procreation-focused race population control. Both forms of control address the analytical question "Who is there?" However, the PRWORA was also concerned with the work effort of welfare recipients. In that instance, consistent with white racist stereotypes of lazy African-American welfare recipients, racial state actors and other political elites were concerned with the second question emanating from concerns with racial control: "What are they doing?"

This concern with work effort was also closely linked to conservative political elites' efforts to frame welfare receipt as welfare "dependency," which they often depicted as "enslaving" poor mothers. Their attacks on dependency led some members of Congress to draw Social Darwinian analogies between welfare recipients and animals, similar to the animal analogy suggested by references to welfare recipients' "breeding" at which procreative race population control policies were aimed.[98] During the House debate on the Republican-proposed Personal Responsibility Act of 1995, Florida Representative Dan Mica spoke in support of the need for mandatory work requirements by comparing welfare recipients to alligators:

> Mr. Chairman, I represent Florida where we have many lakes and natural reserves. If you visit these areas, you may see a sign like this that reads, "Do Not Feed the Alligators." We post these signs for several reasons. First, because if left in a natural state, alligators can fend for themselves. They work, gather food, and care for their young. Second, we post these warnings because unnatural feeding and artificial care creates dependency. When dependency sets in, these otherwise able-bodied alligators can no longer survive on their own.
>
> Now, I know people are not alligators, but I submit to you that with our current handout, nonwork welfare system, we have upset the natural order. We have failed to understand the simple warning signs. We have created a system of dependency.[99]

Throwing her support behind mandatory work requirements, Wyoming Republican Representative Barbara Cubin likened welfare recipients to wolves in the same House debate:

> My home state is Wyoming, and recently the Federal Government introduced wolves into the State of Wyoming, and they put them in pens and they brought elk and venison to them every day. This is what I call the wolf welfare program. The Federal Government

introduced them and they have since provided shelter and they have provided food, they have provided everything that the wolves need for their existence. Guess what? They opened the gate to let the wolves out and now the wolves will not go. They are cutting the fence down to make the wolves go out and the wolves will not go. What has happened with the wolves, just like what happens with human beings, when you take away their incentives, when you take away their freedom, when you take away their dignity, they have to be provided for. The biologists are now giving incentives outside of the gates, trying to get them out.[100]

As Congress moved to approve mandatory work requirements as a condition for the receipt of welfare by allegedly indolent mothers, the racism and classism that helped to shape such provisions of the Personal Responsibility and Work Opportunity Reconciliation Act of 1996 also seemed to immobilize many affluent white feminists, who might have been expected to oppose such punitive requirements for their gender and racial control impact on impoverished mothers of color.

"MISS ANN" REFORMS THE "WELFARE QUEENS"

Ain't I a Woman? Part II

Two basic assertions of the radical black feminist or womanist perspective that we discussed in Chapter 2 are: 1) white racism must be a central focus of any analysis of the oppression of women of color, and 2) the feminist movement itself was constructed on a racist foundation. Given the extent to which welfare and its controlling images have been racialized, if these assertions are valid (and we think they are), they raise serious questions about the amount and quality of support that impoverished welfare-reliant mothers might expect from more affluent white women when public assistance comes under attack. Let us take a closer look at the role of affluent white feminists in the debate over passage of the legislation that abolished the Aid to Families with Dependent Children program.

In chapter 2 we took note of the womanist critique of feminism. In questioning the relevance of what some deemed the "white" feminist movement to their lives, radical black feminists or womanists revisited Sojourner Truth's "Ain't I a Woman?" challenge. Does the contemporary feminist movement appreciate the work, family, and reproductive issues that are particularly important to women of color? Or does it only see issues and stereotypes that are most relevant to the eyes of those who are white and, on average, more socioeconomically privileged? A great racial and class divide became evident early on in the contemporary feminist movement when, to their surprise, white feminists were informed that "Black women don't need liberating. Black women are already liberated."

For black feminists, stating that African-American women are already liberated was not tantamount to rejecting all the goals of feminism. For progressive African-American women, it was an attempt to dislodge white feminists from a position of racial arrogance predicated on the erroneous assumption that the overall social predicament and needs of African-American and European-American women are the same. It was a rejection of the notion that European-American women, as the presumed vanguard of women's liberation, knew what African-American women wanted and could speak for them. In brief, black feminists challenged affluent white feminists' racial and class-based patronizing attitudes and ignorance.

Black Women's Labor Force Attachment

For many affluent white feminists, women's liberation meant the opportunity to avoid full-time child caregiving in favor of choosing paid employment outside of the home. In stark contrast, because of the low socioeconomic status of most African-American families, there has been a long tradition of black women working for wages outside of the home, by necessity and not choice.[101] The jobs typically available to black women—for many years limited largely to working for white employers in low-paid domestic service or agriculture positions—were considered to be pure drudgery, not something to celebrate. On average, black women have historically been more likely than white women to be participants in the labor force.[102] And when white women have needed to work for wages, they have not faced white racist discrimination. Most white women have thus been able to do better than to take "black jobs."

Ironically, for black women one positive consequence of employment outside the home was to raise their status within their families. That is, even when they brought the most meager economic resources home to help meet family needs, they enhanced both their bargaining power with their male partners and their gender autonomy. Yet the dual effects of racism and poverty resulted in other African-American women becoming single mothers who had to function outside the gender-stratified, two-parent nuclear family. Independence was thrust upon them, and they had to make heroic efforts to combine caregiving and labor force participation if they and their children were to survive and thrive.

As many white middle-class and upper-middle-class feminist professionals came to see employment outside the home as inherently of value for women, their advocacy of birth control seemed to be built on the idea that liberated women curtailed their fertility. For impoverished and racially oppressed African-American women, however, the issue was not simply their ability to curtail their

feminist

white racism

fertility but their ability to exercise control over their own reproductive activities rather than have others control them.

Their racist and class-elitist views on work, family, and reproduction led many affluent white feminists to actively support key provisions of the PRWORA, despite their disproportionately adverse effects on impoverished women and children of color. It should be noted, however, that it was not just their relatively privileged locations within the social structure that resulted in significant support for welfare reform by many elite European-American women. There was also a huge ideological divide that was fostered by the contrasting controlling images that have been used to keep European-American women and African-American women subject to male dominance and also racially divided.

feminists strayed from AA women

Historically, more affluent European-American women have been subject to controlling images holding that as women they were too morally pure, weak, and vulnerable to leave their patriarchally erected pedestals for unchaste, manly work worlds. On the other hand, African-American women, poor or not, have long been subject to images portraying them as unfeminine, non-ladylike, and immoral. During the suffrage movement, European-American women chose to keep great distance between themselves and what most European Americans saw as "licentious and immoral" African-American women, lest they risk their own "virtuous, goddess-like" images being tarnished and their movement being lost.[103]

As we noted in chapter 2, African-American feminists found their own womanliness left unacknowledged in some of the rhetoric of this nation's early—and even later—feminists, who compared the problems of "women" with those of "whites" and thus implied that women were white and "blacks" were "male."[104] The combination of gender and racial oppression faced by African-American women long went ignored. Even by the last third of the twentieth century, many white feminists were still ignoring the significance of the triple oppression that poor black women face.

The indifference of many affluent white feminists was not budged, even as the separate equity-oriented goals of the civil rights movement and the feminist movement were challenged by the late 1960s welfare rights movement, which mandated that racial and gender concerns be simultaneously dealt with in the pursuit of economic justice. Nor was it later moved by pleas from civil rights organizations like the National Association for the Advancement of Colored People (NAACP) that drew attention to the race of those who would most be affected by welfare reform. Just six months before President Clinton signed the PRWORA, Wade Henderson, director of the NAACP's Washington, D.C., office, stated: "Many African Americans remember that 'states' rights' were code words for the denial of basic civil rights. We are concerned that this history not return in the context of welfare reform."[105] The NAACP was joined in opposition to the welfare reform proposals by the National Council of Negro Women and other African-American civil rights groups.

No Help from "Ms. Ann"

In the collective memory of African Americans, white "Miss Ann," like her white "Mr. Charlie" male counterpart, rarely proved herself to be a friend or ally. As a symbol, "Miss Ann" was instead, an oppressor, a controller, and an exploiter. Her treatment of African Americans was aimed at bolstering and sustaining her own racial and class privilege. When Miss Ann did see African-American women as women, she generally exploited them as women. She functioned essentially as a white female patriarch who exploited African-American women as free or grossly underpaid mammies for her children or as domestic housekeeping help. *still happening today*

It is not surprising that impoverished mothers and children of color—when threatened in the 1990s with the loss of the frayed safety net that AFDC provided—could not count on support from overtly racist white women, be they Miss, Mrs. or Ms. But what could they expect in the 1990s from women considered to be nonracist feminists? Were the actions of most white feminists in response to punitive welfare reform policies going to be consistent with those of sisters in solidarity across color lines, or those of a "Ms. Ann" update of the old Miss Ann racial icon? Gwendolyn Mink captured what happened:

> Welfare reform did not bear directly on the lives of most white, middle-class feminists, and so they did not mobilize their networks and raise their voices as they have in defending abortion rights or protesting domestic violence. When they did enter the debate, many middle-class feminists prescribed child support and wage work as alternatives to welfare. This echoed policymakers' claims that "real" welfare reform is to be found in the patriarchal family economy and in mothers' work outside of the home.[106] *support welfare reform indirectly*

To be sure, many white middle-class feminists did work tirelessly, if ultimately unsuccessfully, to stop the Personal Responsibility and Work Opportunity Reconciliation Act of 1996 from becoming law.[107] For example, just weeks before President Clinton signed the PRWORA, representatives of women's and civil rights groups rallied with members of the Suffolk Welfare Warriors on the steps of New York City's city hall to urge Clinton not to sign the bill. At that protest, Anne Connors, the president of the New York City chapter of the National Organization for Women, expressed both outrage toward and a sense of betrayal by the president.[108]

However, as Mink has argued, an important reason that the PRWORA passed was the failure of other white feminists, including those in Congress, to value the importance of choice for poor women on welfare.[109] Impoverished mothers with family caregiving responsibilities were not given any choice with regard to the decision of whether or not to work outside of the home. Instead, they were mandated to set aside caregiving activities for employment, or face losing even the meager and time-limited aid that welfare reform provided through the act's Temporary Assistance for Needy Families program.

Mink suggests that white racism subtly played an important part in this failure of many white feminists to question the PRWORA's mandatory work requirements for mothers on the TANF rolls, most of whom were women of color. Too many middle-class white feminists operated under the guiding assumption that employment outside the home, which they believed contributed to gender equality for themselves, would bring equality to all.[110] This "racism-blind" feminist position showed little sensitivity to the African-American experience. Mink points out that in opposition to the "popular feminist claim that women earn independence, autonomy, and equality through wages," poor African-American women have found more inequality than equality in economically exploitative work that keeps them wage-poor. Consequently, for African-American women, "the rights to have and care for their children—to work inside the home—have been touchstone goals of their struggles for equality."[111]

It should be noted, however, that blindness to racism cannot entirely explain support for mandatory work requirements among mainstream white feminists. Influenced in their thinking by this society's racist culture, many of these women no doubt share with European-American males the racist belief that welfare recipients—most likely to be seen as African Americans—are lazy and undeserving, and therefore need to be made to work through punitive welfare reform measures.

By bringing racial inequality and patriarchy into the analysis, a radical black feminist or womanist perspective provides a necessary counterpoint to the equity and mainstreaming focus of an ideology that justifies work-targeted welfare reform as a natural outgrowth of changing work norms for women. That is, white feminists' stress on the liberating value of employment for women implies that it is no longer acceptable for single mothers to receive cash assistance to stay home to take care of their children. Indeed, any priority that welfare-reliant mothers would place on caring for their children at home over engaging in outside employment could be perceived as antifeminist. Moreover, supporting public assistance that allows mothers to remain at home, in the face of the widespread belief that welfare promotes the indolence and other highly racialized pathological behaviors of "welfare queens," could be an embarrassment to the feminist cause.

Racism and class elitism within feminism have blinded many affluent white feminists to the historical and contemporary realities faced by impoverished women of color. For example, in contrast to the notion that employment is liberating for women, it should be noted that whites have *always* expected African-American women to seek employment outside of the home. The feminist ideology that supports wage earning by all women can be used to justify the attack on mothers receiving welfare, but it cannot explain those attacks. Mink concludes that by conflating "their own *right* to work outside the home with poor single mothers' *obligation* to do so" many affluent white feminists, through their support of the racism-driven mandatory work provisions of the 1996 welfare reform bill, forced millions of poor women into a form of "involuntary servitude."[112]

The image of the lazy and promiscuous "welfare queen" and other racist controlling images of African-American women worked very effectively in the political assault on AFDC. They worked so well that many affluent white feminists and other liberal opponents of the PRWORA accepted the mandatory work provisions, and were inclined to express outrage only over what they predicted would be the bill's harmful impact on poor children. On the other hand, the predicament of mothers forced to rely on Temporary Assistance for Needy Families was assumed to be self-inflicted. Their alleged work, family, and reproductive behaviors were thought to be indefensible. Consequently any concern expressed was often only for the innocent child victims of welfare reform, not for despicable welfare queens.[113]

Indeed, some opponents of welfare reform had so completely internalized or been caught up with such racist controlling images—either out of contempt for poor single mothers or fear of having the "legitimate" concerns of feminists tarnished, or both—that they failed to see mothers receiving welfare as women or welfare reform as a women's issue. Consequently, although the targets of punitive welfare reform were clearly impoverished mothers of color, many affluent white feminists failed to fight a piece of landmark welfare reform legislation which, in appearance at least, de-gendered the issue.

With the de-womanization of impoverished women of color and the de-gendering of welfare reform as an issue, the feminist argument that women should be financially compensated for child care and other caregiving work within the home was no longer heard.[114] In chapter 3, we noted that arguments as to the importance of mothers remaining in the home to care for their children were made in connection with the Progressive Era mothers pension movement. But it was generally assumed that the mothers to be given pensions to stay at home and thus "serve the nation" were white. Likewise, when workers' widows were given public assistance under the Social Security Act so they could care for their children, this was instituted at a time when eligible widows were overwhelmingly white. In the 1990s, with the successful racialization of welfare, there were few concerns about the PRWORA's infringement on the maternal responsibilities and contributions of poverty-stricken welfare recipients.[115] There was, for example, little concern that forcing mothers receiving TANF to find employment outside of the home was unlikely to end their poverty status, and that by doing so they would actually be punished for childbearing and child-rearing. Ultimately, even the strategy of opposing the Personal Responsibility and Work Opportunity Reconciliation Act because of the harm it threatened for children was abandoned by many feminists and other liberals. Members of Congress ignored the ominous prediction of the federal Office of Management and Budget that passage of the welfare reform bill would add one million children to the poverty rolls, and overwhelmingly voted for the bill.[116]

In brief, many affluent white feminists who supported the PRWORA by their actions or inactions functioned more as racial and class oppressors than they did as "sisters" united in the struggle for the rights of all women. Their support was were very much in keeping with the popular "Miss Ann" icon of the African-American historical experience, with one major difference: instead of overt hostility to poor women of color, there was largely indifference. To them the answer to Sojourner Truth's "Ain't I a Woman?" challenge was a quiet, but definitive, "No."

7
AFTER AFDC
AND THE RETURN
OF STATES'
RIGHTS-ERA
WELFARE RACISM

When the federal welfare program began with ADC (Aid to Dependent Children) in 1935, there were a lot of ways states could deem under their discretion whole groups of people ineligible for welfare. . . . My concern is now we are returning to this discretionary environment. Of course I recognize this is 1999, we are not in 1935 and we have come a long way in this society. Still, we also know there is hard evidence of present-day housing and labor discrimination. I just wonder, as we return to an environment of discretion have we offered enough protection to make sure that welfare recipients are not discriminated against in terms of race?

Susan Tinsley Gooden,
political scientist,
Virginia Tech University

52:2 52:1

racial state has returned enormous discretion to the individual states. It began this devolution of authority by granting many states waivers to the Social Security Act to experiment with their own welfare programs in the late 1980s and early 1990s. The federal racial state then institutionalized the individual states' authority to form and implement their own welfare programs by passing the Personal Responsibility and Work Opportunity Reconciliation Act of 1996. In doing so, the federal racial state effectively shifted back to the welfare policy approach of the pre-1960s states' rights era.

For decades, local and state governments adapted their welfare policies and practices to prevailing patterns of white racial hegemony. Particularly, but not exclusively, in the South, this concession to states' rights frequently led to the exclusion of African-American and other families of color from public assistance. Until the civil rights and welfare rights movements successfully challenged welfare racism in the streets, legislative bodies, and the courts in the 1960s, public assistance did not become an "entitlement" in real terms for many families of color.[1] As in the states' rights era, the current policy approach allows states and localities license to express welfare racism—often thinly camouflaged as "race-blind" policies and practices—with relatively little federal oversight or effective constraints.

Recent evidence indicates that the so-called race-blind welfare reform policies and practices initiated in the 1990s have a disproportionately adverse effect on members of racially oppressed groups. In many instances these ostensibly race-blind policies and practices have in fact functioned to impede, deny, or reduce the welfare eligibility and benefits of impoverished women and children of color. In some instances, racial discrimination against applicants or recipients has been quite open and direct. The bulk of this chapter is dedicated to showing that welfare racism is thriving in rural and urban settings across the nation.

We are also concerned about the failure of mainstream welfare reform monitoring groups to address these important matters. Their negligence helps to conceal the continuity between welfare racism as we have shown it to be expressed in the states' rights era and the ways in which it is being expressed in the present. Most important, their failure deprives welfare rights organizations of the kinds of knowledge needed for effective educational campaigns, legal and legislative action, grassroots organizing, and social protest.

Let us begin by examining signs that welfare racism is alive and thriving.

WELFARE RACISM AFTER AFDC

The Persistence of Welfare Racism

An overview of expressions of welfare racism accompanying recent welfare reforms is informative. Our evidence is necessarily somewhat limited, given that only a few researchers have chosen to acknowledge the possibility of, much less engage in systematic research on, welfare racism. To their examples we have added others drawn from news media accounts and reports by advocacy groups.[2] But there are clear signs that the same racist attitudes continue to persist that contributed to the abolition of the Aid to Families with Dependent Children program. Indeed, there are a variety of forms of welfare racism that are worthy of the attention of policy analysts and advocacy groups.

Signs of welfare racism include not only individual state and local institutional policies and practices, but also discriminatory acts by welfare caseworkers and employers of welfare recipients or former recipients. African Americans have been affected, as well as Latino/a Americans, Asian Americans, and Native Americans. As we will see, welfare racism has not only caused harm to individual adult recipients of color and their families, but has had negative effects on entire communities of color.

Racial Barriers to People of Color Leaving the Welfare Rolls

One of the most significant phenomena appearing in the post-AFDC era is the changing racial composition of the nation's welfare rolls. Welfare reform researchers have taken little notice of this phenomenon,[3] leaving it to journalists to bring it to public attention. The "darkening" of the welfare rolls and the increasing concentration of welfare caseloads in large cities were addressed in a 1998 article that appeared in the *New York Times* some two years after passage of the PRWORA. That newspaper surveyed fourteen individual states and New York City, whose welfare caseload was larger than that of any state other than California. Together, these fourteen states and New York City accounted for almost 70 percent of the nation's welfare recipients.

Calling its survey findings "new, little-noticed and as yet largely unexplained," the *New York Times* article reported the gist of its findings and some of their implications:

> As the welfare rolls continue to plunge, white recipients are leaving the system much faster than black and Hispanic recipients, pushing the minority share of the caseload to the highest level on record. . . . Some analysts warn that the growing racial and urban imbalance could erode political support for welfare, especially when times turn tight.[4]

While the author of that article did not state this directly, he seems to have been implying that the erosion of (already low) political support for welfare could be tied to racist attitudes, and that such attitudes can be expected to *increase* in the near, post-AFDC future.

In March 1999, an article by the Associated Press described the results of an AP survey of the changing racial composition of individual states' welfare rolls.[5] Citing caseload declines by race, the survey noted that in thirty-three of the forty-two states studied, there had been a drop in the proportion of white (as compared to black and Latino/a) welfare recipients since 1994, a year when AFDC caseloads peaked nationally. The AP survey also found that in fourteen out of sixteen "big states," which together contained 76 percent of the nation's welfare recipients, whites had left faster than blacks and Latinos/as.

The 1999 AP survey also drew attention to what was happening in individual states with significant Native American populations, as whites left the welfare rolls more rapidly than people of color. For example, over a five-year period, the percentage of North Dakota's welfare roll made up of Native Americans increased from 28 to 56, and that of South Dakota rose from 54 to 77.[6] As we will discuss later, many Native Americans living on reservations in such states have been severely disadvantaged in moving off welfare rolls by the scarcity of jobs.

One especially dramatic illustration of racial differences in welfare reform outcomes at the individual state level was provided by the *Columbus Dispatch*. Like many states, Ohio experienced a rapid overall decrease in its welfare rolls under its welfare reform policies. In 1994, Ohio's rolls were 56 percent white and less than 40 percent black. By 1998, the demographic pattern had reversed. The proportion of white welfare recipients had dropped to 44 percent, while blacks made up 51 percent of recipients. Ohio is a predominantly white state. But by 1998, only 1 in 66 whites in Ohio was on the welfare rolls, compared to 1 in 7 blacks.[7]

Yet another example is provided by a study of welfare rolls in Illinois conducted by journalists at the *Chicago Reporter*.[8] In that state, welfare rolls declined significantly between 1997 and 1999, from approximately 191,000 down to 111,000. In July 1997, whites were 26.6 percent of the rolls. By 1999, whites were down to 19.3 percent. While the percentage of Latinos/as hovered around 10.5 percent over this two-year period, the proportion of blacks increased from 61.6 percent of recipients to 69.2 percent.

The *Chicago Reporter* study shed new light on the dynamics surrounding the changing racial composition of the Illinois rolls. Of those who left the welfare rolls between 1997 and 1999, some 40 percent of whites left because they were earning enough money to be ineligible for benefits, compared to only 27 percent of people of color.[9] The latter were more likely to have their cases closed out because they were sanctioned for violating welfare department rules, or otherwise failed to comply with requirements (e.g., by missing appointments or failing to submit paperwork). Only 39 percent of whites had their cases closed for this reason, as opposed to 54 percent of recipients of color. A survey of low-income Illinois families by Work, Welfare, and Families and the Chicago Urban League, in which the vast majority of recipients were people of color, not only found that most Temporary Assistance for Needy Families (TANF) leavers had their cases closed for noncompliance or administrative reasons, but noted that "those families without work or TANF experience extreme hardship and have great difficulty in providing household basics such as housing, groceries, or utilities."[10]

These changes in racial composition of the welfare rolls were generally consistent with national figures compiled by the U.S. Department of Health and Human Services.[11] For example, between 1993 and 1999, the percentage of the national welfare caseload made up of white families dropped from 38.3 to 35.9 percent. In the same period, the percentage of the rolls made up of black families rose, going from 36.6 percent in 1993 to 39 percent in 1999. Latinos/as' proportion on the rolls rose from 18.5 to 22.2 percent; Asians from 2.9 to 3.4 percent; and Native Americans from 1.3 to 1.5 percent. Nationwide, the presence of Latinos/as, Asians, and Native Americans on the rolls grew even faster than that of African Americans. The Latino/a presence grew the fastest.[12]

No definitive reasons were given by the New York Times or the Associated Press that would explain the growing racial imbalance in the welfare roles that their surveys detected, although several possibilities were presented. Many families of color are severely economically disadvantaged, are more likely than whites to be living in extreme poverty (below 50 percent of the official poverty line), and, in comparison to poor white families, are more likely to include small children. They are thus often in even greater need of family income assistance and child care. The concentration of many poor mothers of color in central city areas, away from most job opportunities, together with, frequently, a lack of educational credentials (e.g., a high school diploma) or English language skills, can make it difficult for such mothers to gain employment. Mothers of color are particularly handicapped in responding to pressures to move "from welfare to work" because, since many experience extreme poverty and isolation in racially segregated central city neighborhoods, they are likely to face more barriers to employment than whites.[13] In brief, the same racism-related obstacles that increased their chances of being poor decrease the likelihood of their being able to leave the welfare rolls.

Acknowledging these obstacles and unfavorable conditions, the New York Times speculated that perhaps people of color have faced less pressure from caseworkers to leave the rolls. This explanation does not seem plausible, given the evidence on racial differences in who is likely to face welfare reform sanctions.

Being sanctioned for violation of welfare department rules and removal from the rolls are intended to be punitive measures. Having their cases closed out and being forced to appeal for reinstatement interrupt the flow of meager funds to impoverished families and can create new stresses, even as the outcomes of their reinstatement requests are anxiously awaited. We are left to wonder why these punitive measures were disproportionately directed at recipients of color in Illinois, and why they were demonstrably less likely than whites to leave the rolls due to earnings from employment.

Caseworker largesse as an explanation for the changing racial composition of the welfare rolls also seems somewhat counterintuitive, given decades of racialization of welfare as an issue and the negative racist stereotypes that have accompanied the adoption of punitive welfare reform policies across the country. These are stereotypes to which not only the members of the public and political elites apparently subscribe. Such thinking surely influences many local welfare officials and caseworkers. Indeed, we will shortly provide several examples of local welfare agencies' racially discriminatory treatment of clients. Within the realm of our definition of welfare racism, these are welfare racist *practices.*

It is likely that not only have mothers of color indeed been heavily pressured to abandon welfare for employment, but that they have more obstacles to finding employment and being hired than do whites. They, unlike whites, must contend with racial barriers that are reserved by many white employers for people of color. Their increased presence on the rolls may also in part be a reflection of the fact that mothers of color who leave the welfare rolls are more likely than whites to return to the rolls within a year, as has been found for two individual states, Arizona and Wisconsin, and in the Cleveland, Ohio, area.[14] The role that racial discrimination may play in making it difficult for women of color to support their families while off welfare or to remain employed has yet to be assessed by welfare reform researchers.

Denial of the present-day salience of racism by European Americans is the norm. Thus, it is gratifying that the *New York Times* was willing to speculate that the growing racial imbalance in the rolls may in part reflect "possible discrimination by employers or by landlords in neighborhoods near jobs."[15] This possibility, which was mentioned only in passing, deserves serious attention. For, despite the existence of civil rights and fair housing laws, there is substantial evidence of racist practices being directed at people of color by employers and landlords. Indeed, persons of color who are actively seeking work from white employers or who seek housing in predominantly white residential areas are more likely to experience these racist practices than those who remain in racially isolated situations and do not intrude on "white space."[16]

Race-Based Sanctions and Family Cap Policies: Racial Control Persists

At the same time that impoverished women of color face substantial barriers to participation in the labor force and achievement of economic "self-sufficiency," punitive welfare reform policies make it difficult for mothers who must rely on public assistance to avoid benefit reductions or even loss of benefits.[17] Some insights into the relation between the racial designations of welfare recipients and punitive sanction policies have been provided by researchers interested in the factors that influenced individual states' adoption of such policies.[18]

Joe Soss and his colleagues have taken note of the "devolution revolution" that occurred in the 1990s, wherein the federal racial state returned to the states' rights approach to welfare policy and gave the individual states great discretion in formulating and administering their own welfare reform policies.[19] Under the PRWORA, individual states were encouraged to fashion sanctions to punish those who violated the rules they established for recipients receiving Temporary Assistance for Needy Families. The approach to sanctions taken by individual states has varied. They may entail, for example, the removal of families from the rolls altogether. Or families may be denied some portion of their aid, temporarily or permanently. Or there may be restrictions placed on how much additional aid will be granted if family size increases. Many states have adopted family caps that deny or restrict additional aid to families in which mothers become pregnant and bear children while on the welfare rolls. Family caps are especially punitive because they mean less TANF aid per capita in a family, since the aid provided must be shared by more family members.[20]

Between the time that the Personal Responsibility and Work Opportunity Reconciliation Act passed in 1996 to December 1999 the national welfare rolls declined by 49 percent.[21] Soss and his colleagues observed that decline in the nation's welfare rolls was closely associated with harsh policies that removed whole families from welfare caseloads, often before they were in any position to achieve self-sufficiency. They also noted, however, that the rate at which welfare caseloads had declined was not uniform across the United States. In some states the decline exceeded 60 or even 80 percent. Welfare reform researchers have established that the stricter the sanctions policy, the greater the decline in the rolls.[22] What factors, Soss and his colleagues asked, determined the likelihood that an individual state would adopt strict sanctions policies? Was there, they asked, "a systematic relationship between race and the adoption of welfare reforms"?[23]

After examining various factors possibly associated with policy adoption, these researchers found that an individual state's adoption of the family cap (restricting the amount of aid given when an additional child is conceived and born after a mother is on the welfare rolls) "is most strongly associated with the percentage of recipients who were African-Americans."[24] Although other factors such as having low unemployment rates and a politically conservative citizenry were also found to be important, the welfare rolls of those individual states adopting family caps and other strict sanctions policies were most likely to be disproportionately African-American. One racial control function of punitive sanctions is fulfilled by forcing mothers of color to seek employment. This is an especially important matter in individual states where tight labor markets and worker shortages are putting pressure on employers to raise wages.

In the words of Soss and his colleagues:

> Racial hostility backed by conservative ideology and a growing availability of jobs will lead to a more aggressive approach to welfare reform. Most critically, our findings suggest that in particular a recipient population that is disproportionately composed of African-Americans will be a more vulnerable population, more likely to be subject to the imposition of the harshest sanctions policies. The connection between the racial composition of the recipient population and the adoption of the family cap also suggests that racial hostility and vulnerability are factors affecting whether this particularly harsh policy will be adopted.[25]

In subsequent research, Soss and his colleagues found that the racial composition of the individual states' welfare rolls was correlated not only with harsh sanctions and family cap policies, but also with time limits on cash assistance that are shorter than the maximum five-year limit for federal assistance under TANF that was established under the PRWORA. The strict enforcement of short time limits is another way of pushing mothers of color into the labor market.

Moreover, they found that the presence of Latinos/as on the welfare rolls also influenced individual states to adopt harsh policies: "Indeed, the effects are both independent and additive, suggesting that restrictive TANF policies are most likely to be adopted in states where *both* Hispanics and African Americans receive aid in large numbers [italics theirs]."[26] Soss and his fellow researchers conclude that with the return of authority over public assistance to the states, "the states have returned to some very old and troubling patterns of behavior."[27]

Soss and his colleagues' findings reveal the continuity between recent welfare reform policies and research findings from years ago linking the racial composition of the welfare rolls to the restrictiveness of welfare eligibility policies and benefit generosity levels.[28] There is historical continuity to the welfare racism embedded in individual states' policies that cannot be ignored. The consequences of this welfare racism continue unabated today.

Welfare Racism Devolves to the Local Level: "Diversion" Practices in New York City

The "devolution revolution" returned authority and discretion over welfare policies to the individual states. But consistent with the "welfare localism" of the states' rights era, the states have in turn granted local welfare officials more and more say over the conditions under which public assistance will be extended or denied.[29] And here too welfare racism has played a defining, albeit usually subtle, role.

New York City offers a case in point. While the actions of New York City officials were widely reported upon in the media, the distinctly racial impact of that city's restrictive TANF eligibility policies went largely unreported and ignored even by policy critics. New York City is a racially diverse urban center in which poverty is widespread, particularly among families of color.[30] Three of every ten children in the city are in families that receive welfare assistance. According to a 1998 *New York Times* article on the changing demographics of welfare caseloads, only 5 percent of New York City's TANF caseload were white; 33 percent were black and 59 percent were Latino/a.[31] Given the high poverty rates and rates of welfare reliance among people of color, any adverse effects resulting from punitive welfare policies in New York City had to disproportionately fall upon them.

In the spring of 1998, New York City began to convert welfare offices into "Job Centers," whose acknowledged goal was to "divert" people away from receiving public assistance.[32] Such activities were consistent with the welfare reform policies advocated by Lawrence Mead and other conservative policy analysts who served as consultants and advisers on New York City's welfare programs.[33] The reader will recall that Mead, a New York University political scientist and nationally known advocate of punitive welfare reform, views poverty in highly racialized terms, arguing that "black culture" is the main force behind "nonwork" and "welfare dependency."

Through diversion activities, New York's Republican mayor, Rudolph Giuliani, vowed that "by the year 2000, New York will be the first city in the nation, on its own, to end welfare."[34] He applauded the fact that the approval rate of applications for TANF was being cut in half in those Job Centers that had opened. As is typically the case with diversion strategies, city welfare officials did not seek information on what happened to the families who were diverted.[35]

The new Job Centers intentionally erected a complicated series of bureaucratic hurdles aimed at reducing the likelihood that impoverished mothers and their children would succeed in gaining cash assistance. The horrific process through which mothers were put has been described as "government lawlessness":

> When they first arrive at a job center, receptionists routinely tell
> them that there is no more welfare, that this office exists solely to

see that they get a job, that if they miss any appointments their applications will be denied, that emergency food stamps and cash grants don't exist, that there is a time limit on benefits—without explaining that they can apply for Medicaid or food stamps. [Authors' note: These are both need-based entitlement programs, are not linked to receipt of welfare, and have no time limits.] Receptionists also tell people who arrive after 9:30 AM that they must return another day. If they aren't already deterred, applicants are given a five-page preliminary form to fill out. They must return the next day to get an application. They are fingerprinted, undergo several interviews and are then directed to meet with a financial planner and an employment planner. The financial planner tries to deter people from applying by directing them to churches, charities, and food pantries. At various stages, applicants are orally denied benefits or told they are not eligible to apply, but they receive no written notice of denial or their right to appeal the decision.[36]

As a consequence of such practices, thousands of desperately poor families were forced to apply again and again.[37] Many simply abandoned the TANF application process, often not knowing they were eligible for cash assistance, and having been denied the opportunity to make application for Medicaid and food stamps.

While a federal court found some of the city's diversion tactics to be illegal and demanded that city officials comply with the law,[38] the remedies ordered by this branch of the racial state did not address the racism embedded in New York City's welfare practices or the harmful effects of these practices on impoverished women and children of color who were diverted from receiving aid.

Racially Exclusionary Practices in Idaho

Such denial of poor people of color their rights to information, applications, and assistance is not, of course, limited to New York. Let us move our attention to a drastically different setting—the largely rural, predominantly white, western state of Idaho. By 1998, this state had reduced its welfare rolls by the astonishing figure of 77 percent through the implementation of harsh welfare reform policies. Idaho adopted an extraordinarily restrictive two-year lifetime limit on TANF benefits. The benefit levels for poor families were penurious, limited to $276 per month regardless of family size.[39] A study by Tufts University's Center on Hunger, Poverty, and Nutrition described Idaho as "the state whose policies were most likely to worsen the economic condition of the poor." As the center's research director put it, "Idaho has effectively made itself the worst place in the nation to be poor."[40]

Although Idaho is overwhelmingly white, with people of color making up less than 10 percent of the state's population, in 1998 17.4 percent of the state's TANF recipients were people of color. Most of those recipients, reflecting the composition of Idaho's poor, were Latino/a or Native American; the state's African-American population is quite small.[41] It must be noted here that Idaho is said to possess a particularly intolerant environment when it comes to people of color. The state is, for example, the home of numerous right-wing extremist groups, including highly visible white supremacist organizations. This environment could not help but affect the treatment of poor families of color needing assistance, including assistance with health care.

There has been a sharp drop in Medicaid's coverage of poor families nationally, concurrent with states' implementation of welfare reform policies in the 1990s.[42] Since this drop in health care coverage appears linked to racialized welfare policies and their effects on people of color, we include this example here. Given that people of color are overrepresented in the individual states' poverty populations, this decline in Medicaid participation has exacerbated existing racial disparities in access to health care. Children of color who are living in poor families are especially vulnerable to health problems and thus are disproportionately harmed by a lack of Medicaid coverage.

In 1997 the federal racial state expanded Medicaid to provide health care coverage for the children of those low-income working parents who, while ineligible for standard Medicaid, could not afford to purchase private health care insurance. This included many children of single mothers who moved from welfare to work. By 1999, however, the new Children's Health Insurance Program (CHIP) had enrolled only a fraction of the 3 million to 4 million children estimated to be eligible nationally.

Welfare racism can be considered one important reason for this underenrollment, if racist practices uncovered in Idaho prove to be widespread.[43] A community organization, Idaho Citizen's Action Network (ICAN), sent twenty-five families of different racial backgrounds to three different regions within that state to apply for benefits under CHIP. The organization's purpose was to determine what, if any, barriers to receiving aid these families might encounter, and whether families were treated equally regardless of color. All of the families sent to apply were first carefully screened to make sure they were eligible for CHIP. Twelve of the families chosen were white, ten were Latino/a, two were Native American, and one was African-American. In describing this community group's experiment, one journalist put the outcome this way: "The already dizzyingly complicated and often humiliating process of applying for aid was markedly more so for applicants of color."[44]

treatment different vs. minority

The group found that unless the applicants asked about the CHIP program by name, no information about it was offered. Access to caseworkers was limited to daytime office hours, which discriminated against working parents. Numerous applications and forms, and often four or more trips to the office, were required to determine eligibility for aid. Three weeks after initially requesting assistance, only eight of the twenty-five applicants had even managed to secure a meeting with a caseworker for an application appointment. Six of these applicants were white.

The organization's research revealed overt expressions of welfare racism:

• Unlike white applicants, Latinos/as had to submit documentation of marriage and citizenship before receiving application appointments. Nearly all documents used in the application process were in English (one exception was a flier warning applicants not to bring their children to the office), and bilingual translators were often not available.

• White applicants reported that they heard disparaging remarks about Latino/a families while they were in the department offices. Most of the twenty-five applicants reported to researchers that they believed welfare department members practiced racial discrimination and that they looked down upon people based on their appearance and their poverty.

• Applicants of color were at times openly subjected to intimidation: "Hispanic applicants were threatened with deportation. One applicant had her [17-page] application torn up when the caseworker determined it was inaccurate, and another was required to verbally report on her sexual history in a public waiting room," supposedly in order to establish the exact date of her child's conception.[45]

In the western states, Latinos/as have long faced racial discrimination and exclusion when it comes to welfare. This fact has for the most part gone little noticed and little studied.[46] In Idaho, however, ICAN managed to generate a good deal of publicity for its findings. Indeed, the U.S. Department of Health and Human Services' Office of Civil Rights pronounced the findings to be "alarming" and intervened. Idaho's Department of Health and Welfare was forced to make changes in its handling of CHIP, but there is no sign that other individual states have moved against racial disparities in state-administered health care coverage for poor people of color.

Sabotaging "Welfare to Work" Efforts of Black and Latino/a Recipients in Florida

In Florida's welfare caseload black people have long outnumbered whites and Latinos/as. Reflecting national trends, the proportion of blacks and Latinos/as on the Florida rolls has increased. From 1996 to 1999, 68 percent of whites left the rolls, compared to 60 percent of blacks and 48 percent of Latinos/as. In 1999, blacks receiving welfare in the state of Florida outnumbered whites and Latinos/as by a ratio of more than 2 to 1. The darkening of the welfare rolls was especially apparent in and around Miami where, by 1999, blacks and Latinos/as together made up 94 percent of the welfare population.[47] As in New York City, ostensibly "race-blind" but punitive welfare policies cannot help but disproportionately adversely affect people of color if they make up the vast bulk of the poverty population and the welfare rolls.

The implementation of Florida's welfare reform was overseen by twenty-three Work and Gain Economic Self-Sufficiency (WAGES) boards, which were set up by the state in 1996 to administer TANF in local areas. Under Florida's policies, welfare recipients could receive cash assistance for two consecutive years if they participated in WAGES programs, which required them to either enter "workfare" jobs to earn their TANF benefits (averaging $6.09 per hour) or enroll in training courses. Failure to participate in WAGES programs meant loss of assistance. Recipients leaving the rolls, if eligible, were allowed to return again for no more than an additional two-year period, with the possibility of assistance for one more year under a hardship exemption. Recipients were limited to five years of assistance in their lifetime.

Under the programs administered by the Miami-Dade County WAGES board, welfare caseloads dropped over 50 percent between 1996 and 1999, from roughly 47,000 recipients down to 17,600. While some people who left the welfare rolls found jobs, the jobs they found often proved to be unstable, without benefits, and short term. Many of the recipients who left the rolls had dropped out of WAGES programs, were sanctioned, and were denied further TANF assistance. Elements of the area's overwhelmingly black and Latino/a welfare population became increasingly restive over the job situation, and expressed anger over the WAGES program's failure to provide support and opportunities for recipients of color who were expected to make the transition from welfare to work.

Minority Families Fighting Against WAGES was a grassroots community organization that arose from Miami's impoverished and racially segregated Liberty City section, where neighborhood unemployment rates were as high as 26 percent. The organization denounced the WAGES program for providing poor-quality services that were not really helping recipients achieve independence from welfare. Its members charged that "entire families, ill-prepared to make the transition from dependency to self-reliance, are unfairly cut from the welfare rolls."[48] Without any welfare recipient representatives on the local WAGES board, or any other way to get board members to listen to them, recipients were forced to organize at the grassroots level and to engage in demonstrations and other protest activity. The actions of Minority Families Fighting Against WAGES were an indication of the unwillingness of impoverished women of color to be passive recipients of Florida racial state actors' racial mistreatment and indifference to their families' survival.

The concerns expressed by Minority Families Fighting Against WAGES received support from the Qualitative Study of WAGES, conducted in four areas of the state, including Miami–Dade County, by researchers from several Florida universities. Those looking at the Miami area, where just about all welfare recipients were of people of color, found that many recipients had difficulty getting assistance from WAGES offices in obtaining job leads or referrals, finding jobs, or obtaining correct information about the educational, child care, and transportation services for which they were eligible. Caseworkers were often found to be either unknowledgeable or failing to apply WAGES policies uniformly. Consequently, many recipients left the Miami–Dade County WAGES program out of frustration, despite the threat this posed to their benefits.[49]

How Welfare Racism Violates Human Rights: The Case of Mississippi

The Kensington Welfare Rights Union (KWRU) is a multiethnic group of poor and homeless families in Philadelphia that has worked to mobilize poor people and their allies across the United States around the premise that attacks on the poor, including racial state welfare reform legislation like the PRWORA, are a violation of human rights. While recognizing that such attacks harshly affect impoverished white people as well, KWRU has addressed both the racialization of welfare as a political issue and the disproportionate impact of welfare reform on people of color.[50] KWRU has petitioned international bodies to intervene on behalf of poor people in the United States, declaring that actions by the federal racial state have been contrary to international human and civil rights covenants to which it is a signatory.

One example of welfare policy–related human rights violations cited by KWRU was the state of Mississippi, the poorest state in the nation and the one that provides the lowest welfare benefits.[51] Mississippi has the largest proportion of African-American residents of any of the fifty states. In the late 1990s, almost 40 percent of Mississippians were black, and many were extremely impoverished. Consequently, black families made up more than 80 percent of the state's welfare caseload. An impoverished mother of two typically received $120 a month in cash assistance, an amount that had not changed since 1985. Welfare has long provided Mississippi's politicians with fodder for their political rhetoric and campaigns. It has enabled them to play the "race card" without necessarily being overt when making appeals to sentiments of white supremacy. When it came to the harmful effects of welfare reform, KWRU expressed fear that "So goes Mississippi, so goes the South. So goes the South, so goes the Nation."[52]

Mississippi began its "WorkFirst" welfare reform program in 1995, prior to the passage of the Personal Responsibility and Work Opportunity Reconciliation Act. By 1997, welfare officials in the rural Mississippi Delta region were dropping recipients from the rolls twice as fast as those on the rolls were finding jobs. In many instances, the jobs that former recipients did find proved temporary. In a region in which joblessness is endemic, particularly for poor African-American residents, those on welfare faced "the nation's toughest penalties" for violating welfare department rules. Those who missed appointments or declined work assignments surrendered their entire cash grant.[53] Jobs were scarce, and the child care and public transportation that many poor residents needed to help them hold jobs hardly existed. Racist stereotypes and reluctance of the region's largely white-run businesses to hire black workers added to the stresses that those facing loss of assistance through sanctions or time limits had to endure.[54]

The federal racial state's elimination of welfare as an entitlement offered Mississippi political elites an opportunity they could not refuse—the removal of the safety net from under its large and disproportionately African-American poverty population. Indeed, between 1993 and 1998, Mississippi's welfare caseload was reduced 71 percent! Most of this decline occurred in the last two years of this period. Mississippi led the South, which saw greater caseload declines in 1993–98 than any other section of the nation.[55] One welfare reform researcher, after documenting the declines in the South, commented, "This raises important questions about how the region in the U.S. with the highest poverty rate, with the lion's share of persistent poverty areas, and with a spatial mismatch between welfare dependence and employment, can also become the region with the largest welfare declines."[56] Such questions cannot be answered without attention to welfare racism.

From KWRU's perspective, Mississippi's oppressive posture toward welfare recipients threatened to influence other states, especially those experiencing economic downturns, since "states with the toughest welfare reform are able to provide the most desperate and docile labor force, with workers prepared to take jobs which pay slave wages."[57] Given the preponderance of poor people of color on the welfare rolls in Mississippi and elsewhere, the "slave" reference by KWRU was no frivolous use of rhetoric. By throwing women of color off the welfare rolls in large numbers, white employers of low-wage black labor put themselves in a position to better exploit impoverished African-American mothers' economic desperation. Welfare racism in Mississippi is but one example of human rights violations experienced by poor people of color at the hands of the racial state that has helped inform KWRU's drive to make welfare reform a national and international human rights concern.

Racial Discrimination by Employers and Caseworkers in Virginia

Employer Racism

Welfare reform researchers rarely ask recipients or former recipients about experiences with caseworkers and employers that may be related to their skin color. A notable exception to this failure to look into welfare racist practices is found in the work of Susan T. Gooden, who was interested in reversing the lack of attention being given to the racial implications of welfare practices occurring under welfare reform. Her research focused on treatment recipients received under the Virginia Independence Program (VIP), a welfare reform program that began in July 1995 under a federal waiver. The work component of VIP was called the Virginia Initiative for Employment not Welfare (VIEW). Most recipients were eligible for VIEW and were required to be employed within ninety days of receiving benefits. Part of Gooden's inquiry focused on the work experiences of black and white adult welfare recipients living in five Virginia counties with low unemployment rates and stable economies.[58] More than two-thirds of Virginia's welfare recipients were persons of color.

The 233 recipients participating in her study (118 whites and 105 blacks) were similar in age, number of children, and length of time receiving welfare benefits. Black recipients, however, had higher levels of education on average, and were more likely to have graduated from high school, obtained their General Education Degree, or attended college. Yet, Gooden found that employment outcomes were more likely to be negative for blacks than for whites. While a similar percentage of recipients (65 percent of blacks and 60 percent of whites) found jobs, black recipients were less likely to be employed full time (defined as 30 or more hours per week). The average hourly wages for whites with a high school diploma or better were higher than wages for blacks with the same level of education. Whites were far more likely to be working in higher-paying jobs, defined as those paying more than $5 per hour.

In interviewing a subsample of the recipients under study, recipients who were working in two of the five Virginia counties, Gooden also found that black recipients were more likely than whites to be ill treated by employers.[59] Blacks were granted much shorter job interviews, were more likely to be required to take pre-employment drug tests or undergo criminal background checks, were more likely to be given different work tasks and fewer hours than those described when offered the job, were more likely to have to work evening hours, and were more likely to describe their relationships with supervisors as negative. As Gooden noted, "An unfavorable relationship with a supervisor can negatively affect other employment opportunities including job retention, job promotion and job references for use with other employers."[60]

Gooden pointed out that where documented racial discrimination exists in a labor market, employment opportunities for welfare recipients of color are reduced. She suggested that labor market discrimination should be included in Virginia's criteria for granting recipients "hardship exemptions" from the state's two-year benefit time limits, just as state policy included the presence of high local unemployment rates as a hardship factor. The alternative, presumably, was to push recipients of color into a labor market in which it was far more problematic for them to become economically self-sufficient than it was for white recipients, but where their plight could be exploited by white employers.

Caseworker Racism

Working with the same subsample, Gooden also inquired into the level of support that black and white recipients received from caseworkers as they sought to become economically self-sufficient.[61] Given the enormous day-to-day discretion over the interpretation and application of policies that local welfare agencies have been granted, racial disparities in caseworker treatment of recipients can have a devastating effect on recipients of color who are striving to meet mandatory work requirements under welfare reform.

Again, Gooden found significant racial disparities. Whites were more likely to receive help from caseworkers by being notified of potential jobs and to be encouraged by caseworkers to pursue or complete additional education that would improve their job chances. While both blacks and whites had transportation barriers that impeded their work efforts (no driver's license, no vehicle or one in need of repair, lack of gas money), only whites were offered assistance with transportation problems. While 45 percent of black recipients said they felt treated unfairly by their local welfare agency, only 18 percent of white recipients felt this way.

As Gooden put it,

> Taken together, white welfare recipients benefit considerably from the discretionary actions of their caseworkers. If differences in caseworker discretion are not addressed in the early stages of welfare reform, differences in job placement, wages and job retention among black and white welfare clients may be incorrectly attributed to differences in work ethic, personal motivation or attitude.[62]

The Multiple Discriminatory Barriers Put before Poor Women of Color

Susan T. Gooden's findings were based upon a limited sample of welfare recipients residing in several Virginia counties. Although there is a great need to expand such research elsewhere, other evidence suggests that racial discrimination by employers is widespread. Moreover, other forms of discrimination by employers also adversely affect poor women of color. While welfare reform policies demand that mothers leave the rolls and become economically self-sufficient, the policies fail to even acknowledge these discriminatory barriers, much less provide the means to overcome them.

The National Partnership for Women and Families (NPWF) is a Washington, D.C., advocacy organization concerned with problems that low-income people face. The organization gathered survey data from local programs in forty-five states that were charged with assisting poor women in their search for employment. These local service providers were in a position to detect patterns in what happened to the many women they attempted to place in jobs. One of the NPWF's goals in conducting this research was to inquire into the existence of multiple forms of discrimination and their effects on welfare recipients and other low-income women.[63] The NPWF's findings underscored the kinds of employment problems poor women of color face both while they are on welfare and once they leave the rolls.

Service providers responding to the survey reported multiple forms of employment discrimination as serious problems for the low-income women they served.

> About half of providers said that non-welfare clients "often" face one or more of the following types of discrimination when looking for a job or on the job: race/ethnic, gender, pregnancy, or disability discrimination or sexual/racial harassment. More than half said their welfare clients "often" encounter at least one such form of discrimination.[64]

In addition to the forms of discrimination cited above, the NPWF found that simply being a welfare recipient often posed a serious barrier to employment.[65] Almost 60 percent of service providers said employers were often reluctant to hire recipients, and almost a quarter of providers said employers often did not want to pay equal wages to welfare recipients and nonrecipients doing identical jobs. This was said to be caused by negative attitudes and stereotypes about welfare recipients as a group. However, it should be noted that it is difficult to separate racist stereotypes from stereotypes about welfare recipients generally. Racism may well hide behind the latter.

One form of discrimination against welfare recipients of color that we have not yet addressed is that based on nationality, language, or citizenship status. Such discrimination was fostered and legitimated by the immigration-focused race population control provisions of the PRWORA that we discussed in chapter 6. As we will see in the next section, discrimination against immigrants is not uncommon.

Welfare Reform's Attack on Immigrants of Color

Federal racial state actors stripped many immigrants of eligibility for the PRWORA's Temporary Assistance for Needy Families or set strict conditions under which they may receive TANF. These included tying eligibility for benefits to residency and citizenship status. Nonetheless, many immigrants, including refugees and asylum seekers, are on the welfare rolls.[66] Reflecting the composition of the vast majority of the immigrant population in recent years, many are women and children of color from Latin America, the Caribbean, and Asia. Recent research has underscored the fact that welfare reform is having a "profound impact" on the nation's immigrants. As Lynn H. Fujiwara put it, "Racial backlash has materialized in an attack on the politically most disenfranchised and we have yet to learn the full effects imposed by welfare reform."[67]

Discrimination against Mexican and Asian Immigrants in California

As part of its Immigrant Women and Welfare Project, Equal Rights Advocates (ERA), a San Francisco–based advocacy group, conducted interviews with seventy-five Mexican and seventy-five Vietnamese women who were receiving welfare in Santa Clara County, California. Immigrants make up a quarter of California's highly multiethnic population and almost a fifth of its welfare recipients, most of whom are from Latin American and Asian countries. Mexican and Vietnamese women are the largest two immigrant groups on welfare in Santa Clara County. The advocacy group's goal in conducting this research was to see how such women and their families were faring under "CalWORKS," California's welfare reform program.

The program made it mandatory for welfare recipients to engage in state-approved "work activities" or find paid employment. Local CalWORKS offices often forced recipients to take the first job they found open. Parents could lose aid if they did not find work within twenty-four months (for current recipients) or eighteen months (for new applicants). California counties were given a good deal of discretion as to whether to approve certain skill development courses as work activities for those who spoke little English or had other barriers to regular employment. All recipients had a lifetime limit of five years of cash assistance.

The women participating in this research were almost all receiving cash assistance. While proficiency in English was poor to nonexistent for both groups, Vietnamese mothers were particularly limited in this regard. Almost half of the mothers were engaged in some kind of employment at the time of the study, but the work usually entailed low-skill, dead-end, often temporary jobs with poor pay and working conditions. Consistent with our earlier discussion of multiple forms of discrimination experienced by welfare recipients seeking employment, the interviews revealed that the immigrant mothers suffered multiple forms of discrimination based on their being welfare recipients, people of color, immigrants, and women. In addition to experiencing discrimination, both Mexican and Vietnamese mothers felt they lacked the support and skills to become employed in jobs with adequate pay and health benefits. They also doubted that they would be able to gain such employment within the strict time limits for assistance established by the state. These findings led ERA to conclude that without major changes in the welfare system, such immigrant women "will continue in dire poverty once their access to welfare ends."[68]

In December 1999, a group of legal aid attorneys filed a civil rights complaint with the U.S. Department of Health and Human Services' Office of Civil Rights, claiming that welfare agencies in the Los Angeles County area were denying job training and other services to welfare recipients who did not speak English.[69] While in this particular case the county's welfare-to-work program was said to be capable of handling Spanish-speaking people, it was not meeting the language needs of those speaking many other languages—including families from Cambodia and Vietnam.

Insofar as it did not provide forms and other written materials in languages that recipients could understand, bilingual translators or interpreter services, language-accessible training and education programs, and bilingual providers of county welfare-to-work services such as child care and mental health assessment, the county's Department of Public Social Services was said to be engaged in language discrimination. The latter has been interpreted by federal courts as a violation of the Civil Rights Act of 1964. If non–English-speaking welfare recipients do not get necessary support services and receive them in a timely manner because of language discrimination, they are impeded in their efforts to enter the labor market, much like the Mexican and Vietnamese women described in the Santa Clara County study. Failure to meet work requirements means they may suffer sanctions or termination of benefits, and thus lose out on the limited years of assistance that California's welfare reform policies provided.

We noted earlier that exercising racial control over "Who is there?" on the basis of punitive welfare reform policies is unlikely to keep immigrants of color from coming to the United States or get them to leave. But under the PRWORA, many thousands of immigrant families have lost crucial benefits, ranging from cash assistance to food stamps to health care. Their suffering simply makes them more economically desperate and vulnerable to labor exploitation. This is true not only of states like California, where there are large and heavily concentrated populations of immigrants of color, but wherever such immigrants have tried to settle.

The Struggles of Hmong Refugees in Wisconsin

In 1999, findings from a study by the Institute for Wisconsin's Future[70] prompted the U.S. Department of Health and Human Services' Office of Civil

Rights to investigate language discrimination in the treatment of welfare recipients who are Hmong immigrants. Many of these political refugees from Laos settled in Wisconsin following the war in Vietnam. In 1997 Wisconsin implemented a work-based assistance program—"Wisconsin Works" or "W-2"—that offered eligible recipients who faced barriers to employment up to two years of job training and work experience to help them make a transition off the welfare rolls.

Most of the Hmong immigrant families in the Wisconsin study contained two parents. Unlike many other states, Wisconsin's welfare policy allowed some two-parent families to receive assistance.[71] Hmong parents receiving aid tended to have large families with demanding child-care needs. More than half had five or more children under eighteen, and many had eight or more. Employment was difficult for Hmong parents because they often had few marketable skills and little ability with the English language, and they frequently lacked literacy skills, even in their native Hmong language.

Despite these obvious barriers to employment, W-2 programs were said to provide Hmong aid recipients with little or no useful work experience or skill development. The vast majority of Hmong welfare recipients were found to have caseworkers who were incapable of communicating with them in person or by phone. Recipients also had to contend with English-language forms and instructions that they could not understand. The pay they received from work placements under W-2 was lower for most recipients than the assistance they had received under the Aid to Families with Dependent Children program. Many families did not have sufficient income to meet basic subsistence needs. When interviewed, a third revealed that their families had run out of food in the previous six months, and almost 90 percent said they could not afford to buy clothing for family members.[72] Under Wisconsin's welfare rules, these families were set to lose all cash assistance shortly because of the state's two-year time limit for benefits.

In response to publicity about the plight of the Hmong, Wisconsin state officials quickly went on the counterattack, declaring the research by the Institute for Wisconsin's Future to be faulty and politically biased. Newspaper reports, however, subsequently indicated that Wisconsin's welfare reform program had actually been under Office of Civil Rights review for possible civil rights violations since 1998.[73] In late 2000 the OCR concluded that violations did occur and that, as a result, Hmong clients lost or were denied benefits. Federal officials announced they would work with the state to develop a voluntary plan to prevent unlawful practices that harmed language minorities such as the Hmong.[74] The Hmong situation is but one in a growing list of examples of language discrimination and other forms of mistreatment of immigrants of color around the nation.

Abuse of and Disrespect for Spanish-Speaking Immigrants in New York City

In 1999, an advocacy organization called Make the Road by Walking issued a scathing report on the hostile treatment of immigrants by the New York City welfare system. Interviewing welfare recipients in various neighborhoods around the Brooklyn area, Make the Road by Walking found that the most pressing concerns of people were inadequate translation services and failure of the staff of Human Resources Administration offices, which implemented welfare reform policies, to treat recipients with respect.

Many Spanish-speaking recipients had problems communicating with their caseworkers about benefits their families needed for survival, and most recipients felt frustrated by the treatment they received at welfare offices. Even people who spoke English complained that they could not reach their caseworkers by telephone, found their workers to be rude, or went to appointments with caseworkers but found them absent. Recipients reported "being verbally abused by their caseworkers, misinformed about their legal rights and unable to obtain attention or assistance from their caseworkers in emergency situations."[75] As we noted earlier, the majority of those on New York City's welfare rolls—some 59 percent—were Latino/a.

With the assistance of legal services groups in New York City, Make the Road by Walking filed a civil rights complaint with the U.S. Department of Health and Human Services' Office of Civil Rights. That complaint charged that language discrimination was impeding immigrants from obtaining benefits for which they were eligible. After months of inaction by the OCR, Make the Road by Walking engaged in demonstrations at the office of the city's Human Resources Administration. Growing press coverage, especially in the Spanish media, put pressure on the OCR to respond, and in October 1999 "OCR validated all of the issues raised by Make the Road by Walking."[76] Even while OCR, under continued pressure from Make the Road by Walking, subsequently prodded New York City racial state actors several times to conform to federal civil rights law regarding language access, the problems remained. According to one grassroots organizing newsletter, "Some Make the Road staff called welfare offices speaking Spanish, and of the few instances they got through to a worker, half the time they were hung up on."[77]

The Impact of Welfare Reform on People of Color in Hawaii

In 1998 the Hawai'i Area Program of the American Friends Service Committee interviewed a small random sample of welfare recipients in and around Honolulu in order to assess the impact of Hawaii's welfare reform policies. Few who were interviewed were white; most were Filipino, Hawaiian, Japanese, Laotian, Puerto Rican, Samoan, Tongan, Vietnamese, or Marshallese. This composition was a reflection of both immigration to the islands and the ethnically diverse native-born Hawaiian population.

As in other individual states, welfare recipients in Hawaii were under pressure to make a transition from welfare receipt to economic self-sufficiency. And, as was also true elsewhere, welfare reform policies in Hawaii were insensitive to the inhospitable climate of limited employment opportunities and lack of adequate social service support programs within which recipients often had to meet mandatory work requirements.[78]

Most of the recipients interviewed found their welfare office to be anything but "user friendly." Most had little contact with caseworkers. Few felt their caseworkers were helpful or supportive, and many hesitated to bring up questions. Recipients were fearful of the discretionary power that caseworkers had to cut off their assistance. Immigrants in particular lacked a strong support network of family and friends, and they needed language translators to help not only with welfare matters but in accessing other services.

Cultural insensitivity was apparent too, especially in the ways in which Hawaii's welfare officials communicated with its ethnically diverse recipients. This insensitivity was a source of recipient alienation from the state's welfare bureaucracy. As the study noted, "There is no distinction being made [by officials] between cultural expectations for face to face 'talk story' contexts to communicate vital information, and more formal written correspondence."[79] Failure to understand official communications from the state or their implications for program eligibility put recipients in the position of being sanctioned and losing assistance for not responding to letters. Moreover, many recipients were said to not understand or appreciate the implications of the state's policy of a five-year limit on assistance. Cultural "insensitivity" in the area of welfare policy is but another way in which welfare racism is expressed by racial state actors. It is part of the experience of Native American populations as well.

The Oppression of Native Americans by Welfare Reform

The disruptive and punishing effects of welfare reform are felt not only by people of color who have recently arrived in the United States as immigrants (including political refugees and asylum seekers), but by native peoples whose ancestors were in North America well before the United States existed. Like Latinos/as, impoverished Native Americans are typically ignored in discussions of welfare policy, whether they live on or off tribal reservations.[80] As Layne K. Stromwall and his colleagues have pointed out, "The poorest populations and those most severely limited in employment opportunities will be the most affected by these changes. Among the poorest groups in the U.S. are American Indians. Consequently, the effects of 'welfare reform' may be the greatest on the native people of this country."[81]

We said early in the chapter that whites have left the welfare rolls at faster rates than people of color and cited statistics from North Dakota and South Dakota to show that this trend has been particularly noticeable in states with significant Native American populations. Federal data also show an increase for Native Americans in Montana from 27 percent in 1994 to 45 percent in 1998. Other states reporting significant proportions of Native American recipients are Alaska, Arizona, New Mexico, Oklahoma, and Wyoming.[82]

The situation of reservation residents is not unlike the "internal colonialism" of Washington, D.C., African Americans that we discussed earlier. Dominated socially, economically, and politically by whites, Native Americans have had to deal with the top-down imposition of racialized welfare reform policies and their behavioral requirements. Racial control extends even into remote reservation lands, where many native peoples live miles from welfare offices, lack private or public transportation and phones, have no job prospects, and confront abject poverty in their everyday lives.

Under provisions of the PRWORA, tribes may develop and implement their own welfare reform programs on their reservations if they wish, but to date most have chosen not to do so. By early 2000, the U.S. Department of Health and Human Services had approved only twenty-two tribal TANF programs in twelve states. These plans covered some 4,480 families on Native American reservations or in Alaska Native villages—little more than 10 percent of all reservation families who were on welfare.[83]

Developing and administering their own programs could give tribes degrees of flexibility and independence they otherwise do not have by remaining totally under restrictive, "internal colonial"-like federal and state welfare reform policies. However, under the PRWORA, tribes that run their own welfare programs were not made eligible for all of the types of financial assistance that the federal government provided the individual states, nor were state governments obligated to provide tribes with financial support to run their own programs. Thus, while there may have been definite advantages to devolution of authority over welfare administration to tribal organizations, many tribes have chosen not to participate. Most Native American welfare recipients, whether reservation residents or not, are colonial-like subjects, forced to rely on TANF programs run by the individual state in which they reside.

The federal racial state provided minimal recognition of the dire economic circumstances existing on many Native American reservations when Congress passed the Balanced Budget Act of 1997. A provision of that act allowed Native American recipients to be exempt from the PRWORA five-year benefit time limit for every month they reside on a reservation having an unemployment rate higher than 50 percent. In addition, individual states were allowed to provide hardship extensions to recipients who ran up against state time limits. The

PRWORA already allowed individual states to provide hardship exemptions from the five-year federal time limit of up to 20 percent of a state's welfare case-load.[84] In reality, however, most Native American recipients are subject to time limits for receipt of assistance, and all recipients must conform to the rules and regulations of federal and state welfare reform policies—including work-related requirements—or be sanctioned and lose aid.

Aside from occasional newspaper reports from one or another individual state, the most systematic information about what has happened to Native Americans has come from scholars who have examined the impact of welfare reform in Arizona.[85] Although that state's 200,000 Native Americans make up only about 6 percent of its population, they make up close to 18 percent of Arizona's poverty population. Many Native Americans in Arizona live on one of the state's twenty-one reservations, where the average poverty rate exceeds 50 percent. Even those who live off the reservation are far more likely to be poor than whites and other people of color. Native American families who subsist in extreme poverty circumstances, like other poor families of color, have little choice but to look to welfare for assistance. Consequently, Native American mothers and children on reservations are said to be affected by welfare reform "more severely than any other racial or ethnic group in the U.S."[86] In many respects, the harsh impact of internal colonial-like welfare reform policies on Native Americans in Arizona is an intense version of its negative impact on impoverished families of color across the nation.

The state of Arizona began its welfare reform under a federal waiver in 1995, at a time when almost half of its reservations had unemployment rates of between 50 and 90 percent.[87] Only three tribes out of twenty-one opted to administer their own welfare programs. Most of Arizona's Native Americans were therefore subject to the state program, called "Employing and Moving People Off Welfare and Encouraging Responsibility," or EMPOWER. The program allowed adult recipients to receive only two years of cash assistance over a five-year period, unless they were granted month-to-month hardship exemptions. If adult recipients met the state's mandatory work requirements, their children could continue to receive cash assistance beyond the two-year time limit. If work requirements were not met, both parents and children could lose all benefits, which would occur progressively over a three-month period.

Given the high unemployment rates on and near most of Arizona's reservations, one might consider the imposition of mandatory work requirements on mothers who lack basic means of subsistence for themselves and their children to be bizarre. Shanta Pandey and her colleagues found that poor families on reservations faced the same kinds of barriers to employment as other recipients of color that we have mentioned in this chapter, including the lack of job opportunities for those who wished to and were able to work, lack of child-care facilities and transportation, and employment discrimination. Many families on the reservations lacked telephones, a necessity for communicating with welfare caseworkers, child-care providers, or employers. While mothers living on reservations clearly tried to conform to Arizona's mandatory work requirements, many could not, were subject to punitive sanctions, and lost welfare assistance. Pandey's research team found "evidence that families are living under extreme financial hardship—lacking the ability to purchase basic household supplies including food, fuel, and clothing."[88]

Mothers and children living off reservations who fall victim to sanctions or state time limits may find themselves forced to move back and find family members to take them in. If they reside on a reservation with a 50 percent or higher unemployment rate, they may be able to take advantage of the special time-limit exemption and regain benefits. Movements back, however, put additional stress on families, exacerbate already poor housing conditions, and create an additional burden on hard-pressed reservation tribal governments and tribal service infrastructures.

On the other hand, mothers living on reservations may feel compelled to leave in the face of scarce employment opportunities and no place to apply the limited job training they may be fortunate enough to somehow acquire. Such outmigration from reservations also places stress on families, both those who stay and those who feel they are being forced to leave. The impact of welfare racism on the social stability, cultural cohesion, and morale of Native American reservation communities has yet to be fully assessed.

Our closing comments on the disruptive effects of welfare reform on Native American reservation communities raise an important issue. Welfare racism does not simply hurt individuals or individual families, but disproportionately harms whole communities of people of color. Because little attention has been given to community analyses by those groups monitoring the outcomes of welfare reform, we present an illustration below of welfare racism's effects on one state's communities.

Unraveling Neighborhood Infrastructures in Massachusetts Communities of Color

James Jennings has examined the impact of welfare reform on poor and working-class neighborhoods, especially those that are predominantly African American or Latino/a. Jennings was particularly interested in how welfare reform affected the operation and effectiveness of community-based organizations (CBOs) in neighborhoods of color. Such organizations have played a crucial role in fostering community development and strategies for neighborhood revitalization that involve the participation and empowerment of local residents.[89]

On the basis of a preliminary study in African-American and Latino/a communities in Massachusetts, Jennings found that welfare reform was diverting CBOs away from their work in community development and revitalization. Instead, many CBOs found themselves in an entirely new role, scrambling to help impoverished African-American and Latino/a families meet welfare reform's work requirements and find some way to move "from welfare to work," and trying to assist recipients with everything from job referrals to food and child-care assistance. Yet, in taking on such demanding tasks, CBOs received little in the way of resources, up-to-date information, or support from Massachusetts welfare officials. Jennings found CBOs taking on burdens that were having destructive consequences for both these organizations and for the residents they sought to serve.

Welfare reform, Jennings noted, was aimed at changing the "presumed self-destructive and dependent behavior of poor individuals."[90] This focus does not produce more jobs or housing, or the resources and dynamics needed to vitalize impoverished communities of color. But these were precisely the goals that CBOs were created to pursue. Jennings observed that welfare reform was undercutting the community-building function of CBOs: "Welfare reform 'as we know it' discourages civic participation and collaboration in building strategies to resolve neighborhood problems. Instead, it encourages a specter of big government and mistrust, as well as racial and ethnic conflict among citizens."[91]

This ends our overview of recent expressions of welfare racism. Let us now turn to the failure of mainstream policy analysts and groups that advocate on behalf of the poor to address racism and its effects in monitoring the outcomes of welfare reform.

MORE DENIAL OF RACISM: MAINSTREAM MONITORING
OF THE OUTCOMES OF WELFARE REFORM

Race-Blind Pretensions

We noted earlier that racist stereotypes and negative controlling images regarding the alleged laziness, immorality, and promiscuity of African-American women helped to shape the rationale for and thus the goals of recent welfare reform initiatives. With the help of conservative policy analysts, political elites had great success in portraying the values and behaviors of poor people of color as the causes of their poverty, not white racism. By attacking the alleged cultural deficiencies of the poor and camouflaging their racial sentiments, political elites managed to craft the goals of the Personal Responsibility and Work Opportunity Reconciliation Act of 1996 in "race-blind" terms.[92]

The principal problems to be solved by the PRWORA were said to be welfare "dependency" and "illegitimacy" (problems framed largely by racist stereotypes regarding African Americans' work effort and sexual morality). To racial state actors, these were problems that impoverished individuals could presumably overcome by behaving in accordance with "higher-level" cultural values. Supposedly, welfare reform "wasn't about race," but about "personal responsibility."

The PRWORA and the restrictive, paternalistic welfare reform policies that preceded it were indeed about race. The act itself was an expression of welfare racism masked by the use of race-neutral language. More specifically, the act was an expression of gendered racism. The PRWORA was not primarily aimed at the two-thirds of welfare recipients who were children, or even at their fathers. It was primarily aimed at these children's mothers. And because the act was neither race blind nor gender neutral in its formation by racial state actors, it could not be race blind or gender neutral in its implementation and outcomes. Under the Personal Responsibility and Work Opportunity Reconciliation Act, both the work and reproductive behaviors of impoverished women of color were to be regulated by the racial state.

In our view, much of the research that has been conducted on the impact of welfare reform in recent years can be viewed as a dimension of racial control. Whether funded, shaped, or otherwise influenced by the federal racial state, most of this research has sought to measure the state's success in effecting and thus controlling what welfare recipients of color are doing. Most recent analyses bear on work behavior, an area in which racial state actors at the federal and individual state levels might most easily hope to fine-tune welfare policies and their administration. Work behavior is also an area that is less politically sensitive for racial state actors to evaluate than are the PRWORA's provisions encouraging procreation-focused race population control.

The vast bulk of welfare reform research has been conducted without any attention to race or racism, gender or sexism, as if the simultaneous oppression of racial inequality and patriarchy were simply irrelevant to poor women's lives. In effect, the subjects of welfare reform research have been de-raced and de-gendered. Treating impoverished women of color as if they had no race or gender obscures the role that welfare reform plays as an expression of gendered racism. It prevents consideration of how patriarchy and racial inequality interact with the conditions imposed by welfare reform in determining the daily lived experiences of poor women of color. Such research also diverts attention away from how welfare reform contributes to white racial hegemony. Indeed, considering the role that gendered racism played in rallying support for punitive welfare reform measures, it seems as if some perverse accountability shell game is being played when research into the consequences of reforms pretends to be race- and gender-blind.

Welfare reform research has been race blind, however, only in the sense that policy analysts have largely ignored race or racism and focused their inquiries on supposedly race-neutral topics such as "welfare dependency." But in focusing on such topics, researchers have in effect bought into or otherwise aligned themselves with prevailing racist stereotypes regarding African Americans' lack of work effort. In studying trends in welfare dependency, researchers cannot help but implicitly objectify and reify stereotypes and controlling images of welfare-reliant mothers' assumed laziness and irresponsibility, behaviors that welfare reform is presumably there to alter. Policy analysts do this by their choice of research questions, as well as their use of research terminology, methods, forms of data, and variables that avoid opening up the issues of how patriarchy and racial inequality contribute to the maintenance of a seemingly permanent population of poor families with dark skin.

While most welfare reform analysts would no doubt be shocked to hear their efforts described in this way, we believe that much of their research has functioned to reinforce the racial state's portrayal of welfare recipients as deviant and threatening Others who are in need of the control to be provided by welfare reform. The bulk of welfare reform monitoring has quietly institutionalized gendered racism in the realm of welfare reform discourse through the application of the professional ideology of "value-free" social science. Welfare reform research is far from being value free, from the premises on which it proceeds to the uses to which it gets put.

De-Racing and De-Gendering the Consequences of Welfare Reform

Most major studies of the outcome or effects of welfare reform have been conducted under the auspices of the federal racial state. Given the central role played by federal racial state actors in formulating and implementing welfare reform, their interest in framing research questions to produce findings bearing on its "success" may be as dispassionate and unbiased as the proverbial fox's interest in the occupants of a hen house. The racial state has been aided and abetted in evaluating welfare reform outcomes by policy research organizations, "think tanks," and university-based researchers who, in return for acceptance into the public policy mainstream, often share racial state actors' frames of reference for measuring success. Research notably critical of both the premises and outcomes of welfare reform has come primarily from groups that advocate on behalf of the poor, such as faith-related or children's rights organizations. Such organizations tend to rely less (sometimes not at all) on racial state funding and often operate in accordance with moral principles and political agendas over which the federal racial state has little direct influence.

We have examined numerous reports on the consequences of welfare reform with the following questions in mind: Has research conducted on welfare reform shown signs of being helpful in uncovering and challenging welfare racism? Or has this research simultaneously reflected and obscured welfare racism's existence? Has the research that has been conducted adequately attended to the question of how welfare reform has affected impoverished families of color? Or has this research tended to proceed from a position of "color blindness," effectively denying that the skin color of the poor is of any policy significance? Has the research on welfare reform shown sensitivity to special problems that women of color may face as a consequence of the fact that they simultaneously occupy subordinate positions in U.S. society's systems of gender, race, and class inequality? Or has their status within this matrix of inequalities gone ignored by researchers?

We will answer these questions here with reference to major welfare reform "outcome studies" that have appeared since the passage of the PRWORA in 1996. The level of activity in this area has exploded to the point that we might almost speak of the emergence of a welfare reform research "industry." Obviously the effects of welfare policy changes of the magnitude of the PRWORA take time to appear. We thus limit our discussion to a dozen or so major outcome studies and outcome research overviews issued from mid-1998 to early 2000 by federal agencies, major policy research organizations, and national advocacy groups.

In this 1998–2000 period, the principal federal agencies conducting, funding, or compiling overviews of welfare reform research were the U.S. Department of Health and Human Services and the U.S. Government Accounting Office.[93] Policy research organizations prominent in the conduct of welfare reform research included the Center on Budget and Policy Priorities,[94] The Urban Institute,[95] and the Center for Law and Social Policy.[96] Reports on the outcomes of welfare reform, often critical of reform policies, were also issued by national advocacy groups such as the Children's Defense Fund,[97] Unitarian Universalist Service Committee,[98] NETWORK,[99] Children's Rights Inc.,[100] and Families USA.[101] What did outcome studies from these various agencies and organizations have to say about racism and the impact of welfare reform on impoverished mothers of color?

Important Questions for Welfare Reform Outcome Studies

1. Was the Possible Effect of Race on Welfare Reform Outcomes Recognized?

In the research reports we examined, those conducting welfare reform research rarely even used the race of welfare applicants or recipients, or of those who had left welfare, as a key variable when tracking the outcomes of welfare reform. In some research, mention was made of the racial composition of the population under study, usually in the context of introducing the research that was undertaken. But the attention researchers devoted to race as a variable was typically very brief and did not carry over into the analysis of welfare reform's outcomes.[102] The race of recipients or former recipients otherwise was rarely accorded any recognition in these reports, leaving the overall impression that all of those under study were interchangeable or "universal" poor people whose biographies and daily lived experiences were unaffected by race-based disadvantage or privilege.

2. Did Welfare Reform Outcome Research Address Barriers Faced by People of Color?

We know that the probability of being poor, and especially of being extremely poor, is much higher for people of color than it is for whites. According to the U.S. Bureau of the Census, in 1998 only 3.2 percent of whites had family incomes of less than half of the official poverty line, as opposed to 11.2 percent of African Americans and 9.8 percent of Latinos/as.[103] Their high rates of extreme poverty explain in part why some two-thirds of mothers receiving Temporary Assistance for Needy Families, and an even higher proportion of children in TANF families, were of color.

Indeed, as we saw earlier in this chapter, the proportion of people of color on the welfare rolls actually increased in conjunction with the welfare reforms of the 1990s. This increase raises the important question of whether racially discriminatory barriers to leaving welfare and achieving economic self-sufficiency exist. There is compelling evidence that gendered racism disadvantages African-American and Latina women in the labor market.[104] The research reports we examined, however, were unable to shed light on this phenomenon, since they failed to address racism or to attach any special significance to racial differences among those they were studying.

3. Were Special or Unique Problems Faced by Poor Women of Color Addressed?

Even as they are overrepresented in the poverty population, poor women of color simultaneously bear the burdens of being both female and of color in a predominantly white, male-dominated society. As such, they face somewhat different problems in daily living from those faced by poor white women, particularly since women of color have to contend with the past consequences and present effects of racism, including gendered racism. The research reports we examined failed to look at how poor women of color were socially positioned, or to address whether the status of those studied (disadvantageously situated as they were within the social matrix of racial, gender, and class inequalities) posed special or unique obstacles to rising above poverty. Researchers seemed to assume that all poor women were basically the same, for example, when it came to the ability to attain family self-sufficiency and rise above the poverty line.[105]

4. Was Racism a Concern of Mainstream Watchdogs?

The reports we examined either attempted to provide a national overview of some aspect of welfare reform's impact or draw attention to its impact in a particular group of individual states. In no instance was racism in the realm of welfare reform made the subject of study. Indeed, it was extremely rare to even see the word mentioned. The typical outcome study left the impression that welfare reform was being implemented in a racism-free society, without racial bias or discrimination, and that it was therefore being experienced—for better or worse—in the same ways across color lines. Moreover, most analyses tend to show little concern for whether the socioeconomic conditions of working mothers who must rely on welfare have gotten better or worse.

Why Do Welfare Reform Monitoring Groups Ignore "Race" and Racism?

How are we to understand the marked tendency of welfare reform monitoring groups to ignore race and racism, and to fail to address the ramifications of welfare policy for the daily experiences of people of color? Sanford E. Schram has asserted that "the microdiscourse of the social science of poverty is influenced by the macrodiscourse of the broader society."[106] We have discussed the white intellectual backlash against the notion that racism remains a serious social problem. This backlash has received support from throughout much of the European-American community, and the dismissal of racism as in any way important has become a canon of contemporary racist culture.

As an element of racist culture, the denial of racism's salience is so widespread and pervasive, and so unsuccessfully challenged by racially subordinated groups and their supporters, that we should not be surprised if race and racism are "out of mind" and thus "out of sight" to most researchers.[107] Moreover, as we pointed out above, welfare reform research is often conducted in conformity with the ways in which problems are framed by the racial state, which—itself informed by racist culture—generally only acknowledges racism episodically, when under pressure to do so, and with great caution and reluctance.

Policy outcome analysis that is conducted on welfare reform is thus most likely to be consonant with the fundamental assumptions and primary concerns of racial state actors, who, like most welfare reform researchers, are overwhelmingly members of this society's racially dominant European-American population. Besides their centrality in formulating and implementing welfare reform, these racial state actors have implicitly set the agenda for its evaluation. The criteria for "success" or "failure" of welfare reform policies have been informed by the so-called color-blind goals of welfare reform legislation (e.g., to end welfare "dependency"), and these criteria place political constraints on what research will be funded or deemed credible by racial state actors.

In Schram's words, "All the while aspiring to scientific impartiality, welfare policy research achieves political credibility not by its objectivity, but by its consistency with the prevailing biases of welfare policy discourse."[108] For decades these biases have reflected a preoccupation with the alleged cultural deficiencies of poor people of color, whose supposedly pathological behaviors in the areas of work, family, and reproduction are said to be responsible for their poverty. We examined earlier how racial state officials played upon these allegedly race-based cultural deficiencies in justifying the need for welfare reform.

It is thus no accident that the bulk of welfare reform research focuses on tracking the behavior of impoverished persons without due regard for the varied social, economic, and political contexts within which they struggle to function. Welfare reform is framed so as to suggest that poverty is a matter of individual responsibility, not dominant group exploitation or oppression. To acknowledge that poor people are affected by societal organizing principles of race and gender would mean having to address the consequences of racial and gender inequalities in interpreting the effects of welfare reform policies. Having aligned themselves with the logic of the PRWORA and unquestioningly accepted such racialized concepts as "welfare dependency" (a code term for black laziness), welfare reform researchers are unlikely to enter into such structural interpretations.

To illustrate the effects of race- and gender-blind welfare reform monitoring, take for example the question of whether or not, and how rapidly, mothers receiving TANF are taking up employment and ending their so-called dependency on welfare. In pursuing this question, welfare policy researchers typically tally up the percentage of welfare recipients and welfare leavers who are employed, along with their average hours of employment and hourly earnings. These statistics are presented and interpreted as measures of welfare reform's "success rate" without any concern for the obstacles those mothers face in trying to function within this nation's highly racialized and gendered secondary labor market.[109] Moreover, analyses tend to show little concern for whether the actual socioeconomic conditions of working, welfare-reliant mothers have gotten better or worse. Within this secondary market, impoverished mothers of color have always been devalued and underpaid, and have routinely suffered systematic exploitation of their labor.[110]

Most single mothers receiving TANF are highly disadvantaged when it comes to competing in the primary labor market, where being white, male, middle class, and college educated are important forms of social capital for those wishing to attain decent-paying, relatively secure, white-collar jobs. Lacking sufficient social capital, especially white skin and a male gender, impoverished mothers of color find themselves largely limited to jobs in the secondary labor market. There the jobs available are low wage, usually without benefits, frequently part time or of unstable duration, often dangerous or dirty or physically demanding, and of low social status. Secondary labor market jobs (e.g., day-care helpers, hospital orderlies, food workers, retail store checkout clerks, hotel room maids, unskilled factory operatives) offer little chance of advancement or upward mobility. The precarious economic safety net offered by such jobs has never really been adequately compensated for by supplemental welfare assistance, and it certainly is not now under the conditions of recent welfare reform.

Under the 1996 federal welfare reform law, entitlement to even inadequate cash assistance was abolished. Mothers receiving welfare have been told they must forgo it and attain economic self-sufficiency for their families on their own. However, the racialized and gendered secondary labor market in which mothers of color have been ordered to function has received little or no attention in the reports on the outcomes of welfare reform. Presumably the assumption is that ours is a free market economy in which skin color and gender do not really matter, and "anyone can make it if they really try." If mothers of color who receive welfare do not get jobs, or fail to earn enough to allow their families to become economically self-sufficient, there is consequently nowhere else for welfare reform researchers and racial state actors to place the blame but on the mothers' assumed value and behavioral deficiencies. Racist culture would blame lack of effort on deficiencies of the Other.

Most welfare reform research has been profoundly conservative, for it uses outcome measures that produce findings which do little more than reinforce the status quo. By continuing to conform their inquiries to the limited "success" criteria embedded in the goals of reform legislation, and ignoring gender and racial inequalities, welfare reform researchers are unlikely to find reason for the radical policy changes that would be necessary to eliminate poverty. Rather, by limiting the realm of discourse within which research findings are sought and interpreted, all they can recommend is modest fine-tuning of present welfare reform policies to better exercise control over poor mothers. Much debate is likely to revolve around how to better provide incentives to change poor people's work behavior, and whether it would be more effective to increase the carrot or the stick. This fine-tuning is likely to occur with little knowledge or understanding of how it will affect mothers and children of color. Again, the greatest bias here is in the questions that go unasked, and therefore unanswered.

While the numerous welfare reform research reports that appeared from 1998 to 2000 to which we referred above are largely racism blind, many reveal crucial problems that welfare reform has created or left unaddressed for poor people regardless of their skin color. Taken as a whole, the reports we scrutinized show that welfare reform has exacerbated income difficulties for many poor mothers, placed increased stress on family members, and inadequately addressed impoverished families' needs for child care, transportation, housing, health care, and nutrition. While welfare reform researchers generally did not address the degree to which these problems were distributed along racial lines, it is safe to conclude that people of color were disproportionately hurt.

We have shown in this chapter that, despite the failure of welfare reform monitors to address it, there is abundant evidence that welfare racism is thriving across the nation. With the return to a states' rights approach to welfare policy, discussed at the beginning of this chapter, we should expect welfare racism to increase significantly.

POST-AFDC RACISM: THE ROUTE TO INCREASED RACIAL AND CLASS BALKANIZATION

The states' rights approach to welfare policy that was institutionalized by the Personal Responsibility and Work Opportunity Reconciliation Act of 1996 has done more than allow welfare racism to persist. It has helped welfare racism to increase. The numerous and varied expressions of welfare racism we have presented in this chapter should certainly make clear that ignoring race and racism in analyses of welfare reform proposals and legislation is one way of ignoring their racial consequences.

As we have shown, most mainstream welfare reform research is being performed, if not by or under the aegis of the racial state, then within domain assumptions that are often informed by racist culture. These assumptions include the notion that welfare reform is "race blind," and that federal and individual state TANF policies—from conception to execution—have nothing to do with race. Nonetheless, it is apparent from welfare researchers' own policy outcome reports that the impact of these policies has proved to be destabilizing, disruptive, and harmful to millions of impoverished mothers and children. As oblivious to the fact as most welfare reform researchers might be, there is no way to hide that those being directly and most adversely affected are disproportionately families of color.

While he did not address the racial impact of present-day welfare reform policy, in *Race, Money, and the American Welfare State* historian Michael Brown drew attention to the economic significance that welfare has long had for impoverished African-American mothers. Although Brown limited his comments to African Americans, they no doubt apply to other poor mothers of color as well. Brown noted that black and white women have had different kinds of experiences with federal racial state programs, since many function in ways that favor white women. Notably, "black women find themselves relying upon welfare more than white women." [111] While racist culture might support the notion that this reliance has been a matter of choice, the truth is more complicated.

White mothers have been more likely than black mothers to have access to sources of federal racial state aid besides AFDC or TANF, such as Social Security disability or survivor's benefits, unemployment compensation, and veterans benefits. Not only have whites had more access to such non-means-tested forms of income, but these forms of aid have generally provided higher benefits than those that were means tested. They have thus done a better job than public assistance in helping to move white families out of poverty. The cash assistance available to black mothers under welfare, in contrast, has tended to "merely reshuffle black mothers along the poverty line; rather than being raised out of poverty, they are made less poor, an important but nevertheless insufficient outcome." [112]

What happens, though, when racial state actors remove the welfare safety net, upon which mothers of color are by necessity more reliant than are white mothers? How are families of color to rise above poverty, given that they have less access to alternative income and wealth sources on which whites can more frequently rely?[113] Under current policy conditions, impoverished mothers of color are indeed more dependent upon welfare, but not by choice. The racial state now wants them off public assistance, but is consigning them to a market economy that does not want them either, except as easily exploitable labor. For many mothers and children of color, income impoverishment is being institutionalized under racial state welfare reform policies, just as wealth impoverishment was institutionalized by racial state bank and housing policies for African Americans.[114]

While much has changed over the last sixty-five years with regard to particular expressions of welfare racism, its overall continuity is obvious. Racialized attitudes, policy making, and administrative practices—whether overtly race based or more subtly—continue to afflict public assistance programs, and to have a disproportionately adverse affect on eligibility and benefit levels for racially oppressed groups. Insofar as present-day welfare reform policies of the federal racial state do not reduce poverty among people of color, and insofar as the failure of people of color to rise above poverty is successfully explained away as due to their deficits, notions of white superiority will be legitimated and racist culture will be strengthened. This racist culture, in turn, reinforces the very welfare policies that function to maintain racial control over poor people of color. It is imperative that scholars, welfare reform policy analysts, advocacy groups, and journalists work to break this cycle. All need to make the connection between the racial inequalities that prevail in U.S. society and the harm now being done to people of color by welfare reform.

Denial of the salience of welfare racism, along with racism in other realms of social life, will have consequences. The likelihood that contemporary welfare reform will fail to make inroads into poverty among people of color, together with the eradication of welfare as an entitlement and a safety net, will worsen racial inequalities and stratification. It will also contribute to the racial and class Balkanization of U.S. society and the conflict to which this will give rise.

The conditions faced by millions of impoverished families and the millions more threatened with impoverishment—European Americans as well as people of color—demand that we place antipoverty and antiracism programs on the racial state agenda. In the next chapter, we suggest some ways in which those who are outraged by these conditions can help to push the racial state and other key societal actors in that direction.

8
CONFRONTING
WELFARE RACISM

Poverty in the United States is not color-blind. The debate preceding the 1996 welfare law made the color of poverty the fault of the poor. We insist that the color of poverty is the consequence of racism and related forms of discrimination. Accordingly, our proposal proceeds from the recognition that race affects the material basis for caregiving, privileging some women at the expense of others. We call for policies that address the shared vulnerabilities of women of all races, beginning with the particular vulnerabilities of the poorest caregivers, especially poor women of color.

Women's Committee of 100

the organization of racialized public assistance attitudes, policy making, and administrative practices. For people of color, poverty and racism are simply different sides of the same racial oppression coin. As was evident, however, in the abolition of the Aid to Families with Dependent Children (AFDC) program, welfare racism is now so central to U.S. welfare policy that it directly affects all of the poor, not just those of color. Indeed, the majority of this nation's poor, European Americans, suffer greatly from the poverty-policy racism that results in *all* poor people being treated as social, political, and economic "niggers." Consequently, any serious movement for economic justice in the United States must have as a core value and goal the eradication of racism and its consequences.

Our final chapter is devoted exclusively to what can be done to confront welfare racism. We begin by stressing the urgency of moving beyond the popular societal predisposition to deny the existence and significance of white racism and its catastrophic effect on the U.S. response to poverty. We conclude by briefly sharing our vision of the type of commitment needed to seriously embark on that journey and what U.S. poverty policy might look like if, indeed, it were able to move beyond racism.

As we have shown, welfare racism helped shape the formation, implementation, and outcomes of the AFDC program, and later contributed mightily to its demise. However, as we also make clear, the abolition of AFDC ended neither public assistance programs nor welfare racism. Welfare racism was integral to the formation of the Temporary Assistance for Needy Families program (TANF) that replaced AFDC, and continues to play a major role in TANF's operation and evolution. True to its history, the "shape shifter" we call welfare racism has once again transformed itself in ways that will ensure its persistence. Today, as was the case prior to the civil rights movement and successful legal challenges to punitive welfare policies, welfare racism's primary base of operation is the individual state and local levels of the racial state. The need to confront welfare racism is evident when we examine recent poverty and economic inequality statistics.

THE GOOD TIMES: A CLOSER LOOK

The Personal Responsibility and Work Opportunity Reconciliation Act of 1996 has been widely acclaimed as a success. Consistent with the prevailing conservative ideology that welfare dependency is the problem and not poverty, the claim for the act's success is based almost entirely on its reduction of the welfare rolls. Indeed, the drop in the size of the welfare rolls has been dramatic. Between 1996 (the year the PRWORA was passed) and 1999, there was a 58 percent decline in the average monthly number of families enrolled in AFDC or its successor, TANF.[1] Whites have left welfare more rapidly than persons of color; in

1999, two-thirds of TANF families were of color. The largest category of recipients was black, 38 percent, followed by white recipients with 31 percent. Twenty-five percent were Latino/a, 3 percent were Asian and Pacific Islanders, and 1.5 percent were classified as American Indian or Alaskan Native.[2]

Those who argue that welfare dependency is the primary cause of poverty may be tempted to believe that the PRWORA has resulted not only in a major reduction in the public assistance case rolls, but, indeed, in a significant reduction in poverty itself. To support that view they might point to recent statistics on the decline of poverty rates in the United States. For example, in 1999 there were 32.3 million poor people in the United States, or 11.8 percent of the total population, the lowest poverty rate since 1979. There was also good news for African Americans. In 1999 the black poverty rate fell to a record low of 23.6 percent.[3]

Is welfare reform responsible for this overall decline in poverty? No. The reduction of poverty is primarily the result of the longest and most robust expansion of the economy in U.S. history. As of the year 2000, the last time the U.S. economy was in recession was March 1991. The economic boom of the 1990s was accompanied by the lowest unemployment rates in three decades.[4] Not only did recent racial state welfare reform policies not reduce poverty, but one consequence of both those policies and the 1990s economic boom has been increased income and wealth inequality.[5]

Despite the overall decline in poverty and unemployment, conditions have worsened in recent years for those families who need welfare and other forms of help the most. While the PRWORA is an antiwelfare program, it is clearly not an antipoverty program. Rather than significantly reducing the number of poor people in poverty as the "work opportunity" portion of its title suggests, the act has simply forced a larger proportion of the poor from welfare to work that pays poverty-level wages, and has left many without Medicaid or food stamps.[6] That is, it has forced them into the growing ranks of the working poor.[7] Many other mothers are even less fortunate. They have been forced off the welfare rolls without a job.[8]

Not surprisingly, there has been an increase in the incidence of "extreme child poverty" in mother-headed families, those whose incomes are one-half of the federal poverty line or below. The Children's Defense Fund has noted that while children who receive public assistance benefits are poor, they do not necessarily fall into the ranks of "extreme poverty." Consequently, the extreme poverty measure is a better indicator of the effects of welfare reform on the poverty circumstances of children. Employing this measure and U.S. Census Bureau data in its analysis, the Children's Defense Fund found that "among children in single-mother families—the group most affected by the welfare law—the number of children living below one-half the poverty line rose by 26 percent from 1996 to 1997." The study found this increase in extreme poverty to be directly related to what one of its report's headings referred to as "the weakening protective role of public assistance and food stamps." In 1997 the percent of children in mother-only families with incomes at or less than half of the federal poverty line was especially high for Latinos/as (12 percent), followed by blacks (10.7 percent) and whites (9.5 percent). [9] The increase in extreme child poverty after the passage of the PRWORA is an ominous sign of what might happen when its five-year time limit for benefits begins to take its full effect. [10]

Some welfare policy analysts fear that with the abolition of the Aid to Families with Dependent Children program, as the economy shrinks the situation of the poor will become even more precarious. [11] This is likely to be especially true for people of color. There have been huge racial disparities in poverty and income inequality even during the best of economic times. During economically difficult times, African-American and other workers of color have tended to be "the last hired" and "the first fired." The statistics on poor people of color we have examined here are troubling. While these figures show a decline in the overall percentage of people of color in poverty, a closer look reveals that many millions remain trapped in a very precarious and ominous situation even in a period of sustained economic growth.

Important lessons arise from consideration of these poverty and economic inequality data that need to be communicated effectively in movements against welfare racism. These lessons include the following. "Race" and racism still play a major role in determining who is poor, who is in need of public assistance, who faces extreme poverty, and who is likely to be most hurt as the economic cycle enters its next recession. Moreover, in evaluating the effects of welfare reform on poor people of color as well as whites, it is essential to examine its consequences for those who are diverted from receiving welfare at all, as well as for former welfare recipients, not just its effectiveness in reducing the size of the welfare rolls.

With welfare reform pushing poor mothers from welfare to work without changing their poverty status, antipoverty and antiracism initiatives must include targeting the working poor and the problems they face. The plight of poor whites and poor people of color cannot be understood apart from the issue of economic inequality and the policy decisions that tend to exacerbate it. In recent years a booming economy, not welfare reform or what some falsely argue is the de-racialization of U.S. society, has been responsible for declines in poverty. Both poverty rates and racial discrimination in employment can be expected to rise with economic recessions. Moreover, when recessions hit, many of the customary safety nets will no longer be in place. The needs will be greatest, of course, for those facing extreme poverty.

BEYOND THE POLITICS OF DENIAL

As we have shown, the link between poverty and skin color is strong. This fact is one of many reflections of white racism. Unfortunately, as we discussed earlier, the dominant European-American response to racism today is denial.[12] To the frustration of grassroots community organizers who were asked "to speak out on race" for the Applied Research Center's *ColorLines* magazine, all too often people refuse to see the racism that blocks the way of effective progressive social movement organizing.[13]

Elaborate ideological schemes have been developed by dominant racial group members to justify the denial of the existence and significance of white racism. These range from the extremely antisociological "there is no systemic racism: we are all just individuals" color-blind ideology advocated by the political right; to the "let's just try to get along" avoidance of needed challenges to the racial status quo of political moderates and liberals; to the "close your eyes for the revolution" class-consciousness wishful thinking of the political left.[14] Consequently, the denial of racism seems to ultimately be an issue of racial politics, not what we ordinarily think of as left, right, or center political ideology. Again, regardless of political orientation and specific ideological reasons for doing so, the general tendency among those designated as "white" when it comes to acknowledging the existence of racism is the same: denial.

Since the political left may be most inclined to challenge welfare racism if it were able to free itself of immobilizing ideologies, let's take a closer look at its ideological fetters. The dominant left political ideology assumes that if it can just, somehow, move beyond "race" and whatever else divides it, the working class could be united in a broad-based movement for economic justice. Jill Quadagno's *The Color of Welfare* is a case in point. While Quadagno's book makes some noteworthy contributions to our understanding of welfare racism, it is clearly limited by her preoccupation with white working-class attitudes. Despite its title, Quadagno's study focuses more on negative white reactions to the civil rights movement as an obstacle to the evolution of the U.S. welfare state than it does on systemic white racism and the support it receives from racial state elites. Indeed, the moral of Quadagno's analytical story seems to be that white people should not be challenged or provoked. The goal of progressive poverty policy should be to avoid white political backlashes.[15]

Central to the denial of the existence or significance of racism is the tendency to ignore the fact that race and racism are essential components of the organization of racialized societies. In such societies it is, by definition, *impossible* to move "beyond race." Unfortunately, there is a "culture of silence" in contemporary U.S. society regarding white racism. That profound silence has enveloped the highly careerist and politically opportunistic mainstream of U.S. contemporary social science and public policy analysis.[16] Sometimes that silence takes a more active turn as denial, and on occasion the denial becomes militant. The "race" and urban poverty writings of African-American sociologist William J. Wilson are a case in point of the militant denial of the significance of systemic racism in contemporary U.S. society and in its antipoverty policies.

Just as Wilson confused the ever-changing nature of U.S. racism with what he deemed "the declining significance of race," he is also wrong in his advocacy of racism-blind poverty policies to address the high rates of African-American urban poverty. Neither the "disappearance" of work in racially segregated neighborhoods or its consequences are "race neutral."[17] Moreover, it is most improbable that the so-called "race-neutral programs" that Wilson advocates would, indeed, be race neutral in a society where virtually every significant social structure is highly racialized.[18]

Racism-blind public policies are often offered in the name of being politically practical. That is, it is claimed that racism-focused programs cannot work, politically. All too often in social science policy-related research such political choices are treated as value-neutral social science. Career benefits like large research grants and being included as a part of the public policy mainstream are most likely to accrue to those who locate themselves within the center of existing political discourse, even if such discourse is fundamentally racist and in other ways inhumane in its basic assumptions and outcomes.

Color-blind economic justice strategies can work only in color-blind societies. There is no evidence that the United States is color-blind or will be so in the foreseeable future. Color blindness in a highly racialized society—a society which is structured around "race"—is, rather, *racism blindness*. Racism blindness is an increasingly essential ingredient in the ideological glue that holds such societies together. Racism blindness not only ignores the powerful impact that systemic white racism has on determining who is poor in the United States, but damages all poor people by helping to shape this nation's response to poverty.[19]

Conceptually, welfare and other poverty-focused policies and programs may be placed along a continuum based on their response to systemic white racism. This continuum ranges from racism-based action to racism-blind inaction, to racism-cognizant acknowledgment of the existence of racism, to prevention-focused racism-sensitive safeguards, to racism-targeted interventions.[20]

Continuum of Public Policy Response to Racism

Racism-driven policies and programs are significantly influenced by racist sentiments, attitudes, and goals. Racism-blind policies and programs do nothing to challenge welfare racism. Indeed, as a policy ideology[21] of denial they reinforce it. Racism-cognizant policies and programs acknowledge racism as a cause of

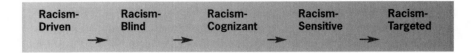

Racism-Driven	Racism-Blind	Racism-Cognizant	Racism-Sensitive	Racism-Targeted
→	→	→	→	

poverty and punitive welfare policies, but offer little if anything to specifically challenge that racism. Racism-sensitive *safeguards*, like the inclusion of strong preventative antidiscrimination provisions as part of public assistance legislation, or the media's self-monitoring of its racial depictions of the poor, can challenge welfare racism. Finally, racism-targeted *interventions* are needed to address racism-specific causes of poverty and to challenge existing racialized poverty policy when there are no internal racism-sensitive safeguards in place or they do not work effectively.

In contrast to prevention-focused internal racism-sensitive safeguard mechanisms, racism-targeted interventions come from outside the entity to be challenged. A political movement to pass laws to better monitor and prosecute racial discrimination in the implementation of existing welfare policies, and citizen groups' monitoring of the media's racial portrayal of the poor, are examples of racism-targeted interventions. Challenges to welfare racism cannot be racism blind. Racism cognizance is merely a start. Effective challenges to welfare racism *must be* either racism sensitive or racism targeted.

As long as welfare racism is allowed to go unconfronted it will continue to have devastating effects for all poor and working-class Americans. In the absence of effective challenges to welfare racism, impoverished Americans will remain deprived of both the welfare state resources they need and opportunities to organize along class, gender, and other lines that go beyond racial identity. In brief, what is ultimately needed is a broad-based movement for economic justice that incorporates into its ideologies, strategies, and tactics specific ways of addressing welfare racist attitudes, policies, and practices. What are needed are anti–welfare racist strategies and tactics.

STRATEGIES AND TACTICS FOR CONFRONTING WELFARE RACISM

> Our three-pronged attack includes the streets, the legislature, and the courts for helping people out of poverty.
>
> Marian Kramer, chair, National Welfare Rights Union, 1994

To this three-pronged attack we would add another important antipoverty strategy: the education that can come, for example, from the informative and inspiring words and actions of welfare rights advocates like Marian Kramer. In this section we will explore four major anti–welfare racism strategies: education, research, and monitoring; legislative policy action; legal remedies; and social protest and grassroots organizing. Rather than being distinct, these four strategies overlap, often joining forces to make a successful strategy possible.

Education, Research, and Monitoring

The cognitive liberation portion of sociologist Doug McAdam's political process model of black insurgency suggests that education and its research and monitoring components can inspire social movement activity. It is in this way that "a significant segment of the aggrieved population" come to "collectively define their situation as unjust and as subject to change through group action."[22] The usefulness of McAdam's model is, of course, not limited to explaining the emergence of social movement activity among African Americans. Because of the racial, class, and gender consequences of welfare racism, educational tactics should be targeted to include not only welfare recipients, but all poor people, people of color, women, and political progressives who might feel aggrieved if made sufficiently aware of the racist, sexist, and class-elitist nature and consequences of welfare racism. Initiatives against welfare racism should therefore strive to inform both the general public and potential activists of the overall impact of welfare racism on poor people of color and the white poor. Central to that educational process are tactics that disseminate information challenging racialized ideologies about poverty and racist controlling images of poor women of color.[23]

It is essential that such educational campaigns make clear that battling welfare racist attitudes does not benefit only poor people of color. When poor people of color are subjected to racist stereotypes that depict them as undeserving, and when public assistance programs are racialized as "black" programs and then attacked, the European-American poor suffer terrible consequences. This fact should be stressed by welfare rights activists and others who work with impoverished European Americans, who may otherwise see campaigns against welfare racism as being irrelevant, if not hostile, to their interests. Finally, successful educational campaigns about the nature, significance, and persistence of welfare racism must also make clear its systemic character (e.g., the fact that it cannot be reduced to a relatively small number of racially bigoted caseworkers); the important social, political, and economic functions welfare racism serves, from which more affluent whites benefit the most; and its ability to manifest itself in different forms as the need arises.

Of course, before information or knowledge can be disseminated it must be gathered. Research activities of various types are needed to collect information on welfare racist attitudes, policies, and practices that can then serve as the basis for educational, legislative policy, legal, and social protest challenges. Since the widespread dissemination of negative controlling images through the media is a major means by which welfare racism is promoted, initiatives are needed to monitor and challenge racist media images. Effective monitoring activities include both the process of educating through research and the use of that knowledge in more direct forms of anti–welfare racism challenges.

A media-focused monitoring initiative was undertaken by *TomPaine.Common-Sense: A Journal of Opinion.* Through its website, that progressive magazine disseminated articles on the findings and implications of political scientist Martin Gilens's important study on the highly racialized magazine portrayals of the poor that we discussed earlier. In one of those articles, Gilens explored possible solutions to "media misrepresentations." Gilens's tactical suggestions were limited to what media organizations themselves could do. They included the hiring of more journalists of color in hopes that this would make those organizations more cognizant of the problem. Consistent with what we would refer to as racism-sensitive internal safeguards, Gilens noted that "photo audits" have already been initiated by some news media entities. Such audits quantify how people of color are depicted in news stories. As an example of this tactic, Gilens noted a photo audit initiated by the *Seattle Times* as early as 1988. That audit's findings of overwhelmingly negative depictions of people of color were followed by a discussion and "consciousness raising" educational tactic within the newspaper that produced dramatically more positive results for the next audit.[24]

While we would not want to discourage effective efforts at self-monitoring on the part of the mass media, we think that greater and more enduring accountability is possible through external monitoring. Such monitoring works best when it is linked to an educational program (e.g., via websites) that can disseminate both the findings and appropriate methods for other groups to engage in similar monitoring tactics. The Applied Research Center–sponsored Grass Roots Innovative Policy Program (GRIPP) has supported such a media monitoring project. Its media associate group, We Interrupt This Message (WITM), examined the media's coverage of TANF over a one-year period. That analysis found that in the wake of the PRWORA, the dominant controlling image of welfare recipients was no longer the highly racialized "welfare queen." Newer, more positive images had appeared, including the "hardworking, happy, *former* recipient." While media welfare images may be undergoing some changes, consistent with both the history of welfare racism we have documented and with what we have concluded about its shape-shifting ability, the newer, more positive images tend to be of white women. So-called hard-core recipients who have not been able to escape their so-called culture of poverty are more likely to be depicted with people of color. We Interrupt This Message expressed concern that the "demonization" of recipients will intensify "as it becomes more widely reported that a lot of the folks still receiving assistance are Black and Latino."[25]

To combat racist media images of welfare recipients, WITM suggested a proactive strategy that includes, but goes beyond, countering negative media images. More stories are needed to communicate what is actually happening to the poor, and to provide alternative ways of framing the causes and solutions of poverty problems and welfare issues. With training and technical support services provided by groups such as WITM, community organizations and public interest groups can be assisted in offering accurate stories about poor people.[26]

Another way of combating negative controlling images of welfare recipients is, of course, through social protest targeted at news organizations that regularly promote racist stereotypes. Social protest tactics could include demonstrations at and boycotts of local newspapers, televison and radio stations; community forums, teach-ins, and speak-outs that focus on media bias; and well-publicized complaints to the Federal Communications Commission.

We will next combine thoughts from our discussion of educational, research, and monitoring challenges to racist media images with our earlier conceptualizations of the functions of welfare racism, the continuum of types of racism-related policy actions, and overlapping anti–welfare racist strategies and tactics. By doing so we hope to at least outline what a systematic challenge to the media's racist controlling images of welfare recipients might look like, and how and why it could work. We also hope that this exercise will suggest how the contours of other systematic anti–welfare racism strategies and tactics could be delineated.

As we noted earlier, welfare racism persists in large part due to the social, economic, and political functions it serves. Since the mass media can benefit economically by disseminating racist media images that bolster white racial identity and prestige at the expense of poor people of color, there is value to such activity. Pursuit of this value is made easy in cooperation with political elites, who need receptive media outlets for welfare racist messages and policies that serve their own and their political party's ambitions. Only through persistent, relentless monitoring and public exposure of media organizations and political elites who exploit racist controlling images of the poor can the social, economic, and political costs of such actions be raised to such a point that their respective values are diminished beyond a level where they are worth pursuing.

That high cost/low rewards threshold is typically the socially disreputable manifestation of overt racism. This threshold can be introduced by making camouflaged racism "overt" through social protest (including, of course, economic boycotts), litigation, and electoral politics. These activities require the backing of education, research, and monitoring campaigns that publicize both the racism inherent in political elites' discourse and the specific benefits that particular groups derive from them. Racism-sensitive safeguards and racism-targeted interventions become possible only after people are made racism cognizant. Achieving racism cognizance entails exposing race-based discourse and actions in such a way that makes racism blindness no longer feasible.

Education, like research, can be formal or informal. College courses and books are part of the structure of formal education that can influence not only voting behavior but, indeed, the next generation of policy makers. Books that are targeted to reach audiences beyond the classroom can also influence current public policy debates. There is also more experientially based education on movement organizing. An example is the political education activities of the Philadelphia-based Kensington Welfare Rights Union (KWRU). For the KWRU, political education is inseparable from organizing.[27]

Somewhere in between education and organizing are the sometimes highly useful reports produced by research- and advocacy-focused organizations like the Children's Defense Fund and the Center on Budget and Policy Priorities. Earlier, we identified groups such as these that have been involved in research and advocacy regarding the harmful effects of welfare reform. Unfortunately, as we noted, welfare racism has tended not to be a focus of their research. The consequences of such racism-blind analyses are often evident in what they propose or do not propose in the way of legislative policy action. Supporters of such groups and the users of their research should ask that they directly address the effects of racism on welfare and poverty policies, and propose appropriate legislative policy solutions.

Legislative Policy Action

The goal of legislation-focused antiracist initiatives should be the enactment of legislation that is explicitly racism sensitive and racism targeted. Antiracism legislation must be targeted at not only intentionally racist actions, but at the racially differential outcomes of institutionalized racism. This is the approach being taken by the British government through its Race Relations Act, largely in response to political pressures following widely publicized incidents of racist police misconduct. All government agencies are to examine the racial composition of their employee populations, their policies and practices, and the effects of those policies and practices on different racial and ethnic groups.[28]

There is a great need for antiracist groups to push for such legislation at the individual state and federal levels in the United States. Noting that individual states now have control of much of welfare reform, the Rainbow/PUSH Coalition argues that states should be pressured to enact legislation calling for a "disparate impact analysis" of the PRWORA. Antidiscrimination legislation and agency training should be provided to reduce racial and gender disparities in welfare reform.[29] Focusing attention on problems at the local level, the Applied

Research Center has called for the development of "equity impact statements" that would address "bias that is firmly rooted in local conditions."[30]

In May 2000, some 2,000 delegates from forty-four states, most of whom were low-income leaders from a wide variety of grassroots groups, met to found the National Campaign for Jobs and Income Support. One of the campaign's platform principles is: "Race and gender equity shall be a central goal of all policies, programs and practices adopted to eliminate poverty." The campaign aims to "ensure equal access to benefits for immigrants, including language accessibility," and to "eliminate discrimination on the basis of race, gender, and sexual orientation in services, jobs, and income support." The National Campaign has begun working with grassroots organizations to document and expose inequitable treatment and the denial of access to food stamps, Medicaid, health and child-care services, and other services needed by the poor.[31] Legislative initiatives could be built around the findings.

Clearly, there is much that can be done by policy research groups and grassroots welfare rights organizations even in the absence of such legislation. Relevant government agencies and those they contract welfare services out to can be publicly pressured to conduct "racial audits" to demonstrate that all poor people are benefiting from programs equally and are making equal use of services.[32] This includes, of course, European-American welfare recipients as well as recipients of color.

Finally, financial incentives could be offered to reward those offices and contractors that find jobs for welfare recipients of color which on average pay the same as those found for European-American welfare recipients.[33] Racism-sensitive monitoring safeguards should be included in all future public assistance legislation. Appropriate government agencies should be made to take racism-targeted actions to ensure that current public assistance policies do not violate existing laws against racial discrimination.

The most direct manifestation of the power behind public policy is electoral politics. Key events in the abolition of AFDC were the election of Bill Clinton as president in 1992, based in part on his promise "to end welfare as we know it" and the election two years later of a conservative Republican–dominated Congress that made punitive welfare reform a part of its "Contract With America." Electoral politics have played a major role in the formulation, enactment, and implementation of welfare racist policies. Indeed, aside from the War on Poverty and other rare exceptions, when the federal racial state has been forced to play an ameliorative role as the political regulator of U.S. race relations, its dominant racial impact has been repressive.

The predicament that poor people and their advocates face is how to affect electoral politics and legislative processes when they lack the substantial economic and other resources that are needed to do so. Is it possible, for example, for poor people and people of color to join with small numbers of relatively affluent antiracist European Americans to challenge the "tyranny of the majority" inherent in this nation's highly racialized democracy and win more progressive and humane welfare policies?[34] Since their combined numbers do not add up to make them a decisive political force, how do they ensure that their voices are heard? Unlike the wealthy, the poor do not have the money to employ media and policy organizations, or to buy the backing of politicians and other political elites to shape welfare discourse and policy. So what can poor people do?

For the poor, influencing electoral politics and ultimately public policy legislation may require using social protest, which is often the only resource available to them. Piven and Cloward suggest that through the strategic use of social protest the poor can disrupt, or threaten to disrupt, the political coalitions that politicians count on to win elections.[35] In this way the political value of welfare racism can be diminished in direct proportion to the increase in its political costs.

Most European Americans do not wish to be seen as supporting a political system that has been demonstrated to be overtly racist and where there is no attempt at reform. Overtly racist actions by the racial state and its political elites are an embarrassment and threat to the stratification beliefs (beliefs about who gets what and why) and self-esteem of European Americans that many will not normally endure. Social protests by the poor and their supporters that make politicians appear as racially meanspirited as their actions therefore threaten their political survival.

Legal Remedies

Legal challenges to welfare racism are often inextricably intertwined with educational, legislative policy, and social protest remedies. We noted earlier that lawsuits and legal briefs prepared for administrative hearings were successful tactics in eliminating many of the most punitive public assistance provisions in the 1960s. We also discussed how in Louisiana a racist welfare law was passed in response to successful legal challenges to that state's system of white racial supremacy, and how organizations like the American Civil Liberties Union and the National Urban League then filed briefs challenging the Louisiana law at administrative hearings held by what was then known as the U.S. Department of Health, Education, and Welfare. We also noted earlier that it was legal challenges by New York state welfare officials which ultimately resulted in a permanent injunction by the courts that stopped the racist Newburgh welfare reform initiative aimed at blocking what was perceived as a flood of southern African-American migrants to that city.

Many of the civil rights movement–era lawsuit challenges to welfare racism were a part of the same welfare rights movement that benefited from activist social science and involved extensive use of social protest. For example, from the mid-1960s through the early 1970s, the National Welfare Rights Organization and the War on Poverty's Legal Services Program worked together on class action suits aimed at reforming the welfare system through the courts.[36] A landmark welfare racism decision was rendered in 1975 when a three-judge U.S. District Court ruled in favor of a class action suit filed in the name of black recipients of Aid to Families with Dependent Children against the Alabama Department of Pensions and Security. That suit challenged racial discrimination in both "purpose" and "effect" in the "allocation" and "payment" of the predominantly black AFDC program, compared to the mostly white Old Age Assistance program in that state. The testimony of a former commissioner of the Department of Pensions and Security was noted to be "perhaps the most striking evidence in this case" in which it was found that disparity of treatment of people in the two programs "violated the equal protection clause of the Fourteenth Amendment" of the U.S. Constitution. In a statement which he later elaborated on to confirm that such views had been expressed by Alabama state legislators, the former commissioner stated that a specific criticism of the program was that "most of the people in this state and, I think, throughout the country think that most of the people on AFDC are colored."[37]

Some federal racial state actors and policy analysts have acknowledged that greater civil rights protections are needed. For example, researchers at the Urban Institute, with support from the U.S. Department of Housing and Urban Development, have expressed interest in developing new measures of racial and ethnic discrimination with an eye toward possibly developing a "national report card" on how the United States is doing in this regard. A volume of papers presented at a 1998 conference on this topic suggested that, among other things, the report card on discrimination could help "identify barriers to the achievement of important social objectives (such as promoting work among former welfare recipients)." The following argument was made for the importance of monitoring racial disparities in work outcomes under welfare reform:

> Welfare reform, for example, is spurring the entry of a new cohort of low-wage, low-skilled workers into the labor force. Most of the new entrants are women; many are members of racial and ethnic minorities. The success of the policies designed to promote welfare-to-work transitions is premised upon low barriers to labor force entry, including low levels of workplace discrimination.[38]

The existence of race-based employment discrimination is especially unfortunate, given the high stakes involved for impoverished families. As the quote above suggested, welfare-to-work policies made mandatory under recent welfare reforms were premised on low levels of racial and gender discrimination. Poor mothers of color who can barely support their children on TANF, and who are sanctioned off or run out their time limits for TANF eligibility, have very few options for their families' survival other than to find work somewhere. Being turned away from employment opportunities because they are not "white" makes survival extremely difficult.

When the PRWORA was passed in 1996, federal racial state welfare officials should have been clearly aware of the likelihood of racially discriminatory treatment, not only by employers, but also by individual state and local welfare agencies administering welfare reform policies. Yet, it was three full years after passage of the PRWORA before the Office for Civil Rights of the U.S. Department of Health and Human Services formally advised the individual states of the federal protections afforded poor people who apply for or receive aid through state-run TANF programs.[39] In August 1999, notice of the need to comply with civil rights laws was directed at welfare providers, caseworkers, and both public and private contractors hired by state or local welfare agencies to help implement welfare reform.

Clearly cognizant of possible ways in which racism could be expressed in the implementation of welfare reform policies, the DHHS's Office of Civil Rights offered those notified many examples of prohibited practices, such as the following:

• "Welfare workers may not reject an applicant for benefits because he is or appears to be an African-American, Hispanic, Asian, American Indian, Alaskan Native, or a member of another racial or ethnic minority."

• Welfare programs may not "impose different standards or procedures to determine who may receive benefits on the basis of race, color, national origin, disability, or age, or on the basis of sex in education programs."

• "A welfare office may not refuse to provide translated written materials to applicants when a significant proportion are limited English proficient."

• "Employees should not question the authenticity of documents submitted by applicants who are or who appear to be Hispanic, in the absence of independent evidence to warrant such inquiry."

• "Employees must provide complete information to all persons who ask questions about the type of benefits, including job training assistance, placement, and other services, and not fail or refuse to provide the same, complete information on opportunities to persons who are or appear to be Asian."

- "Individuals who refer welfare participants to an employer may not make assignments on the basis of race, color, national origin, citizenship status, religion, sex, age, or disability. Thus, for example, a job placement service for welfare recipients may not assign African-Americans to janitorial and sanitation positions and whites with similar backgrounds to entry-level office positions."

- "Employers and those referring welfare recipients to employers may not discriminate on the basis that a person looks 'foreign' or has an accent."

- "Employers may not discriminate on the basis of race, color, national origin, citizenship status, sex, age, religion, or disability in the payment of wages."

- "A contractor that provides jobs training or referral services may not use a high school diploma requirement for participation in training programs, or use another requirement that excludes disproportionate numbers of minorities, unless such a requirement is job related and consistent with business necessity."[40]

In any kind of situation in which racial discrimination occurs, people of color are often unsure as to whether they have in truth been treated illegally, why, or what recourse they have under the law. Moreover, remedies to allegedly unlawful discrimination require that individuals file formal complaints with racial state agencies and get involved with bureaucratic legal processes, which many victims of discrimination often do not know how to do or may be reluctant to do. Protecting impoverished families against racial discrimination is especially difficult, given that many single mothers of color have limited formal education and little understanding of civil rights laws. Poor people in general are not only less likely to be aware of their legal rights than members of more affluent classes; they have less of a sense of efficacy when it comes to "working the system" of law and government. Single mothers are also likely to have many immediate day-to-day personal and family problems that steal energy away from doing battle with welfare bureaucracies. Thus, while legal protection of the civil rights of poor mothers of color under welfare reform is absolutely imperative, systematic enforcement of existing protections is highly problematic.

One of the fears of critics of the Personal Responsibility and Work Opportunity Reconciliation Act of 1996 has been realized. As we have pointed out, the PRWORA places the poor—especially poor people of color—under the type of "states' rights" control that made welfare racist practices commonplace in the past. Thus it is important to demand enforcement of civil rights protections for welfare program applicants and recipients, such as those that have now been outlined by the U.S. Department of Health and Human Services.[41] Specific examples of forbidden welfare racist practices, such as those listed above, should be made available to all welfare rights organizations. Lists of those explicitly prohibited practices can be used in educational, research, and monitoring campaigns.

Today, welfare rights and legal services groups work together through Internet communication links (e.g., www.lincproject.org) organized by activist groups like the New York City-based Welfare Law Center (www.welfarelaw.org), the Center for Community Change (www.commchange.org), and the Applied Research Center (www.arc.org) to use existing civil rights laws to challenge welfare racist practices through administrative hearings and in the courts. The Welfare Law Center stresses that such challenges serve multiple purposes. First, they provide needed relief for low-income people. Second, litigation promotes government accountability by putting welfare agencies on notice that their actions are being observed. Finally, legal challenges help educate the public as to changes needed in public policies.[42]

Given what the historical evidence suggests about the importance of legal challenges to welfare racism, welfare rights advocacy groups should pressure federal-level politicians to significantly increase the resources available to the U.S. Department of Health and Human Services' Office of Civil Rights to investigate discriminatory practices nationwide. Political pressure and monitoring may also be needed to ensure that these additional resources are directed toward this end. There is also a need for racism-sensitive safeguards. We have mentioned the need to build stronger antidiscrimination provisions into all new welfare-related legislation. There is also a need for racism-targeted actions such as the extensive use of federally assigned antidiscrimination testers in welfare offices.

Similar actions should be pushed for at the individual state and local levels. Such efforts are especially needed now since, with the elimination of AFDC, public assistance is no longer a federal entitlement and many of the old federal protections for welfare recipients are no longer in place. Left unconfronted, welfare racism at individual state and local levels may see a return of its "good ole days."

There are limits to what can be achieved today through legal challenges to welfare racism. The courts are, of course, a part of the larger racialized society. When the racial state and the larger society move toward actions that strengthen rather than challenge racism, the courts are inclined to follow suit. In recent years the civil rights movement has reached an impasse as it has found that it can no longer depend on support from the courts in fighting racism. As the political composition of the courts has changed in response to white backlash politics, so has their tendency to require "intent" burdens of proof, usually impossible to meet, for the existence of racism in welfare policies and practices. Increasingly, racially disparate outcomes are not proof enough. This decline in the helpfulness of the court system in combating welfare racism has made social protest even more important as a strategy.

Social Protest and Grassroots Organization

> This is a new millennium. . . . We must make office holders accountable. We must educate and organize our friends, neighbors and strangers. We must unite with other like-minded organizations. We must take advantage of every media opportunity that presents itself. We must demand what we need. We must be heard in the courts, in the legislature, and in the streets. We must get access to the internet and organize with it. We must organize, mobilize rally, march, chant, pray, sit-in, and do whatever is necessary to change the status quo.[43]

With these words, Dottie Stevens, a well-known activist on behalf of economic justice and welfare rights, has issued a call to arms to all persons who are concerned with the harm that punitive welfare reform is doing to the poor. Her eloquent call in the year 2000 is informed by years of struggle along with and on behalf of the poor, a struggle which clearly needs to widen and escalate in intensity in the new millennium.

The Legacy and Lost Lessons of the National Welfare Rights Organization

Business as usual when it comes to U.S. welfare policy is that the voices of the poor, including poor people of color, are unheard. There are, however, rare moments in history when such voices are heard, even if they go unheeded. The brief history of the National Welfare Rights Organization (NWRO) is a case in point.

In the late 1960s, the NWRO was one of the most militant components of the growing "black power" phase of the African-American freedom movement. Through its contentious and often flamboyant tactics it managed to antagonize some of the most powerful members of Congress. These included Representative Wilbur Mills of Arkansas and Senator Russell Long of Louisiana. It was Senator Long, the majority whip[44] and chair of the Senate Finance Committee, who is said to have referred to a group of NWRO members, who staged a "wait-in" to demand that their views on the Mills-drafted 1967 Amendment to the Social Security Act be heard, as "brood mares."[45]

In these congressmen's minds, and in the thinking of other segregationist congressional leaders, welfare, the NWRO, that summer's "riots," and black militancy were all inseparable. It was within this white political backlash environment that the amendment was enacted. It contained a funding "freeze" provision to limit the number of AFDC recipients. The freeze would have hampered the NWRO's efforts to encourage those who qualified for welfare benefits, but who did not already receive them, to apply for welfare and join the NWRO. In brief, the legislation threatened the NWRO's membership campaign. It also placed new and unprecedented work requirements on mothers who received welfare. Senator Robert Kennedy referred to the law as "the most punitive measure in the history of the country."[46]

Ironically, a significant event in the history of the National Welfare Rights Organization was its involvement in the late 1960s with the Poor People's Campaign. We say ironically, because while the National Welfare Rights Organization participated in the Poor People's Campaign and made Martin Luther King Jr.'s highly publicized goal of the attainment of a guaranteed annual family income its primary demand, both were done reluctantly by NWRO leader George Wiley. Wiley was pressured by King into having the NWRO participate in the campaign for the good of the then-struggling civil rights movement.

Wiley disagreed with a one-shot national demonstration and with tactics that centered on broad ideas or goals like a guaranteed annual income. Instead, he preferred more specific battles, where needed, with a major focus on grassroots organization building. At that time the NRWO membership was especially interested in having the new, largely punitive, welfare amendment repealed and in pressuring the federal racial state to force individual states to comply with federal laws protecting the rights of welfare recipients.[47]

The 1968 Poor People's Campaign was aimed at the twin targets of racism and poverty. Unfortunately, its symbolic tent city set up in the nation's capital became hopelessly bogged down in rain and mud; a crisis of leadership in the wake of King's assassination; class and racial divisiveness; violence; and, federal racial state paranoia and repression.[48] Some of that government paranoia and repression came from Senator Robert C. Byrd. In the wake of a violent outbreak of black anger and frustration in Memphis that he and other racial conservatives blamed on King, Senator Byrd led emotional congressional attacks on the planned Poor People's Campaign. Byrd referred to King as "a self-seeking rabble-rouser" and called on the U.S. Department of Justice to seek an injunction to block the campaign, if King led it.[49]

Despite its failure on some levels, the Poor People's Campaign did have its positive moments. One of those came when the National Welfare Rights Organization presented its demands in a 1968 meeting with Wilber Cohen, secretary of the U.S. Department of Health, Education, and Welfare. The "principal demand" was "immediate administrative support for a national guaranteed minimum income of at least $4,000 for every American family." The dollar figure was based on what was estimated to be needed to raise a family of four out of poverty at that time. The proposed policy would also have allowed for annual cost-of-living increases and provided "a work incentive allowing families to keep all earnings up to 25% of their guaranteed minimum income and some portion of additional earnings."[50]

Eligibility for the NWRO-proposed guaranteed minimum income program was to be based on a simple affidavit much like an income tax form.[51] The initiation of such a program would have had profound implications for welfare racism. First, welfare as we know it would have been eliminated. Second, much of the racial discrimination in the administration of aid programs would have been eradicated. There would have been little racial state discretion in determining who was eligible for public assistance or the benefit levels to be provided. Had the voices of the NWRO welfare recipients been heeded, it is unlikely that the problems of welfare policy racism and welfare practices racism would be as serious as they are today.

In addition to the demand for a guaranteed minimum income, other demands were made that did not necessitate congressional approval.[52] Those demands focused on needed changes in the existing AFDC system. All were relevant to the reduction of welfare racist practices.

What the NWRO actually won as a part of its participation in the Poor People's Campaign was limited, but was consistent with the organization's proclivity for achieving practical, concrete, and specific objectives. The federal racial state did pressure the individual states to stop abusing AFDC laws. The U.S. Department of Health, Education, and Welfare agreed to rule changes that were important to welfare recipients, including mandates that individual states not terminate AFDC grants without giving recipients prior notice and that states take action on applications within thirty days. Both provided some protection from welfare racist policies and practices.[53]

In August 1969, racial politics again came into play, after the Nixon administration proposed its Family Assistance Plan (FAP), a negative income tax program that would have provided poor families a guaranteed annual income. Not surprisingly, racial politics influenced analyses of the reasons for the congressional rejection of FAP that were offered by poverty policy scholars. A good place to begin is with Jill Quadagno's *The Color of Welfare*.[54]

In her analysis of the FAP's failure Quadagno stresses the bill's racial origins. The guaranteed annual income idea picked up support only after economic inequality was cited as a cause of urban "riots" by the National Advisory Committee on Civil Disorders. Quadagno notes that while the NWRO mothers favored the concept of a guaranteed income over welfare, they ultimately opposed the Nixon administration's FAP plan for very specific, practical, and concrete reasons: they believed that the administration's bill set minimum benefit levels too low and that its work requirements were too punitive.

In brief, as brilliant as the social policy theory behind the proposal may have been, the welfare recipients decided that they could not live off of social policy theory alone. Moreover, those mothers who were reliant on welfare saw racism as being behind the stinginess and punitiveness of the plan. Quadagno quotes a magazine article on the dispute over the FAP: "In the eyes of the NWRO, the FAP was 'anti-poor, and anti-black . . . a flagrant example of institutional racism,' leading to slavery."[55] An example of the type of racial politics which enveloped the bill was briefly mentioned in a *Newsweek* article. It referred to an unaccepted offer made to the Nixon administration by a "Western Republican to support the bill if it gave Indians only half the regular payment."[56]

The rejection of the FAP by the NWRO upset elite policy analysts like Daniel Patrick Moynihan and James Patterson, who in their writings seem to shake their heads in disbelief and to wag their fingers in disgust at what they suggest was the ignorance, shortsightedness, and ingratitude of the NWRO mothers. They imply that the militant mothers helped defeat perhaps the only chance the United States had to adopt a sensible poverty policy consistent with that of more advanced, Western European welfare states. The following is Patterson's bottom-line assessment of the consequences of "loud protests of the NWRO" which he situates within "the national revolution of expectations, which so often centered on getting more money out of Washington."

> Their efforts were possibly counterproductive. Congressmen did not relish the "invasion," as they saw it, of black welfare clients, and they resented the rhetorical excesses. One contemporary complained bitterly of [NWRO head] Wiley's "diverse Mau Mau tactics." Most important, the stand of the NWRO divided liberals.[57]

What might women on welfare who opposed the FAP have said if Professor Patterson had allowed their voices to be heard in his analysis? Here is what one welfare rights activist had to say about the FAP.

> Who is it that had the audacity to sit down over Scotch on the rocks or whatever you have, pills or Benzedrine or whatever it is, and even consider in this affluent and rich country, where we waste over $70 billion a year on the military, that a family of four should live on $1600? I want to get to him.[58]

Patterson does a much better job of representing the sentiments of affluent European Americans of various political persuasions, which cast highly racialized dispersions on the actions of the NWRO, than he does of articulating the bottom line of the NWRO mothers who relied on welfare. In doing so, he provides ideological justification for the white political backlash in which FAP was caught up without even acknowledging that such a backlash existed. In Patterson's America, while there are fears of black welfare recipients' "Mau Mau" invasions, there is no race and no racism.[59] In this way he privileges analysis of the conduct of noisy black welfare recipients over that of the often quiet operations of white racial hegemony.

Unlike Patterson, Quadagno focused more on the policy demands of the NWRO mothers, which she found to be "realistic," than she did on their tactics and behavior.[60] Quadagno's analysis of the defeat of the FAP also closely examines the opposition of southern conservatives and the effect of Nixon's sudden fear that the passage of the FAP might threaten his racially charged "New Majority" political coalition. Also, unlike Patterson, Quadagno stresses more the political economic reasons for the bill's defeat. This included opposition from the U.S. Chamber of Commerce and from southern politicians who feared that a guaranteed minimum income would threaten the low-wage labor system of the South and might level its racial disparities. In short, that the bill might imperil the South's overall system of racial inequality.[61]

Quadagno notes that for these reasons there was intense opposition from powerful southern Democrats.[62] In what appears to be a clear example of welfare policy racism déjà vu, that opposition was reminiscent of the racialization of the Social Security Act of 1935 which established the Aid to Dependent Children program. In brief, affluent and powerful white male political elites and the major economic interests behind them clearly had a greater say in determining the fate of the FAP than did an organization of angry black mothers who were reliant on welfare. Unfortunately, the same would be true for the federal welfare reform legislation enacted in the mid-1990s.

The Economic Justice Lessons of the National Welfare Rights Union

Two years prior to the enactment of the Personal Responsibility and Work Opportunity Reconciliation Act of 1996, Marian Kramer identified six proposals that the National Welfare Rights Union considered to be essential to any program of genuine welfare reform. The NWRU's first two recommendations were the passage of a minimum wage of $15 per hour and the enactment of enforceable "child-support legislation based on the cost of living." The implementation of those two recommendations would challenge welfare racism in much the same way that the National Welfare Rights Organization's guaranteed annual income would have. They would greatly reduce the need for welfare, and thus the racism that goes with it.

The third National Welfare Rights Union recommendation entailed the nationalization of all forms of public assistance programs. The implementation of this recommendation would take away individual state and local discretion, and with it some of the welfare racism that pervades public assistance. Welfare racism would also be challenged though the implementation of the fourth proposal, which calls for the establishment of "uniform standards for eligibility above the poverty line for all public assistance recipients at the state and federal levels," and by the fifth recommendation that all grant-level penalties be abolished." The sixth and final NWRU proposal was an end to various individual states' fraud-targeted, punitive welfare policies (e.g., mandatory fingerprinting or digital imaging, and lie detector tests) that treat families receiving welfare like criminals. This proposal would also challenge welfare racism at the individual state and local levels.[63]

The Kensington Welfare Rights Union's Battle for Human Rights for the Poor

Many challenges to welfare racism will originate and be fought at the grassroots level by welfare rights organizations like the NWRU-affiliated Kensington Welfare Rights Union. While the KWRU prides itself in being a "multiracial group of poor and homeless families" and is headed by a woman who is of European-American and some Native-American descent, the organization is neither racism blind in its tactics nor in its ideology. The group's organizational tactics are influenced by those developed by the Black Panther Party, and one of its organizational papers is framed around the metaphor of recent welfare reform as a slave auction.[64]

Let's take a closer look at the KWRU's "The New Welfare Reform: Delivering Slaves to the Auction Block." The Kensington Welfare Rights Union has argued that under articles of the 1993 Vienna World Conference on Human Rights, passage of the Personal Responsibility and Work Opportunity Reconciliation Act of 1996 and other punitive welfare reforms was a violation of human rights. In an address at the United Nations, Cheri Honkala, the director of the KWRU, called for the organization to monitor such government actions.[65] Within the United States, the KWRU has organized a national Poor People's Economic Human Rights Campaign "to raise the issue of poverty as a human rights violation."[66] Behind the violation, enabling it, are the racist attitudes that economic and political elites have exploited to initiate punitive welfare policies:

> The rhetoric behind these attacks has played on and encouraged racist fears and myths, in violation of Article 4 of the International Convention on the Elimination of All Forms of Racism, which condemns "all propaganda . . . which are based on ideas of superiority of one race . . . or which attempt to justify or promote racial hatred and discrimination in any form." The effect of this propaganda has been to portray poverty as only a problem of racial minorities, when in fact most people in poverty are white.[67]

Using its slavery metaphor, the NWRU draws parallels between the historic oppression of people of African descent in the United States and the racial state's current treatment of all its poor. For example, just as the Dred Scott decision ruled in 1857 that black people had no rights that whites were bound to respect, today in violation of international human rights provisions the U.S. racial state acts in ways consistent with the view that the poor have no rights (or entitlements) it must respect. Beginning with slavery, the KWRU article also locates the condition of the poor and the government response to them in a changing but always highly racialized political economy. In this way, KWRU places contemporary welfare reform in the context of technological advances that have made increasingly low-skilled workers and people, especially those of color, economically obsolete.[68]

The KWRU's international human rights remedy is important because it brings both a global perspective and international eyes to bear on racist U.S. poverty policies. As a result, actions that might ordinarily be accepted as normal within the context of a highly racialized, conservative-dominated nation like the United States may be seen for what they are, racist violations of human rights. Moreover, an international human rights strategy provides a venue for protest, ethical condemnation, and litigation that rests, at least in part, outside the white supremacist U.S. political economy. Such a venue is especially important when most white people in the United States and their racial state actors are not inclined to hear the voices of racially and economically oppressed peoples. To this end the KWRU, along with other organizations of low-income people from throughout the nation that have joined the Poor People's Economic Human Rights Campaign, is filing international petitions (e.g., with the Organization of American States) as a way of bringing into play international scrutiny of the United States' treatment of its poor.[69]

The KWRU's lessons for challenging welfare racism are especially intriguing because they run counter to elitist notions that poor people are not capable of addressing complex issues like racism, and must therefore be protected from attempts to do so for fear that they may cause permanent racial divisions within their own ranks. To antiracism historian Herbert Aptheker, however, the KWRU's actions would come as no surprise. In *Anti-Racism in U.S. History: The First Two Hundred Years*, Aptheker found that European-American antiracists were most likely to be from the lower classes, to be female, and to have had significant contact with people of African-American descent.[70]

Contrary to the "Archie Bunker" myth held by many of society's elites,[71] the likelihood that people will be antiracist is not determined by formal education but by their location in the social structure and their life experiences; in brief, their relationship to social privilege and oppression. This suggests that there may be a greater inclination among European-American welfare recipients to both acknowledge and to challenge welfare racism than among economically affluent elites who have not had much contact with poor people of color. This potential can be enhanced through educational initiatives like those of the Kensington Welfare Rights Union that make clear that racism harms *all* poor people and that racism-blind strategies do not and cannot work.

Racism-targeted initiatives can actually increase the membership and support of grassroots welfare rights organizations like the KRWU. We mentioned earlier the important welfare racism–related work of the Grass Roots Innovative Policy Program (GRIPP). The organization has placed on its website a detailed document called "Putting Welfare Reform to the Test: A Guide to Uncovering Bias and Unfair Treatment in Local Welfare Programs." That guide provides the information that grassroots welfare rights organizations need (including a recruitment and training manual for testers and sample postappointment questions) to document welfare practices racism.[72] By organizing campaigns to expose and otherwise challenge welfare racist practices, grassroots organizations can demonstrate to welfare recipients of color that they realize how racism affects their daily lives and are willing to work with them to take appropriate action. This can be especially helpful in boosting the number of people of color in organizations whose participants are underrepresentative of the actual numbers of welfare recipients of color in their given geographical areas.

The Applied Research Center's publication *ColorLines* devoted much of its fall 2000 issue to challenges to punitive welfare reform. In one article, center director Gary Delgado proposed that grassroots organizations combine with progressive legal defense organizations to take a "civil rights" strategy. That strategy would combine educational, legislative policy, legal, and social protest challenges to racial and gender discrimination in welfare reform.[73] Some thirty grassroots welfare rights organizations have organized themselves into Grass Roots Organizing for Welfare Leadership. A project of the Center for Third World Organizing, GROWL, is specifically interested in challenging racial, class, and gender discrimination, as well as discrimination against immigrants.[74]

Racism-focused monitoring and other tactics can also help build support for welfare rights organizations among working-class and more affluent classes of people of color who are affected culturally, politically, and economically by welfare racist attitudes, policies, and practices. Educational campaigns are needed to show people of color that racist stereotypes generated by the racialization of welfare images by the media and politicians stereotype all people of color, not just the poor. In *Shadows of Race and Class*, Raymond S. Franklin argues that racist stereotypes targeted at low-income African Americans ultimately cast a shadow over all African Americans regardless of their class position.[75] This can be seen in the "welfare queen" stereotype encountered by many affluent African-American women.[76] This stereotype was both reinforced and expanded upon in the 1990s when conservative politicians blocking attorney Lani Guinier's appointment to the U.S. Department of Justice depicted her as a "quota queen." In another instance, Jocelyn Elders's removal as U.S. Surgeon General was aided by conservatives' derisive depiction of her as a "condom queen."

Educational campaigns can also help to counter the tendency of some people of color (including some who are poor) to accept the negative stereotypes of poor people of color and the repressive welfare polices targeted at them. Their rejection is made easier in an environment where the underlying racist assumptions of such controlling images and policies are made explicit and challenged. Such challenges provide an alternative to either accepting these assumptions or going even further by trying to boost one's self-esteem by acquiescence to and identification with the views of one's racial oppressors. Finally, there is a need for educational campaigns that focus attention on the economic and social damage that welfare racist policies do to entire communities of color. In this way, people in those communities can be mobilized to join with grassroots welfare rights organizations to confront such policies.[77]

THE JOURNEY CONTINUES: BEYOND WELFARE RACISM

An adequate guaranteed annual family income—combined with racism-sensitive monitoring safeguards and appropriate racism-targeted legal and legislative policy interventions—could offer the single best remedy to most forms of welfare policy and welfare practices racism. However, the guaranteed income component of such a remedy is unlikely to happen without effective challenges to the widespread racist attitudes toward the poor and antipoverty programs that are generated by the racial state, the media, and other key institutions of U.S. society. In the meantime, while the poor must depend on public assistance, welfare racist attitudes, policies, and practices should be confronted through appropriate racism-sensitive safeguards and racism-targeted interventions. By combating welfare racism, we can remove a major roadblock from the path to economic justice for all.

In this, our final chapter, we have explored the need for educational, legislative policy, legal, and social protest–based challenges to the great shape shifter, welfare racism. While such challenges are absolutely essential to obtain fair and humane welfare policies and practices, welfare racism, as we have seen, is remarkably adaptable. When confronted it continues to find new ways to manifest itself. Challenging welfare racism can only ameliorate some of the suffering caused by racism and the structures and processes that perpetuate it.

such challenges are consistent with the current badly needed efforts of welfare rights advocates to reform punitive welfare reform measures and to ameliorate their harmful effects by advocating for additional support services or time extensions for mothers being forced off the welfare rolls and into poorly paid work. Those who engage in such good and necessary efforts at reform of current policies should be ever mindful, however, that equity-focused struggles whose reform objectives are achievable only within systems of highly structured inequality are just the beginning for those fully committed to economic justice. Reforms of existing welfare reform measures alone cannot take us where we need to go in terms of the elimination of poverty and racism and the reduction of gender and class inequalities. As Randall Robinson puts it, "Lines, begun parallel and left alone, can never touch."[78]

The actual elimination of racism—in all of its many forms and manifestations—requires nothing less than a radical transformation of U.S. society and what is now its racial state. While this task is, indeed, a daunting one, the prize is even greater, and the journey has already begun. Those who embark on this adventure do so in the belief that confronting welfare racism is another step along the path toward the full realization of our humanity. It is through this hope and determination that we dare envision a time when welfare racism will be nothing more than an unpleasant historic memory. Let the journey continue.

Notes

CHAPTER 1

The epigram at the opening of this chapter is drawn from Francis Calpotura and Bob Wing, "The View from the Ground: Organizers Speak Out on Race," *ColorLines*, Summer 2000, 3 (2). Available at www.arc.org/C_Lines/CLArchive/story3_2_02.html.

1. In this book we treat the terms *race, white,* and *black* as being erroneous and injurious ideological constructs. Consequently, whenever they are used they should be read as if they appear within quotation marks.

2. The term *welfare mother* suggests a master status that carries many stereotypes and which overrides all other human features of mothers receiving public assistance. For this reason, we choose to avoid using that term in this book unless stereotypical thinking is being portrayed.

3. National Public Radio, Weekend Edition, September 5, 1992.

4. Annual reports on the characteristics and financial circumstances of welfare recipients are available from the U.S. Department of Health and Human Services. Racial breakdowns for 1983–96 show African-American and white families to have each constituted between 35 and 41 percent of the recipients in various years during that time period, and their proportion was usually within a percent of one another. See U.S. Department of Health and Human Services, *Aid to Families with Dependent Children: The Baseline* (Washington, D.C.: DHHS, June 1998), p. 57, at http://aspe.hhs.gov/hsp/afdc/afdcbase98exhib.htm.

5. Martin Gilens, *Why Americans Hate Welfare: Race, Media, and the Politics of Anti-Poverty Policy* (Chicago: University of Chicago Press, 1999).

6. When President Clinton signed the Personal Responsibility and Work Opportunity Reconciliation Act in 1996, 36 percent of the nation's 4.6 million families receiving AFDC that year were white. The majority were of color, but were not all African-American: thirty-seven percent were black; 21 percent were Latino/a; 3 percent were Asian; and 1.4 percent were Native American. See U.S. Department of Health and Human Services, Administration for Children and Families, *Characteristics and Financial Circumstances of AFDC Recipients, FY 1996* (Washington, D.C.: DHHS, 1997), p. 10. The public policy discourse preceding passage of the Personal Responsibility and Work Opportunity Reconciliation Act pointedly ignored any acknowledgment of the fact that 1.7 million white families were receiving AFDC assistance at the time, close to the number of black families receiving aid.

7. In 1993, only 5.1 percent of all AFDC mothers, European Americans included, were nineteen years of age or younger. The mean age of African-American mothers was 29.9 years. See U.S. Bureau of the Census, "Mothers Who Receive AFDC Payments: Fertility and Socio-economic Characteristics," *Statistical Brief* (March 1995).

8. See *Poverty in the United States*, an annual report issued by the U.S. Bureau of the Census.

9. U.S. Department of Health and Human Services, *Characteristics and Financial Circumstances of AFDC Recipients*, p. 10.

10. Anti-Defamation League, *Highlights from an Anti-Defamation League Survey on Racial Attitudes in America* (New York: ADL, 1993).

11. Lawrence Bobo and James R. Kleugel, "Modern American Prejudice: Stereotypes,

Social Distance, and Perceptions of Discrimination toward Blacks, Hispanics, and Asians." Paper presented at the 1991 Meetings of the American Sociological Association, Cincinnati.

12. CBS News/New York Times Poll, December 6–8, 1994; Maureen Dowd, "Americans Like G.O.P. Agenda but Split on How to Reach Goals," *New York Times*, December 15, 1994, p. A1.

13. Gilens, *Why Americans Hate Welfare*.

14. Tom Smith, *Taking America's Pulse II: A Survey of Intergroup Relations* (New York: National Conference for Community and Justice, 2000); Joe R. Feagin and Melvin P. Sikes, *Living with Racism: The Black Middle-Class Experience* (Boston: Beacon Press, 1994), pp. 4–12; Paul Kivel, *Uprooting Racism: How White People Can Work for Racial Justice* (Philadelphia: New Society Publishers, 1996), pp. 40–46.

15. Melvin Thomas, "Anything but Race: The Social Science Retreat from Racism," *African American Research Perspectives* 6 (winter 2000): 79–96.

16. Joe R. Feagin and Hernán Vera, *White Racism: The Basics* (New York: Routledge, 1995), p. 7.

17. Kivel, *Uprooting Racism*, pp. 44–45.

18. George Lipsitz, *The Possessive Investment in Whiteness: How White People Profit from Identity Politics* (Philadelphia: Temple University Press, 1998), pp. 1–24.

19. See, for example, Joe R. Feagin, *Racist America: Roots, Current Realities, and Future Reparations* (New York: Routledge, 2000); Feagin and Sikes, *Living with Racism*; Feagin and Vera, *White Racism*; Christopher Bates Doob, *Racism: An American Cauldron* (New York: HarperCollins, 1996); Andrew Hacker, *Two Nations: Black and White, Separate, Hostile, Unequal* (New York: Charles Scribner's Sons, 1992); Robert C. Smith, *Racism in the Post–Civil Rights Era: Now You See It, Now You Don't* (Albany: State University of New York Press, 1995); and, Carter A. Wilson, *Racism: From Slavery to Advanced Capitalism* (Thousand Oaks, CA: Sage, 1996), chapter 7.

20. See Stephen Steinberg, *Turning Back: The Retreat from Racial Justice in American Thought and Policy* (Boston: Beacon Press, 1995); Thomas, "Anything but Race."

21. Steinberg, *Turning Back*, p. 126.

22. William J. Wilson, *The Declining Significance of Race: Blacks and Changing American Institutions* (Chicago: University of Chicago Press, 1978), p. xi.

23. Amy Elizabeth Ansell, *New Right, New Racism: Race and Reaction in the United States and Britain* (New York: New York University Press, 1997), pp. 49–73; Michael Omi and Howard Winant, *Racial Formation in the United States: From the 1960s to the 1990s* (New York: Routledge, 1994), pp. 113–36.

24. Steinberg, *Turning Back*, p. 153.

25. Dinesh D'Souza, *The End of Racism: Principles for a Multiracial Society* (New York: Free Press, 1995), p. 525.

26. Dinesh D'Souza, "Black America's Moment of Truth," *The American Spectator*, October 1995, p. 35.

27. See, for example, Charles Murray, *Losing Ground: American Social Policy, 1950–1980* (New York: Basic Books, 1984), and Lawrence M. Mead, *The New Politics of Poverty: The Nonworking Poor in America* (New York: Basic Books, 1992).

28. Richard J. Herrnstein and Charles Murray, *The Bell Curve: Intelligence and Class Structure in American Life* (New York: Free Press, 1994).

29. The term *racial realism* has been attributed to Alan Wolfe. See his "Enough Blame to Go Around," *New York Times*, June 21, 1998, sec. 7, p. 12. See also Philip Klinkner, "The 'Racial Realism' Hoax," *The Nation*, December 14, 1998, pp. 33–34, 36–38.

30. Stephan Thernstrom and Abigail Thernstrom, *America in Black and White: One Nation, Indivisible* (New York: Simon & Schuster, 1997), p. 534.

31. Ibid., pp. 16–17.

32. Shelby Steele, *A Dream Deferred: The Second Betrayal of Black Freedom in America* (New York: HarperCollins, 1998), p. 78.

33. Gilens, *Why Americans Hate Welfare*.

34. Indeed, the word *racism* is listed in the book's index only once.

35. Gilens, *Why Americans Hate Welfare*. p. 3.

36. Ibid.

37. Gilens does not acknowledge, much less address, *any* form of systemic oppression. His book has been criticized for ignoring gender relations in understanding negative attitudes toward welfare. See Susan L. Thomas's review of *Why Americans Hate Welfare* in the *Journal of Politics* 62 (February 2000): 267–269. Gilens's book also ignores class inequality.

38. Gilens, *Why Americans Hate Welfare*, p. 5.

39. April 1968 "Dear Friend" letter from Martin Luther King Jr., p. 2. Highlander Research and Education Center 1977 Addition, 1936–1978, Box 105, Folder 12, Material re: Poor People's Campaign, State Historical Society of Wisconsin, Madison.

40. See, for example, Sylvia B. Weinberg, "Mexican American Mothers and the Welfare Debate: A History of Exclusion," *Journal of Poverty* 2 (1998): 53–76.

41. Jacqueline Johnson, Sharon Rush, and Joe Feagin, "Doing Anti-Racism: Toward an Egalitarian American Society," *Contemporary Sociology* 29 (January 2000): 95–96.

CHAPTER 2

1. See Clyde W. Barrow, *Critical Theories of the State* (Madison: University of Wisconsin Press, 1993).

2. G. William Domhoff, *The Power Elite and the State: How Policy Is Made in America* (New York: Aldine de Gruyter, 1990); Ian Gough, *The Political Economy of the Welfare State* (London: Macmillan, 1979).

3. Gosta Esping-Anderson, *The Three Worlds of Welfare Capitalism* (Princeton, NJ: Princeton University Press, 1990); James O'Connor, *The Fiscal Crisis of the State* (New York: St. Martin's Press, 1973); Claus Offe, *Contradictions of the Welfare State* (Cambridge: MIT Press, 1984).

4. Rhonda Levine, *Class Struggle and the New Deal* (Lawrence: University Press of Kansas, 1988).

5. Frances Fox Piven and Richard A. Cloward, *Regulating the Poor: The Functions of Public Welfare* (New York: Vintage Books, 1993).

6. Mimi Abramovitz, *Regulating the Lives of Women: Social Welfare Policy from Colonial Times to the Present* (Boston: South End Press, 1996); Mimi Abramovitz, *Under Attack, Fighting Back: Women and Welfare in the United States* (New York: Monthly Review Press, 1996); Linda Gordon, ed., *Women, the State, and Welfare* (Madison: University of Wisconsin Press, 1990).

7. Abramovitz, *Regulating the Lives of Women*.

8. Peter Evans, Dietrich Rueschemeyer, and Theda Skocpol, eds., *Bringing the State Back In* (New York: Cambridge University Press, 1985).

9. Theda Skocpol, *Protecting Soldiers and Mothers: The Political Origins of Social Policy in the United States* (Cambridge, MA: Belknap Press of Harvard University Press, 1992); Theda Skocpol, *Social Policy in the United States: Future Possibilities in Historical Perspective* (Princeton, NJ: Princeton University Press, 1995); Margaret Weir, Ann Orloff, and Theda Skocpol, eds., *The Politics of Social Policy in the United States* (Princeton, NJ: Princeton University Press, 1988).

10. Skocpol, *Protecting Soldiers and Mothers*.

11. Ibid., p. 32.

12. Theda Skocpol, "African Americans in U.S. Social Policy," in Paul E. Peterson, ed., *Classifying by Race* (Princeton, NJ: Princeton University Press, 1995), pp. 129–155.

13. Jill Quadagno, *The Color of Welfare: How Racism Undermined the War on Poverty* (New York:

Oxford University Press, 1994). Quadagno takes a more class-centered perspective in "Race, Class, and Gender in the U.S. Welfare State: Nixon's Failed Family Assistance Plan," *American Sociological Review* 55 (February 1990): 11–28, and in "Welfare Capitalism and the Social Security Act of 1935," *American Sociological Review* 49 (October 1984): 632–647.

14. Robert C. Lieberman, *Shifting the Color Line: Race and the American Welfare State* (Cambridge, MA: Harvard University Press, 1998).

15. Michael Brown, *Race, Money, and the American Welfare State* (Ithaca, NY: Cornell University Press, 1999).

16. Ibid., p. 7.

17. To these exceptions we would add Charles Noble, *Welfare As We Knew It: A Political History of the American Welfare State* (New York: Oxford University Press, 1997). Noble attempts a synthesis of state- and class-centered approaches with racism. He does not address gender or patriarchy.

18. Jack Niemonen, "The Role of the State in the Sociology of Racial and Ethnic Relations: Some Theoretical Considerations," *Free Inquiry in Creative Sociology* 23 (1995): 28.

19. Amy Ansell, *New Right, New Racism: Race and Reaction in the United States and Britain* (New York: New York University Press, 1997); David R. James, "The Transformation of the Southern Racial State," *American Sociological Review* 53 (1988): 191–208.; Michael Omi and Howard Winant, *Racial Formation in the United States: From the 1960s to the 1990s* (New York: Routledge, 1994).

20. Melvin L. Oliver and Thomas M. Shapiro, *Black Wealth, White Wealth: A New Perspective on Racial Inequality* (New York: Routledge, 1995).

21. Wahneema Lubiano, "Black Ladies, Welfare Queens, and State Minstrels," in *Race-ing Justice, En-gendering Power*, ed. Toni Morrison (New York: Pantheon Books, 1992), p. 331.

22. Charles W. Mills, *The Racial Contract* (Ithaca, NY: Cornell University Press, 1997).

23. John Solomos, "Varieties of Marxist Conceptions of 'Race,' Class, and the State: A Critical Analysis," in *Theories of Race and Ethnic Relations*, ed. John Rex and David Mason (Cambridge, England: Cambridge University Press, 1986), pp. 84–109.

24. Centre for Contemporary Cultural Studies, *The Empire Strikes Back* (London: Hutchinson, 1982); John Gabriel and Gideon Ben–Tovim, "Marxism and the Concept of Racism," *Economy and Society* 7 (1978): 118–154; Stuart Hall, "Race, Articulation, and Societies Structured in Dominance," in UNESCO, *Sociological Theories: Race and Colonialism* (Paris: UNESCO, 1980); Solomos, "Varieties of Marxist Conceptions of 'Race,' Class and the State."

25. Stuart Hall et al., *Policing the Crisis* (London: Macmillan, 1978); Robert Miles, *Racism after "Race Relations"* (London: Routledge, 1993); John Solomos, *Black Youth, Racism, and the State* (Cambridge, England: Cambridge University Press, 1988); Rob Witte, *Racist Violence and the State* (London: Longman, 1996).

26. Eduardo Bonilla-Silva, "Rethinking Racism: Toward a Structural Interpretation," *American Sociological Review* 62 (1997): 465–480.

27. Thomas F. Gossett, *Race: The History of an Idea in America* (New York: Schocken Books, 1965).

28. Audrey Smedley, *Race in North America: Origin and Evolution of a Worldview*, 2nd ed. (Boulder, CO: Westview Press, 1999).

29. Ashley Montague, *Man's Most Dangerous Myth: The Fallacy of Race*, 6th ed. (Walnut Creek, CA: AltaMira Press, 1997), p. 515; Smedley, *Race in North America*, pp. 39 and 281.

30. Carter A. Wilson, *Racism: From Slavery to Advanced Capitalism* (Thousand Oaks, CA: Sage Publications, 1996), pp. 16–36. Wilson draws heavily upon ideas associated with the theories of Karl Marx, Max Weber, and Antonio Gramsci.

31. Key tenets of this racist culture were strongly in place both in the North and in the South

after the 1830s. See George M. Frederickson, *The Black Image in the White Mind: The Debate on Afro-American Character and Destiny, 1817–1914* (New York: Harper & Row, 1971), p. 321.

32. C. Wilson, *Racism*, p. 106.

33. Ibid.

34. See, for example, Richard Delgado and Jean Stefancic, eds., *Critical White Studies: Looking Behind the Mirror* (Philadelphia: Temple University Press, 1997); Mike Hill, ed., *Whiteness: A Critical Reader* (New York: New York University Press, 1998); Michelle Fine et al., eds., *Off White: Readings on Race, Power, and Society* (New York: Routledge, 1997).

35. See George Lipsitz, *The Possessive Investment in Whiteness: How White People Profit from Identity Politics* (Philadelphia: Temple University Press, 1998).

36. Ansell, *New Right, New Racism*; Teun van Dijk, *Elite Discourse and Racism* (Newbury Park, CA: SAGE Publications, 1993).

37. C. Wilson, *Racism*, p. 165.

38. James, "The Transformation of the Southern Racial State."

39. Teresa L. Amott and Julia A. Matthaei, *Race, Gender, and Work: A Multicultural Economic History of Women in the United States* (Boston: South End Press, 1996).

40. Philomena Essed, *Understanding Everyday Racism: An Interdisciplinary Theory* (Newbury Park, CA: Sage Publications, 1991).

41. Richard Schmitt, "A New Hypothesis about the Relations of Class, Race and Gender: Capitalism as a Dependent System," *Social Theory and Social Practice* 14 (1988): 345–346. See also Karen Brodkin Sacks, "Toward a Unified Theory of Class, Race, Gender," *American Ethnologist* 16 (1989): 534–550.

42. On the importance of a multidimensional sensitivity, see Leith Mullings, *On Our Own Terms: Race, Class, and Gender in the Lives of African American Women* (New York: Routledge, 1997). See also Essed, *Understanding Everyday Racism*.

43. bell hooks, *Ain't I a Woman: Black Women and Feminism* (Boston: South End Press, 1981), p. 159.

44. Elizabeth Cady Stanton, Susan B Anthony, and Matilda Jaslin Gage, eds., *History of Woman Suffrage*, Vol. 1 (New York: Source Book Press, 1970), p. 115.

45. Patricia Hill Collins, *Black Feminist Thought: Knowledge, Consciousness, and the Politics of Empowerment* (New York: Routledge, 2000), p. 42.

46. Ibid., p. 41.

47. Dorothy E. Roberts, "Racism and Patriarchy in the Meaning of Motherhood," in *Mothers in Law: Feminist Theory and the Legal Regulation of Motherhood*, ed. Martha Fineman and Isabel Karpin (New York: Columbia University Press, 1995), p. 224.

48. Collins, *Black Feminist Thought*, p. 42.

49. Essed, *Understanding Everyday Racism*, p. 31.

50. Ibid., p 5.

51. Susan Thomas, "Race, Gender, and Welfare Reform: The Antinatalist Response," *Journal of Black Studies* 28 (March 1998): 441.

52. Cheryl Townsend Gilkes, "From Slavery to Social Welfare: Racism and the Control of Black Women," in *Class, Race, and Sex: The Dynamics of Control*, ed. Amy Swerdlow and Hanna Lessinger (Boston: G.K. Hall & Co., 1983), p. 289.

53. Howard S. Becker, *Outsiders* (New York: Free Press, 1963).

54. Gilkes, "From Slavery to Social Welfare," p. 289.

55. Ibid., pp. 289–290.

56. Dorothy Roberts, *Killing the Black Body: Race, Reproduction, and the Meaning of Liberty* (New York: Vintage Books, 1997), pp. 5–6, 21.

57. Ibid., p. 10.

58. Ibid,, pp. 104–149.

59. Barbara Cruikshank, "Welfare Queens: Policing by the Numbers," in *Tales of the State: Narrative in Contemporary U.S. Politics and Public Policy*, ed. Sanford Schram and Philip Neisser (Lanham, MD: Rowman & Littlefield, 1997), p. 113.

60. Collins, *Black Feminist Thought*, pp. 5, 69. Similarly, K. Sue Jewell focuses on "how the privileged class uses images and ideology to maintain its social power and economic wealth, while consigning African-American women to a depressed socioeconomic status." See *From Mammy to Miss America and Beyond: Cultural Images and the Shaping of U.S. Social Policy* (New York: Routledge, 1993), p. 1.

61. Collins, *Black Feminist Thought*, p. 72.

62. Ibid., p. 73.

63. Ibid., p. 72.

64. Ibid.

65. See U.S. Department of Labor, *The Negro Family: The Case for National Action* (Washington, D.C.: U.S. Government Printing Office, 1965), and Lee Rainwater and William L. Yancey, *The Moynihan Report and the Politics of Controversy* (Cambridge: MIT Press, 1967).

66. Robin D. G. Kelley, *Yo' Mama's Disfunktional!: Fighting the Culture Wars in Urban America* (Boston: Beacon Press, 1997), p. 5.

67. Collins, *Black Feminist Thought*, p. 77.

68. Ibid.

69. Ibid., pp. 76–77.

70. Ibid., p. 78.

71. Ibid., p. 79.

72. Ibid.

73. Ibid., p. 81.

74. C. Wilson, *Racism*, p. 106.

75. Our structural and multidimensional definition of welfare racism was influenced by the work of Joe Feagin. See, for example, the definition of white racism in Joe R. Feagin, Hernán Vera, and Pinar Batur, *White Racism: The Basics* (New York: Routledge, 2001), p. 17.

76. In the view of Raymond S. Franklin, racist stereotypes about the African–American poor cast "shadows" of inferiority over middle-class African Americans. See his *Shadows of Race and Class* (Minneapolis: University of Minnesota Press, 1991).

CHAPTER 3

The opening quote is cited in Winifred Bell, *Aid to Dependent Children* (New York: Columbia University Press, 1965), pp. 34–35.

1. Angela Y. Davis, "Race and Criminalization: Black Americans and the Punishment Industry," in *The House That Race Built*, ed. Wehneema Lubiano (New York: Pantheon, 1997), p. 264.

2. James T. Patterson, *America's Struggle against Poverty, 1900–1994* (Cambridge, MA: Harvard University Press, 1994), p. 13.

3. In 1900, some 77 percent of all mother-headed families in the United States were led by widows. Most other such families were headed by deserted wives, few of whom were legally divorced. Only a small percentage of families were headed by women who had never married. See Mimi Abramovitz, *Under Attack, Fighting Back: Women and Welfare in the United States* (New York: Monthly Review Press, 1996), p. 59.

4. Walter I. Trattner, *From Poor Law to Welfare State: A History of Social Welfare in America*, 4th ed. (New York: Free Press, 1989), pp. 200–201.

5. Theda Skocpol, *Protecting Soldiers and Mothers: The Political Origins of Social Policy in the United States* (Cambridge, MA: Belknap Press of Harvard University Press, 1992).

6. Linda Gordon, *Pitied but Not Entitled: Single Mothers and the History of Welfare, 1890–1935* (New York: Free Press, 1994), p. 43. See also Theda Skocpol, *Protecting Soldiers and Mothers*, chapter 8. At different times and places mothers pensions were also called widows pensions or mother's aid.

7. Barbara J. Nelson, "The Gender, Race, and Class Origins of Early Welfare Policy and the Welfare State: A Comparison of Workmen's Compensation and Mother's Aid," in *Women, Politics, and Change*, ed. Louise A. Tilly and Patricia Gurin (New York: Russell Sage Foundation, 1990), p. 423.

8. Ibid., p. 426.

9. Grace Abbott, *The Child and the State*, vol. 2 (Chicago: University of Chicago Press, 1938), p. 229. Passage of mothers pension legislation tended to lag and occur later in the southern states. As late as 1934, South Carolina and Georgia still had not adopted such laws. For a table showing time period and region, see Mark H. Leff, "Consensus for Reform: The Mothers'-Pension Movement in the Progressive Era," in *Compassion and Responsibility: Readings in the History of Social Welfare Policy in the United States*, ed. Frank R. Breul and Steven J. Diner (Chicago: University of Chicago Press, 1980), p. 248.

10. Gordon, *Pitied but Not Entitled*, p. 63.

11. Bruce S. Jansson, *The Reluctant Welfare State: A History of American Social Welfare Policies* (Belmont, CA: Wadsworth, 1988), p. 106.

12. Skocpol, *Protecting Soldiers and Mothers*.

13. Andrew Billingsley and Jeanne M. Giovannoni, *Children of the Storm: Black Children and American Child Welfare* (New York: Harcourt Brace Jovanovich, 1972), p. 72.

14. Ibid., p. 73.

15. Bell, *Aid to Dependent Children*, p. 9.

16. Ibid., pp. 9–10. Bell's racial composition data are drawn from U.S. Department of Labor, *Mothers' Aid, 1931*, Children's Bureau Publication No. 220 (Washington, D.C.: Government Printing Office, 1933).

17. Gordon, *Pitied but Not Entitled*, pp. 47–48.

18. See, for example, Theodore Allen, *The Invention of the White Race: Racial Oppression and Social Control* (London: Verso Press, 1994), and Noel Ignatiev, *How the Irish Became White* (New York: Routledge, 1995).

19. Gordon, *Pitied but Not Entitled*, pp. 46–47.

20. Ibid., p. 47. The nativist view that the United States should deny "racial defectives" entry into this country was part of the rationale underlying the U.S. Congress's passage of the Immigration Act of 1924, which drastically reduced the legal quotas of Jews, Italians, Russians, Poles, Hungarians, Spaniards, Greeks, and other eastern and southern Europeans who could be admitted. See Allan Chase, *The Legacy of Malthus: The Social Costs of the New Scientific Racism* (New York: Alfred A. Knopf, 1977), pp. 289–291. The desirability of race population control has long been an issue connected with immigration. In the 1990s federal racial state actors adopted legislation to deny welfare benefits to immigrants as one way of discouraging the heavy influx of poor families of color from Asia and Latin America.

21. Gordon, *Pitied but Not Entitled*, pp. 46–47; Bell, *Aid to Dependent Children*, p. 19.

22. Bell, *Aid to Dependent Children*, p. 15.

23. Gordon, *Pitied but Not Entitled*, pp. 46–48, 84–88; Gwendolyn Mink, *The Wages of Motherhood: Inequality in the Welfare State, 1917–1942* (Ithaca, NY: Cornell University Press), pp. 27–52.

24. Joanne L. Goodwin, *Gender and the Politics of Welfare Reform: Mothers Pension in Chicago, 1911–1929* (Chicago: University of Chicago Press, 1997), pp. 163–164.

25. Mink, *Wages of Motherhood*, p. 50.

26. Bell, *Aid to Dependent Children*, pp. 9 and 19.

27. Mink, *Wages of Motherhood*, p. 51.

28. Bell, *Aid to Dependent Children*, p. 9.

29. Ibid., p. 19.

30. Steve Valocchi, "The Racial Basis of Capitalism and the State, and the Impact of the New Deal on African Americans," *Social Problems* 41 (August 1994): 347.

31. Edwin E. Witte, *The Development of the Social Security Act* (Madison: University of Wisconsin Press, 1962), p. 164.

32. Ibid., p. 144.

33. For a view that argues that economic considerations may better explain revisions made in the Social Security Act than do "racially deterministic approaches," see Gareth Davies and Martha Derrick, "Race and Social Welfare Policy: The Social Security Act of 1935," *Political Science Quarterly* 112 (summer 1997): 217–235.

34. Witte, *Development of Social Security Act*, p. 144.

35. White House capitulation to white racial hegemony was neither new to this historical period, nor would it ever wholly cease. See Kenneth O'Reilly, *Nixon's Piano: Presidents and Racial Politics from Washington to Clinton* (New York: Free Press, 1995).

36. Dorothy K. Newman et al., *Protest, Politics, and Prosperity: Black Americans and White Institutions, 1940–75* (New York: Pantheon, 1978), p. 256.

37. Abbott, *Child and the State*, p. 240.

38. Ibid.

39. Newman et al., *Protest, Politics*, p. 256.

40. Jill Quadagno, "Welfare Capitalism and the Social Security Act of 1935," *American Sociological Review* 49 (1984): 643. See also Jill Quadagno, *The Transformation of Old Age Security: Class and Politics in the American Welfare State* (Chicago: University of Chicago Press, 1988).

41. Abbott, *Child and the State*, p. 240.

42. Paul H. Douglas, *Social Security in the United States: An Analysis and Appraisal of the Federal Social Security Act* (New York: Whittlesey House, 1936), pp. 100–101.

43. Newman et al., *Protest, Politics*, p. 256.

44. Susan Tinsley Gooden, "Local Discretion and Welfare Policy: The Case of Virginia (1911–1970)," *Southern Studies* 6 (1995): 79–110.

45. Dona Cooper Hamilton, "The National Association for the Advancement of Colored People," *Social Service Review* (December 1994): 488. See also Dona Cooper Hamilton and Charles V. Hamilton, *The Dual Agenda: Race and Social Welfare Policies of Civil Rights Organizations* (New York: Columbia University Press, 1997).

46. Hamilton, "The National Association for the Advancement of Colored People," p. 489.

47. U.S. Congress, House of Representatives, *Economic Security Act, Hearings before the Committee on Ways and Means*, Seventy-Fourth Congress, First Session (Washington, D.C.: U.S. Government Printing Office, 1935), p. 798.

48. For insight into the U.S. Supreme Court as a component of the racial state, see Ian F. Harvey Lopez, *White by Law: The Legal Construction of Race* (New York: New York University Press, 1996).

49. U.S. Congress, House of Representatives, *Economic Security Act*, p. 597.

50. Ibid., p. 598.

51. Ibid., p. 609.

52. Vallochi, "Racial Basis of Capitalism and the State," pp. 355–357.

53. Douglas, *Social Security in the United States*, p. 193.

54. Gilbert F. Steiner, *Social Insecurity: The Politics of Welfare* (Chicago: Rand McNally, 1966), p. 257.

55. Douglas, *Social Security in the United States*, pp. 193–195.

56. Ibid., pp. 194–195.

57. Abbott, *Child and the State*, p. 311.

58. Gunnar Myrdal, *An American Dilemma, Volume 1, The Negro in a White Nation* (New York: McGraw-Hill, 1964), p. 359. At the end of the 1930s, approximately 30 percent of African-American families were "broken," compared to 20 percent of native white families; 19 percent of African-American families were female headed. The latter families were on average larger than white families, particularly in the southern states. See Richard Sterner, *The Negro's Share: A Study of Income, Consumption, Housing and Public Assistance* (New York: Harper & Brothers, 1943), pp. 280–281.

59. Sterner, *The Negro's Share*, pp. 281–282.

60. Myrdal, *An American Dilemma*, p. 359.

61. Sterner, *The Negro's Share*, p. 283.

62. Ibid., pp. 282 and 284.

63. Ibid., p. 285.

64. Ibid., p. 284.

65. Ibid, pp. 284–285.

66. Ibid., p. 285.

67. Frances Fox Piven and Richard A. Cloward, *Regulating the Poor: The Functions of Public Welfare* (New York: Vintage Books, 1993), p. 133.

68. See also Mink, *Wages of Motherhood*, p. 142.

69. Vincent J. and Vee Burke, *Nixon's Good Deed: Welfare Reform* (New York: Columbia University Press, 1974), pp. 7–8; Joe R. Feagin, *Subordinating the Poor: Welfare and American Beliefs* (Englewood Cliffs, NJ: Prentice Hall, 1975), p. 59.

70. Theda Skocpol, *Social Policy in the United States: Future Possibilities in Historical Perspective* (Princeton, NJ: Princeton University Press, 1995), p. 164.

71. Jane Hoey, oral history interview, Social Security Project, Columbia University Library (March 10, 1965), pp. 43–44.

72. Ibid., p. 44.

73. Ibid.

74. Ibid., p. 45

75. Ibid., p. 47.

76. Steiner, *Social Insecurity*, p. 89.

77. Gooden, "Local Discretion," p. 90.

78. Ibid., pp. 90–91.

79. Bell, *Aid to Dependent Children*, p. 223, fn 33.

80. Ibid., p. 35.

81. Ibid., p. 46.

82. Ibid.

83. Ibid., p. 34.

84. Myrdal, *An American Dilemma*, p. 360.

85. Quadagno, *The Transformation of Old Age Security*.

86. Gwendolyn Mink, *Welfare's End* (Ithaca, NY: Cornell University Press), p. 133.

87. Jill Quadagno, *The Color of Welfare: How Racism Undermined the War on Poverty* (New York: Oxford University Press, 1994), p. 119.

88. Agnes Leisy, *Families Receiving Aid to Dependent Children. Part I. Race, Size, and Composition of Families and Reasons for Dependency* (Washington, D.C.: Social Security Board, 1942), p. 41.

89. Newman et al., *Protest, Politics*, p. 257.

90. Kenneth J. Neubeck and Jack L. Roach, "Racism and Poverty Policies," in *Impacts of Racism on White Americans*, ed. Benjamin P. Bowser and Raymond J. Hunt (Beverly Hills, CA: Sage, 1981), p. 160.

91. Rickie Solinger, *Wake Up Little Suzie: Single Pregnancy and Race before Roe v. Wade* (New York: Routledge, 1992), pp. 7 and 17.

92. Mimi Abramovitz, *Regulating the Lives of Women: Social Welfare Policy from Colonial Times to the Present* (Boston: South End Press, 1996), pp. 323–326.

93. Solinger, *Wake Up Little Suzie*, p. 53.

94. Abramovitz, *Regulating the Lives of Women*, p. 323.

95. Piven and Cloward, *Regulating the Poor*, p. 144.

96. James Graham, *The Enemies of the Poor* (New York: Vintage Books, 1970), p. 61.

97. See Robert C. Lieberman, *Shifting the Color Line: Race and the American Welfare State* (Cambridge, MA: Harvard University Press, 1998), chapter 8.

98. Bobbie Green Turner, *Federal/State Aid to Dependent Children Program and Its Benefits to Black Children in America, 1935–1985* (New York: Garland, 1993), pp. 140 and 149.

99. Douglas S. Massey and Nancy A. Denton, *American Apartheid: Segregation and the Making of the Underclass* (Cambridge, MA: Harvard University Press, 1993), pp. 43–59.

100. Turner, *Federal/State Aid*, p. 140.

101. Edgar May, *The Wasted Americans: Costs of Our Welfare Dilemma* (New York: Harper & Row, 1964), p. 45.

102. Newman et al., *Protest, Politics*, p. 260.

103. U.S. Commission on Civil Rights, *Children in Need* (Washington, D.C.: U.S. Government Printing Office, 1966).

104. A. L. Schorr and C. Wagner, *Cash and Food Programs in Virginia* (Washington, D.C.: U.S. Senate, Select Committee on Nutrition and Human Needs, 1969).

105. Michael Reich, "Who Benefits from Racism? The Distribution Among Whites of Gains and Losses from Racial Inequality," *Journal of Human Resources* 13 (1978): 524–544.

106. Kirsten A. Grönbjerg, *Mass Society and the Extension of Welfare* (Chicago: University of Chicago Press, 1977).

107. Newman et al., *Protest, Politics*, p. 283; Larry L. Orr, "Income Transfers as a Public Good: An Application to A.F.D.C.," *American Economic Review* 66 (June 1976): 359–371; John E. Tropman and A. Gordon, "The Welfare Threat: AFDC Coverage and Closeness in the American States," *Social Forces* 57 (1978): 697–712. Such welfare benefit disparities have been detected as recently as 1990. See Christopher Howard, "The American Welfare State, or States?" *Political Research Quarterly* 52 (June 1999): 421–442.

108. Gerald C. Wright, "Racism and Welfare Policy in America," *Social Science Quarterly* 57 (1977): 718–730.

CHAPTER 4

The epigraph is taken from Michael K. Brown, *Race, Money, and the American Welfare State* (Ithaca, NY: Cornell University Press, 1999), p. 350.

1. Gilbert F. Steiner, *Social Insecurity: The Politics of Welfare* (Chicago: Rand McNally, 1966), pp. 99–101; Winifred Bell, *Aid to Dependent Children* (New York: Columbia University Press, 1965), pp. 137–151.

2. See Michael L. Kurtz, "Reform and Race: 1950–1960," in *Louisiana: A History*, ed. Bennett H. Wall (Arlington Heights, IL: Forum Press, 1990), pp. 320–329.

3. Michael L. Kurtz, "The Rise and Fall of Racism, 1960–1972," in *Louisiana: A History*, ed. Bennett H. Wall (Arlington Heights, IL: Forum Press, 1990), p. 337.

4. Adam Fairclough, *Race and Democracy: The Civil Rights Struggle in Louisiana, 1915–1972* (Athens: University of Georgia Press, 1995), pp. 232–233.

5. Ibid., pp. 306–307.

6. State of Louisiana, *Louisiana Revised Statutes of 1950: 1962 Cumulative Summary*, vol. 1, Act No. 305, pp. 564–565.

7. U.S. Department of Health, Education, and Welfare, Social Security Administration, "Decision of Commissioner of Social Security; In the Matter of: The Conformity of the Louisiana Plan for Aid to Dependent Children Under Title IV of the Social Security Act," Washington, D.C., January 16, 1961, p. 3.

8. Ibid.

9. Sam A. Hanna, "Statute Removing 23,000 from Welfare Rolls Gets New Fed'l Govt. Scrutiny," *Baton Rouge Morning Advocate*, September 2, 1960, p. 1A.

10. State of Louisiana, *Official Journal of the Proceedings of the Senate of Louisiana*, 23rd Regular Session, May 16, 1960, p. 48.

11. "Davis Hits Mothers of La. Illegitimates: Terms Applicants as 'Professional Prostitutes,'" *Baton Rouge Morning Advocate*, September 23, 1960, p. 1A.

12. "Davis Hits Mothers of La. Illegitimates," p. 5A.

13. Fairclough, *Race and Democracy*, p. 277.

14. Phone interview with attorney Risley C. Triche conducted by Noel A. Cazenave on June 20, 1994, while Triche was at his law office in Napoleanville, Louisiana. In contrast, another of the legislation's sponsors, former Louisiana state Senator William T. Carpenter, stated that the bill was not aimed at any particular group, but affected African Americans more because they had higher rates of "illegitimacy." In his view, the issue was not racial, but moral. Phone interview with Carpenter conducted by Cazenave while Carpenter was at his home in Bastrop, Louisiana, on June 8, 1994.

15. National Urban League, "The Current Attack on ADC in Louisiana." Memorandum to National Agencies, National Leaders, Local Urban Leagues, dated September 19, 1960, New York City, p. 3.

16. Ibid., p. 2.

17. "Example of States' Rights—Southern Style," *Louisiana Weekly*, September 17, 1960, p. 11.

18. "Hate Move Doomed to Fail," *Afro-American*, September 17, 1960, reprinted in *Louisiana Weekly*, September 24, 1960, p. 18.

19. Robert E. Moran, *One Hundred Years of Child Welfare in Louisiana, 1860–1960* (Lafayette: Center for Louisiana Studies, University of Southwestern Louisiana, 1980), p. 34.

20. "Source Materials: The 'Suitable-Home' Requirement," *Social Service Review* 35 (1961): 204.

21. Sam A. Hanna, "Kennon Battles Federal Officials on Welfare Law; Witnesses Mustered to Refute Charges Inequities Intended," *Baton Rouge Morning Advocate*, November 15, 1960, p. 1A.

22. Ibid., p. 8A.

23. "Memorandum of the American Civil Liberties Union Filed With the Department of Health, Education, and Welfare With Reference to the Louisiana Plan for Aid to Dependent Children," November 22, 1960, p. 2.

24. Ibid., p. 3.

25. "Statement by Lisle C. Carter Jr., legal counsel, National Urban League, at a Hearing Pursuant to Title IV of the Social Security Act, Sec. 404, In the Matter of the State of Louisiana, Before the Commissioner of Social Security, Department of Health, Education, and Welfare, Washington, D.C.," November 16, 1960, p. 4.

26. U.S. Department of Health, Education, and Welfare.

27. State Letter No. 452 from Kathryn D. Goodwin, director, Bureau of Public Assistance,

Social Security Administration, U.S. Department of Health, Education, and Welfare, "Aid to Dependent Children—'Suitable Home' Requirements," January 17, 1961, pp. 1–2.

28. Lucy Komisar, *Down and Out in the U.S.A.: A History of Public Welfare* (New York: Franklin Watts, 1977), p. 76.

29. Bell, *Aid to Dependent Children*, pp. 140–141.

30. Ibid., p. 147.

31. Steiner, *Social Insecurity*, p. 101.

32. Joe R. Feagin, *Subordinating the Poor: Welfare and American Beliefs* (Englewood Cliffs, NJ: Prentice Hall, Inc., 1975), p. 72.

33. Moran, *One Hundred Years*, pp. 99–100.

34. Joseph P. Ritz, *The Despised Poor: Newburgh's War on Welfare* (Boston: Beacon Press, 1966); Steiner, *Social Insecurity*, pp. 110–112.

35. Edgar May, *The Wasted Americans: Costs of Our Welfare Dilemma* (New York: Harper & Row, 1964), p. 17.

36. Conditions in Newburgh are drawn from Ritz, *The Despised Poor*, pp. 3–8, and an interview with Joseph P. Ritz conducted by Kenneth J. Neubeck on July 19, 1994, at Ritz's home in Hamburgh, New York.

37. In 1960 Newburgh had thirty-one thousand residents. Between 1950 and 1960 the city's African-American population rose by more than 151 percent, from approximately two thousand to five thousand. In that same decade the white population underwent a 13.6 percent decline, as about four thousand whites left the city. See Ritz, *The Despised Poor*, p. 71.

38. Ritz, *The Despised Poor*, p. 8.

39. Interview with Joseph P. Ritz on July 19, 1994.

40. Ibid.

41. "McKneally Hits 'Gang Attacks'; City Neglect Charged by NAACP," *Newburgh News*, March 24, 1959, p. 9.

42. Ibid.

43. Ibid.

44. "McKneally Rejects Invitation to Debate on 'Gang Incidents'," *Newburgh News*, March 25, 1959, p. 16.

45. Rev. Lee Clinton Siler, "Wrong to Condemn Group Because of One's Fault," *Newburgh News*, March 28, 1959, p. 6.

46. Richard Carroll, "No Indian Solution," *Newburgh News*, March 30, 1959, p. 4.

47. "McKneally Offers Rebuttal in Controversy," *Newburgh News*, April 8, 1959, p. 13.

48. Ibid.

49. Ibid.

50. "McKneally Rejects Invitation to Debate on 'Gang Incidents,'" p. 16.

51. William B. Rollins and Bernard Lefkowitz, "Welfare a la Newburgh," *The Nation*, September 16, 1961, p. 158. See also Ritz, *The Despised Poor*, p. 22.

52. Ibid.

53. Ibid.

54. May, *The Wasted Americans*, p. 22.

55. Ritz, *The Despised Poor*, p. 34.

56. Ibid., pp. 36–37.

57. Ibid., pp. 37–38.

58. "Newburgh News Backs Stiff Welfare Code," *Editor & Publisher*, August 5, 1961, p. 16.

59. Rollins and Lefkowitz, "Welfare a la Newburgh," p. 159.

60. "Newburgh Stirs New Relief Rift," *New York Times*, May 19, 1961, p. 33.

61. Ritz, *The Despised Poor*, pp. 40–44.

62. Eve Edstrom, "Newburgh Is a Mirror Reflecting on Us All," *Washington Post*, August 6, 1961, p. E1.

63. Ritz, *The Despised Poor*, p. 76.

64. "13 Changes in Welfare Rules Set in Newburgh to Cut Costs," *New York Times*, June 21, 1961, p. 22.

65. The Council of the City of Newburgh, Proceedings for 1961, "New Business," June 19, 1961, pp. 141–142. See also Ritz, *The Despised Poor*, pp. 50–53.

66. "Newburgh Manager Vows Fight to Keep New Welfare Curb," *New York Times*, June 22, 1961, p. 33.

67. See Ritz, *The Despised Poor*, pp. 50–54.

68. Ibid., p. 51.

69. Ibid., p. 77.

70. Interview with Joseph P. Ritz, July 19, 1994.

71. Meg Greenfield, "The 'Welfare Chiselers' of Newburgh, N.Y.," *The Reporter* 35, August 17, 1961, p. 37.

72. Ritz, *The Despised Poor*, p. 68.

73. May, *The Wasted Americans*, p. 29. According to May, "Among the letters were the printed hate sheets that social controversy seems to lure out from under the damp rocks. The words 'black bastards' were so prevalent that city hall secretaries joked about it."

74. Joseph McDowell Mitchell, "The Revolt in Newburgh: The Failure of the Welfare Program," *Vital Speeches* 28 (1962), p. 214.

75. Indeed, welfare policy historian Edward D. Berkowitz has argued that Mitchell took his suitable-home proposal from the Louisiana initiative. See his *America's Welfare State from Roosevelt to Reagan* (Baltimore: Johns Hopkins University Press, 1991), p. 104.

76. Greenfield, " The 'Welfare Chiselers,'" p. 37.

77. Warren Weaver Jr., "Newburgh Plan on Welfare Held Illegal by Panel," *New York Times*, July 8, 1961, p. 1.

78. "Newburgh Ordered to Drop Relief Plan," *New York Times*, July 13, 1961, p. 37. The Democratic mayor of Newburgh wrote to Republican Governor Nelson Rockefeller asking his help in halting implementation of the thirteen-point plan. See "Mayor Asks Governor's Help," *New York Times*, July 13, 1961, p. 37.

79. "Goldwater Hails Plan," *New York Times*, July 8, 1961, p. 16.

80. Greenfield, " The 'Welfare Chiselers,'" p. 38.

81. See "Goldwater Hails Newburgh Plan as Welfare Ideal for All Cities," *New York World-Telegram*, July 19, 1961, p. 1, and "Javits Rejects Goldwater's View of Newburgh's Relief as a Model," *New York Times*, July 21, 1961, p. 12.

82. Warren Weaver, "Governor Scores Newburgh's Code," *New York Times*, July 14, 1961, p. 10.

83. "Javits Rejects Goldwater's View," p. 12.

84. "Newburgh to Use Pictures of Needy," *New York Times*, August 15, 1961, p. 20.

85. George Gallup, "Public Favors a Stronger Local Say on Relief Programs," *Chicago Sun-Times*, August 11, 1961, p. 10.

86. Kathryn D. Goodwin, director, Bureau of Public Assistance, memo to U.S. Social Security Commissioner William L. Mitchell, "New York—Summary Report of Newburgh Situation," July 21, 1961, p. 6.

87. "Newburgh Barred from Enforcement of New Relief Code," *New York Times*, August 19, 1961, p. 1.

88. "Wilkins Accuses Newburgh of Bias," *New York Times*, August 22, 1961, p. 16.

89. "Governor Orders Welfare Inquiry," *New York Times*, August 31, 1961, pp. 1 and 25.

90. "Ribicoff Orders 10 Steps to Halt Welfare Abuses," *New York Times*, December 12, 1961, p. 1.

91. Ibid., pp. 1 and 46.

92. Ibid., p. 46.

93. "Court Overturns Newburgh Rules Limiting Welfare," *New York Times*, December 20, 1961, p. 1.

94. "Scorching Indictment," *New York Times*, January 29, 1962, p. 45.

95. Will Lissner, "State Condemns Newburgh Relief," *New York Times*, March 30, 1962, p. 22.

96. J. Anthony Lukas, "Year-Long Fight Tires Newburgh," *New York Times*, July 20, 1962, p. 27.

97. "Mitchell, Newburgh Aide, Arrested in Bribery Case," *New York Times*, December 8, 1962, p. 1.

98. Ritz, *The Despised Poor*, p. 184.

99. Ibid., p. 68.

100. See, for example, Ed Shanahan, "30 Years Later, 'Battle' Echoes; U.S. Saw Newburgh Fight," *Middletown Times Herald Record*, January 26, 1992, p. 3, and Sam Roberts, "Spirit of Newburgh Past Haunts Political Present," *New York Times*, March 9, 1992, p. B2.

101. May, *The Wasted Americans*, p. 37.

102. Roberts, "Spirit of Newburgh Past." He notes as well, "What is so striking about the 13 welfare regulations [Mitchell] sought to impose three decades ago is not how Draconian they seem in retrospect, but how many of them have been adopted, proposed, or rationally discussed . . . by Republicans and more than a few Democrats."

103. See Mario Barrera, *Race and Class in the Southwest: A Theory of Racial Inequality* (Notre Dame, IN: University of Notre Dame Press, 1979), p. 202. Barrera divides the internal colonialism literature into two camps: the "right," "non-class differentiated" approach which assumes that all "whites" benefit from colonialism, and the "left," "class-differentiated" approach which assumes that only the dominant class of "whites" benefit.

104. Harold Cruse, *Rebellion or Revolution?* (New York: William Morrow, 1968), p. 74. Chapter 7 discusses "domestic colonialism" and was originally published in *Studies on the Left* 2, 3 (1962).

105. Ibid., p. 76.

106. Ibid.

107. Ibid., p. 77. Critics of the internal colonialism analogy have often insisted that geographic distance of the colonized from the home country is a key element of colonization. This observation, however, misses the point that internal colonialism is just an analogy. As such it implies only that similar, not identical, conditions tend to exist for both external colonies as they are conventionally conceived, and domestic or internal colonies. Neither full-blown colonial dependence nor distinct geographical boundaries are required for the metaphor of internal colonialism to be analytically useful for understanding the plight of African Americans. See, for example, Robert Blauner, *Racial Oppression in America* (New York: Harper & Row, 1972).

108. Martha Derthick, *City Politics in Washington, D.C.* (Cambridge, MA: Joint Center for Urban Studies, 1962), p. 1.

109. Ibid.

110. Constance McLaughlin Green stresses the social distance between black and white Washington by referring to the former as "The Secret City." See her *The Secret City: A History of Race Relations in the Nation's Capital* (Princeton, NJ: Princeton University Press, 1967).

111. Sam Smith, *Captive Capital: Colonial Life in Modern Washington* (Bloomington: Indiana University Press, 1974), p. ix. Even by the time that Smith's book was published—after Wash-

ington, D.C., had been granted "the right to elect a mayor and city council"—Smith observed that because the city still lacked "control over the budget, courts, prosecutor's office, police and planning," as well as "voting representation in either the Senate or the House," the "limited suffrage" it was granted by Congress in 1973 could best be defined as "participatory colonialism" (pp. ix–x, 135).

112. Green, *Secret City*, p. 316, and Derthick, *City Politics*, p. 126.

113. Derthick, *City Politics*, pp. 48–49.

114. Ibid., p. 48.

115. Ibid., p. 37.

116. Ibid., p. 48.

117. Ibid, p. 129. Prior to the Kennedy administration, for example, African Americans held few positions of importance in the city's government departments.

118. Smith, *Captive Capital*, pp. 37–38. Among the racial forces at play was "fear of black local political power in the nation's capital" (p. 149).

119. Harry S. Jaffe and Tom Sherwood, *Dream City: Race, Power, and the Decline of Washington, D.C.* (New York: Simon & Schuster, 1994), p. 24.

120. Ibid., p. 30.

121. See Derthick, *City Politics*, p. 48. Derthick writes there,

> In the eyes of its many local critics, the committee plays an obstructionist role in District government, willfully and maliciously frustrating the best interests of the District. It has consistently blocked home rule. . . . In general it acts to exclude the Negro from participation in local government and to limit the benefits Negroes derive from government.

122. Ibid., pp. 48–49. While the composition of the House District Committee's leadership explains much of its racial bias, Derthick argues (pp. 70–72) that conservative "biases" are built into the very structure of governance for Washington, D.C.

123. Ibid., p. 54.

124. Ibid., pp. 48, 56–57.

125. Jaffe and Sherwood, *Dream City*, p. 27.

126. Keesing's Research Report, *Race Relations in the USA: 1954–68* (New York: Charles Scribner's, 1970), pp. 71, 148, 152, 154.

127. Derthick, *City Politics*, p. 73.

128. Ibid., pp. 71–72.

129. Theodore C. Sorensen, *Kennedy* (New York: Harper & Row, 1965), p. 141; Arthur Schlesinger Jr., *Robert Kennedy and His Times* (New York: Ballantine, 1978), p. 232.

130. Frances Fox Piven and Richard A. Cloward, *Regulating the Poor: The Functions of Public Welfare* (New York: Vintage Books, 1993), pp. 149–150.

131. *District of Columbia Appropriations for 1963. Hearings before the Subcommittee of the Committee on Appropriations, United States Senate*. Eighty-Seventh Congress. Second Session on H.R. 12276. Part 2. Washington, D.C., 1962. U.S. Government Printing Office, p. 1411.

132. Ibid., Part 1, p. 115.

133. Steiner, *Social Insecurity*, pp. 62–63.

134. Ibid., p. 63.

135. Ibid., Steiner notes that Senator Byrd "dropped his bomb" just "a few months" after the enactment of the 1962 Kennedy administration's welfare amendments.

136. *District of Columbia Appropriations for 1963*, Part 2, p. 1029.

137. David M. Chalmers, *Hooded Americanism: The History of the Ku Klux Klan* (Chicago, Quadrangle, 1968), p. 326; Patsy Sims, *The Klan* (New York: Stern and Day, 1978), pp. 12, 39;

Schlesinger Jr., *Robert Kennedy*, p. 232; Sorensen, *Kennedy*, p. 146; William P. Hoar, "Senator Bobby Byrd: The Exalted Cyclops of Ku Klux Populism," *Conservative Digest*, January 1988, pp. 37–39.

138. In 1964 Byrd filibustered against the Civil Rights Bill and opposed both the Voting Rights Bill of 1965 and its extension in 1970 (Hoar, "Senator Bobby Byrd," p. 38). Byrd also voted against the confirmation of African-American Thurgood Marshall as Supreme Court justice. See Thomas R. Dye, *Who's Running America? The Conservative Years* (Englewood Cliffs, NJ: Prentice Hall, 1986), p. 106.

139. George P. Rawick, *From Sundown to Sunup: The Making of the Black Community* (Westport, CT: Greenwood, 1972), p. 143.

140. "How Big Is the Scandal in Relief? What the Nation's Capital Found Out," *U.S. News and World Report*, November 1962, pp. 84–88. See also May, *The Wasted Americans*, pp. 13–14. Of twenty-three cities he listed, May reported that Washington, D.C., had both the highest percentage of African-American population (53.9) and the highest percentage of Aid to Dependent Children who were African-American (92.9) in 1960 and 1961. May also noted that segregationists frequently used the high proportion of ADC recipients who were African American to support their arguments for segregation.

141. *District of Columbia Appropriations for 1963*, Part 2, p. 1255.

142. Ibid.

143. Ibid.

144. Ibid., p. 1257.

145. Audrey Smedley, *Race in North American: Origin and Evolution of a Worldview* (Boulder, CO: Westview, 1999), p. 8.

146. *District of Columbia Appropriations for 1963*, Part 2, p. 1257.

147. Kai Erikson, *Wayward Puritans: A Study in the Sociology of Deviance* (New Haven, CT: Yale University Press, 1966).

148. *District of Columbia Appropriations for 1963*, Part 2, p. 1308.

149. Citing recent research by Kathryn Edin, a *New York Times* reporter concluded that "AFDC typically provided just 34 percent of the average recipient's monthly income." Other sources of income were food stamps, "boyfriends, charities, relatives, and jobs, including under-the-table work." Jason DeParle, "Bold Effort Leaves Much Unchanged for the Poor," *New York Times*, December 30, 1999, p. A12. See also Kathryn Edin and Laura Lein, *Making Ends Meet: How Single Mothers Survive Welfare and Low-Wage Work* (New York: Russell Sage, 1997), and Carol B. Stack, *All Our Kin: Strategies for Survival in a Black Community* (New York: Harper & Row, 1974). 150. May, *Wasted Americans*, p. 38.

151. *District of Columbia Appropriations for 1963*, Part 2, p. 903.

152. Ibid.

153. Ibid.

154. Ibid., p. 1025.

155. Ibid., p. 1026.

156. Ibid., p. 1031.

157. Ibid., p. 1032.

158. Ibid., p. 1308.

159. Russell Baker, "Washington's Welfare Program Is Upset by Senate Critic," *New York Times*, June 12, 1963, p. 22.

160. *District of Columbia Appropriations for 1963*, Part 2, p. 1308.

161. Ibid., p. 1307.

162. Ibid., p. 1309.

163. Ibid.

164. Ibid.

165. Ibid.

166. Baker, "Washington's Welfare Program Is Upset by Senate Critic."

167. Ibid.

168. Ibid.

169. "How Big Is the Scandal in Relief?" p. 88.

170. Piven and Cloward, *Regulating the Poor*, p. 150.

171. Steiner, *Social Insecurity*, pp. 158–159.

172. *District of Columbia Appropriations for 1963*, Part 2, p. 1222.

173. Ibid., p. 1238.

174. Ibid., pp. 915, 1089, 1092. It was noted that in stark contrast to the estimated average of only five hours a year District social workers spent on each case, the special investigators spent an average of thirty-one man-hours on the cases closed as a result of their investigation (p. 907).

175. Baker, "Washington's Welfare Program Is Upset by Senate Critic."

176. Ibid.

177. *District of Columbia Appropriations for 1963*, Part 2, p. 1093.

178. Steiner, *Social Insecurity*, p. 176.

179. *District of Columbia Appropriations for 1963*, Part 1, pp. 359–360.

180. Ibid., Part 1, p. 360.

181. Baker, "Washington's Welfare Program Is Upset by Senate Critic"; Steiner, *Social Insecurity*, pp. 68–69.

182. Komisar, *Down and Out in the U.S.A.*, p. 90.

183. Steiner, *Social Insecurity*, p. 66.

184. Ibid., pp. 68–69.

185. Derthick, *City Politics*, p. 86.

186. Ibid, p. 87.

187. Baker, "Washington Welfare Program Is Upset by Senate Critic"; Derthick, p. 86.

188. Derthick, *City Politics*, p. 55.

189. Ibid., p. 86.

190. Piven and Cloward, *Regulating the Poor*, pp. 173–174.

191. Joel F. Handler and Yeheskel Hasenfeld, *The Moral Construction of Poverty: Welfare Reform in America* (Newbury Park, CA: Sage Publications, 1991), p. 18. Emphasis is theirs.

192. *District of Columbia Appropriations for 1963*, Part 2, p. 2327.

193. Green, *The Secret City*.

194. Piven and Cloward, *Regulating the Poor*, p. 174.

195. Ibid., p. 150.

196. May, *Wasted Americans*, pp. 38–39. That study found a national ineligibility rate of only 1 in 20, with the highest rate being in Senator Byrd's home state of West Virginia. Moreover, when the percentage of ineligibles was limited to those suspected of cheating, thirty–four states had rates of less than 2 percent (p. 39).

197. Mimi Abramovitz, *Regulating the Lives of Women: Social Policy from Colonial Times to the Present* (Boston: South End Press, 1996), p. 327.

198. Rickie Solinger, *Wake Up Little Suzie: Single Pregnancy and Race before Roe v. Wade* (New York: Routledge, 1992), p. 43.

199. Ibid., p. 42.

200. James T. Patterson, *America's Struggle against Poverty 1900–1985*, (Cambridge, MA: Harvard University Press, 1986), p. 110.

201. Ibid., p. 108.

202. Ibid., p. 110.

203. Piven and Cloward, *Regulating the Poor*, p. 169.

204. Patterson, *America's Struggle against Poverty*, p. 110.

205. Ritz, *The Despised Poor*, p. 84.

206. Ibid., p. 85.

207. Ibid., p. 214.

CHAPTER 5

1. Thomas Byrne Edsall with Mary D. Edsall, *Chain Reaction: The Impact of Race, Rights, and Taxes on American Politics* (New York: W.W. Norton, 1992); Jill Quadagno, *The Color of Welfare: How Racism Undermined the War on Poverty* (New York: Oxford University Press, 1994); and James T. Patterson, *Grand Expectations: The United States, 1945–1974* (New York: Oxford University Press, 1996). All of these authors make reference to what they typically refer to as a "backlash," as opposed to a *white* backlash. This is particularly noteworthy given the title of Quadagno's book. The Edsalls, Quadagno, and Patterson focus their analyses on federal policies targeted to benefit African Americans or on their perceived behavior rather than on white racism. In all three books African Americans are portrayed as being on the wrong side of cherished national values.

2. Michael J. Klarman, "How *Brown* Changed Race Relations: The Backlash Thesis," *Journal of American History* (June 1994): 81–118.

3. David Levering Lewis, *W.E.B. DuBois: Biography of a Race, 1869–1919* (New York: Henry Holt, 1993), p. 579; Klarman, "How *Brown* Changed Race Relations," pp. 92–93.

4. Anthony W. Marx, *Making Race and Nation* (Cambridge: Cambridge University Press, 1988), p. 235.

5. Newman et al. showed that during the two-decade period from 1953 to 1973 the percentage of African–American AFDC families residing in large cities increased from 56 percent to 73 percent, while the proportion living in nonmetropolitan areas declined from 37 percent to 16 percent. See Dorothy K. Newman et al., *Protest, Politics, and Opportunity: Black Americans and White Institutions, 1940–75* (New York: Pantheon, 1978), p. 281.

6. Ibid., p. 198.

7. For more on racial inclusion and welfare racism see Robert C. Lieberman, *Shifting the Color Line: Race and the American Welfare State* (Cambridge, MA: Harvard University Press, 1998), pp. 3, 8, and Michael K. Brown, *Race, Money and the American Welfare State* (Ithaca, NY: Cornell University Press, 1999), pp. 8–9.

8. Bobbie Green Turner, *Federal/State Aid to Dependent Children and Its Benefits to Black Children in America, 1935–1985* (New York: Garland, 1993), pp. 164, 167.

9. Mimi Abramovitz, *Regulating the Lives of Women: Social Welfare Policy from Colonial Times to the Present* (Boston: South End Press, 1996), p. 321.

10. Frances Fox Piven and Richard A. Cloward, *Regulating the Poor: The Functions of Public Welfare* (New York: Vintage Books, 1993).

11. Republican Vice President Dan Quayle articulated such thinking in framing his explanation for the massive Los Angeles urban rebellion that occurred in 1992. Andrew Rosenthal, "Quayle Says Riots Sprang from Lack of Family Values," *New York Times*, March 20, 1992, p. A1.

12. Peter Steinfels, *The NeoConservatives: The Men Who Are Challenging America's Politics* (New York: Simon & Schuster, 1979).

13. James A. Morone, *The Democratic Wish: Popular Participation and the Limits of American Government* (New York: Basic Books, 1990); Quadagno, *The Color of Welfare*.

14. Marx, *Making Race*, pp. 236–237.

15. Daniel Bell, *The Coming of Post-Industrial Society: A Venture in Social Forecasting* (New York: Basic Books, 1973), p. 365.

16. Piven and Cloward, *Regulating the Poor*.

17. *CNN Morning News*, "President Johnson Fights War on Poverty in His Efforts to Create The Great Society." John Holliman, CNN national correspondent. Donna Kelley, CNN anchor. October 18, 1996. Transcript # 96101815V29. Video based on secretly recorded tapes of President Lyndon Baines Johnson.

18. Michael Goldfield, *The Color of Politics: Race and the Mainsprings of American Politics* (New York: New Press, 1997), p. 311.

19. Tom W. Smith, "America's Most Important Problem—A Trend Analysis, 1946–1976," *Public Opinion Quarterly* (1980): 166.

20. Edsall and Edsall, *Chain Reaction*, p. 59.

21. Robert Weisbrot, *Freedom Bound: A History of America's Civil Rights Movement* (New York: Plume, 1991), p. 220.

22. Smith, "America's Most Important Problem," p. 166.

23. Edward G. Carmines and James A. Stimson, *Issue Evolution: Race and the Transformation of American Politics* (Princeton, NJ: Princeton University Press, 1989), p. xii.

24. Ibid., pp. xii–xiii.

25. Thomas Byrne Edsall and Mary D. Edsall, "When the Official Subject Is Presidential Politics, Taxes, Welfare, Crime, Rights, or Values . . . the Real Subject Is Race," *Atlantic Monthly*, May 1991: 53.

26. Goldfield, *The Color of Politics*, p. 309.

27. Ibid.

28. Ibid., p. 314; Harvard Sitkoff, *The Struggle for Black Equality: 1954–1980* (New York: Hill and Wang, 1981), p. 223.

29. Goldfield, *The Color of Politics*, p. 312.

30. Ibid.

31. Dan T. Carter, *The Politics of Rage: George Wallace, the Origins of the New Conservatism and the Transformation of American Politics* (New York: Simon & Schuster, 1995), pp. 27, 30; Goldfield, *The Color of Politics*, p. 312.

32. H. R. Haldeman, *The Haldeman Diaries: Inside the Nixon White House* (New York: G. P. Putnam, 1994), p. 53. Emphasis is his.

33. Frances Fox Piven and Richard A. Cloward, "National Welfare Rights Organization," in *Civil Rights in the United States, Volume 2*, ed. Waldo E. Martin Jr. and Patricia Sullivan (New York: Macmillan, 2000), pp. 536–537.

34. Harry A. Ploski and James D. Williams, *The Negro Almanac: A Reference Work on the African-American*, 5th ed. (Detroit: Gale Research, 1989), p. 272.

35. Piven and Cloward, "National Welfare Rights Organization," p. 537.

36. Goldfield, *The Color of Politics*, p. 314.

37. Ibid., p. 314. Edsall and Edsall, *Chain Reaction*, p. 148.

38. "'Welfare Queen' Becomes Issue in Reagan Campaign," *New York Times*, February 15, 1976, p. 51.

39. Ibid.

40. See Raymond S. Franklin, "White Uses of the Black Underclass," in *A New Introduction to Poverty: The Role of Race, Power, and Politics*, ed. Louis Kushnick and James Jennings (New York: New York University Press, 1999), pp. 119–145; Keith M. Kilty and Eric Swank, "Institutional Racism and Media Representations: Depictions of Violent Criminals and Welfare Recipients," *Sociological Imagination* 34, 2–3 (1997): 105–128; and Coramae Richey Mann and Marjorie S. Zatz, eds., *Images of Color, Images of Crime* (Los Angeles: Roxbury, 1998).

41. Martin Gilens, *Why Americans Hate Welfare: Race, Media, and the Politics of Antipoverty Policy* (Chicago: University of Chicago, 1999), p. 111.

42. Ibid., pp. 113, 115.

43. Ibid., p. 114.

44. Ibid.

45. Ibid., pp. 114–115.

46. Ibid., p. 117.

47. Ibid., p. 118.

48. Ibid., p. 119.

49. Ibid., p. 122.

50. Ibid., pp. 122, 125.

51. Ibid., p. 123.

52. Ibid.

53. Ibid., pp. 114,126, 127.

54. Ibid., pp. 140–153.

55. Martin Gilens, "Media Misrepresentations: Is There a Solution?" *TomPaine.Common Sense: A Journal of Opinion* (October 20, 1999), pp. 1–3, at www.tompaine.com/features/1999/10/20/1.html..

56. Ibid., pp. 2–3.

57. Ibid., p. 3.

58. The concept of racist culture and its importance to racial oppression is discussed in Carter A. Wilson, *Racism: From Slavery to Advanced Capitalism* (Thousand Oaks, CA: Sage, 1996). See also Teun A. van Dijk, *Elite Discourse and Racism* (Newbury Park, CA: Sage, 1993); Sue K. Jewell, *From Mammy to Miss America and Beyond: Cultural Images and the Shaping of U.S. Social Policy* (New York: Routledge, 1993); Lucy A. Williams, "Race, Rat Bites and Unfit Mothers: How Media Discourse Informs Welfare Legislation Debate," *Fordham Urban Law Journal* 22 (summer 1995): 1159–1196.

59. Holly Sklar, *Chaos or Community: Seeking Solutions, Not Scapegoats for Bad Economics* (Boston: South End Press, 1995), p. 95.

60. Turner, *Federal/State Aid*, p. 166.

61. U.S. Department of Health and Human Services, *Characteristics and Financial Circumstances of AFDC Recipients* (Washington, D.C.: DHHS, 1997), p. 10.

62. *NBC News*, Racial Attitudes and Consciousness Exam, August 1989, Roper Center Archives.

63. Edsall and Edsall, *Chain Reaction*.

64. Anti-Defamation League, *Highlights from an Anti-Defamation League Survey on Racial Attitudes in America* (New York: ADL, June 1993). The percentage of people believing this varied by age: under thirty, 36 percent; thirty to forty-nine, 29 percent; fifty and over, 42 percent.

65. See Lawrence Bobo and James R. Kluegel, "Modern American Prejudice: Stereotypes, Social Distance, and Perceptions of Discrimination toward Blacks, Hispanics, and Asians." Paper presented at the annual meetings of the American Sociological Association, Cincinnati, Ohio, August 23–27, 1991. Their data are derived from James A. Davis and Tom W. Smith, *The General Social Survey: Cumulative Code Book and Data File* (Chicago: National Opinion Research Center, 1990).

66. *CBS News/New York Times* Poll, "The Public Weighs In on the Republican Agenda," December 6–9, 1994. See also Maureen Dowd, "Americans Like G.O.P. Agenda but Split on How to Reach Goals," *New York Times,* December 15, 1994, pp. A1, A24.

67. *CBS News/New York Times Poll*, December 14, 1994, Roper Center Archives.

68. Ibid.

69. Richard L. Berke, "Survey Finds Voters in U.S. Rootless and Self Absorbed," *New York Times*, September 21, 1994, p. A21.

70. Edsall and Edsall, *Chain Reaction*; Sklar, *Chaos or Community?*

71. Lucy A. Williams, "The Right's Attack on Aid to Families with Dependent Children," *The Public Eye* (fall/winter 1996): 1–18.

72. For an analysis of the evolution from political domination to "moral/psychological" conceptualizations of dependency, see Nancy Frazier and Linda Gordon, "A Genealogy of Dependency," *Signs* 19 (fall 1994): 309–336. In their discussion of the origins of the contemporary negative connotation of economic dependency among the poor, Frazier and Gordon discuss various images they trace to "the colonial native" and "the slave." These images include "savage," "childlike," and "submissive." They conclude that consistent with these stereotypes, "it was the intrinsic, essential dependency of natives and slaves that justified their colonization and enslavement" (p. 317).

73. AFDC recipients included some 5 million families representing 14.3 million people, primarily women and children. See "Welfare as We've Known It," *New York Times*, June 19, 1994, p. E4.

74. The philosophical foundations of New Paternalism were established by Lawrence Mead in *Beyond Entitlement: The Social Obligations of Citizenship* (New York: Basic Books, 1986). See also Mead's "The New Welfare Debate," *Commentary* 85 (March 1988): 44, and *The New Politics of Poverty* (New York: Basic Books, 1992). Mead's views, along with those of other New Paternalism advocates, are also found in "The New Paternalism," a special issue of *Public Welfare* (spring 1992), and in Lawrence M. Mead, ed. *The New Paternalism: Supervisory Approaches to Poverty* (Washington, D.C.: Brookings Institution Press, 1997).

75. Gwendolyn Mink, *Welfare's End* (Ithaca, NY: Cornell University Press, 1998), p. 127.

76. Fred Block et al., eds., *The Mean Season: The Attack on the Welfare State* (New York: Pantheon Books, 1987). See also Frances Fox Piven and Richard A. Cloward, *The New Class War: Reagan's Attack on the Welfare State and Its Consequences* (New York: Pantheon, 1985).

77. For more on this concept see Frazier and Gordon, "A Genealogy of Dependency."

78. Quadagno, *The Color of Welfare*, p. v.

79. Abramovitz, *Regulating the Lives of Women*, pp. 357–361.

80. Williams, "The Right's Attack on Aid to Families with Dependent Children."

81. Edsall and Edsall, *Chain Reaction*.

82. Mead, *Beyond Entitlement*; Mead, *The New Politics of Poverty*; "Welfare Reform: Should Welfare Benefits Be Used to Change Recipients' Behavior?" *CQ Researcher* (April 10, 1992): 313–336; "The New Paternalism," special issue of *Public Welfare*.

83. For an overview of policies, see Paul Taylor, "Welfare Policy's 'New Paternalism' Uses Benefits to Alter Recipients' Behavior," *Washington Post*, June 8, 1991, p. A3; U.S. Senate, Committee on Finance, Hearing Before the Subcommittee on Social Security and Family Policy, *Changes in State Welfare Reform Programs* (Washington, D.C.: U.S. Government Printing Office, 1992); "Welfare Reform"; David Whitman, "War on Welfare Dependency," *U.S. News and World Report*, April 20, 1992, pp. 34–35; John S. DeMott, "States Act to Reform Welfare," *Nation's Business* (August 1992), pp. 32–34; Gloria Negri and Anthony Flint, "States Take Hard Line on Dependency: Punitive Actions Gaining Favor," *Boston Globe*, May 16, 1994, pp. 1, 8; and various publications of the Center on Social Policy and Law in Washington, D.C.

84. See Mimi Abramovitz, "Why Welfare Reform Is a Sham," *The Nation*, September 26, 1988, pp. 221, 240–241. Some called for mandatory full–time community service for those who failed to hold a job; see Sara Rimer, "Welfare Plan Places Limit on Cash Grants," *New York Times*, January 14, 1994, p. A12.

85. See, for example, Susan Chira, "A Welfare Experiment for Teen-Age Mothers," *New York Times,* April 28, 1993, p. A12.

86. Jason DeParle, "States' Eagerness to Experiment on Welfare Jars Administration," *New York Times,* April 14, 1994, p. B10.

87. U.S. Senate, *Changes in State Welfare Reform Programs.*

88. "Welfare Reform Plan Sets Sights on Fathers," *Hartford Courant,* December 16, 1993, p. A8.

89. Isabel Wilkerson, "Wisconsin Makes Truancy Costly by Tying Welfare to Attendance," *New York Times,* December 11, 1989, p. A1.

90. U.S. Senate, *Changes in State Welfare Reform Programs.*

91. June M. Axinn and Amy E. Hirsch, "Welfare and the 'Reform' of Women," *Families in Society* (November 1993): 563–572.

92. Jason DeParle, "Clinton Idea Used to Limit Welfare: States Issue Their Own Plans to Put Two-Year Curbs on Those Getting Benefits," *New York Times,* June 2, 1993, p. A12.

93. Wanda Motley, "Legislator Pushes for Fingerprinting of Welfare Recipients," *Philadelphia Inquirer,* October 14, 1993, p. B3; "A Welfare Fingerprint Program," *New York Times,* March 1, 1994, p. A14.

94. U.S. Senate, *Changes in State Welfare Reform Programs.*

95. See Lynn Martin, "For Children Who Have Children," *New York Times,* September 8, 1993, p. A23.

96. Charles Murray, "The Coming White Underclass," *Wall Street Journal,* October 29, 1993, p. A14; George F. Will, "End Government Support for Single Mothers," *Hartford Courant,* November 18, 1993, p. C17; Jason DeParle, "An Idea Becomes a Cause," *New York Times,* April 22, 1994, p. A14.

97. Murray, "The Coming White Underclass."

98. See Tamar Lewin, "Implanted Birth Control Device Renews Debate," *New York Times,* January 10, 1991, p. A20, and "The Norplant Debate," *Newsweek,* February 15, 1993, pp. 37, 40–41.

99. Murray, "The Coming White Underclass." See also Taylor, "Welfare Policy's 'New Paternalism'," and Will, "End Government Support for Single Mothers." The state of Wisconsin passed legislation that required the state to withdraw from the AFDC program within five years. See Jason DeParle, "Wisconsin Pledges to Exit U.S. System of Public Welfare," *New York Times,* December 14, 1993, p. 1A.

100. Nick Kotz and Mary Lynn Kotz, *A Passion for Equality: George A. Wiley and the Welfare Rights Movement* (New York: Norton, 1977), p. 251.

101. Jason DeParle, "Counter to Trend, a Welfare Program in California Has One Idea: Get a Job," *New York Times,* May 16, 1993, p. A14.

102. For examples of such stereotypes and counterevidence, see Dorothy K. Seavey, "Women and Welfare: Popular Conceptions vs. Facts," in Randy Albelda and Chris Tilly, *Glass Ceilings and Bottomless Pits: Women's Work, Women's Poverty* (Boston: South End Press, 1997), Appendix B, and Tufts University Center on Hunger, Poverty, and Nutrition Policy, *Statement on Key Welfare Reform Issues: The Empirical Evidence* (Medford, MA: Tufts University, 1995).

103. Abramovitz, *Regulating the Lives of Women,* pp. 352–358.

104. See Richard J. Herrnstein and Charles Murray, *The Bell Curve: Intelligence and Class Structure in American Life* (New York: Free Press, 1994). Their analysis implies the desirability of restricting reproduction within "cognitively limited" groups, reproduction that the availability of welfare benefits allegedly encourages.

105. David Theo Goldberg, *Racist Culture: Philosophy and the Politics of Meaning* (Cambridge, MA: Blackwell, 1993).

106. Such views and stereotypes are common in contemporary white supremacist discourse and publications. See the discussion of the racist imagery used to depict the

stereotypical African-American "welfare queen" in Jessie Daniels, *White Lies: Race, Class, Gender, and Sexuality in White Supremacist Discourse* (New York: Routledge, 1997).

107. See Noel A. Cazenave, "Commentary: People of Color Become Scapegoats at the Polls," *Hartford Courant*, November 13, 1994, Section C, p. 1.

108. Edsall and Edsall, *Chain Reaction*.

109. See Edward C. Banfield, *The Unheavenly City Revisited* (Boston: Little, Brown, 1974); Ken Auletta, *The Underclass* (New York: Random House, 1982); Christopher Jencks, *Rethinking Social Policy: Race, Poverty, and the Underclass* (Cambridge, MA: Harvard University Press, 1992); Mickey Kaus, *The End of Inequality* (New York: Basic Books, 1992); and Mead, *The New Politics of Poverty*.

110. Mead, *The New Politics of Poverty*, pp. 148–149. Unlike other advocates of the culture of poverty view that poverty is passed on from one generation to the next through the patho-logical attitudes and behavior of the poor, Mead focuses on that negative, self-perpetuating poverty lifestyle exclusively among African Americans. He traces this pathology not to lower-class status but to "black" and Third World culture. According to Mead (p. 148), "The culture of black America is the most significant factor for an understanding of today's nonwork and poverty."

111. Ibid., p. 148.

112. Ibid., p. 2.

113. Mead, "The New Welfare Debate," p. 44.

114. Lawrence M. Mead, "Jobs Programs and Other Bromides," *New York Times*, May 19, 1992, p. 23.

115. U.S. Senate, *Changes in State Welfare Reform Programs* ("Prepared Statement of Lawrence M. Mead"). For a detailed analysis of racism and the Willie Horton representation, see Joe R. Feagin and Hernán Vera, *White Racism: The Basics* (New York: Routledge, 1995), chapter 6.

116. See Noel A. Cazenave, "Mean-Spirited Political Assault on Welfare Increases Suffer-ing," *Hartford Courant*, May 20, 1994, B13; Laurie Udesky, "How Workfare Hurts Kids: Welfare Reform and Its Victims," *The Nation*, September 24, 1990, pp. 302–304, 306; "Welfare Reform Done Harshly," *New York Times*, November 8, 1993, p. A18; Todd Barrett, "Getting Tough on the Poor: Tommy Thompson's Wisconsin Welfare Lab," *Newsweek*, October 15, 1990, p. 33; Axinn and Hirsch, "Welfare and the 'Reform' of Women."

117. Newt Gingrich, et al., *Contract With America: The Bold Plan* (New York: Times Books, 1994).

118. Sanford F. Schram argues that the emphasis on "personal responsibility" in welfare discourse and policy is both a way to blame the poor for their poverty and a means by which the cultural image of the "welfare queen" is continually re-created. See his *After Wel-fare: The Culture of Postindustrial Social Policy* (New York: New York University Press, 2000), chapter 2.

119. Dorothy Roberts, *Killing the Black Body: Race, Reproduction, and the Meaning of Liberty* (New York: Pantheon, 1997), pp. 5–6, 21.

120. Brown, *Race, Money*, pp. 2–3, 6.

121. Jewell, *From Mammy to Miss America*, pp. 1–2.

122. Lieberman, *Shifting the Color Line*, pp. 5–6.

CHAPTER 6

1. Lawrence Bobo and James M. Kluegel, "Modern American Prejudice: Stereotypes, Social Distance, and Perceptions of Discrimination toward Blacks, Hispanics, and Asians." Paper presented at the 1991 meetings of the American Sociological Association, Cincinnati.

2. Amy Ansell, *New Right, New Racism: Race and Reaction in the United States and Britain* (Washington Square: New York University, 1997), p. 230.

3. Personal Responsibility and Work Opportunity Reconciliation Act of 1996 (Enrolled bill sent to president) 104th Congress, at http://thomas.loc.gov.

4. Ibid.

5. Peter Brimelow, *Alien Nation: Common Sense about America's Immigration Disaster* (New York: Random House, 1995), p. xvii. We are not suggesting, however, that Peter Brimelow's works represent the views articulated by most conservatives who have addressed the issue. Some conservatives are in favor of the relatively open new immigration policies which they feel strengthen the economy and provide powerful evidence that with the proper motivation and work ethic anyone can achieve affluence in the United States, a land of extraordinary opportunity. Economic conservatives are likely to favor policies that encourage open immigration, whereas social conservatives are more likely to oppose such policies. For an example of a pro-immigration conservative view, see Ron K. Unz, "Immigration or the Welfare State: Which Is Our Enemy?" *Policy Review* (fall 1994): 33–38. Also see George Gilder's and Jack Kemp's comments in "Immigration: Where to Go from Here," *Wall Street Journal*, November 27, 1995.

6. Brimelow, *Alien Nation*, p. 65.

7. *Congressional Record*, "Immigration: Where to Go from Here?" (Senate—November 29, 1995), pp. S17790–S17791. http://thomas.loc.gov.

8. Nina Perales, "A Tangle of Pathology: Racial Myth and the New Jersey Family Development Act," in *Mothers in Law: Feminist Theory and the Legal Regulation of Motherhood*, ed. Martha Fineman and Isadore Karpin (New York: Columbia University Press, 1995), pp. 258–259. The poem at the opening of this chapter is cited by Perales. She also discusses a much more sophisticated expression of anti-immigration and antiwelfare sentiment. She cites a *New York Times* op-ed essay by a Nobel Prize–winning economist as "using the image of the immigrant on welfare to symbolize a racial threat to the country." In that October 14, 1992, essay Gary Becker argued that to keep immigrants from poor countries from coming to the United States in search of welfare benefits, immigration permits should be auctioned.

9. The conservative anti-immigrant sentiment in the Congress was not only reflected in the PRWORA. In 1996, the Republican-dominated Congress also passed the Illegal Immigrant Reform and Immigrant Responsibility Act. This act expanded the grounds for deportation of immigrants, drastically reduced their rights to appeal, and speeded up the deportation process. The result has been a sharp rise in deportations, particularly of recent immigrants. See Eric Rich, "Deportations Soar under Rigid Law," *Hartford Courant*, October 8, 2000, pp. A1, A8.

10. On debunking the myth that poor residents migrate within the United States to get better welfare benefits, see Sanford F. Schram, Lawrence Nitz, and Gary Krueger, "Welfare Migration as a Policy Rumor: A Statistical Accounting," in *Tales of the State: Narrative in Contemporary U.S. Politics and Public Policy*, ed. Sanford F. Schram and Philip T. Neisser (Lanham, MD: Rowman & Littlefield, 1997), pp. 139–149.

11. Susan Thomas, "Race, Gender, and Welfare Reform: The Antinatalist Response," *Journal of Black Studies* 28 (March 1998): 420.

12. Quoted in Nancy Gibbs, "The Vicious Cycle," *Time,* June 1994, pp. 25–32.

13. Linda Burton et al., *What Welfare Recipients and the Fathers of Their Children Are Saying about Welfare Reform* (June 1998), p. 11. This is the first report from "Welfare Reform and Children: A Three-City Study," a project conducted in Baltimore, Boston, and Chicago. Available from www.jhu.edu/~welfare/.

14. Thomas, "Race, Gender, and Welfare Reform," p. 437. For more on racism and eugenics see Steven Selden, *Inheriting Shame: The Story of Eugenics and Racism in America* (New York: Teachers College Press, 1999). In a broadcast by popular radio talk-show host Bob Grant, Grant was quoted mimicking the dialect of an African-American welfare recipient who laments, "I

don't have no job, how'm I gonna feed my family?" In explaining what he saw as their great reproductive proclivities and the need for the "Bob Grant Mandatory Sterilization Act," Grant stated, "It's like maggots on a hot day. You look back one minute and there are so many there, and you look again and, wow, they've tripled!" Quoted in Dorothy Roberts, *Killing the Black Body: Race, Reproduction, and the Meaning of Liberty* (New York: Vintage Books, 1997), p. 18.

15. Thomas, pp. 420, 426.

16. Lee Rainwater and William L. Yancey, *The Moynihan Report and the Politics of Controversy* (Cambridge: MIT Press, 1967).

17. Ibid. See also Noel A. Cazenave, "Race, Class, Ideology and Changing Black Family Structures and Processes," in *Institutional Racism and Black America: Challenges, Choices, Change*, ed. Mfanya Donald Tryman (Lexington, MA: Ginn, 1985), p. 40.

18. Cazenave, "Race, Class, Ideology," p. 41.

19. Rainwater and Yancey, *The Moynihan Report*, p. 5.

20. Cazenave, "Race, Class, Ideology," p. 41.

21. Roberts, *Killing the Black Body*, p. 16.

22. Rainwater and Yancey, *The Moynihan Report*.

23. Thomas, "Race, Gender, and Welfare Reform."

24. For a critique of this view of the culture of poverty, see Elliot Liebow, *Tally's Corner: A Study of Negro Streetcorner Men* (Boston: Little, Brown, 1967).

25. Thomas, "Race, Gender, and Welfare Reform," p. 426. See also Susan L. Thomas, "From the Culture of Poverty to the Culture of Single Motherhood: The New Poverty Paradigm," *Women & Politics* 14 (1994): 65–97.

26. Thomas, "Race, Gender, and Welfare Reform," pp. 419–420, 426.

27. Comments made in the presence of Noel A. and Anita Washington Cazenave.

28. Consistent with this approach, Thomas defines racism as "a process of systematic oppression directed against people who are defined as inferior, usually in pseudobiological terms such as skin color." Thomas, "Race, Gender, and Welfare Reform," p. 441, note 4.

29. Thomas M. Shapiro, *Population Control Politics: Women, Sterilization and Reproductive Choice* (Philadelphia: Temple University Press, 1985), pp. 9, 29. His analysis of population control efforts targeted at low-income women of color influenced our use of the term *race population control*.

30. Ibid., p. 23.

31. Shapiro makes the latter point. Ibid.

32. Ibid., p. 5. Shapiro cites a 1974 federal court ruling that found: "Over the last few years, an estimated 100,000 to 150,000 low-income persons have been sterilized annually under federally funded programs," and "an indefinite number of poor people have been improperly coerced into accepting a sterilization operation under the threat that various federally supported welfare benefits would be withdrawn" (p. 5). See also Roberts, *Killing the Black Body*, pp. 90–91.

33. J. Philippe Rushton, *Race, Evolution, and Behavior* (New Brunswick, NJ: Transaction Publications, 1995), p. 4.

34. Ibid., p. xiii.

35. Adam Miller, "Professors of Hate," *Rolling Stone*, October 20, 1994, pp. 107–108, 110, 112–114.

36. Ibid., p. 112.

37. Ibid., pp. 107, 114.

38. Ibid., pp. 107, 113.

39. Ibid., p. 108.

40. Joseph F. Sullivan, "Whitman Apologizes for Remarks on Blacks," *New York Times*, April 14, 1995, p. B6; "New Jersey Gov. Christie Whitman Apologizes for Racial Slur," *Jet*, May 1, 1995, p. 6.

41. "News of the Weak in Review," *The Nation*, May 20, 1996, p. 7.

42. Paul Foy, "Bennett Apologizes to Black Leaders," Associated Press, August 24, 1999.

43. Roberts, *Killing the Black Body*, p.104.

44. Ibid., pp. 105–106.

45. Sally Quinn, "Childhood's End," *Washington Post*, November 20, 1994, p. C1.

46. Roberts, *Killing the Black Body*, p. 106.

47. Ibid., p. 107.

48. Ibid., p. 108.

49. Ibid., p. 109; Thomas, "Race, Gender, and Welfare Reform," p. 434.

50. Roberts, *Killing the Black Body*, pp. 112, 144–147.

51. Charles V. Zehren, "Changing of the Species? Moynihan Suggests Illegitimacy May Lead to New Type of Human," *Newsday*, July 14, 1994, p. A4.

52. Roberts, *Killing the Black Body*, p. 110; Thomas, "Race, Gender, and Welfare Reform," p. 432.

53. Perales, "A Tangle of Pathology," p. 251. The New Jersey family cap legislation and its advocates are discussed in detail (if in generally laudatory tones) in Ted George Goertzel and John Hart, "New Jersey's $64 Question: Legislative Entrepreneurship and the Family Cap," *The Politics of Welfare Reform*, ed. Donald F. Norris and Lyke Thompson (Thousand Oaks, CA: Sage, 1995), pp. 109–145.

54. Jesse Daniels, *White Lies: Race, Class, Gender, and Sexuality in White Supremacist Discourse* (New York: Routledge, 1997), pp. 95, 98.

55. Ibid., p. 94.

56. Julius L. Chambers et al., Administrative Complaint Submitted to the U.S. Department of Health and Human Services Regarding the "Additional Child Provision" (A–4703) of New Jersey Family Development Act by the NAACP Legal Defense and Educational Fund, the NOW Legal Defense and Educational Fund, and the Puerto Rican Legal Defense and Educational Fund.

57. Ibid., p. 15.

58. Ibid., p. 9.

59. Ibid., p. 11.

60. Ibid., p. 12.

61. Mimi Abramovitz, *Regulating the Lives of Women: Social Welfare Policy from Colonial Times to the Present* (Boston: South End Press, 1996), p. 13.

62. Ibid., p. 313.

63. Ibid., pp. 33, 35.

64. Perales, "A Tangle of Pathology," pp. 251, 264.

65. For more on the reasons why such legislation may be supported by African-American and Latino males, see Perales, "A Tangle of Pathology," p. 261.

66. Personal communication to Kenneth J. Neubeck from Robert F. Bacigalupi, Legal Support Unit, Legal Services for New York City, July 3, 2000.

67. Roberts, *Killing the Black Body*, p. 212.

68. Ibid., p. 111.

69. Personal Responsibility Act of 1995 (introduced in the House), H.R. 4. 104th Cong., 1st sess., March 24, 1995. http://thomas.loc.gov.

70. Personal Responsibility and Work Opportunity Reconciliation Act of 1996.

71. Personal Responsibility Act of 1995, pp. 2, 3, 4–7. We do not think that any children should be labeled as "illegitimate." We prefer the term *nonmarital* (or *out-of-wedlock*) births to "illegitimate."

72. Personal Responsibility Act of 1995, pp. 4, 6.

73. Personal Responsibility Act of 1995.

74. Work Opportunity Act of 1995 (introduced in the Senate), S. 1120. August 3, 1995 104th Congress. http://thomas.loc.gov. Work Opportunity Act of 1995 (introduced in the House), H.R. 2915. January 31, 1996 104th Congress. http://thomas.loc.gov.; Personal Responsibility and Work Opportunity Reconciliation Act of 1996.

75. Robert Pear, "Debate in House on Welfare Bills G.O.P. Bloc," *New York Times*, March 23, 1995, pp. A1, A23.

76. Robert Pear, "Catholic Bishops Challenge Pieces of Welfare Bill," *New York Times*, March 19, 1995, p. A1.

77. Steven A. Holmes, "Clinton Says He May Veto Welfare Bill," *New York Times*, April 9, 1995, p. A 23.

78. Robert Pear, "G.O.P. Governors Urge Big Changes for Welfare Bill," *New York Times*, April 13, 1995, pp. A1, B9.

79. Work Opportunity Act of 1995 (introduced in the House).

80. "Republican Welfare Bill Gets a Boost," *New York Times*, September 8, 1995, p. A10.

81. Robin Toner, "Senators Gain in Move to Pass a Welfare Bill," *New York Times*, September 15, 1995, pp. A1, A30.

82. Ibid., p. A30.

83. Abramovitz, *Regulating the Lives of Women*, p. 319.

84. Martha A. Fineman, "Images of Mothers in Poverty Discourse," in *Mothers in Law*, ed. Fineman and Karpin, pp. 205, 222.

85. Johnnie Tillman, "Welfare Is a Women's Issue," in *America's Working Women*, ed. Rosalyn Baxandall, Linda Gordon, and Susan Reverby (New York: Random House, 1976), pp. 356–357.

86. Selden, *Inheriting Shame*, p. 25.

87. Shapiro, *Population Control Politics*, p. 18.

88. Dwight J. Ingle, *Who Should Have Children? An Environmental and Genetics Approach* (Indianapolis: Bobbs-Merrill, 1973), p. xiii.

89. Ibid., p. 1.

90. Ibid., pp. 100–101.

91. Alan Chase, *The Legacy of Malthus: The Social Costs of the New Scientific Racism* (New York: Alfred A. Knopf, 1977), p. xv.

92. Charles Murray, "The Time Has Come to Put Stigma Back on Illegitimacy," *Sacramento Bee*, November 7, 1993. See also Charles Murray, "The Coming White Underclass," *Wall Street Journal*, October 29, 1993, p. A14.

93. Murray, "The Coming White Underclass."

94. After noting what they saw as the dangers of government efforts to affect fertility, Herrnstein and Murray complained that "American fertility policy" "subsidizes births among poor women, who are also disproportionately at the low end of the intelligence distribution." Richard J. Herrnstein and Charles Murray, *The Bell Curve: Intelligence and Class Structure in American Life* (New York: Basic Books, 1994), pp. 548–549.

95. Murray, "The Time Has Come to Put Stigma Back on Illegitimacy."

96. Ibid.

97. Daniels, *White Lies*, p. 98.

98. See Charles Derber, "The Politics of Triage: The Contract with America's Surplus Populations," *Tikkun* 10 (May 1995): 40.

99. *Congressional Record*, U.S. House of Representatives, 104th Congress, March 24, 1995, p. H3766.

100. Ibid., p. H3772.

101. See Jacqueline Jones, *Labor of Love, Labor of Sorrow: Black Women, Work, and the Family, from Slavery to the Present* (New York: Vintage Books, 1995).

102. Teresa Amott and Julie Matthaei, *Race, Gender, and Work: A Multi-cultural Economic History of Women in the United States* (Boston: South End Press, 1996), chapter 6.

103. Referring to the segregation of women's suffrage clubs and more antiblack feelings directed toward African American women than men, bell hooks states, "Many white women felt that their status as ladies would be undermined were they to associate with black women." See hooks's *Ain't I A Woman: Black Women and Feminism* (Boston: South End Press, 1981), pp. 130–131.

104. Ibid., p. 136.

105. Robert Pear, "Governors' Plan on Welfare Attacked; Civil Rights Groups Say Minority Children Would Suffer Unduly," *New York Times*, February 14, 1996, p. A12.

106. Gwendolyn Mink, *Welfare's End* (Ithaca, NY: Cornell University Press, 1998), p. 7. See also Rinku Sen, "The First Time Was Tragedy . . . " *ColorLines* 3, fall 2000, pp. 18–23, also available as "The First Time Was Tragedy, Will the Second Be Farce? Fighting Welfare 'Reform,'" at www.arc.org/C_Lines/CLArchive/story3_3_07.html.

107. See Mimi Abramovitz, *Under Attack, Fighting Back: Women and Welfare in the United States* (New York: Monthly Review Press, 1996), pp. 133–137.

108. Michael O. Allen, "Welfare Bill Stirs a Storm; Protestors Urge Prez to Veto," (New York) *Daily News*, August 3, 1996, p. 8.

109. Gwendolyn Mink, "Aren't Poor Single Mothers Women? Feminists, Welfare Reform, and Welfare Justice," in *Whose Welfare?*, ed. Gwendolyn Mink (Ithaca, NY: Cornell University Press, 1999), pp. 171–188.

110. Mink, *Welfare's End*, p. 23.

111. Ibid., p. 25.

112. Ibid., pp. 26–27.

113. Ibid., pp. 1–2. Mink observed that while there were some feminist activist exceptions, for the most part "among policy makers, even the usual champions of gender equality erased mothers from the debate."

114. Ibid,, p. 25.

115. Ibid., p. 2.

116. Ibid., p. 23.

CHAPTER 7

The interview from which the epigraph is taken, "The Secret Truth about Race and Welfare; An Interview with Dr. Susan Tinsley Gooden," spring 1999, can be found under "newsletters" at the website of the Grass Roots Innovative Policy Program, www.arc.org/gripp.

1. Gwendolyn Mink, *Welfare's End* (Ithaca, NY: Cornell University Press, 1998), pp. 50–53.

2. Many examples to be discussed here were referenced in "Impact of Recent Changes in Welfare Programs on Racial and Ethnic Communities: Selected List of Resource Materials," compiled in May 2000 by the National Partnership for Women and Families, Washington, D.C. The resource materials above may be found on www.nationalpartnership.org by searching under "racial and ethnic". The NPWF has had an active interest in research on and advocacy against welfare racism.

3. One exception is Elizabeth Lower-Basch, "'Leavers' and Diversion Studies: Preliminary Analysis of Racial Differences in Caseload Trends and Leaver Outcomes." Paper presented at the fall 1999 Office of the Assistant Secretary for Planning and Evaluation Outcomes Grantee Meeting. Washington, D.C.: U.S. Department of Health and Human Services, October 1999.

4. Jason DeParle, "Shrinking Welfare Rolls Leave Record High Share of Minorities," *New York Times*, July 28, 1998, p. A1.

5. Laura Meckler, "Whites Beat Minorities Off Welfare," Associated Press Online Report, March 29, 1999, pp. 1–3.

6. Ibid., p. 2.

7. Darrel Rowland, "As Welfare Caseloads Shrink, the Racial Makeup Is Reversed," *Columbus Dispatch*, August 2, 1998, p. 1A.

8. Sarah Karp, "Minorities Off Welfare Get Few Jobs," *Chicago Reporter*, January 2000, available at www.chicagoreporter.com.

9. Ibid. The Illinois Department of Human Services reported data in two categories, "whites" and "non-whites."

10. Suzanne Armato, Jim Lewis, and Tim Lohrentz, *Living with Welfare Reform: A Survey of Low Income Families in Illinois* (Chicago: University of Illinois Center for Urban Economic Development, 2000), p. 6.

11. National and some state data on the racial composition of AFDC and TANF recipients are available from the U.S. Department of Health and Human Services, Administration of Children and Families. See, for example, the DHHS website at www.acf.dhhs.gov.

12. Alexandra Starr, "Left Behind; Everybody's Leaving the Welfare Rolls—Except Latinas," *Washington Monthly*, April 1999, pp. 18–22. See also Rachel L. Swarns, "Hispanic Mothers Lagging as Others Escape Welfare," *New York Times*, September 15, 1998, p. A1.

13. On barriers to employment, see Krista Olson and LaDonna Pavetti, *Personal and Family Challenges to the Successful Transition from Welfare to Work* (Washington, D.C.: Urban Institute,1996). See also Deborah L. Puntenney, "The Work of Mothers: Strategies for Survival in an Inner-City Neighborhood," *Journal of Poverty* 3 (1999): 63–92. Race aside, the more barriers a recipient has, the less likely she is to successfully become employed. See Sandra Danziger et al., *Barriers to the Employment of Welfare Recipients* (Ann Arbor: University of Michigan, Poverty Research and Training Center, 1999).

14. Lower-Basch, "'Leavers' and Diversion Studies," p. 6.

15. DeParle, "Shrinking Welfare Rolls," p. A1.

16. On employment discrimination, see Irene Browne, ed., *Latinas and African American Women at Work: Race, Gender, and Economic Inequality* (New York: Russell Sage Foundation, 1999), and Philip Moss and Charles Tilly, *Stories Employers Tell: Race, Skill, and Hiring in America* (New York: Russell Sage Foundation, 2001). On housing discrimination, see Douglas S. Massey and Nancy A. Denton, *American Apartheid: Segregation and the Making of the Underclass* (Cambridge, MA: Harvard University Press, 1993).

17. Barbara Vobejda and Judith Havermann, "Sanctions: A Force behind Falling Welfare Rolls," *Washington Post*, March 23, 1998, p. A1. Families on the welfare rolls that face the most serious problems or barriers to employment are most likely to experience punitive sanctions by welfare officials for violating welfare department rules. There are very little data on how the imposition of sanctions breaks down along racial lines.

18. Joe Soss et al., "Predicting Welfare Reform Retrenchment: Race, Ideology, and Economy in the Devolution Revolution," 1999. Unpublished paper made available by coauthor Sanford Schram, Graduate School of Social Work and Social Research, Bryn Mawr College.

19. Ibid. See also Sanford F. Schram, *After Welfare: The Culture of Postindustrial Social Policy* (New York: New York University Press, 2000), chapter 4.

20. Dorothy Roberts, *Killing the Black Body: Race, Reproduction, and the Meaning of Liberty* (New York: Vintage Books, 1997), pp. 210–211.

21. U.S. Department of Health and Human Services, *Temporary Assistance for Needy Families, Third Annual Report to Congress* (Washington, D.C.: DHHS, August 2000), p. 3. On the decline of

the rolls, see also Julie N. Zimmerman, "Counting Cases: Changes in Welfare Recipiency since 1993," *Southern Rural Development Center Information Brief* (January 1999), p. 2.

22. States with the most punitive sanctions appear to have the greatest caseload declines. See Robert E. Rector and Sarah E. Yousef, *The Determinants of Welfare Caseload Decline* (Washington, D.C.: The Heritage Foundation, 1999).

23. Soss et al., "Predicting Welfare Reform Retrenchment," p. 9.

24. Ibid., pp. 12–13.

25. Ibid., p. 13.

26. Joe Soss et al., "Setting the Terms of Relief: Political Explanations for State Policy Choices in the Devolution Revolution," 2000, p. 28. Unpublished paper made available by coauthor Sanford Schram, Graduate School of Social Work and Social Research, Bryn Mawr College. See also Joe Soss et al., "Setting the Terms of Relief: Explaining State Policy Choices in the Devolution Revolution," *American Journal of Political Science* 45 (April 2001).

27. Soss et al., "Setting the Terms of Relief" (2000), p. 32.

28. See also Martin Gilens, *Why Americans Hate Welfare: Race, Media, and the Politics of Antipoverty Policy* (Chicago: University of Chicago Press, 1999), pp. 175–178; Larry Orr, "Income Transfers as a Public Good: An Application to AFDC," *American Economic Review* 66 (June 1976): 359–371; Christopher Howard, "The American Welfare State, or States?" *Political Research Quarterly* 52 (June 1999): 421–422.

29. Richard P. Nathan and Thomas L. Gais, "Early Findings about the Newest New Federalism For Welfare," in *Welfare Reform: A Race to the Bottom*, ed. Sanford F. Schram and Samuel H. Beer (Washington, D.C: Woodrow Wilson Center Press, 1999), pp. 129–137.

30. Anthony Ramirez, "Rise in Number of Children Born into Poverty in New York City," *New York Times*, February 4, 1999, p. B9. New York City possesses 41 percent of New York state's population and a disproportionate share of the state's welfare caseload. Some 70 percent of New York state's welfare recipients live in the city. Consistent with overall national trends, the city's welfare population dropped drastically with welfare reform. Between 1994 and 1998, the number of families receiving assistance dropped by 26 percent, to 230,942; see the Brookings Institution, *The State of Welfare Caseloads in America's Cities: 1999* (Washington, D.C.: Brookings Institution, 1999), pp. 5 and 7. One observer attributed much of this decline to "an increase in denials to needy, financially eligible persons resulting from stricter verification requirements and stricter administration of the work rules [resulting in increasing numbers of sanctions]." Timothy J. Casey, *Welfare Reform and Its Impact in the Nation and in New York* (New York: Federation of Protestant Welfare Agencies, 1998), p. 8.

31. DeParle, "Shrinking Welfare Rolls," p. A1.

32. Barbara Vobejda and Judith Havermann, "States' Welfare Shift: Stop It Before It Starts; 'Diversion' to Alternatives Cuts Caseloads," *Washington Post*, August 12, 1998, p. A1. With the knowledge and approval of the federal racial state, many individual states and localities adopted "diversion" policies intended to keep people from getting on the welfare rolls in the first place, in addition to punitive sanctions that push recipients off the rolls. By 1998, well over thirty states were using some kind of diversion practices.

33. In 1998 Mead was a consultant to New York City's Human Resources Administration. Another advisor was Heather MacDonald, a fellow at the Manhattan Institute, a policy research center described by New York City's Welfare Reform Network as "a right-wing think tank that has been an influential force behind many of the Mayor's harshest initiatives." See "Who Is Heather MacDonald and Why Is Mayor Giuliani Listening to Her?" *Bully Pulpit: The Welfare Reform Network Media Watch* 1 (October 1998): 1. MacDonald was also said to be a con-

tributor of "inflammatory, racially coded articles" about welfare and the city's poor to the Manhattan Institute's magazine, *City Journal*, and other media outlets (p. 2).

34. Nina Bernstein, "Giuliani Proclaims Success on Pledge 'to End Welfare,'" *New York Times*, December 29, 1999, p. A1.

35. Casey, *Welfare Reform and Its Impact*, p. 8.

36. Karen Houppert, "You're Not Entitled! Welfare 'Reform' Is Leading to Government Lawlessness," *The Nation*, October 25, 1999, pp. 12–13. For more on law violations by welfare program officials, see the special issue on the implementation of welfare reform entitled "Lawlessness," *Organizing* (February 2000), published by Center for Community Change, at www.commchange.org.

37. Welfare Law Center, *The Role of the Courts in Securing Welfare Rights and Improvements in Welfare and Related Programs* (New York: Welfare Law Center, 1999), p. 33.

38. Welfare Law Center, *Federal Court Finds New York City Illegally Deters and Denies Food Stamps, Medicaid, and Cash Assistance Applications and Bars Expansion of "Job Centers"* (New York: Welfare Law Center, 1999).

39. Timothy Egan, "As Idaho Booms, Prisons Fill and Spending on Poor Lags," *New York Times*, April 16, 1998, p. A1.

40. Ibid.

41. Ibid.

42. Robert Pear, "A Million Parents Lost Medicaid, Study Says," *New York Times*, June 20, 2000, p. A12.

43. For research into exclusion from Medicaid and other programs for the poor, see Lissa Bell and Carson Strege-Flora, "Access Denied: Federal Neglect Gives Rise to State Lawlessness: Families Denied Access to Medicaid, Food Stamps, CHIP, and Child Care" (Northwest Federation of Community Organizations and National Campaign for Jobs and Income, May 2000), and the Grassroots Collective and the National Campaign for Jobs and Income, "Access Denied in Illinois: State Practices, Lawlessness Deny Health Insurance to Parents and Children in Illinois/Significant Disparity in Enrollment between Cook County and Rest of State Raises Concerns of Racial Impact" (Chicago: NCJI, May 2000). The reports are on www.nationalcampaign.org.

44. Alison Mann, "CHIP Discriminates," *The Nation*, October 25, 1999, p. 15.

45. Rebecca Bauen, "All Kids Need a Healthy Start: DH&W Doesn't Play Fair with Children's Health" (ID:Northwest Federation of Community Organizations and the Idaho Community Action Network, 1999). Quote is from p. 2. The study findings are also posted at www.arc.org.

46. One exception is a study by Sylvia B. Weinberg, "Mexican American Mothers and the Welfare Debate: A History of Exclusion," *Journal of Poverty* 2 (1998): 53–76.

47. Elizabeth Bettendorf, "Hispanics Slower to Get Off Welfare," *Tampa Tribune*, April 5, 1999, p. 1.

48. Lissette Corsa, "Wages of Welfare War," *Miami New Times*, January 20–26, 2000, pp. 1–11; p. 3. Story available at www.miaminewtimes.com/issues/2000–01–20/feature2.html-page1.html.

49. Researchers also uncovered racial disparities in welfare leavers' experiences in five rural Florida counties. Leslie L. Clarke et al., "People Who Have Left WAGES," *A Qualitative Study of WAGES* (Florida State University: Inter-University Welfare Reform Collaborative, fall 1999).

50. See Kensington Welfare Rights Union, "The New Welfare Reform: Delivering Slaves to the Auction Block," (1998) and the Poor People's Economic Human Rights Campaign petition to the Inter-American Commission on Human Rights (1999), available at www.kwru.org/educat/werfrm.html.

51. Kensington Welfare Rights Union, "The New Welfare Reform," pp. 3–4. On Mississippi, see also Jason DeParle, "Welfare Law Weighs Heavy in Delta, Where Jobs Are Few,"*New York Times*, October 16, 1997, p. A1, and Gretchen G. Kirby et al., *Income Support and Social Services for Low-Income People in Mississippi* (Washington, D.C.: Urban Institute, 1999).

52. Kensington Welfare Rights Union, "The New Welfare Reform," p. 3.

53. Jason DeParle, "Welfare Law Weighs Heavy in Delta."

54. Ibid.

55. Zimmerman, "Counting Cases," pp. 3–4.

56. Ibid., p. 4.

57. Kensington Welfare Rights Union, "The New Welfare Reform," p. 3.

58. See Susan Tinsley Gooden, "Race and Welfare: Examining Employment Outcomes of White and Black Welfare Recipients," *Journal of Poverty* 4 (2000): 21–41, and Susan Gooden, "Examining Racial Differences in Employment Status among Welfare Recipients," January 1, 1997, located under Race and Welfare Report at www.arc.org.

59. See Gooden, "Race and Welfare," and Susan T. Gooden, "The Hidden Third Party: Welfare Recipients' Experiences with Employers," *Journal of Public Management and Social Policy* 5 (1999): 75.

60. Gooden, "The Hidden Third Party," p. 78.

61. Susan T. Gooden, "All Things Not Being Equal: Differences in Caseworker Support toward Black and White Welfare Clients," *Harvard Journal of African American Public Policy* 4 (1998): 23–33. This issue of the journal was devoted to "Welfare Reform and the Black Community."

62. Ibid., p. 32.

63. National Partnership for Women and Families, *Detours on the Road to Employment: Obstacles Facing Low-Income Women* (Washington, D.C.: NPWF, 1999).

64. Ibid., p. 2. Similar findings on multiple forms of discrimination affecting people of color emerged in focus group research conducted in California. See Doris Y. Ng and Ana J. Matosantos, *The Broken Promise:Welfare Reform Two Years Later* (San Francisco: Equal Rights Advocates, 2000), pp. 26–28. Such discrimination was also found in a survey by the Applied Research Center, as reported in Rebecca Gordon, "Cruel and Usual: How Welfare 'Reform' Punishes Poor People" (2001), at www.arc.org.

65. National Partnership for Women and Families, p. 8.

66. See Wendy Zimmerman and Karen C. Tumlin, *Patchwork Policies: State Assistance for Immigrants under Welfare Reform* (Washington, D.C.: Urban Institute, 1999).

67. Lynn H. Fujiwara, "The Impact of Welfare Reform on Asian American Communities," *Social Justice* 25 (1998): 101. See also Lynn H. Fujiwara, "Asian American Communities and the Racial Politics of Welfare Reform," in *Whose Welfare?*, ed. Gwendolyn Mink (Ithaca, NY: Cornell University Press, 1999), pp. 100–131.

68. Doris Y. Ng, *From War on Poverty to War on Welfare: The Impact of Welfare Reform on the Lives of Immigrant Women* (San Francisco: Equal Rights Advocates, 1999), p. 4.

69. "Non-English Speakers Denied Welfare-to-Work Services, Suit Says," *Los Angeles Times*, December 16, 1999, Metro Section, p. 4.

70. Thomas Moore and Vicky Selkowe, *The Impact of Welfare Reform on Wisconsin's Hmong Aid Recipients* (Milwaukee: Institute for Wisconsin's Future, 1999).

71. Under both AFDC and TANF, all states were given the option of adopting welfare policies that provide aid to two-parent househoulds. Many declined.

72. Ibid., p. 4.

73. "Hmong Study Should Serve as Valuable Research Tool," *Milwaukee Journal Sentinel*,

December 27, 1999, p. 10, and Steve Schultz, "Washington Has Been Watching W-2 Results," *Milwaukee Journal Sentinel,* December 29, 1999, p. 1.

74. Steve Schultze, "U.S. Criticizes W-2 Dealings with Hmong," *Milwaukee Journal Sentinel,* December 8, 2000, p. 3B. Wisconsin Governor Tommy Thompson had publicly derided the Institute's report, whose warnings of civil rights violations were confirmed by the Office of Civil Rights. In January 2001 the U.S. Senate approved President George W. Bush's nomination of Thompson as secretary of the U.S. Department of Health and Human Services, thus providing him with authority over federal welfare policy nationally as well as the activities of OCR. On Thompson's recored in his home state, including more on the civil rights violations, see "Credit Where Blame Is Due: The Reality behind the Rhetoric about Governor Thompson's Record in Wisconsin, " January 16, 2001, at www.nationalcampaign.org/action/thompsonum.htm.

75. Make the Road by Walking, *System Failure* (Brooklyn, NY: Make the Road by Walking, 1999), p. 6. This report is available at www.maketheroad.org.

76. "Lawlessness," *Organizing,* p. 14.

77. Ibid., p. 15.

78. Sharon Ehia, June Shimokawa, and Jim Shon, *How Hawai'i Families on Public Assistance Are Responding to Welfare Reform* (Honolulu: American Friends Service Committee, 1999), p. 1.

79. Ibid.

80. For more on the absence of Latinos/as in treatments of welfare policy, see Weinberg, "Mexican American Mothers and the Welfare Debate," pp. 53–76.

81. Layne K. Stromwall, Stephanie Brzuzy, Polly Sharp, and Celina Andersen, "The Implications of 'Welfare Reform' for American Indian Families and Communities," *Journal of Poverty* 2 (1998): 2.

82. See U.S. Department of Health and Human Services AFDC and TANF caseload statistics, by race, available through www.acf.dhhs.gov.

83. U.S. Department of Health and Human Services, "HHS Issues New Rules Governing Tribal Welfare Programs," Press release dated February 18, 2000.

84. "Notes on Welfare Reform from Indian Country," *Organizing* (May 1998): 1. Issues of this newsletter, issued by Center for Community Change, can be accessed at www.commchange.org.

85. See Shanta Pandey et al., *Implementation of the Temporary Assistance for Needy Families (TANF) on American Indian Reservations: Early Evidence from Arizona* (St. Louis: Washington University, Center for American Indian Studies, 1999); Shanta Pandey et al., "Promise of Welfare Reform: Development through Devolution on Indian Reservations," *Journal of Poverty* 3 (1999): 37–61; Stephanie Brzuzy et al., "The Vulnerability of American Indian Women in the New Welfare State," unpublished paper, Arizona State University, and Stromwall, Brzuzy, Sharp, and Andersen, "Implications of 'Welfare Reform,'" pp. 1–15.

86. Pandey et al., *Implementation of the Temporary Assistance for Needy Families,* p. 8.

87. On Arizona's welfare reform policy, see Stromwall, Brzuzy, Sharp, and Andersen, "Implications of 'Welfare Reform,'" pp. 6–10.

88. Pandey et al., *Implementation of the Temporary Assistance for Needy Families,* p. ii.

89. James Jennings, "The End of Welfare As We Know It? Or Ending Neighborhoods As We Have Come to Know Them?" *NFG Reports* 6 (winter 1999): 1. This newsletter is available through Neighborhood Funders Group, McLean, VA 22101. See also www.nfg.org.

90. Jennings, "The End of Welfare as We Know It?," p. 1.

91. Ibid., p. 5.

92. For treatment of "color blindness" as a racist ideology, see Leslie G. Carr, *Color-Blind Racism* (Thousand Oaks, CA: Sage, 1997).

93. U.S. Department of Health and Human Services, *Temporary Assistance for Needy Families (TANF), Second Annual Report to Congress, August 1999* (Washington, D.C.: DHHS, 1999). U.S. Government Accounting Office, *Welfare Reform: Information on Former Recipients' Status, Report to the Chairman, Committee on Finance, U.S. Senate, and the Chairman, Subcommittee on Human Resources, Committee on Ways and Means, House of Representatives* (Washington, D.C.: U.S. Government Accounting Office, April 1999), and *Welfare Reform: States's Implementation Progress and Information on Former Recipients, Testimony before the Subcommittee on Human Resources, Committee on Ways and Means, House of Representatives* (Washington, D.C.: U.S. Government Accounting Office, May 27, 1999).

94. Wendell Primus, Lynette Rawlings, Kathy Larin, Kathryn Porter, *The Initial Impacts of Welfare Reform on the Incomes of Single-Mother Families* (Washington, D.C.: Center on Budget and Policy Priorities, August 1999), and Sharon Parrott, *Welfare Recipients Who Find Jobs: What Do We Know about Their Employment and Earnings?* (Washington, D.C.: Center for Budget and Policy Priorities, November 1998).

95. Sarah Brauner and Pamela Loprest, *Where Are They Now? What States' Studies of People Who Left Welfare Tell Us* (Washington, D.C.: Urban Institute, May 1999), and Pamela Loprest, *Families Who Left Welfare: Who Are They and How Are They Doing?* (Washington, D.C.: Urban Institute, 1999).

96. Rachel Schumacher and Mark Greenberg, *Child Care After Leaving Welfare: Early Evidence from State Studies* (Washington, D.C.: Center for Law and Social Policy, October 1999).

97. Children's Defense Fund and National Coalition for the Homeless, *Welfare to What? Early Findings on Family Hardship and Well-Being* (Washington, D.C.: Children's Defense Fund, December 1998).

98. Unitarian Universalist Service Committee, *Is It Reform? The Welfare and Human Rights Monitoring Report* (Boston: Unitarian Universalist Service Committee, 1998).

99. NETWORK, *Poverty amid Plenty: The Unfinished Business of Welfare Reform* (Washington, D.C.: NETWORK, 1999).

100. Children's Rights Inc., *Working without a Net: Children, Welfare Reform, and the Child Welfare System* (New York: Children's Rights Inc., September 1999).

101. Families USA Foundation, *Losing Health Insurance: The Unintended Consequences of Welfare Reform* (Washington, D.C.: Families USA Foundation, May 1999).

102. For an exception to this statement, see Pamela J. Loprest and Sheila R. Zedlewski, *Current and Former Welfare Recipients: How Do They Differ?* (Washington, D.C.: Urban Institute, November 1999). Interest in race as a variable was expressed in 1999 by a member of the research staff at the U.S. Department of Health and Human Services. See Lower-Basch, "'Leavers' and Diversion Studies."

103. U.S. Census Bureau, *Poverty in the United States, 1998* (Washington, D.C.: U.S. Government Printing Office, 1999), p. xiii.

104. See Browne, *Latinas and African American Women at Work*, and Moss and Tilly, *Stories Employers Tell*. The competition for limited numbers of low-wage jobs that people of color living in depressed urban areas face is described in Katherine S. Newman, *No Shame in My Game: The Working Poor in the Inner City* (New York: Alfred A. Knopf and Russell Sage Foundation, 1999). On the absolute dearth of jobs in many such areas, see William J. Wilson, *When Work Disappears: The World of the New Urban Poor* (New York: Knopf, 1996), chapters 1 and 2.

105. The experiences of women of color from different racial/ethnic groups may be similar, but are not interchangeable. Groups may, for example, differ in the availability of family support networks. See Anne R. Roschelle, *No More Kin: Exploring Race, Class, and Gender in Family Networks* (Thousand Oaks, CA: Sage, 1997).

106. Sanford E. Schram, *Words of Welfare: The Poverty of Social Science and the Social Science of Poverty* (Minneapolis: University of Minnesota Press, 1995), p. xxviii.

107. See Melvin Thomas, "Anything but Race: The Social Science Retreat from Racism," *African American Research Perspectives* 6 (winter 2000): 79–96.

108. Schram, *Words of Welfare*, p. 6.

109. See Browne, *Latinas and African American Women at Work*; Moss and Tilly, *Stories Employers Tell*; Donald Tomaskovic-Devey, *Gender and Racial Inequality at Work: The Sources and Consequences of Job Segregation* (Ithaca, NY: ILR Press, 1993).

110. See Teresa L. Amott and Julie Matthaei, *Race, Gender, and Work: A Multicultural Economic History of Women in the United States* (Boston: South End Press, 1996).

111. Michael Brown, *Race, Money, and the American Welfare State* (Ithaca, NY: Cornell University Press, 1999), p. 335.

112. Ibid., p. 340.

113. On the importance of the possession of wealth assets in avoiding reliance on welfare, see Dalton Conley, *Being Black, Living in the Red: Race, Wealth, and Social Policy in America* (Berkeley: University of California Press, 1999), pp. 120–122.

114. See Melvin Oliver and Thomas M. Shapiro, *Black Wealth/White Wealth: A New Perspective on Racial Inequality* (New York: Routledge, 1995).

CHAPTER 8

The epigraph opening the chapter is taken from "An Immodest Proposal: Rewarding Women's Work to End Poverty," *Survival News* (summer 2000), p. 18. This proposal was prepared by a distinguished group of "feminist academics, professionals, and activists who are concerned with the relationship between women, economic survival, and the work of caregiving" (p. 18). It was issued in anticipation of the debate over the 2002 congressional reauthorization of the Personal Responsibility and Work Opportunity Reconciliation Act of 1996. For information see www.welfare2002.org.

1. That decline was from a peak of 5 million families in 1994 to 3.2 million in 1998 and 2.6 million in 1999 (numbers are by fiscal year). U.S. Department of Health and Human Services, Administration for Children and Families, *Temporary Assistance for Needy Families (TANF) Program, Third Annual Report to Congress* (Washington, D.C.: DHHS, August 2000), Table 10: 1: a. See also www.acf.dhhs.gov/programs/opre/annual3.pdf.

2. U.S. Department of Health and Human Services.

3. U.S. Department of Commerce, U.S. Census Bureau, *Poverty in the United States 1999* (Washington, D.C.: U.S. Government Printing Office, 2000), p. v.

4. Louis Uchitelle, "Rising Incomes Lift 1.1 Million out of Poverty; 107 Months, and Counting," *New York Times*, January 30, 2000, section 3, pp. 1, 14.

5. Chuck Collins, Chris Hartman, and Holly Sklar, "Divided Decade: Economic Disparity at the Century's Turn." United for a Fair Economy, December 15, 1999. http://www.ufenet.org/press/divided_decade.html. See also Center on Budget and Policy Priorities. "Gaps between High-Income and Other Americans Will Reach Record Level in 1999, Analysis Finds." September 4, 1999, at www.cbpp.org/9-4-99tax.htm.

6. See Arloc Sherman, "Extreme Child Poverty Rises Sharply in 1997," Children's Defense Fund, August 22, 1999, p. 3, at http://www.childrensdefensefund.org/release990822.htm. Robert Pear, "A Million Parents Lost Medicaid, Study Says,"*New York Times*, June 20, 2000, p. A12; and Wilde Parke et al., *The Decline in Food Stamp Program Participation in the 1990s*, Food Assistance and Nutrition Research Report No. 7 (Washington, D.C.: U.S. Department of Agriculture, June 2000).

7. A joint report by the Children's Defense Fund and the National Coalition for the Homeless said, "Only a small fraction of welfare recipients' new jobs pay above-poverty wages; most of the new jobs pay far below the poverty line." That report also found that "Many families leaving welfare report struggling to get food, shelter, or needed medical care; many are suffering even more hardships than before." *Welfare to What? Early Findings on Family Hardship and Well-Being* (Washington, D.C.: Children's Defense Fund and National Coalition for the Homeless, December 1998), pp. 2, 3. The report is at http://www.childrensdefensefund.org/fair-start-welfare2what.htm. It found, for example, that "Among recipients who find jobs, 71 percent earn below the three-person poverty level ($250 per week)," p. 2.

8. See Jason DeParle, "Success and Frustration, as Welfare Rules Change," *New York Times*, December 30, 1997, pp. A1, A16–17. Commenting on the effects of the PRWORA, DeParle concluded that "the early evidence suggests that only about half of those leaving the rolls have jobs" (p. A16).

9. See Sherman, "Extreme Child Poverty Rises Sharply in 1997." The increase of 372,000 children living in extreme poverty in 1997 brought the total number of such children in mother-only families to 1.8 million. The Children's Defense Fund report emphasizes the suddenness of the increase: "Prior to increasing in 1997, this measure had been falling for four straight years." It is important to reiterate that the PRWORA was passed in August 1996, just before the extreme child poverty rate shot up. The report noted also that the extreme child poverty finding "runs counter to broad economic trends. . . . The increase coincided with an unusually strong, sustained, and widespread economic boom."

10. Peter Edelman, "Clinton Fudged on the Facts about Poverty," *Plain Dealer*, July 10, 1999, p. B8.

11. Sheldon H. Danziger, ed., *Economic Conditions and Welfare Reform* (New York: W.E. Upjohn Institute, 1999).

12. For both a discussion of the literature on the denial of white racism and a case analysis of such denial see Noel A. Cazenave and Darlene Alvarez Maddern, "Defending the White Race: White Male Faculty Opposition to a 'White Racism' Course," *Race and Society* 2 (1999): 25–50.

13. Frances Calpotura and Bob Wing, "The View from the Ground: Organizers Speak Out on Race," *ColorLines* 3 (summer 2000), www.arc.org/C_Lines/CLArchive/story3_2_02.html.

14. There are, of course, noteworthy exceptions. This chapter discusses the important work of the Applied Research Center. Another example is the New Abolitionist Movement and its journal *Race Traitor*.

15. Jill Quadagno, *The Color of Welfare: How Racism Undermined the War on Poverty* (New York: Oxford University Press, 1994).

16. Paulo Freire, *Pedagogy of the Oppressed* (New York: Continuum, 1989), p. 11. For more on how American social science contributes to this "culture of silence," see Cazenave and Maddern, "Defending the White Race."

17. See William Julius Wilson, *The Declining Significance of Race: Blacks and Changing American American Institutions* (Chicago: University of Chicago Press, 1980), and William Julius Wilson, *When Work Disappears: The World of the New Urban Poor* (New York: Alfred A. Knopf, 1996), pp. 235–238. One among many critiques of the logical and empirical flaws of Wilson's "declining significance of race" argument is contained in Noel A. Cazenave, "Race, Class, Ideology and Changing Black Family Structures and Processes: Challenges for the Future," in *Institutional Racism and Black America: Challenges, Choices, Change*, ed. Mfanya Donald Tryman (Lexington, MA: Ginn Press, 1985), pp. 43–50. For other articles that challenge Wilson's thesis see Charles V. Willie, ed., *The Caste and Class Controversy* (Bayside, NY: General Hall, 1979). For data on the

profound link between racism, housing segregation, and the high poverty rates of urban African Americans, see Douglas S. Massey and Nancy A. Denton, *American Apartheid: Segregation and the Making of the Underclass* (Cambridge, MA: Harvard University Press, 1993).

18. "Race-neutrality" was certainly not true for the programs initiated in the United States as part of the New Deal. See Steve Valocchi, "The Racial Basis of Capitalism and the State, and the Impact of the New Deal on African Americans," *Social Problems* 41 (1994): 347–362.

19. For a discussion of how U.S. society is structured around "race," see Audrey Smedley, *Race in North America: Origin and Evolution of a Worldview* (Boulder, CO: Westview, 1999), p. 22, and David T. Wellman, *Portraits of White Racism* (New York: Cambridge University Press, 1993), pp. 54–55. See also Leslie G. Carr, *Color-Blind Racism* (Thousand Oaks, CA: Sage, 1997).

20. The first three of these possible responses were influenced by Ruth Frankenberg's "essentialist racism," "color- and power-evasiveness," and "race-cognizant" forms of thinking about race and racism. Ruth Frankenberg, *White Women, Race Matters: The Social Construction of Whiteness* (Minneapolis: University of Minnesota Press, 1993), p. 140.

21. See Dorothy Roberts, *Killing the Black Body: Race, Reproduction, and the Meaning of Liberty* (New York: Pantheon, 1997), pp. 5–6.

22. Doug McAdam, *Political Process and the Development of Black Insurgency, 1930–1970* (Chicago: University of Chicago Press, 1999), pp. 48–51.

23. Patricia Hill Collins, *Black Feminist Thought: Knowledge, Consciousness, and the Politics of Empowerment* (New York: Routledge, 2000), p. 5.

24. Martin Gilens, "Media Misrepresentations: Is There a Solution?" *TomPaine.Common Sense: A Journal of Opinion* (October 20, 1999), at www.tompaine.com/features/1999/10/20/1.html.

25. Makani Themba-Nixon, "The Stories They Tell: Media Coverage of Welfare," *GRIPP News and Notes* 2, 1 (spring 2000). Available from the GRIPP website at www.arc.org/gripp.

26. Ibid. The We Interrupt This Message website is www.interrupt.org. On another front, in 2000 more than ninety organizations joined in a national "Welfare Made a Difference Campaign," aimed at challenging stereotypes about women who receive welfare and addressing the need for more effective antipoverty strategies. The campaign's website is www.wmadcampaign.org.

27. For more on education/empowerment strategies of social change see again Freire, *The Pedagogy of the Oppressed*. Also see John Gaventa, *Power and Powerlessness: Quiescence and Rebellion in an Appalachian Valley* (Urbana: University of Illinois Press, 1980), and David Reed, *Education for Building a People's Movement* (Boston: South End Press, 1981). For an account of KWRU's methods, see Willie Baptist, "Willie Baptist on Organizing the Poor: The Experience of Kensington." http://www.Kwru.org/educat/orgmod2.html.

28. See the Race Relations Act, as amended, at www.cre.gov.uk/law/rev_rra.html.

29. Rinku Sen, "The First Time Was Tragedy . . . , " *ColorLines* 3 (summer 2000): 20, also available as "The First Time Was Tragedy, Will the Second Time Be Farce? Fighting Welfare 'Reform,'" at www.arc.org/C_Lines/CLArchive/story3_3_07.html.

30. Applied Research Center, "Developing an Equity Impact Statement: A Tool for Local Policymaking," Draft dated May 2000. See www.arc.org under "research publications".

31. National Campaign for Jobs and Income Support at www.nationalcampaign.org.

32. The need for racial audits was stressed in Susan T. Gooden, "All Things Not Being Equal: Differences in Caseworker Support toward Black and White Welfare Clients," *Harvard Journal of African American Public Policy* 4 (1998): 23–33. Some of the issues raised there are taken up in "Putting Welfare Reform to the Test: A Guide to Uncovering Bias and Unfair Treatment in Local Welfare Programs," Grass Roots Innovative Policy Program,

Applied Research Center, January 2000. www.arc.org/gripp under "research publications". See also Susan Gooden, "Race and Welfare Report: Examining Racial Differences in Employment Status among Welfare Recipients," January 1, 1997, at www.arc.org/gripp/researchPublications/reports/goodenReport/reportTitlePg.html; "Race and Welfare: Examining Employment Outcomes of White and Black Welfare Recipients," *Journal of Poverty* 4 (fall 2000): 21–41, and "The Hidden Third Party: Welfare Recipients' Experiences with Employers," *Journal of Public Management and Social Policy* 5 (summer 1999): 69–83.

33. Gooden, "Race and Welfare Report."

34. Lani Guinier, *The Tyranny of the Majority: Fundamental Fairness in Representative Democracy* (New York: Free Press, 1994).

35. Frances Fox Piven and Richard A. Cloward, *Regulating the Poor: The Functions of Public Welfare* (New York: Vintage Books, 1993). Frances Fox Piven and Richard A. Cloward, *Poor People's Movements: Why They Succeed, How They Fail* (New York: Vintage Books, 1979).

36. Guida West, *The National Welfare Rights Movement: The Social Protest of Poor Women* (New York: Praeger, 1981), p. 326.

37. *Annie Lee Whitfield et al., Plaintiffs v. Julia J. Oliver et al, Defendants.* Civ. A. No. 3330–N. United States District Court, M.D. Alabama, N.D. Aug 1, 1975, *399 Federal Supplement,* (1975:348).

38. Michael Fix and Margery Austin Turner, eds., *A National Report Card on Discrimination in America: The Role of Testing* (Washington, D.C.: Urban Institute, 1999), pp. 1, 9.

39. U.S. Department of Health and Human Services, "HHS Office for Civil Rights Issues Guidance on Civil Rights Laws and Welfare Reform," *HHS* News (August 27, 1999), p. 1. See U.S. Department of Health and Human Services, Office for Civil Rights, *Technical Assistance for Caseworkers on Civil Rights Laws and Welfare Reform* (Washington, D.C.: DHHS, 1999), available from the OCR at www.ocr.hhs.gov/ocr. Additional guidance is provided in NOW Legal Defense and Education Fund, *Civil Rights Laws and Welfare* (New York: NOW LDEF, 1999), and by National Partnership for Women and Families, *Preventing Discrimination: A Guide for Caseworkers and Others Helping Welfare Recipients Enter the Workforce* (Washington, D.C.: NPWF, 1999).

40. U.S. Department of Health and Human Services, *Technical Assistance for Caseworkers*, Section III on "What Conduct Is Prohibited in Federally Funded Programs and Activities?" and Section IV on "What Type of Conduct Is Prohibited in Employment Settings?"

41. U.S. Department of Health and Human Services. "HHS Office for Civil Rights Issues Guidance on Civil Rights Laws." U.S. Department of Health and Human Services, Office for Civil Rights, *Technical Assistance for Caseworkers*.

42. Welfare Law Center, *The Role of the Courts in Securing Welfare Rights and Improvements in Welfare and Related Programs* (May 1999), pp.11–12. Available at www.welfarelaw.org.

43. Dottie Stevens, "Which Way Welfare Rights?" *Survival News* (summer 2000), p. 7. That same issue of *Survival News*, published in Boston, Massachusetts, contains another article by Stevens on the plans of the Massachusetts Welfare Rights Union and nine other groups from across the nation to work with the Applied Research Center to collect data on racial, gender, and immigration discrimination in the implementation of welfare reform. "The Welfare Bias Civil Rights Survey," p. 9. For survey results, see www.arc.org.

44. Daniel P. Moynihan, *The Politics of a Guaranteed Income: The Nixon Administration and the Family Assistance Plan* (New York: Vintage, 1973), p. 336.

45. Letter from George A. Wiley, Director, Poverty/Rights Action Center to Welfare Rights Leaders and Friends published in *NOW! National Welfare Leaders Newsletter*, September 22, 1967, Vol. 1, no 19. Available in the George Wiley Papers, the State Historical Society of Wisconsin, Madison; Eve Edstrom, "Irate Welfare Mothers Hold 'Wait-In'," *Washington Post*, September 20,

1967, pp. A1, A7; Eve Edstrom, "Protesting Welfare Mothers Rebuked," *Washington Post*, September 21, 1967, p. A2.

46. Nick Kotz and Mary Lynn Kotz, *A Passion for Equality: George Wiley and the Movement* (New York: Norton, 1977), pp. 249–251.

47. Ibid., pp. 248, 252–253.

48. "Poor Campaign Is Found Failing," *Baltimore Sun*, June 9, 1968; "Stumbling Crusaders. Poor People's Campaign Attempts to Overcome Confusion, Gain Aims," *Wall Street Journal*, May 29, 1968. See also Charles Fager, *Uncertain Resurrection: The Poor People's Washington Campaign* (Grand Rapids, MI: Eerdmans,1969), and Harvard Sitkoff, *The Struggle for Black Equality 1954–1980* (New York: Hill and Wang, 1981), p. 222.

49. Gerald D. McKnight, *The Last Crusade: Martin Luther King, Jr., the FBI, and the Poor People's Campaign* (Boulder, CO: Westview, 1998), p. 63.

50. "National Welfare Rights Organization HEW Demands Presented at Poor People's Campaign Meeting with Hon. Wilber Cohen, Secretary, U.S. Dept. of Health, Education, and Welfare," p.1. Domestic Crises. Poor People's Campaign. May 11–May 20, 1968. Lyndon Baines Johnson Library, Austin, Texas. Secretary Cohen said to President Johnson at a cabinet meeting:

> I met with them for two hours. I found their specific complaints valid. I feel that a lot more can be achieved through administrative action, such as revisions in the welfare system and changes in legislative recommendations. We will have to try harder, and we will.

"The Cabinet Meeting of May 1, 1968." The White House. p. 4. Domestic Crises. Poor People's Campaign. May 11–May 20, 1968. Lyndon Baines Johnson Library, Austin, Texas.

51. Ibid.

52. Ibid., pp. 1–2.

53. Kotz and Kotz, *Passion for Equality*, p. 258.

54. See especially Quadagno's discussion on pp. 118ff.

55. Ibid., p. 133.

56. "Why the Welfare Bill Is Stuck," *Newsweek*, December 7, 1970, pp. 22–23.

57. James T. Patterson, *America's Struggle against Poverty 1900–1994* (Cambridge, MA: Harvard University Press, 1994), p. 195. Also see "The Welfare Militants" chapter of Moynihan, *The Politics of a Guaranteed Income.*

58. Statement by Mrs. Roxanne Jones, a Philadelphia welfare rights activist, in Milwaukee County Welfare Rights Organization, *Welfare Mothers Speak Out: We Ain't Gonna Shuffle Anymore* (New York: W. W. Norton, 1972), p. 107.

59. Indeed, neither the words *white backlash* nor *racism* appear in the index of Patterson's racism-blind analysis of U.S. poverty attitudes throughout most of the twentieth century. While there is a listing for "Blacks" there is no "white" listing of any kind. Indeed the word *race* is not even listed in his index. Patterson, *America's Struggle against Poverty.*

60. Quadagno, *The Color of Welfare*, p. 133.

61. For some other political economic factors that worked against this and other guaranteed income proposals, see Kenneth J. Neubeck and Jack L. Roach, "Income Maintenance Experiments, Politics, and the Perpetuation of Poverty," *Social Problems* 28 (February 1981): 308–320, and Kenneth J. Neubeck, "Income Maintenance Experimentation: Cui Bono," in *Applied Poverty Research*, ed. Richard Goldstein and Stephen M. Sachs (New York: Rowman and Allenheld, 1983), pp. 253–259.

62. Quadagno, *The Color of Welfare*, pp. 128–131.

63. Marian Kramer, "Remarks on the National Welfare Rights Union," *Social Justice* 21, 1: 9–10.

64. Baptist, "Willie Baptist on Organizing the Poor." "Protest" and "Political Education" are two of "The Six Panther P's" KWRU incorporates into its organizational strategy. See Kensington Welfare Rights Union, "The New Welfare Reform: Delivering Slaves to the Auction Block." www.kwru.org/educat/welrfrm.html.

65. Cheri Honkala, "Kensington Welfare Rights Union and the Economic Human Rights Campaign," at www.kwru.org/educat/cheriun2.html.

66. Kensington Welfare Rights Union, "What Is the Campaign?" http://www.kwru.org/ehrc/ehrc–q1.html.

67. Kensington Welfare Rights Union, "The New Welfare Reform."

68. Ibid.

69. Kristen Lombardi, "Welfare Outrage Goes Global: A Grassroots Campaign to Restore Welfare Benefits to America's Poor Takes Its Case to the International Court of Public Opinion," *Boston Phoenix*, June 1–8, 2000, at www.bostonphoenix.com/archive/features/00/06/01/welfare.html. For a hard copy version of this article see *Boston Phoenix*, June 2, 2000, pp. 26–27.

70. Herbert Aptheker, *Anti-Racism in U.S. History: The First Two Hundred Years* (Westport, CT: Greenwood, 1992), p. xiv.

71. Archie Bunker was a racially bigoted European-American character on the popular 1970s show *All in the Family*.

72. "Putting Welfare Reform to the Test."

73. Gary Delgado, "Racing the Welfare Debate," *ColorLines* 3 (fall 2000): 13–17, available at www.arc.org/c-Lines/CLArchive/story3_3_04.html.

74. See the Grass Roots Organizing for Welfare Leadership website at www.ctwo.org/growl/.

75. Raymond S. Franklin, *Shadows of Race and Class* (Minneapolis: University of Minnesota, 1991). See also Joe R. Feagin and Melvin P. Sikes, *Living with Racism: The Black Middle-Class Experience* (Boston: Beacon, 1994), pp. 61–62.

76. See, for example, Joe R. Feagin and Melvin P. Sikes, *Living With Racism: The Black Middle-Class Experience* (Boston: Beacon Press, 1994), pp. 61–62.

77. See James Jennings, "The End of Welfare As We Know It? Or Ending Neighborhoods As We Have Come to Know Them?" *NFG Reports* 6 (winter 1999): 1, 3–5. Also available at www.nfg.org.

76. Randall Robinson, *The Debt: What America Owes to Blacks* (New York: Dutton, 2000), p. 74.

Index

abolitionists, 28
abortion, 60, 161, 173
Abraham, Senator Spencer, 164–65
Abramovitz, Mimi: *Regulating the Lives of Women*, 18, 111, 160–61, 165
ACLU (American Civil Liberties Union), 75–76, 228
activism, 223, 229, 232; political, 42
ADC (Aid to Dependent Children) (*see also* welfare), 13, 41, 46, 48, 50–53, 54–64, 69, 71–79, 82, 85–86, 88–89, 92, 96, 98, 100–102, 105–108, 110, 149, 165, 177, 237, 258nn. 140; and the racial state, 50–51, 54–57; eligibility and benefits, 46, 52–57, 60, 62, 64, 72, 100–103, 105, 107–109; in Louisiana, 69–78; racial exclusion from, 54–57, 62, 74–75; rolls, 57, 59–60, 62–65, 78; welfare racism in, 51–54, 57–59
adoption, 42, 138, 163, 168
advocacy groups, 180, 195, 199, 207, 226, 232
AFDC (Aid to Families with Dependent Children) (*see also* welfare), 4–5, 13–14, 20–21, 107, 117–18, 121, 125, 127, 131–33, 136–38, 143, 148, 159, 165, 166, 168, 173, 175, 177, 181, 198, 213, 217, 219, 229, 235, 243n. 6, xi; -UF (Unemployed Fathers), 107; abolition of, 12, 14, 37, 115–44, 165, 170, 180, 217, 227, 232; benefits and eligibility rules for, 120, 132, 138–39, 143, 159, 165, 168, 233–34; policies, 138, 141; post-, 212–14, xi; racial composition of recipients, 14, 121, 132, 271n. 11; racist attitudes toward, 123, 133, 135, 136; recipients, 120–21, 133, 233, 263n. 73; rolls, 119–21, 132, 165
affirmative action, 9, 144
Africa, 22
African Americans (*see also* blacks; people of color), 3–6, 8–11, 13, 14, 19–20, 23, 24, 29, 31, 33, 36–38, 41, 43, 47, 48, 49, 56–60, 62–64, 69, 71, 79–80, 83–88, 92–93, 99, 109–110, 113, 118, 120–22, 124–25, 128–29, 133, 139, 141, 144, 148, 150, 156, 160, 162, 172, 174, 180, 186, 188, 201, 213, 218, 223, 230–31, 239, 241, 253n. 14, 256n. 107, 260n. 1, 265n. 110; affluent, 241, 248n. 75; as the Other, 31; disenfranchised, 14, 54, 94; exploitation of, 18, 24, 31; families receiving welfare, 5, 82–83; impoverished, 8, 9, 14, 18, 33, 54, 117, 129, 131, 133, 135, 158, 163; low-income, 240–41; middle-class, 106, 248n. 75; migration from the South to the North, 14, 62–63, 111, 120, 228; mothers (*see* African-Ameri-

can mothers); racist stereotypes of, 3, 4, 5, 134; reproduction control of, 151–70
African-American: children (*see* children, African-American); communities, 60, 74, 81–82, 85, 160, 203–204; freedom movement, 28, 233; households, 60–61; men, 19, 38, 63, 153, 156, 163; populations, 44, 51, 55, 69, 79, 94–95, 188, 254n. 37, 258n. 140; semi-colonial status of, 93 (*see also* Washington, D.C.); social workers, 56–57; socioeconomic status of, 10, 133, 171; southern, 80, 82; veterans, 118; work ethic of, 11
African-American mothers, 3–4, 32, 34, 43, 44–45, 53, 60, 62, 65, 73, 76, 111, 151–53, 155, 167, 213, 237; impoverished, 7, 11, 57, 154, 213; receiving welfare, 3, 137, 140, 147; single, 33, 60
African-American women, 3, 4, 19, 20, 27–28, 30, 32–35, 44–45, 53, 59–61, 65, 130, 139, 171, 173–75, 208, 213, 248n. 60, 270n. 103; as Other, 32; gender oppression of, 29 (*see also* gendered racism); impoverished, 47, 57, 139, 172; labor force attachment, 171–73; low-income, 152–53, 155, 165; moral stigmatization of, 31, 32; negative controlling images of (*see also* controlling images; stereotypes), 37, 41, 43, 97, 99, 123, 139, 152–53, 175, 204; racist stereotypes of, 30, 32, 35, 45, 62, 140, 155, 204; restricting reproductive choices of, 143, 152, 159–70, 205
Alabama, 94, 95–96, 229; Birmingham, 123
Alaska, 42, 201
Alien Nation, 150
aliens: illegal, 148; legal, 148
Allott, Senator, 105
American Eugenics Society, 166
Anglo-Saxon Europeans, 44–45
Anti-Defamation League, 133
antidiscrimination, 222; legislation, 226, 232
antipoverty, 14, 214, 222; programs, 144, 219, 221, xi
antiracism, 214
antiracist(s), 226, xii; European Americans, 228, 239; legislation-focused initiatives, 226–28
antiwelfare: programs, 109, 218–19, xi; racism challenges, 223; racist actions, 225; sentiments, 112–13, 222
Applied Research Center, the, 224, 226–27, 232, 280n. 43, xi; *ColorLines*, 220
Aptheker, Herbert: *Anti-Racism in U.S. History*, 239
Arizona, 55–56, 61, 183, 201, 202; welfare reform in, 202–203

Hmong, 197–98, 275n. 74; in California, 196–97; Indian, 8; Laotian, 197; Latin American, 196; Latino/a, 150; Mexican, 196–97; of color, 149–50, 196–200; poor European, 44–45; refugees, 200; resentment toward, 134; southern and eastern European, 44–45; Spanish-speaking, 199
immigration, 148, 200, 249n. 20; -focused control, 61, 148–51; anti-, 9, 266nn. 8; policy, 9, 87, 266nn. 5; welfare inducement for, 148
Immigration Act of 1924, 249n. 19
impoverished: culture of the, 140–43
income assistance, 83
Indian People's Action, 1
individual states. *See* states, individual
Ingle, Dwight: *Who Should Have Children?,* 166–67
injustice: economic and social, 144
Institute for Wisconsin's Future, 197–98
integration: racial, 95; school, 73
Ireland, 75

Jansson, Bruce S.: *The Reluctant Welfare State,* 43
Javits, Senator Jacob, 89
Jennings, James, 203–204
Jensen, Arthur, 156
Jewell, K. Sue, 248n. 60
Jim Crow segregation laws, 43, 69
job: benefits, 197; leads or referrals, 191; opportunities, 182, 203; programs, 138; referrals, 204; skills, 10; training, 138, 190, 194, 197–98, 203, 230–31
Job Centers, 186
jobs (*see also* employment; labor): agricultural, 47, 61, 171; domestic service, 32, 42, 61, 171, 173; exploitive, 174; finding, 191; for welfare recipients, 227; low-wage, 42, 47, 150; scarcity of, 181, 192; temporary, 192, 196; transportation to, 192, 194; white-collar, 211; without benefits, 190, 211; workfare, 190
Johnson administration, 33, 121–22, 124, 129, 153
Johnson, President Lyndon B., 122–23, 125
Joint Committee on Segregation, 70
justice: economic, 11–12, 14, 33, 117, 120–22, 142, 153, 172, 217, 220–22, 233, 237–38, 241–42, x, xiii; racial, 11, 25, 50, x; social, 29

Kennedy administration, 76, 106–107, 121, 129, 257n. 135
Kennedy, President John F., 90, 96, 122
Kennedy, Senator Robert, 234
Kensington Welfare Rights Union. *See* KWRU
Kentucky, 52
King, Martin Luther, Jr., 12, 234, x
Knight, William, 145
Kramer, Marian, 222, 237
Ku Klux Klan, 70, 97, 99, 137
KWRU (Kensington Welfare Rights Union), 191–92, 226, 238–41, xi

labor (*see also* employment; jobs), 24, 27, 229; African-American mothers', 65; agricultural, 58, 61; black, 53; cheap domestic, 151; dis-

crimination (*see* discrimination, labor); exploitation of, 24, 26, 31, 61–62, 65, 150, 174, 197, 210, 213; immigrant, 147; low-wage, 47, 53, 58, 109, 147, 161, 237; market, 108, 185, 194, 208, 210–11; menial, 53; non-union, 79; regulation, 109; slave, 147; unpaid, 147; unskilled, 109
landlords, 183; slum, 123
language: discrimination, 197–99, 230; minorities, 198; skills, 182, 197
Latin America, 150, 196
Latinos/as: Americans, 13, 23, 64, 121, 148, 150, 160, 180, 185, 186, 188–89, 199, 200, 218–19; communities, 203–204
Levin, Michael, 156
Lieberman, Robert C.: *Shifting the Color Line,* 20, 144
local: communities, 53; government, 27, 41, 42, 44, 86
Long, Senator Russell, 139, 233
Los Angeles, 45, 124–25, 129, 197, 260n. 11
Louisiana, 58, 96, 109, 110–14, 117, 125, 137, 139, 233, 253n. 14; ADC program, 69–78, 86; Board of Welfare, 74–75; criminal justice system of, 71; state legislature, 70, 72, 155; welfare racism in, 69–78, 88, 92, 228
Louisiana Weekly, 74
Lower-Basch, Elizabeth, 270n. 3
lynching, 99

MacDonald, Heather, 272n. 32
Make the Road by Walking, 199
male dominance, 18–19, 21, 172
mammy, the, 32–33
man-in-the-house policies, 60–61, 101–103, 107
mandatory: birth control, 158, 159–60; drug testing, 143; fingerprinting, 238; work requirements, 14, 58–59, 62, 88, 132, 137, 139, 150, 154, 163, 165, 169–70, 174–75, 185, 200, 202–203, 234, 242
Manhattan Institute, 272n. 32
March on Washington, D.C., 123
marriage: common-law, 71, 72; for poor women, 161; public-policy pressured, 153, 161, 166
Marshall, Justice Thurgood, 258n. 138
Maryland, 91
mass media, 14, 23, 25, 30, 31, 86, 87, 112, 116, 118, 127–33, 223, 225, 241, xi; external monitoring of, 224; misrepresentations, 224–25; organizations, 225, 228; poverty photos in, 128–29; racial bias of, 128–32, 223–25; racism-sensitive internal safeguards, 222, 224; racist images in, 223–25, 240
Massachusetts: communities of color in, 203–204; Welfare Rights Union, 280n. 43; welfare system, 204
maternal responsibilities, 176
maternity homes, 60
matriarchy: black, 32, 34–35, 153, 163
May, Edgar, 79, 91, 255n. 73, 258n. 140
McAdam, Doug, 223
McGuire, Robert G., 106
McKneally, George F., 80–84, 91

Mead, Lawrence M., 136, 272n. 32; *The New Politics of Poverty,* 115, 141–42, 186, 265n. 110
Medicaid, 187–88, 218, 227
men of color, 30
merit-based hiring, 56–57
Mexican Americans, 48
Mexicans, 87
Mica, Representative Dan, 169
Michigan, 75, 164
migrants, 62, 83, 87, 228
Mills, Representative Wilbur, 233
Mink, Gwendolyn, 59; *Welfare's End,* 15, 136, 173–75, 270n. 113
minorities, 134 (*see also* individual ethnic groups by name; people of color; women)
Minority Families Fighting Against WAGES, 190–91
miscegenation laws, 113
Mississippi, 52, 54–55, 57, 71, 75; welfare racism in, 191–92
Mitchell, Joseph McDowell, 83–90, 91–92, 113, 255n. 75, 256n. 102
Mitchell, William L., 76, 89
Montana, 201
moral standards, 41, 45, 73, 84, 88, 108, 121
morality: racialized, 136, 166, 205
Morgan, Senator John Tyler, 94
mothers, 3, 218, ix; AFDC, 127, 130, 132, 137–39 161; African American (*see* African-American mothers); divorced, 18; employable, 58–59, 62, 101, 108; immigrant, 44, 196–97; impoverished, 41–42, 61, 108–109, 111, 117, 159, 164, 168–70, 175, 182, 186, 207, 210–11, 212–13, 219, 230–31, xi; inner city, 151; militant, 236; morality of, 77; Native American, 203; NWRO, 235–37; of children receiving aid, 117; of color, 5, 154, 170, 173, 175, 182, 185, 207, 210–11, 213, 230–31; single, 5, 35, 41–42, 73, 138, 151, 161, 164, 166, 168, 171, 174–75, 188, 231; stereotypes of bad, 34; TANF, 210–11; teenage, 138, 163; unwed, 18, 45, 60, 72, 86, 138, 143, 163, 168; welfare reliant, 35, 102, 136, 157, 159, 161, 170, 174–75, 206, 210, 236, 243n. 2; white, 44, 48, 167–68, 176, 213; with disabilities, 63; working, 209; young, 138, 151
Mothers Pension Movement, 43, 44, 46, 175–76
mothers pension programs, 13, 41–43, 44, 48, 50, 55, 58, 69, 249n. 9; eligibility for, 45; racial exclusion from, 43–46, 55
Moynihan Report, the, 33, 152–53, 154–55, 163
Moynihan, Daniel Patrick, 33, 122, 158–59, 236
Mr. Charlie, 173
Ms. Ann, 170–76
Murray, Charles, 138, 167; *Losing Ground,* 168
Myrdal, Gunnar: *An American Dilemma,* 51–52, 58

NAACP (National Association for the Advancement of Colored People), 49, 50, 80, 88, 90, 159–60, 168, 172–73
National: Advisory Committee on Civil Disorders, 235; Campaign for Jobs and Income

Support, 226; Coalition for the Homeless, 278n. 7; Council of Negro Women, 173; Opinion Research Center, 5, 133; Organization for Women (NOW), 173; Partnership for Women and Families, 195, 270n. 2; Urban League, 74–76, 104, 106, 228; Welfare Rights Organization (NWRO), 126, 229, 233–41, x; Welfare Rights Union (NWRU), 222, 237–39
Native American(s), 13, 23, 48, 55, 64, 180–82, 188, 200–202, 218, 230; reservations, 200–203
NETWORK, 207
Nevada, 56
New Deal, the, 13, 20–21; and white racial hegemony, 46–48, 54; assistance program, 48
New Jersey: Family Development Act, 159–60, 161; legislature, 159–60
New Mexico, 55–56, 201
New Orleans, 72, 74–76
New Paternalism, 135–43, 150, 153, 263n. 74; welfare policies, 154
New York, 52, 78–92; State Supreme Court, 90; Welfare Board, 88, 89, 228
New York City, 180, 190; diversion practices in, 186–87, 272n. 32; welfare system in, 32, 33, 199, 272nn. 30
Newburgh News, 81
Newburgh, New York, 78–92, 109, 110–14, 117, 125, 129, 228, 254n. 37, 255n. 78
Niemonen, Jack, 22, 23
Nixon administration, 121, 235
Nixon, President Richard, 3, 33, 121, 124–27, 237
Norplant, 138, 157–59
North: Carolina, 44, 52; Dakota, 181, 201
North, the, 61, 63, 121, 126; migration to, 62–63, 78–92; racism in, 122; whites in, 63, 126
NPWF (National Partnership for Women and Families), 195, 270n. 2

Office: for Civil Rights, 230, 232, 275n. 74; of Management and Budget, 176
Ohio, 44, 181, 183; Cleveland, 64
Old Age: Assistance, 47, 49, 58, 229; Insurance, 20–21, 58, 63
oppression, 29, 210, 239, 245n. 37, ix; class, 167, 176; economic, 29, 135; racial, 13, 48–50, 77, 92, 158, 167, 170, 176, 179, 217, 239, 241
orphanages, 42, 138, 143, 163, 168
Other, the: racialized, 147, 149, 206, 211
out-of-wedlock births. *See* children, out-of-wedlock

Pacific Islanders, 218
Pandey, Shanta, 202–203
parents: African-American, 80; deserting, 90; employable, 101, 107–109; unemployed, 123; white, 70; working, 188–89
paternalism, 135–43
patriarchy, 18, 21, 30–31, 33–34, 160–61, 165–68, 174, 205; familial, 160–61, 173; leg-

movement); women's, 173, 176
riots, 119, 129, 142, 233, 235 (*see also* protest, social; urban rebellions)
Ritz, Joseph, 80, 82, 87, 112
Roberts, Dorothy, 29, 31–32, 143, 162; *Killing the Black Body*, 158
Robideau, Janet, 1
Robinson, Randall, 242
Rockefeller Foundation, 158
Rockefeller, Nelson, 89, 90, 255n. 78
Rockefeller, Senator Jay, 159
Roosevelt administration, 50
Roosevelt, President Franklin D., 46, 47, 50
Rushton, J. Philippe: *Race, Evolution, and Behavior*, 155–56

safety net, 6, 37, 173, 213–14, 219, xi
Schram, Sanford E., 209–210, 265n. 118
segregated: communities, 43, 63, 80, 221; housing, 63; schools, 69, 74
segregation, 21, 43, 49, 57, 69–70, 73, 76, 111, 122, 140, 258n. 140, 270n. 103; African-American litigation and protest against, 73–74; laws, 43; of labor market, 24; package, 70, 71–72, 74; racial, 43, 54, 70, 73–74
segregationists: congressional, 233; white southern, 3, 48, 73, 95, 97, 122
self-sufficiency, 123, 149, 209, x; economic, 5, 184, 200, 211
Senate: Committe on Appropriations, 97, 103, 105; District Committee, 95; Finance Committee, 164, 233
Sense of Congress, 162–63
separate but equal doctrine, 49, 54
sexism, 28, 30, 167, 205
Shapiro, Tom, 267n. 32, xi
Shea, Gerard M., 100
Shockley, William, 156, 158
single motherhood: culture of, 153–55, 163; poverty as a problem of, 155, 166
Skocpol, Theda, 43, 54; *Protecting Soldiers and Mothers*, 19
slavery, 10, 24, 32, 33–34, 43, 45, 93, 97, 99, 140–41, 236, 239, 263n. 72
social: control, 30–31, 136 (*see also* racial, as social control), control; racism; Darwinism, 169; movements, 25, 26, 148, 223; policy, 8–9, 19, 121, 236, xii; reformers, 42, 43; scientists, 8, 22, 31, 117, 140, 152, ix; structures, 12, 23, 26, 31, 154, 239, xii; welfare, 49, 135
social science, 7–8, 153, 206, 221, x; racism-blind, 10–11; research, 7; U.S., 8; welfare racism (*see* welfare racism, social science)
Social Security Act: 1967 Amendment to the, 233; of 1935, 46–48, 50–51, 53, 54, 56, 57–58, 61, 63, 76–78, 85, 90, 132, 176, 237; waivers, 138, 179
Social Security Board, 50–52, 54–56, 59, 76; Bureau of Public Assistance, 54
Social Security disability, 213
social workers, 98; African-American, 105–107; racial control, 104–106
societies: racialized, 11–12, 232
socioeconomic status, 3, 10, 24

Solinger, Rickie, 61, 111
Soss, Joe, 184–85
South Carolina, 52, 249n. 9
South Dakota, 181, 201
South, the, 43, 47–48, 52–54, 58, 61, 63, 69–78, 80, 97, 113, 120, 122, 125, 179, 191–92, 237; Jim Crow, 99
southern: freedom rides, 95; states, 44, 47, 50, 51–52, 54, 60–61, 64, 69–78, 84, 249n. 9, 251n. 58
southwestern states, 55
state: actors, 19–21, 22, 25–27, 30, 36, 112, 161 (*see also* racial state, actors); funding, 50, 57; government, 27, 42; media, 23; power, 26; racial, 22–24, 26; racism, 22, 27; welfare programs, 41, 52, 54–57, 58, 142, 177–214
states: individual, 49–50, 51, 54, 57, 59–61, 63–64, 142, 179, 186–87, 202
states' rights, 47–48, 53, 69–70, 74, 77, 172, 184, 231; approach to welfare policy, 14, 49, 186–87, 212; era, 177–214; welfare racism, 177–214
Steele, Shelby: *A Dream Deferred*, 9–10
Steiner, Gilbert, 78, 105, 257n. 135
Steinfels, Peter: *The Neoconservatives*, 122
stereotypes: gendered racist, 31–32, 41, 53; of blacks, 10, 41, 140 (*see also* controlling images); of poor people of color, 15, 142, 241, 248n. 75; of women on welfare, 5, 142, 148, 206, 241, 279n. 26 (*see also* welfare, queens); racist, 3, 5, 7, 32, 61, 240, 248n. 75, 263n. 72, 264n. 106
sterilization, 267n. 32; bonus plan, 156; involuntary, 152, 155–56, 157–59, 168; temporary, 157
Sterner, Richard, 52–53
Stevens, Dottie, 233, 280n. 43
Stromwell, Layne K., 200
substitute father policies, 60
Suffolk Welfare Warriors, 173
suffrage movement, the, 172, 270n. 103
suitable: home policies, 45, 58–59, 60, 61, 71, 73, 75–78, 255n. 75; work policies, 57
supplemental welfare assistance, 211
Survival News, 277, 280n. 43
survivor's benefits, 213

TANF (Temporary Assistance to Needy Families program) (*see also* welfare), 143, 147, 150, 174–76, 182, 184–85, 190, 196, 201, 208, 210–11, 212, 213, 217–18, 224; benefits, 187, 190; eligibility policies, 186–89, 230; recipients, 188, 208
taxes, 30, 108; and spending, 21
taxpayers, 21, 113, 149
Texas, 52, 56, 75
Thernstrom, Stephan and Abigail: *America in Black and White*, 9
think tanks, 25, 31, 206, 272n. 32
Thirteen-Point Program, 85–87, 90–91, 255n. 78
Thomas, Justice Clarence, 159
Thomas, Susan L., 30, 151–52, 163, 267n. 28
Thomson, Governor Tommy, 275n. 74
Tillman, Johnnie, 160, 166